The Secrets of Mind Power

The Secrets of
Mind Power

The Secret of Success and
Other Essential Works

WILLIAM WALKER ATKINSON

ST. MARTIN'S
ESSENTIALS
NEW YORK

Published in the United States by St. Martin's Essentials, an imprint of St. Martin's Publishing Group

FOREWORD. Copyright © 2021 by Joel Fotinos. All rights reserved. Printed in the United States of America. For information, address St. Martin's Publishing Group, 120 Broadway, New York, NY 10271.

Your Mind and How to Use It was first published in 1911
The Keynote—I Can! was first published in 1902
The Art of Logical Thinking was first published in 1909
The Secret of the "I Am" was first published in 1902
Dynamic Thought, or the Law of Vibrant Energy was first published in 1906
Let a Little Sunshine In was first published in 1902
Practical Mental Influence was first published in 1908
Look Aloft! was first published in 1902
The Secret of Success was first published in 1908
The Hunger of the Soul was first published in 1902

www.stmartins.com

Designed by Steven Seighman

The Library of Congress Cataloging-in-Publication Data is available upon request.

ISBN 978-1-250-78005-8 (hardcover)
ISBN 978-1-250-78006-5 (ebook)

NOTE: This edition seeks to faithfully reproduce the original editions of the author's work and so has maintained the original spelling and grammar throughout, with only minor alterations for clarity or content.

Our books may be purchased in bulk for promotional, educational, or business use. Please contact your local bookseller or the Macmillan Corporate and Premium Sales Department at 1-800-221-7945, extension 5442, or by email at MacmillanSpecialMarkets@macmillan.com.

First St. Martin's Essentials Edition: 2021

10   9   8   7   6   5   4   3   2   1

Contents

Foreword

William Walker Atkinson might be the most famous and influential inspirational writer you have never heard of.

I say that because Atkinson at one time was extremely popular, but somehow while his ideas have continued to flourish, his name has been largely forgotten. With one exception (which I'll mention later), his books are difficult to find, relegated to print-on-demand status. It is my hope that this volume—one of the inaugural books in the Library of Spiritual Wisdom series, which was created to bring the spiritual classics of the 19th and 20th Centuries to modern readers—brings some of Atkinson's most potent and timeless books to many new readers. He deserves a wide readership.

His Life

Atkinson was a lawyer, author, publisher, editor, and speaker. Born in Baltimore in 1862, Atkinson married Margaret Foster Black, had two children, became a lawyer, and moved to Chicago. That last sentence sums up years of his life in just a few words, but there is much about Atkinson that we do not know.

What we do know, mostly through his articles and writings, is that at one point his life took a difficult turn. He suffered a physical and emotion breakdown, as well as financial ruin. It was then that he found books on mental healing. Chicago at that time was a hot spot for the fast-growing New Thought philosophy, the philosophy based on transcendentalism as well as mesmerism and mental science. He studied with two of New Thought's most formidable and influential leaders, Helen Wilmans and Emma Curtis Hopkins.

MAGAZINES AND BOOKS

Atkinson's mind, body, and finances were all healed using the ideas from New Thought. He began writing articles about his experiences and about the metaphysical ideas that he now embraced. And shortly after that, he began writing books.

He also began working with several New Thought magazines, including *New Thought Magazine*, *Advanced Thought*, and eventually *Nautilus* magazine, which was founded and headed by early New Thought publisher Elizabeth Towne.

Eventually he began to publish books through his own publishing companies, the Yogi Publication Society and Advance Thought Publishing Company.

Here's where his story gets interesting, at least to me. Atkinson was incredibly prolific, and he wrote many books about his main interests, which included mental science, New Thought, psychic studies, numerology, the occult, natural health and wellness, and also Eastern philosophy, especially Hinduism, which he had become interested in. During his lifetime, he wrote well over a hundred books, which is a remarkable achievement.

However, instead of just publishing them all under his own name, he evidently created a series of pseudonyms, each with a different emphasis. For example, the books under his own name dealt with mental sciences, the occult, divination, and spiritual success. His books with Eastern and Hindu influences were written under the name Swami Ramachakara. He also published under the names Swami Bhakta Vishita and Swami Panchadasi, and these books were largely about clairvoyance, psychic thought, and life after death. His pseudonym Theron Q. Dumont focused on mental power, self-improvement, self-confidence, memory, and concentration. The health and wellness titles were published under the name of Theodore Sheldon, and the esoteric studies, such as Rosicrucianism, were published with the name Magus Incognito. There were other pseudonyms as well.

Notice that I said he evidently published books with pseudonyms. He never revealed one way or another if he authored those, and in fact even created elaborate stories of who some of these "authors" were. However, there doesn't seem to be evidence of these "other" authors actually existing. Not to mention, those books all had the same "feel" as the books published under his own name. It is widely accepted that he was the author of the books under these pseudonyms.

His most famous pseudonym, was known as "the Three Initiates," who authored a book that claimed to be of authentic Hermetic wisdom, called *The Kybalion*. This book ended up being his bestseller, the book that he is best known for today, though most readers of the book don't know that the name of the author is actually William Walker Atkinson. There is some question as to the authorship, whether he wrote the book by himself, or with others, or even at all, but careful study of *The Kybalion* reveals that there is a vast probability that Atkinson was the sole author of the book. (*The Kybalion* is available as a part of the Essential Wisdom Library series from St. Martin's Essentials, with a foreword by me as well).

THIS VOLUME

While his pseudonyms are fascinating, the books he wrote under his own name are equally fascinating.

In one of his earliest books, under his own name, he discussed the concept of "the law of attraction," one of the first writers to use that term, which has become widely known and taught in recent years, through books such as *The Secret*, and those written by Wayne Dyer and others. Many of his other ideas are now commonplace as well, and some are still ahead of their time.

The ten books in this volume—each original and complete—showcase a man with a brilliant mind and charismatic personality. While the language is of the times when he wrote them, his ideas are timely and practical and valuable. You can tell as you read these books that he truly *wants* to help readers improve their lives. They are written in a motivational, personal style, totally graspable and applicable for the modern reader.

Yes, some of the stories or examples are dated, but the ideas behind those examples transcend the time he wrote them. After all, Atkinson would be the first to tell us that he didn't invent these ideas, he only wrote about them in a way that made them understandable.

He was incredibly clear in his writing. Look at even the titles he used:

- Your Mind and How to Use It: A Manual of Practical Psychology
- The Keynote—I Can!
- The Art of Logical Thinking
- The Secret of the "I AM"
- Dynamic Thought, or the Law of Vibrant Energy
- Let a Little Sunshine In
- Practical Mind Influence
- Look Aloft!
- The Secret of Success
- The Hunger of the Soul

The reader can tell exactly what each book is about, and Atkinson more than delivers. His confidence in and love of the ideas in his books burst forth from every paragraph. Reading his books is more than instructional, it is joyful.

His Legacy

In Atkinson's later years, he become involved in the International New Thought Alliance, and in fact was their president at one point. He ran his publishing businesses, remained an active lawyer, popular speaker, and influential New Thought teacher.

He died in 1932, just shy of his 70th birthday. His publishing company continued to publish his books for decades, but otherwise he left behind no organization or "center" that taught his principles and ideas. Perhaps that is why his name isn't well known in this time. His books didn't have an author or organization to keep them fresh in the minds of readers. However, as you read his books, you'll begin to see his ideas, from these books written more than a century ago, in today's current bestsellers. Whenever I notice it, I pause and smile, knowing that Atkinson's influence is still being felt today.

As I mentioned at the start of this foreword, nearly all of his books, most in the public domain, are today only available in often-substandard print-on-demand editions, or error-filled ebooks. This volume, which I hope is the first of many, aims to not only bring his books back, but do so in a way that honors his work as it deserves. The plan is to publish future volumes, keeping his books separated by his pseudonyms.

My hope is that as you read the ten books in the volume, you will discover the very principles that speak directly to you, and inspire you to live a deeper, richer, more joyous life. Atkinson may have died and his name has seemed to fade, but his ideas can come alive within you, and within me. In that way, Atkinson is still with us, still doing what he strove to do his entire adult life, which was to help readers live the life they were meant to live. With that thought in mind, turn the page and let the adventure—*your* adventure—begin. . . .

—Joel Fotinos

YOUR MIND AND HOW TO USE IT

A Manual of Practical Psychology

Contents

1

What Is the Mind?

Psychology is generally considered to be the science of mind, although more properly it is the science of mental states—thoughts, feelings, and acts of volition. It was formerly the custom of writers on the subject of psychology to begin by an attempt to define and describe the nature of mind, before proceeding to a consideration of the subject of the various mental spates and activities. But more recent authorities have rebelled against this demand, and have claimed that it is no more reasonable to hold that psychology should be held to an explanation of the ultimate nature of mind than it is that physical science be held to an explanation of the ultimate nature of matter. The attempt to explain the ultimate nature of either is futile—no actual necessity exists for explanation in either case. Physics may explain the phenomena of matter, and psychology the phenomena of mind, without regard to the ultimate nature of the substance of either.

The science of physics has progressed steadily during the past century, notwithstanding the fact that the theories regarding the ultimate nature of matter have been revolutionized during that period. The facts of the phenomena of matter remain, notwithstanding the change of theory regarding the nature of matter itself. Science demands and holds fast to facts, regarding theories as but working hypotheses at the best. Someone has said that "theories are but the bubbles with which the grown-up children of science amuse themselves." Science holds several well-supported, though opposing, theories regarding the nature of electricity, but the *facts* of the phenomena of electricity, and the application thereof, are agreed upon by the disputing theorists. And so it is with psychology; the facts regarding mental states are agreed upon, and methods of developing mental powers are effectively employed, without regard to whether mind is a product of the brain, or the brain merely an organ of the mind. The fact that the brain and nervous system are employed in the phenomena of thought is conceded by all, and that is all that is necessary for a basis for the science of psychology.

Disputes regarding the ultimate nature of mind are now generally passed over to the philosophers and metaphysicians, while psychology devotes its entire attention to studying the laws of mental activities, and to discovering methods of mental development. Even philosophy is beginning to tire of the eternal "why" and is devoting its attention to the "how" phase of things. The pragmatic spirit has invaded the field of philosophy, expressing itself in the words of Prof. William James, who said: "Pragmatism is the attitude of looking away from first things, principles, categories, supposed necessities; and of looking forward toward last things, *fruits, consequences, facts*." Modern psychology is essentially pragmatic in its treatment of the subject of the mind. Leaving to metaphysics the old arguments and disputes regarding the ultimate nature of mind, it bends all its energies upon discovering the laws of mental activities and states, and developing methods whereby the mind may be trained to perform better and more work, to conserve its energies, to concentrate its forces. To modern psychology the mind is *something to be used*, not merely something about which to speculate and theorize. While the metaphysicians deplore this tendency, the practical people of the world rejoice.

MIND DEFINED

Mind is defined as "the faculty or power whereby thinking creatures, feel, think, and will." This definition is inadequate and circular in nature, but this is unavoidable, for mind can be defined only in its own terms and only by reference to its own processes. Mind, except in reference to its own activities, cannot be defined or conceived. It is known to itself only through its activities. Mind without mental states is a mere abstraction—a word without a corresponding mental image or concept. Sir William Hamilton expressed the matter as clearly as possible, when he said: "What we mean by mind is simply *that which* perceives, thinks, feels, wills, and desires." Without the perceiving, thinking, feeling, willing, and desiring, it is impossible to form a clear conception or mental image of mind; deprived of its phenomena it becomes the merest abstraction.

"THINK ABOUT THAT WHICH THINKS."

Perhaps the simplest method of conveying the idea of the existence and nature of the mind is that attributed to a celebrated German teacher of psychology who was wont to begin his course by bidding his students think of something, his desk, for example. Then he would say, "Now think of *that which thinks about the desk.*" Then, after a pause, he would add, "This thing which thinks about the desk, and about which you are now thinking, is the subject matter of our study of psychology." The professor could not have said more had he lectured for a month.

Professor Gordy has well said on this point: "The mind must either be *that which* thinks, feels, and wills, or it must be the thoughts, feelings, and acts of will of which we are conscious—mental facts, in one word. But what can we know about *that which* thinks, feels, and wills, and what can we find out about it? Where is it? You will probably say, in the brain. But, if you are speaking literally, if you say that it is in the brain, as a pencil is in the pocket, then you must mean that it takes up room, that it occupies space, and that would make it very much like a material thing. In truth, the more carefully you consider it, the more plainly you will see what thinking men have known for a long time— that we do not know and cannot learn anything about the thing which thinks, and feels, and wills. It is beyond the range of human knowledge. The books which define psychology as the science of mind have not a word to say about that which thinks, and feels, and wills. They are entirely taken up with these thoughts and feelings and acts of the will—mental facts, in a word—trying to tell us what they are, and to arrange them in classes, and tell us the circumstances or conditions under which they exist. It seems to me that it would be better to define psychology as *the science of the experiences, phenomena, or facts of the mind, soul, or self—of mental facts, in a word.*"

In view of the facts of the case, and following the example of the best of the modern authorities, in this book we shall leave the consideration of the question of the ultimate nature of mind to the metaphysicians, and shall confine ourselves to the *mental facts*, the laws governing them, and the best methods of governing and using them in "the business of life."

The classification and method of development to be followed in this book is as follows:

I. The mechanism of mental states, *i.e.*, the brain, nervous system, sense organs, etc.

II. The fact of Consciousness and its planes.

III. Mental processes or faculties, *i.e.*, (1) Sensation and Perception; (2) Representation, or Imagination and Memory; (3) Feeling or Emotion; (4) Intellect, or Reason and Understanding; (5) Will or Volition.

Mental states depend upon the physical mechanism for manifestation, whatever may be the ultimate nature of mind. Mental states, whatever their special character, will be found to fit into one of the above five general classes of mental activities.

2

The Mechanism of Mental States

The mechanism of mental states—the mental machinery by means of which we feel, think, and will—consists of the brain, nervous system, and the organs of sense. No matter what may be the real nature of mind—no matter what may be the theory held regarding its activities—it must be admitted that the mind is dependent upon this mechanism for the manifestation of what we know as mental states. Wonderful as is the mind, it is seen to be dependent upon this physical mechanism for the expression of its activities. And this dependence is not upon the brain alone, but also upon the entire nervous system.

The best authorities agree that the higher and more complex mental states are but an evolution of simple sensation, and that they are dependent upon sensation for their raw material of feeling and thought. Therefore it is proper that we begin by a consideration of the machinery of sensation. This necessitates a previous consideration of the nerves.

THE NERVES

The body is traversed by an intricate system of nerves, which has been likened to a great telegraph system. The nerves transmit sensations from the various parts of the body to the great receiving office of the brain. They also serve to transmit the motor impulses from the brain to the various parts of the body, which impulses result in motion of appropriate parts of the body. There are also other nerves with which we have no concern in this book, but which perform certain physiological functions, such as digestion, secretion, excretion, and circulation. Our chief concern, at this point, is with the sensory nerves.

The sensory nerves convey the impressions of the outside world to the brain. The brain is the great central station of the sensory nerves, the latter having countless sending stations in all parts of the body, the "wires" terminating in the skin. When these nervous terminal stations are irritated or excited, they send to the brain messages calling for attention. This is true not only of the nerves of touch or feeling, but also of those concerned with the respective senses of sight, smell, taste, and hearing. In fact, the best authorities hold that all the five senses are but an evolution of the primary sense of touch or feeling.

THE SENSE OF TOUCH

The nerves of the sense of touch have their ending in the outer covering or skin of the body. They report *contact* with other physical objects. By means of these reports we are aware not only of contact with the outside object, but also of many facts concerning the nature of that object, as for instance, its degree of hardness, roughness, etc., and its temperature. Some of these nerve ends are very sensitive, as, for example, those of the tip of the tongue and finger ends, while others are comparatively lacking in sensitiveness, as, for illustration, those of the back. Certain of these sensory nerves confine themselves to reporting contact and degrees of pressure, while others concern themselves solely with reporting the degrees of temperature of the objects with which their ends come in contact. Some of the latter respond to the higher degrees of heat, while others respond only to the lower degrees of cold. The nerves of certain parts of the body respond more readily and distinctly to temperature than do those of other parts. To illustrate, the nerves of the cheek are quite responsive to heat impressions.

THE SENSE OF SIGHT

The nerves of the sense of sight terminate in the complex optical apparatus which in popular terminology is known as "the eye." What is known as "the retina" is a very sensitive nervous membrane which lines the inner, back part of the eye, and in which the fibers of the optic nerve terminate. The optical instrument of the eye conveys the focused light vibrations to the nerves of the retina, from which the impulse is transmitted to the brain. But, contrary to the popular notion, the nerves of the eye do not gauge distances, nor form inferences of any kind; that is distinctly the work of the mind. The simple office of the optical nerves consists in reporting color and degrees of intensity of the light waves.

THE SENSE OF HEARING

The nerves of the sense of hearing terminate in the inner part of the ear. The tympanum, or "ear drum," receives the sound vibrations entering the cavities of the ear, and, intensifying and adapting them, it passes them on to the ends of the auditory nerve in the internal ear, which conveys the sensation to the brain. The auditory nerve reports to the brain the degrees of pitch, intensity, quality, and harmony, respectively, of the sound waves reaching the tympanum. As is well known, there are certain vibrations of sound which are too low for the auditory nerve to register, and others too high for it to record, both classes, however, capable of being recorded by scientific instruments. It is also regarded as certain that some of the lower animals are conscious of sound vibrations which are not registered by the human auditory nerves.

THE SENSE OF SMELL

The nerves of the sense of smell terminate in the mucous membrane of the nostrils. In order that these nerves report the odor of outside objects, actual contact of minute particles of the object with the mucous membrane of the nostrils is necessary. This is possible only by the passage through the nostrils of air containing these particles; mere nearness to the nostril will not suffice. These particles are for the most part composed of tenuous gases. Certain substances affect the olfactory nerves much more than do others, the difference arising from the chemical composition of the substance. The olfactory nerves convey the report to the brain.

THE SENSE OF TASTE

The nerves of the sense of taste terminate in the tongue, or rather in the tiny cells of the tongue which are called "taste buds." Substances taken into the mouth chemically affect these tiny cells, and an impulse is transmitted to the gustatory nerves, which then report the sensation to the brain. The authorities claim that taste sensations may be reduced to five general classes, viz.: sweet, bitter, sour, salty, and "hot."

There are certain nerve centers having important offices in the production and expression of mental states, located in the skull and in the spinal column— the brain and the spinal cord—which we shall consider in the following chapter.

3

The Great Nerve Centers

The great nerve centers which play an important part in the production and expression of mental states are those of the brain and spinal cord, respectively.

THE SPINAL CORD

The spinal cord is that cord or rope of nerve substance which is inclosed in the spinal column or "backbone." It leaves the lower part of the skull and extends downward in the interior of the spinal column for about eighteen inches. It is continuous with the brain, however, and it is difficult to determine where one begins and the other ends. It is composed of a mass of gray matter surrounded by a covering of white matter. From the spinal cord, along its length, emerge thirty-one pairs of spinal nerves which branch out to each side of the body and connect with the various smaller nerves, extending to all parts of the system. The spinal cord is the great central cable of the nervous telegraphic system, and any injury to or obstruction of it cripples or paralyzes those portions of the body the nerves of which enter the spinal cord below the seat of the injury or obstruction. Injuries or obstructions of this kind not only inhibit the sensory reports from the affected area, but also inhibit the motor impulses from the brain which are intended to move the limbs or parts of the body.

THE GANGLIA OR "TINY BRAINS"

What are known as ganglia, or tiny bunches of nerve cells, are found in various parts of the nervous system, including the spinal nerves. These groups of nerve cells are sometimes called "little brains," and perform quite important offices in the mechanism of thought and action. The spinal ganglia receive sensory reports, and issue motor impulses, in many cases, without troubling the central brain regarding the matter. These activities are known as "reflex nervous action."

REFLEX ACTION

What is known as reflex nervous action is one of the most wonderful of the activities of the nervous and mental mechanism, and the knowledge thereof usually comes as a surprise to the average person, for he is generally under the impression that these activities are possible only to the central brain. It is a fact that not only is the central brain really a trinity of three brains, but that, in addition to these, every one has a great number of "little brains" distributed over his nervous system, any and all of which are capable of receiving sensory reports and also of sending forth motor impulses. It is quite worth while for one to become acquainted with this wonderful form of neuro-mental activity.

A cinder enters the eye, the report reaches a ganglion, a motor impulse is sent forth, and the eyelid closes. The same result ensues if an object approaches the eye but without actually entering it. In either case the person is not conscious of the sensation and motor impulse until the latter has been accomplished. This is reflex action. The instinctive movement of the tickled foot is another instance. The jerking away of the hand burnt by the lighted end of the cigar, or pricked by the point of the pin, is another instance. The involuntary activities, and those known as unconscious activities, result from reflex action.

More than this, it is a fact that many activities originally voluntary become what is known as "acquired reflexes," or "motor habits," by means of certain nervous centers acquiring the habit of sending forth certain motor impulses in response to certain sensory reports. The familiar movements of our lives are largely performed in this way, as, for instance, walking, using knife and fork, operating typewriters, machines of all kinds, writing, etc. The squirming of a decapitated snake, the muscular movements of a decapitated frog, and the violent struggles, fluttering, and leaps of the decapitated fowl, are instances of reflex action. Medical reports indicate that in cases of decapitation even man may manifest similar reflex action in some cases. Thus we may see that we may *feel* and *will* by means of our "little brains" as well as by the central brain or brains. Whatever mind may be, it is certain that in these processes it employs other portions of the nervous system than the central brain.

THE THREE BRAINS

What is known as the brain of man is really a trinity of three brains, known respectively as (1) the *medulla oblongata*, (2) the *cerebellum*, and (3) the *cerebrum*. If one wishes to limit the mental activity to conscious intellectual effort, then and then only is he correct in considering the cerebrum or large brain as "the brain."

- *The Medulla Oblongata*—The medulla oblongata is an enlargement of the spinal cord at the base of the brain. Its office is that of controlling the involuntary activities of the body, such as respiration, circulation, assimilation, etc. In a broad sense, its activities may be said to be of the nature of highly developed and complex reflex activities. It manifests chiefly through the sympathetic nervous system which controls the vital functions. It does not need to call on the large brain in these matters, ordinarily, and is able to perform its tasks without the plane of ordinary consciousness.

- *The Cerebellum*—The cerebellum, also known as "the little brain," lies just above the medulla oblongata, and just below the rear portion of the cerebrum or great brain. It combines the nature of a purely reflex center on the one hand, with that of "habit mind" on the other. In short, it fills a place between the activities of the cerebrum and the medulla oblongata, having some of the characteristics of each. It is the organ of a number of important acquired reflexes, such as walking, and many other familiar muscular movements, which have first been consciously acquired and then become habitual. The skilled skater, bicyclist, typist, or machinist depends upon the cerebellum for the ease and certainty with which he performs his movements "without thinking of them." One may be said never to have thoroughly acquired a set of muscular movements such as we have mentioned, until the cerebellum has taken over the task and relieved the cerebrum of the conscious effort. One's technique is never perfected until the cerebellum assumes control and direction of the necessary movements and the impulses are sent forth from below the plane of ordinary consciousness.

- *The Cerebrum*—The cerebrum, or "great brain" (which is regarded as "the brain" by the average person), is situated in the upper portion of the skull, and occupies by far the larger portion of the cavity of the skull. It is divided into two great divisions or hemispheres. The best of the modern authorities are agreed that the cerebrum has zones or areas of specialized functioning, some of which receive the sensory reports of the nerves and organs of sense, while others send forth the motor impulses which result in voluntary physical action. Many of these areas or zones have been located by science, while others remain as yet unlocated. The probability is that in time science will succeed in correctly locating the area or zone of each and every class of sensation and motor impulse.

THE CORTEX

The area of thought, memory, and imagination has not been clearly located, except that these mental states are believed to have their seat in the *cortex* or outer thin rind of gray brain matter which envelopes and covers the mass of brain substance. It is, moreover, considered probable that the higher processes of reasoning are performed in or by the cortex of the frontal lobes. The cortex of a person of average intelligence, if spread out on a flat surface, measures about four square feet. The higher the degree of intelligence possessed by a lower animal or human being, as a rule, the deeper and more numerous are the folds or convolutions of the cortex, and the finer its structure. It may be stated as a general rule, with but very few exceptions, that the higher the degree of intelligence in a lower animal or human being, the greater is the area of its cortex in proportion to the size of the brain. The cortex, it must be remembered, is folded into deep furrows or convolutions, the brain in shape, divisions, and convolutions resembling the inner portion of an English walnut. The interior of the two hemispheres of the cerebrum is composed largely of connective nerves which doubtless serve to produce and maintain the unity of function of the mental processes.

While physiological psychology has performed great work in discovering brain-centers and explaining much of the mechanism of mental processes, it has but touched the most elementary and simple of the mental processes. The higher processes have so far defied analysis or explanation in the terms of physiology.

4

Consciousness

The fact of consciousness is the great mystery of psychology. It is difficult even to define the term, although every person of average intelligence understands what is sought to be conveyed by it. Webster defines it as "knowledge of one's own existence, sensations, mental operations, etc.; immediate knowledge or perception of any object, state, or sensation; being aware; being sensible of." Another authority defines the term as "the state of being aware of one's sensations; the power, faculty, or mental state of being aware of one's own existence, condition at the moment, thoughts, feelings, and actions." Halleck's definition is: "That indefinable characteristic of mental states which causes us to be aware of them."

It will be seen that the idea of "awareness" is the essence of the idea of consciousness. But, at the last, we are compelled to acknowledge that it is impossible to closely define consciousness, for it is something so entirely unique and different from anything else that we have no other terms at all synonymous to it. We can define it only in its own terms, as will be seen by reference to the definitions above given. And it is equally impossible to clearly account for its appearance and being. Huxley has well said: "How it is that anything so remarkable as a state of consciousness comes about by the result of irritating nervous tissue, is just as unaccountable as the appearance of the jinnee when Aladdin rubbed his lamp." All that we can ever know regarding the nature of consciousness must be learned from turning the consciousness in ourselves back upon itself—by focusing consciousness upon its own mental operations by means of introspection. By turning inward the conscious gaze we may perceive the flow of the stream of thought from its rise from the subconscious regions of the mind to its final disappearance in the same region.

It is a common error to suppose that we are directly conscious of objects outside of ourselves. This is impossible, for there is no direct knowledge of such outside objects. We are conscious merely of our sensations of, or mental images of, the outside objects. All that it is possible for us to be directly conscious of are our own mental experiences or states. We cannot be directly conscious of anything outside of our own minds. We are not directly conscious of the tree which we *see*; we are directly conscious merely of the sensation of the nerves arising from the impact of the light waves carrying the image of the tree. We are not directly conscious of the tree when we touch it and perceive its character in that way; we are directly conscious merely of the sensation reported by the nerves in the finger tips which have come in contact with the tree. We are directly conscious even of our own bodies only in the same way. It is necessary for the mind to experience that of which it may become conscious. We are conscious only of (1) that which our mind is experiencing at this moment, or (2) that which it has experienced in the past, and which is being re-experienced this moment by the process of the memory, or which is being re-combined or re-arranged this moment by the imagination.

SUBCONSCIOUS PLANES

But it must not be thought that every mental state or mental fact is in the field of consciousness. This error has been exploded for many years. The fact is now recognized that the field of consciousness is a very narrow and limited one, and that the great field of mental activity lies outside of its narrow limits. Beyond and outside of the narrow field of consciousness lies the great subconscious storehouse of memory in which are stored the experiences of the past, to be drawn again into the field of consciousness by an effort of the will in the act of recollection, or by association in ordinary remembrance. In that great region, also, the mind manifests many of its activities and performs much of its work. In that great region are evolved the emotions and feelings which play such an important part in our lives, and which often manifest a vague disturbing unrest long before they rise to the plane of consciousness. In that great region are produced the ideas, feelings, and conceptions which arise to the plane of consciousness and manifest that which men call "genius."

On the subconscious plane the imagination does much of its work, and startles its owner by presenting him with the accomplished result in the field of consciousness. In the subconscious field is performed that peculiar process of mental mastication, digestion, and assimilation with which all brain workers are familiar, and which absorbs the raw mental material given it, separates, digests, and assimilates it, and re-presents it to the conscious faculties sometime after as a transformed substance. It has been estimated that at least eighty-five per cent of our mental activities are performed below or outside of the field of consciousness. The psychology of today is paying much attention to this formerly neglected great area or areas of the mind. The psychology of tomorrow will pay still greater attention to it.

The best of the modern authorities agree that in the great field of subconscious mentation is to be found the explanation of much that is unexplainable otherwise. In fact, it is probable that before long consciousness will be regarded as a mere *focusing of attention* upon mental states, and the objects of consciousness merely as that portion of the contents of the mind in the field of mental vision created by such focusing.

5

Attention

Intimately connected with the object of consciousness is that process of the mind which we call "attention." Attention is generally defined as "the application of the mind to a mental state." It is often referred to as "concentrated consciousness," but others have ventured the somewhat daring conjecture that consciousness itself is rather the result of attention, instead of the latter being an incident of consciousness. We shall not attempt to discuss this question here, except to state that consciousness depends very materially upon the degree of attention bestowed upon its object. The authorities place great importance upon the intelligent direction of the attention, and hold that without this the higher forms of knowledge are impossible.

It is the common belief that we feel, see, hear, taste, or smell whenever objects affecting those senses come in contact with the organs of sense governing them. But this is only a partial truth. The real truth is that we become conscious of the report of these senses only when the attention is directed toward the sensation, voluntarily or involuntarily. That is to say, that in many cases although the sense nerves and organs report a disturbance, the mind does not become consciously aware of the report unless the attention is directed toward it either by an act of will or else by reflex action. For instance, the clock may strike loudly, and yet we may not be conscious of the fact, for we are concentrating our attention upon a book; or we may eat the choicest food without tasting it, for we are listening intently to the conversation of our charming neighbor. We may fail to perceive some startling occurrence happening under our very eyes, for we are buried in deep thought concerning something far removed from the present scene. There are many cases on record showing that one may be so interested in speaking, thinking, or acting that he will not experience pain that would otherwise be intolerable. Writers have forgotten their pain in the concentrated interest bestowed upon their work; mothers have failed to feel pain when their infants required urgent attention; orators have been so carried away by their own eloquence that they have failed to feel the pricking of the pin by means of which their friends have sought to attract their attention. Not only perception and feeling depend largely upon attention, but the processes of reasoning, memory, and even of will, depend upon attention for much of their manifestation.

Psychologists divide attention into two general classes, viz.: (1) voluntary attention and (2) involuntary attention.

Voluntary attention is attention directed by the will to some object of our own more or less deliberate selection. It requires a distinct effort of the will in order to focus the attention in this way, and many persons are scarcely aware of its existence, so seldom do they manifest it. Voluntary attention is the result of training and practice, and marks the man of strong will, concentration, and character. Some authorities go so far as to say that much of that which is commonly called "willpower" is really but a developed form of voluntary attention, the man of "strong will" holding before him the one idea which he wishes to realize.

Involuntary attention, often called "reflex attention," is attention called forth by a nervous response to some sense stimulus. This is the common form of attention, and is but the same form which is so strongly manifested by children whose attention is caught by every new object, but which cannot be held for any length of time by a familiar or uninteresting one.

It is of the utmost importance that one should cultivate his power of voluntary attention. Not only is the willpower strengthened and developed in this way, but every mental faculty is developed by reason thereof. The training of the voluntary attention is the first step in mental development.

TRAINING THE ATTENTION

That the voluntary attention may be deliberately trained and developed is a fact which many of the world's greatest men have proved for themselves. There is only one way to train and develop any mental power of faculty—and that is *by practice and use*. By practice, interest may be given to objects previously uninteresting, and thus the use of the attention develops the interest which further holds it. Interest is the natural road over which attention travels easily, but interest itself may be induced by concentrated attention. By studying and examining an object, the attention brings to light many new and novel features regarding the thing, and these produce a new interest which in turn attracts further and continued attention.

There is no royal road to the development of voluntary attention. The only true method is *work, practice, and use*. You must practice on uninteresting things, the primary interest being your desire to develop the power of voluntary attention. But as you begin to attend to the uninteresting thing you will become interested in the task for its own sake. Take some object and "place your mind upon it." Think of its nature, where it came from, its use, its associations, its probable future, of things related to it, etc., etc. Keep the attention firmly upon it, and shut out all outside ideas. Then, after a little practice of this kind, lay aside the object for the time being, and take it up again the next day, endeavoring to discover new points of interest in it. The main thing to be sought is *to hold the thing in your mind*, and this can be done only by *discovering features of interest in it*. The interest-loving attention may rebel at this task at first, and will seek to wander from the path into the green pastures which are found on each side thereof. But you must bring the mind back to the task, again and again.

After a time the mind will become accustomed to the drill, and will even begin to enjoy it. Give it some variety by occasionally changing the objects of examination. The object need not always be something to be looked at. Instead, select some subject in history or literature, and "run it down," endeavoring to bring to light all the facts relating to it that are possible to you. *Anything* may be used as the subject or object of your inquiry; but what is chosen must be held in the field of conscious attention firmly and fixedly. The habit once acquired, you will find the practice most fascinating. You will invent new subjects or objects of inquiry, investigation, and thought, which in themselves will well repay you for your work and time. But never lose sight of the main point—the development of the power of voluntary attention.

In studying the methods of developing and training the voluntary attention, the student should remember that *any* exercise which develops the will, will result in developing the attention; and, likewise, any exercise which develops the voluntary attention will tend to strengthen the will. The will and attention are so closely bound together that what affects one also influences the other. This fact should be borne in mind, and the exercises and practices based upon it.

In practicing concentration of voluntary attention, it should be remembered that concentrating consists not only of *focusing* the attention upon a given object or subject, but also of the *shutting out* of impressions from other objects or subjects. Some authorities advise that the student endeavor to listen to one voice among many, or one instrument among the many of a band or orchestra. Others advise the practice of concentrating on the reading of a book in a room filled by persons engaged in conversation, and similar exercises. Whatever aids in *narrowing the circle* of attention at a given moment tends to develop the power of voluntary attention.

The study of mathematics and logic is also held to be an excellent practice in concentration of voluntary attention, inasmuch as these studies require close concentration and attention. Attention is also developed by any study or practice which demands *analysis* of a whole into its parts, and then the *synthesis* or building up of a whole from its scattered parts. Each of the senses should play a part in the exercises, and in addition to this the mind should be trained to concentrate upon some one idea held within itself—some mental image or abstract idea existing independently of any object of immediate sense report.

6

Perception

IT is a common mistake that we *perceive* everything that is reported to the mind by the senses. As a matter of fact we perceive but a very small portion of the reports of the senses. There are thousands of sights reported by our eyes, sounds reported by our ears, smells reported by our nostrils, and contacts reported by our nerves of touch, every day of our lives, but which are not *perceived* or *observed* by the mind. We perceive and observe only when the attention, reflex or voluntary, is directed to the report of the senses, and when the mind interprets the report. While perception depends upon the reports of the senses for its raw material, it depends entirely upon the application of the mind for its complete manifestation.

The student usually experiences great difficulty in distinguishing between *sensation* and *perception*. A sensation is a simple report of the senses, which is received in consciousness. Perception is the *thought* arising from the *feeling* of the sensation. Perception usually combines several sensations into one thought or percept. By sensation the mind *feels*; by perception it *knows* that it feels, and recognizes the object causing the sensation. Sensation merely brings a report from outside objects, while perception identifies the report with the object which caused it. Perception *interprets* the reports of sensation. Sensation reports a flash of light from above; perception interprets the light as starlight, or moonlight, or sunlight, or as the flash of a meteor. Sensation reports a sharp, pricking, painful contact; perception interprets it as the prick of a pin. Sensation reports a red spot on a green background; perception interprets it as a berry on a bush.

Moreover, while we may perceive a simple single sensation, our perceptions are usually of a group of sensations. Perception is usually employed in grouping sensations and identifying them with the object or objects causing them. In its identification it draws upon whatever memory of past experiences the mind may possess. Memory, imagination, feeling, and thought are called into play, to some extent, in every clear perception. The infant has but feeble perception, but as it gains experience it begins to manifest perceptions and form percepts. Sensations resemble the letters of the alphabet, and perception the forming of words and sentences from the letters. Thus *c*, *a*, and *t* symbolize sensations, while the word "cat," formed from them, symbolizes the perception of the object.

It is held that all knowledge begins with sensation; that the mental history of the race or individual begins with its first sensation. But, while this is admitted, it must be remembered that sensation simply provides the simple, elementary, raw material of thought. The first process of *actual thought*, or knowledge, begins with perception. From our percepts all of our higher concepts and ideas are formed. Perception depends upon association of the sensation with other sensations previously experienced; it is based upon experience. The greater the experience, the greater is the possibility of perception, all else being equal.

When perception begins, the mind loses sight of the sensation in itself, for it identifies it as a quality of the thing producing it. The sensation of light is thought of as a quality of the star; the pricking sensation is thought of as a quality of the pin or chestnut burr; the sensation of odor is thought of as a quality of the rose. In the case of the rose, the several sensations of sight, touch, and smell, in their impression of the qualities of color, shape, softness, and perfume, are grouped together in the percept of the complete object of the flower.

A *percept* is "that which is perceived; the object of the act of perception." The percept, of course, is a mental state corresponding with its outside object. It is a combination of several sensations which are regarded as the qualities of the outside object, to which are combined the memories of past experiences, ideas, feelings, and thoughts. A percept, then, while the simplest form of thought, is seen to be a mental state. The formation of a percept consists of three gradual stages, viz.: (1) The attention forms definite conscious sensations from indefinite nervous reports; (2) the mind interprets these definite conscious sensations and attributes them to the outside object causing them; (3) the related sensations are grouped together, their unity perceived, and they are regarded as qualities of the outside object.

The plain distinction between a sensation and a percept may be fixed in the mind by remembering the following: *A sensation is a feeling; a percept is a simple thought identifying one or more sensations.* A sensation is merely the conscious recognition of an excitation of a nerve end; a percept results from a distinct mental process regarding the sensation.

DEVELOPING PERCEPTION

It is of the utmost importance that we develop and train our powers of perception. For our education depends very materially upon our perceptive power. What matters it to us if the outside world be filled with manifold objects, if we do not perceive them to exist? Upon perception depends the material of our mental world. Many persons go through the world without perceiving even the most obvious facts. Their eyes and ears are perfect instruments, their nerves convey accurate reports, but the perceptive faculties of the mind fail to observe and interpret the report of the senses. They see and hear distinctly, but the reports of the senses are not observed or noted by them; they mean nothing to them. One may see many things, and yet *observe* but few. It is not upon what we see or hear that our stock of knowledge depends, so much as it does upon what we perceive, notice, or observe.

Not only is one's stock of practical knowledge largely based upon developed perception, but one's success also depends materially upon the same faculties. In business and professional life the successful man is usually he who has developed perceptive powers; he who has learned to perceive, observe, and note. The man who perceives and takes mental notes of what occurs in his world is the man who is apt to know things when such knowledge is needed. In this age of "book education" we find that the young people are not nearly so observant as are those children who had to depend upon the powers of perception for their knowledge. The young Arab or Indian will observe more in an hour than the civilized child will in a day. To live in a world of books tends, in many cases, to weaken the powers of observation and perception.

Perception may be developed by practice. Begin by taking notice of the things seen and heard in your usual walks. Keep wide open the eyes of the mind. Notice the faces of people, their walk, their characteristics. Look for interesting and odd things, and you will see them. Do not go through life in a daydream, but keep a sharp lookout for things of interest and value. The most familiar things will repay you for the time and work of examining them in detail, and the practice gained by such tasks will prove valuable in your development of perception.

An authority remarks that very few persons, even those living in the country, know whether a cow's ears are above, below, behind, or in front of her horns; nor whether cats descend trees head first or tail first. Very few persons can distinguish between the leaves of the various kinds of familiar trees in their neighborhood. Comparatively few persons are able to describe the house in which they live, at least beyond the most general features—the details are unknown.

Houdin, the French conjurer, was able to pass by a shop window and perceive every article in it, and then repeat what he had seen. But he acquired this skill only by constant and gradual practice. He himself decried his skill and claimed that it was as nothing compared to that of the fashionable woman who can pass another woman on the street and "take in" her entire attire, from head to foot, at one glance, and "be able to describe not only the fashion and quality of the stuffs, but also say if the lace be real or only machine made." A former president of Yale is said to have been able to glance at a book and read a quarter of a page at one time.

Any study or occupation which requires *analysis* will develop the power of perception. Consequently, if we will analyze the things we see, resolving them into their parts or elements, we will likewise develop the perceptive faculties. It is a good exercise to examine some small object and endeavor to discover as many separate points of perception as possible, noting them on a sheet of paper. The most familiar object, if carefully examined, will yield rich returns.

If two persons will enter into a contest of this kind, the spirit of rivalry and competition will quicken the powers of observation. Those who have had the patience and perseverance to systematically practice exercises of this kind, report that they notice a steady improvement from the very start. But even if one does not feel inclined to practice in this way, it will be found possible *to begin to take notice* of the details of things one sees, the expression of persons' faces, the details of their dress, their tone of voice, the quality of the goods we handle, and *the little things especially*. Perception, like attention, follows interest; but, likewise, interest may be created in things by observing their details, peculiarities, and characteristics.

The best knowledge gained by one is that resulting from his own personal perception. There is a nearness and trueness about that which one *knows* in this way which is lacking in that which he merely *believes* because he has read or heard it. One can make such knowledge a part of himself. Not only is one's knowledge dependent upon what he perceives, but his very character also results from the character of his percepts. The influence of environment is great—and what is environment but things perceived about one? It is not so much what lies outside of one, as what part of it gets *inside* of one by perception. By directing his attention to desirable objects, and perceiving as much of them as is possible, one really builds his own character at will.

The world needs good "perceivers" in all the walks of life. It finds a shortage of them, and is demanding them loudly, being willing to pay a good price for their services. The person who can voluntarily perceive and observe the details of any profession, business, or trade will go far in that vocation. The education of children should take the faculty of perception into active consideration. The kindergarten has taken some steps in this direction, but there is much more to be done.

7

Memory

PSYCHOLOGISTS class as "representative mental processes" those known as memory and imagination, respectively. The term "representation" is used in psychology to indicate the processes of re-presentation or presenting again to consciousness that which has formerly been presented to it but which afterward passed from its field. As Hamilton says: "The general capability of knowledge necessarily requires that, besides the power of evoking out of unconsciousness one portion of our retained knowledge in preference to another, we possess the faculty of representing in consciousness what is thus evoked."

Memory is the primary representative faculty or power of the mind. Imagination depends upon memory for its material, as we shall see when we consider that faculty. Every mental process which involves the remembrance, recollection, or representation of a sensation, perception, mental image, thought, or idea previously experienced must depend upon memory for its material. Memory is the great storehouse of the mind in which are placed the records of previous mental experiences. It is a part of the great subconscious field of mental activity, and the greater part of its work is performed below the plane of consciousness. It is only when its results are passed into the field of consciousness that we are aware of its existence. We know memory only by its works. Of its nature we know but little, although certain of its principal laws and principles have been discovered.

It was formerly customary to class memory with the various faculties of the mind, but later psychology no longer so considers it. Memory is now regarded as a power of the general mind, manifesting in connection with every faculty of the mind. It is now regarded as belonging to the great subconscious field of mentation, and its explanation must be sought there. It is utterly unexplainable otherwise.

The importance of memory cannot be overestimated. Not only does a man's character and education depend chiefly upon it, but his very mental being is bound up with it. If there were no memory, man would never progress mentally beyond the mental state of the newborn babe. He would never be able to profit by experience. He would never be able to form clear perceptions. He would never be able to reason or form judgments. The processes of thought depend for material upon the memory of past experiences; this material lacking, there can be no thought.

Memory has two important general functions, viz.: (1) The *retention* of impressions and experiences; and (2) the *reproduction* of the impressions and experiences so retained.

It was formerly held that the memory retained only a portion of the impressions and experiences originally noted by it. But the present theory is that it retains every impression and experience which is noted by it. It is true that many of these impressions are never reproduced in consciousness, but experiments tend to prove, nevertheless, that the records are still in the memory and that appropriate and sufficiently strong stimuli will bring them into the field of consciousness. The phenomena of somnambulism, dreams, hysteria, delirium, approach of death, etc., show that the subconscious mind has an immense accumulation of apparently forgotten facts, which unusual stimuli will serve to recall.

The power of the memory to reproduce the retained impressions and experiences is variously called remembrance, recollection, or memory. This power varies materially in various individuals, but it is an axiom of psychology that the memory of any person may be developed and trained by practice. The ability to recall depends to a great extent upon the clearness and depth of the original impression, which in turn depends upon the degree of attention given to it at the time of its occurrence. Recollection is also greatly aided by the law of association, or the principle whereby one mental fact is linked to another. The more facts to which a given fact is linked, the greater the ease by which it is recalled or remembered. Recollection is also greatly assisted by use and exercise. Like the fingers, the memory cells of the brain become expert and efficient by use and exercise, or stiff and inefficient by lack of the same.

In addition to the phases of retention and reproduction, there are two important phases of memory, viz.: (3) Recognition of the reproduced impression or experience; and (4) localization of the impression, or its reference to a more or less definite time and place.

The recognition of the recalled impression is quite important. It is not enough that the impression be retained and recalled. If we are not able to recognize the recalled impression as having been experienced before, the recollection will be of but little use to us in our thought processes; the purposes of thought demand that we shall be able to identify the recalled impression with the original one. Recognition is really re-cognition—re-knowing. Recognition is akin to perception. The mind becomes conscious of the recalled impression just as it becomes conscious of the sensation. It then recognizes the relation of the recalled impression to the original one just as it realizes the relation of the sensation to its object.

The localization of the recalled and recognized impression is also important. Even if we recognize the recalled impression, it will be of comparatively little use to us unless we are able to locate it as having happened yesterday, last week, last month, last year, ten years ago, or at some time in the past; and as having happened in our office, house, or in such-and-such a place in the street, or in some distant place. Without the power of localization we should be unable to connect and associate the remembered fact with the time, place, and persons with which it should be placed to be of use and value to us in our thought processes.

RETENTION

The retention of a mental impression in the memory depends very materially upon the clearness and depth of the original impression. And this clearness and depth, as we have previously stated, depend upon the degree of attention bestowed upon the original impression. Attention, then, is the important factor in the forming and recording of impressions. The rule is: *Slight attention, faint record; marked attention, clear and deep record.* To fix this fact in the mind, the student may think of the retentive and reproductive phases of memory as a phonographic record. The receiving diaphragm of the phonograph represents the sense organs, and the recording needle represents the *attention*. The needle makes the record on the cylinder deep or faint according to the condition of the needle. A loud sound may be recorded but faintly, if the needle is not properly adjusted. And, further, it must be remembered that the strength of the reproduction depends almost entirely upon the clearness and depth of the original impression on the cylinder; as is the record, so is the reproduction. It will be well for the student to carry this symbol of the phonograph in his mind; it will aid him in developing his powers of memory.

In this connection we should remember that attention depends largely upon interest. Therefore we would naturally expect to find that we remember interesting things far more readily than those which lack interest. This supposition is borne out in actual experience. This accounts for the fact that every one remembers a certain class of things better than he does others. One remembers faces, another dates, another spoken conversation, another written words, and so on. It will be found, as a rule, that each person is interested in the class of things which he most easily remembers. The artist easily remembers faces and details of faces, or scenery and details thereof. The musician easily recalls passages or bars of music, often of a most complicated nature. The speculator easily recalls the quotations of his favorite stocks. The racing man recalls without difficulty the "odds" posted on a certain horse on a certain day, or the details of a race which was run many years ago. The moral is: *Arouse and induce an interest in the things which you wish to remember.* This interest may be aroused by studying the things in question, as we have suggested in a preceding chapter.

VISUALIZATION IN MEMORY

Many of the best authorities hold that original impressions may be made clear and deep, and the process of reproduction accordingly rendered more efficient, by the practice of *visualizing* the thing to be remembered. By visualizing is meant the formation of a *mental image* of the thing in the imagination. If you wish to remember the appearance of anything, look at it closely, with attention, and then turning away from it endeavor to reproduce its appearance as a mental picture in the mind. If this is done, a particularly clear impression will be made in the memory, and when you recall the thing you will find that you will also recall the clear mental image of it. Of course the greater the number of details observed and included in the original mental image, the greater the remembered detail.

PERCEPTION IN MEMORY

Not only is attention necessary in forming clear memory records, but careful perception is also important. Without clear perception there is a lack of detail in the retained record, and the element of association is lacking. It is not enough to merely remember the thing itself; we should also remember *what* it is, and all about it. The practice of the methods of developing perception, given in a preceding lesson, will tend to develop and train the retentive, reproductive, recognitive, and locative powers of the memory. The rule is: *The greater the degree of perception accorded a thing, the greater the detail of the retained impression, and the greater the ease of the recollection.*

UNDERSTANDING AND MEMORY

Another important point in acquiring impressions in memory is this: *That the better the understanding of the subject or object, the clearer the impressions regarding it, and the clearer the recollection of it.* This fact is proved by experiment and experience. A subject which will be remembered only with difficulty under ordinary circumstances will be easily remembered if it is fully explained to the person, and accompanied by a few familiar illustrations or examples. It is very difficult to remember a meaningless string of words, while a sentence which conveys a clear meaning may be memorized easily. If we understand *what a thing is for*, its uses and employment, we remember it far more easily than if we lack this understanding. Elbringhaus, who conducted a number of experiments along this line, reports that he could memorize a stanza of poetry in about one tenth the time required to memorize the same amount of nonsense syllables. Gordy states that he once asked a capable student of the Johns Hopkins University to give him an account of a lecture to which he had just listened. "I cannot do it," replied the student; "it was not logical." The rule is: *The more one knows about a certain thing, the more easily is that thing remembered.* This is a point worth noting.

8

Memory—Continued

THE subject of memory cannot be touched upon intelligently without a consideration of the Law of Association, one of the important psychological principles.

THE LAW OF ASSOCIATION

What is known in psychology as the Law of Association is based on the fact that *no idea exists in the mind except in association with other ideas.* This is not generally recognized, and the majority of persons will dispute the law at first thought. But the existence and appearance of ideas in the mind are governed by a mental law as invariable and constant as the physical law of gravitation. Every idea has associations with other ideas. Ideas travel in groups, and one group is associated with another group, and so on, until in the end every idea in one's mind is associated directly or indirectly with every other idea. Theoretically, at least, it would be possible to begin with one idea in the mind of a person, and then gradually unwind his entire stock of ideas like the yarn on the ball. Our thoughts proceed according to this law. We sit down in a "brown study" and proceed from one subject to another, until we are unable to remember any connection between the first thought and the last. But each step of the reverie was connected with the one preceding and the one succeeding it. It is interesting to trace back these connections. Poe based one of his celebrated detective stories on this law. The reverie may be broken into by a sudden impression from outside, and we will then proceed from that impression, connecting it with something else already in our experience, and starting a new chain of sequence.

Often we fail to trace the associations governing our ideas, but the chain is there nevertheless. One may think of a past scene or experience without any apparent cause. A little thought will show that something seen, or a few notes of a song floating to the ears, or the fragrance of a flower, has supplied the connecting link between the past and the present. A suggestion of mignonette will recall some past event in which the perfume played a part; someone's handkerchief, perhaps, carried the same odor. Or an old familiar tune reminds one of someone, something, or some place in the past. A familiar feature in the countenance of a passer-by will start one thinking of someone else who had that kind of a mouth, that shaped nose, or that expression of the eye—and away he will be off in a sequence of remembered experiences. Often the starting idea, or the connecting links, may appear but dimly in consciousness; but rest assured they are always there. In fact, we frequently accept this law, unconsciously and without realizing its actual existence. For instance, one makes a remark, and at once we wonder, "How did he come to think of that?" and, if we are shrewd, we may discover what was in his mind before he spoke.

There are two general classes of association of ideas in memory, viz.: (1) Association of contiguity, and (2) logical association.

Association of contiguity is that form of association depending upon the previous association in time or space of ideas which have been impressed on the mind. For instance, if you met Mr. and Mrs. Wetterhorn and were introduced to them one after the other, thereafter you will naturally remember Mr. W. when you think of Mrs. W., and vice versa. You will naturally remember Napoleon when you think of Wellington, or Benedict Arnold when you think of Major André, for the same reason. You will also naturally remember b and c when you think of a. Likewise, you will think of abstract time when you think of abstract space, of thunder when you think of lightning, of colic when you recall green apples, of love making and moonlight nights when you think of college days. In the same way we remember things which occurred just before or just after the event in our mind at the moment; of things near in space to the thing of which we are thinking.

Logical association depends upon the relation of likeness or difference between several things thought of. Things thus associated may have never come into the mind at the same previous time, nor are they necessarily connected in time and space. One may think of a book, and then proceed by association to think of another book by the same author, or of another author treating of the same subject. Or he may think of a book directly opposed to the first, the relation of distinct difference causing the associated idea. Logical association depends upon *inner relations*, and not upon the outer relations of time and space. This *innerness* of relation between things not connected in space or time is discovered only by experience and education. The educated man realizes many points of relationship between things that are thought by the uneducated man to be totally unrelated. Wisdom and knowledge consist largely in the recognition of relations between things.

ASSOCIATION IN MEMORY

It follows from a consideration of the Law of Association that when one wishes to impress a thing upon the memory he should, as an authority says, "Multiply associations; entangle the fact you wish to remember in a net of as many associations as possible, especially those that are logical." Hence the advice to place your facts in groups and classes in the memory. As Blackie says: "Nothing helps the mind so much as order and classification. Classes are always few, individuals many; to know the class well is to know what is most essential in the character of the individual, and what burdens the memory least to retain."

REPETITION IN MEMORY

Another important principle of memory is that the impressions acquire depth and clearness by repetition. Repeat a line of poetry once, and you may remember it; repeat it again, and your chances of remembering it are greatly increased; repeat it a sufficient number of times, and you cannot escape remembering it. The illustration of the phonograph record will help you to understand the reason of this. The rule is: *Constant repetition deepens memory impressions; frequent reviewing and recalling what has been memorized tends to keep the records clear and clean, beside deepening the impression at each review.*

GENERAL RULES OF MEMORY

The following general rules will be of service to the student who wishes to develop his memory:

MAKING IMPRESSIONS

(1) Bestow attention
(2) Cultivate interest
(3) Manifest perception
(4) Cultivate understanding
(5) Form associations
(6) Repeat and review

Recalling Impressions

(1) Endeavor to get hold of the loose end of association, and then unwind your memory ball of yarn.

(2) When you recall an impression, send it back with energy to deepen the impression, and attach it to as many new associations as possible.

(3) Practice a little memorizing and recalling each day, if only a line of verse. The memory improves by practice, and deteriorates by neglect and disuse.

(4) Demand good service of your memory, and it will learn to respond. Learn to trust it, and it will rise to the occasion. How can you expect your memory to give good service when you continually abuse it and tell every one of "the wretched memory I have; I can never remember anything"? Your memory is very apt to accept your statements as truth; our mental faculties have an annoying habit of taking us at our word in these matters. Tell your memory what you expect it to do; then trust it and refrain from abusing it and giving it a bad name.

FINAL ADVICE

Finally, remember this rule: You get out of your memory only that which you place in it. Place in it good, clear, deep impressions, and it will reproduce good, clear, strong recollections. Think of your memory as a phonographic record, and take care that you place the right kind of impressions upon it. In memory you reap that which you have sown. You must give to the memory before you can receive from it. Of one thing you may rest assured, namely, that unless you take sufficient interest in the things to be remembered, you will find that the memory will not take sufficient interest in them to remember them. Memory demands interest before it will take interest in the task. It demands attention before it will give attention. It demands understanding before it will give understanding. It demands association before it will respond to association. It demands repetition before it will repeat. The memory is a splendid instrument, but it stands on its dignity and asserts its rights. It belongs to the old dispensation—it demands compensation and believes in giving only in equal measure to what it receives. Our advice is to get acquainted with your memory, and make friends with it. Treat it well and it will serve you well. But neglect it, and it will turn its back on you.

9

Imagination

THE imagination belongs to the general class of mental processes called the representative faculties, by which is meant the processes in which there are re-presented, or presented again, to consciousness impressions previously presented to it.

As we have indicated elsewhere, the imagination is dependent upon memory for its materials—its records of previous impressions. But imagination is more than mere memory or recollection of these previously experienced and recorded impressions. There is, in addition to the re-presentation and recollection, a process of arranging the recalled impressions into new forms and new combinations. The imagination not only gathers together the old impressions, but also *creates* new combinations and forms from the material so gathered.

Psychology gives us many hairsplitting definitions and distinctions between simple reproductive imagination and memory, but these distinctions are technical and as a rule perplexing to the average student. In truth, there is very little, if any, difference between simple reproductive imagination and memory, although when the imagination indulges in constructive activity a new feature enters into the process which is absent in pure memory operations. In simple reproductive imagination there is simply the formation of the mental image of some previous experience—the reproduction of a previous mental image. This differs very little from memory, except that the recalled image is clearer and stronger. In the same way in ordinary memory, in the manifestation of recollection, there is often the same clear, strong mental image that is produced in reproductive imagination. The two mental processes blend into each other so closely that it is practically impossible to draw the line between them, in spite of the technical differences urged by the psychologists. Of course, the mere remembrance of a person who presents himself to one is nearer to pure memory than to imagination, for the process is that of recognition. But the memory or remembrance of the same person when he is absent from sight is practically that of reproductive imagination. Memory, in its stage of recognition, exists in the child mind before reproductive imagination is manifested. The latter, therefore, is regarded as a higher mental process.

But still higher in the scale is that which is known as *constructive imagination*. This form of imagination appears at a later period of child mentation, and is regarded as a later evolution of mental processes of the race. Gordy makes the following distinction between the two phases of imagination: "The difference between reproductive imagination and constructive imagination is that the images resulting from reproductive imagination are *copies of past experience*, while those resulting from constructive imagination are not. * * * To learn whether any particular image, or combination of images, is the product of reproductive or constructive imagination, all we have to do is to learn whether or not it is a copy of a past experience. Our memories, of course, are defective, and we may be uncertain on that account; but apart from that, we need be in no doubt whatever."

Many persons hearing for the first time the statement of psychologists that the imaginative faculties can re-present and re-produce or re-combine only the images which have previously been impressed upon the mind, are apt to object that they can, and frequently do, image things which they have not previously experienced. But can they and do they? Is it not true that what they believe to be original creations of the imagination are merely *new combinations* of original impressions? For instance, no one ever saw a unicorn, and yet someone originally imagined its form. But a little thought will show that the image of the unicorn is merely that of an animal having the head, neck, and body of a horse, with the beard of a goat, the legs of a buck, the tail of a lion, and a long, tapering horn, spirally twisted, in the middle of the forehead. Each of the several parts of the unicorn exists in some living animal, although the unicorn, composed of all of these parts, is non-existent outside of fable. In the same way the centaur is composed of the body, legs, and tail of the horse and the trunk, head, and arms of a man. The satyr has the head, body, and arms of a man, with the horns, legs, and hoofs of a goat. The mermaid has the head, arms, and trunk of a woman, joined at the waist to the body and tail of a fish. The mythological "devil" has the head, body, and arms of a man, with the horns, legs, and cloven foot of the lower animal, and a peculiar tail composed of that of some animal but tipped with a spearhead. Each of these characteristics is composed of familiar images of experience. The imagination may occupy itself for a lifetime turning out impossible animals of this kind, but every part thereof will be found to correspond to something existent in nature, and experienced by the mind of the person creating the strange beast.

In the same way the imagination may picture a familiar person or thing acting in an unaccustomed manner, the latter having no basis in fact so far as the individual person or thing is concerned, but being warranted by some experience concerning other persons or things. For instance, one may easily form the image of a dog swimming under water like a fish, or climbing a tree like a cat. Likewise, one may form a mental image of a learned, bewigged High Chancellor, or a venerable Archbishop of Canterbury, dressed like a clown, standing on his head, balancing a colored football on his feet, sticking his tongue in his cheek and winking at the audience. In the same way one may imagine a railroad running across a barren desert, or a steep mountain, upon which there is not as yet a rail laid. The bridge across a river may be imaged in the same way. In fact, this is the way that everything is mentally created, constructed, or invented—the old materials being combined in a new way, and arranged in a new fashion. Some psychologists go so far as to say that no mental image of memory is an exact reproduction of the original impression; that there are always changes due to the unconscious operation of the constructive imagination.

The constructive imagination is able to "tear things to pieces" in search for material, as well as to "join things together" in its work of building. The importance of the imagination in all the processes of intellectual thought is great. Without imagination man could not reason or manifest any intellectual process. It is impossible to consider the subject of thought without first regarding the processes of imagination. And yet it is common to hear persons speak of the imagination as if it were a faculty of mere fancy, useless and without place in the practical world of thought.

DEVELOPING THE IMAGINATION

The imagination is capable of development and training. The general rules for development of the imagination are practically those which we have stated in connection with the development of the memory. There is the same necessity for plenty of material; for the formation of clear and deep impressions and clear-cut mental images; the same necessity for repeated impression, and the frequent use and employment of the faculty. The practice of visualization, of course, strengthens the power of the imagination as it does that of the memory, the two powers being intimately related. The imagination may be strengthened and trained by deliberately recalling previous impressions and then combining them into new relations. The materials of memory may be torn apart and then re-combined and re-grouped. In the same way one may enter into the feelings and thoughts of other persons by imagining one's self in their place and endeavoring to act out in imagination the life of such persons. In this way one may build up a much fuller and broader conception of human nature and human motives.

In this place, also, we should caution the student against the common waste of the powers of the imagination, and the dissipation of its powers in idle fancies and daydreams. Many persons misuse their imagination in this way and not only weaken its power for effective work but also waste their time and energy. Daydreams are notoriously unfit for the real, practical work of life.

IMAGINATION AND IDEALS

And, finally, the student should remember that in the category of the imaginative powers must be placed that phase of mental activity which has so much to do with the making or marring of one's life—the formation of ideals. Our ideals are the patterns after which we shape our life. According to the nature of our ideals is the character of the life we lead.

Our ideals are the supports of that which we call *character*.

It is a truth, old as the race, and now being perceived most clearly by thinkers, that indeed "as a man thinketh in his heart so is he." The influence of our ideals is perceived to affect not only our character but also our place and degree of success in life. We grow to be that of which we have held ideals. If we create an ideal, either of general qualities or else these qualities as manifested by some person living or dead, and keep that ideal ever before us, we cannot help developing traits and qualities corresponding to those of our ideal. Careful thought will show that character depends greatly upon the nature of our ideals; therefore we see the effect of the imagination in character building.

Moreover, our imagination has an important bearing on our actions. Many a man has committed an imprudent or immoral act which he would not have done had he been possessed of an imagination which showed him the probable results of the action. In the same way many men have been inspired to great deeds and achievements by reason of their imagination picturing to them the possible results of certain action. The "big things" in all walks of life have been performed by men who had sufficient imagination to picture the possibilities of certain courses or plans. The railroads, bridges, telegraph lines, cable lines, and other works of man are the results of the imagination of some men. The good fairy godmother always provides a vivid and lively imagination among the gifts she bestows upon her beloved godchildren. Well did the old philosopher pray to the gods: "And, with all, give unto me a clear and active imagination."

The dramatic values of life depend upon the quality of the imagination. Life without imagination is mechanical and dreary. Imagination may increase the susceptibility to pain, but it pays for this by increasing the capacity for joy and happiness. The pig has but little imagination—little pain and little joy—but who envies the pig? The person with a clear and active imagination is in a measure a creator of his world, or at least a re-creator. He takes an active part in the creative activities of the universe, instead of being a mere pawn pushed here and there in the game of life.

Again, the divine gift of sympathy and understanding depends materially upon the possession of a good imagination. One can never understand the pain or problems of another unless he first can imagine himself in the place of the other. Imagination is at the very heart of sympathy. One may be possessed of great capacity for feeling, but owing to his lack of imagination may never have this feeling called into action. The person who would sympathize with others must first learn to understand them and feel their emotions. This he can do only if he has the proper degree of imagination. Those who reach the heart of the people must first be reached by the feelings of the people. And this is possible only to him whose imagination enables him to picture himself in the same condition as others, and thus awaken his latent feelings and sympathies and understanding. Thus it is seen that the imagination touches not only our intellectual life but also our emotional nature. Imagination is the very life of the soul.

10

The Feelings

In thinking of the mind and its activities we are accustomed to the general idea that the mental processes are chiefly those of intellect, reason, thought. But, as a fact, the greater part of the mental activities are those concerned with feeling and emotion. The intellect is the youngest child of the mind, and while making its presence strenuously known in the manner of all youngest children so that one is perhaps justified in regarding it as "the whole thing" in the family, nevertheless it really plays but a comparatively small part in the general work of the mental family. The activities of the "feeling" side of life greatly outnumber those of the "thinking" side, are far stronger in their influence and effect, as a rule, and, in fact, so color the intellectual processes, unconsciously, as to constitute their distinctive quality except in the case of a very few advanced thinkers.

But there is a difference between "feeling" and "emotion," as the terms are employed in psychology. The former is the simple phase, the latter the complex. Generally speaking, the resemblance or difference is akin to that existing between sensation and perception, as explained in a previous chapter. Beginning with the simple, in order later on to reach the complex, we shall now consider that which is known as simple "feeling."

The term "feeling," as used in this connection in psychology, has been defined as "the simple *agreeable* or *disagreeable* side of any mental state." These agreeable or disagreeable sides of mental states are quite distinct from the act of knowing, which accompanies them. One may perceive and thus "know" that another is speaking to him and be fully aware of the words being used and of their meaning. Ordinarily, and so far as pure thought processes are concerned, this would complete the mental state. But we must reckon on the feeling side as well as on the thinking side of the mental state. Accordingly we find that the knowledge of the words of the other person and the meaning thereof results in a mental state agreeable or disagreeable. In the same way the reading of the words of a book, the hearing of a song, or a sight or scene perceived, may result in a more or less strong feeling, agreeable or disagreeable. This sense of agreeable or disagreeable consciousness is the essential characteristic of what we call "feeling."

It is very difficult to explain feeling except in its own terms. We know very well what we mean, or what another means, when it is said that we or he "*feels* sad," or has "a joyous feeling," or "a feeling of interest." And yet we shall find it very hard to explain the mental state except in terms of feeling itself. Our knowledge depends entirely upon our previous experience of the feeling. As an authority says: "If we have never felt pleasure, pain, fear, or sorrow, a quarto volume cannot make us understand what such a mental state is." Every mental state is not distinguished by strong feeling. There are certain mental states which are concerned chiefly with intellectual effort, and in which all trace of feeling seems to be absent, unless, as some have claimed, the "feeling" of interest or the lack of same is a faint form of the feeling of pleasure or pain. Habit may dull the feeling of a mental state until it is apparently neutral, but there is generally a faint feeling of like or dislike still left.

The elementary forms of feeling are closely allied with those of simple sensation. But experiments have revealed that there is a distinction in consciousness. It has been discovered that one is often conscious of the "touch" of a heated object before he is of the feeling or pain resulting from it. Psychologists have pointed out another distinction, namely: When we experience a sensation we are accustomed to refer it to the outside thing which is the object of it, as when we touch the heated object; but when we experience a feeling we instinctively refer it to ourself, as when the heated object gives us pain. As an authority has said: "My feelings belong to me; but my sensations seem to belong to the object which caused them."

Another proof of the difference and distinction between sensation and feeling is the fact that the same sensation will produce different feelings in different persons experiencing the former, even at the same time. For instance, the same sight will cause one person to feel elated, and the other depressed; the same words will produce a feeling of joy in one, and a feeling of sorrow in another. The same sensation will produce different feelings in the same person at different times. An authority well says: "You drop your purse, and you see it lying on the ground as you stoop to pick it up, with no feeling either of pleasure or pain. But if you see it after you have lost it and have hunted for it a long time in vain, you have a pronounced feeling of pleasure."

There is a vast range of degree and kind in feeling. Gordy says: "All forms of pleasure and pain are called feelings. Between the pleasure which comes from

eating a peach and that which results from solving a difficult problem, or learning good news of a friend, or thinking of the progress of civilization—between
the pain that results from a cut in the hand and that which results from the
failure of a long-cherished plan or the death of a friend—there is a long distance. But the one group are all pleasures; the other all pains. And, whatever
the source of the pleasure or pain, it is alike feeling."

There are many different kinds of feelings. Some arise from sensations of
physical comfort or discomfort; others from purely physiological conditions;
others from the satisfaction of accustomed tastes, or the dissatisfaction arising from the stimulation of unaccustomed tastes; others from the presence or
absence of comfort; others from the presence or absence of things or persons
for whom we have an affection or liking. Over-indulgence often transforms
the feeling of pleasure into that of pain; and, likewise, habit and practice may
cause us to experience a pleasurable feeling from that which formerly inspired
feeling of an opposite kind. Feelings also differ in degree; that is to say, some
things cause us to experience pleasurable feelings of a greater intensity than do
others, and some cause us to experience painful feelings of a greater intensity
than do others. These degrees of intensity depend more or less upon the habit
or experience of the individual. As a general rule, feelings may be classified into
(1) those arising from physical sensations, and (2) those arising from ideas.

The feelings depending upon physical sensations arise either from inherited
tendencies and inclinations or from acquired habits and experience. It is an axiom of the evolutionary school that any physical activity that has been a habit
of the race, long continued, becomes an instinctive pleasure-giving activity in
the individual. For instance, the race for many generations was compelled to
hunt, fish, travel, swim, etc., in order to maintain existence. The result is that
we, the descendants, are apt to find pleasure in the same activities as sport,
games, exercise, etc. Many of our tendencies and feelings are inherited in this
way. To these we have added many acquired habits of physical activity, which
follow the same rule, *i.e.*, that habit and practice impart more or less pleasurable feeling. We find more pleasure in doing those things which we can do
easily or quite well than in the opposite kind of things.

The feelings depending upon ideas may also arise from inheritance. Many
of our mental tendencies and inclinations have come down to us from the past.
There are certain feelings that are born in one, without a doubt; that is to say,
there is a great capacity for such feelings which will be transformed into manifestation upon the presentation of the proper stimulus. Other mental feelings
depend upon our individual past experience, association, or suggestions from
others—upon our past environment, in fact. The ideals of those around us will

cause us to experience pleasure or pain, as the case may be, under certain circumstances; the force of suggestion along these lines is very strong indeed. Not only do we experience feelings in response to present sensations, but the recollection of some previous experience will also arouse feeling. In fact, feelings of this kind are closely bound up with memory and imagination. Persons of vivid imagination are apt to feel far more than others. They suffer more, and enjoy more. Our sympathies, which depend largely upon our imaginative power, are the cause of many of our feelings of this kind.

Many of the facts which we generally ascribe to feeling are really a part of the phenomena of emotion, the latter being the more complex phase of feeling. For the purposes of this consideration we have regarded simple feeling as the raw material of emotion, the relation being compared to that existing between sensation and perception. In our consideration of emotion we shall see the fuller manifestation of feeling, and its more complex expressions.

11

The Emotions

AS we have seen in the preceding lessons, an emotion is the more complex phase of feeling. As a rule an emotion arises from a number of feelings. Moreover, it is of a higher order of mental activity. As we have seen, a feeling may arise either from a physical sensation or from an idea. Emotion, however, as a rule, is dependent upon *an idea* for its expression, and always upon an idea for its direction and its continuance. Feeling, of course, is the elemental spirit of all emotional states, and, as an authority has said, is the thread upon which the emotional states are strung.

Halleck says: "When representative ideas appear, the feeling in combination with them produces emotion. After the waters of the Missouri combine with another stream, they receive a different name, although they flow toward the gulf in as great volume as before. Suppose we liken the feeling due to sensation to the Missouri River; the train of representative ideas to the Mississippi before its junction with the Missouri. Emotion may then be likened to the Mississippi *after* its junction—after feeling has combined with representative ideas. The emotional stream will not be broader and deeper than before. This analogy is employed only to make the distinction clearer. The student must remember that mental powers are never actually as distinct as two rivers before their union. * * * The student must beware of thinking that we have done with feeling when we consider emotion. Just as the waters of the Missouri flow on until they reach the gulf, so does feeling run through every emotional state." In the above analogy the term "representative ideas," of course, means the ideas of memory and imagination as explained in previous chapters.

There is a close relation between emotion and the physical expression thereof—a peculiar mutual action and reaction between the mental state and the physical action accompanying it. Psychologists are divided regarding this relation. One school holds that the physical expression follows and results from the mental state. For instance, we hear or see something, and thereupon experience the feeling or emotion of anger. This emotional feeling reacts upon the body and causes an increased heart beat, a tight closing of the lips, a frown and low-ered eyebrows, and clinched fists. Or we may perceive something which causes the feeling or emotion of fear, which reacts upon the body and produces pallor, raising of the hair, dropping of the jaw, opening of the eyelids, trembling of the legs, etc. According to this school, and the popular idea, the mental state precedes and causes the physical expression.

But another school of psychology, of which the late Prof. William James is a leading authority, holds that the physical expression precedes and causes the mental state. For instance, in the cases above cited, the perception of the anger-causing or fear-causing sight first causes a reflex action upon the muscles, according to inherited race habits of expression. This muscular expression and activity, in turn, is held to react upon the mind and to cause the feeling or emo-tion of anger or fear, as the case may be. Professor James, in some of his works, makes a forcible argument in support of this theory, and his opinions have influenced the scientific thought of the day upon this subject. Others, however, have sought to combat his theory by equally forcible argument, and the subject is still under lively and spirited discussion in psychological circles.

Without taking sides in the above controversy, many psychologists pro-ceed upon the hypothesis that there is a mutual action and reaction between emotional mental states and the appropriate physical expression thereof, each in a measure being the cause of the other, and each likewise being the effect of the other. For instance, in the cases above cited, the perception of the anger-producing or fear-producing sight causes, almost or quite simultaneously, the emotional mental state of anger or fear, as the case may be, and the physical ex-pression thereof. Then rapidly ensues a series of mental and physical reactions. The mental state acts upon the physical expression and intensifies it. The phys-ical expression in turn reacts upon the mental state and induces a more intense degree of the emotional feeling. And so on, until the mental state and physical expression reach their highest point and then begin to subside from exhaustion of energy. This middle-ground conception meets all the requirements of the facts, and is probably more nearly correct than either extreme theory.

Darwin in his classic work, "The Expression of the Emotions in Man and Animals," has thrown a great light on the subject of the expression of emotion in physical motions. The Florentine scientist, Paolo Mantegazza, added to Darwin's work with ideas of his own and countless examples drawn from his own ex-perience and observation. The work of François Delsarte, the founder of the school of expression which bears his name, is also a most valuable addition to the thought on this subject. The subject of the relation and reaction between emotional feeling and physical expression is a most fascinating one, and one in which we may expect interesting and valuable discoveries during the next twenty years.

The relation and reaction above mentioned are interesting not only from the viewpoint of theory but also because of their practicable application in emotional development and training. It is an established truth of psychology that each physical expression of an emotional state serves to intensify the latter; it is pouring oil on the fire. Likewise, it is equally true that the repression of the physical expression of an emotion tends to restrain and inhibit the emotion itself.

Halleck says: "If we watch a person growing angry, we shall see the emotion increase as he talks loud, frowns deeply, clinches his fist, and gesticulates wildly. Each expression of his passion is reflected back upon the original anger and adds fuel to the fire. If he resolutely inhibits the muscular expressions of his anger, it will not attain great intensity, and it will soon die a quiet death. * * * Not without reason are those persons called cold blooded who habitually restrain as far as possible the expression of their emotion; who never frown or throw any feeling into their tones, even when a wrong inflicted upon some one demands aggressive measures. There is here no wave of bodily expression to flow back and augment the emotional state."

In this connection we call your attention to the familiar and oft-quoted passage from the works of Prof. William James: "Refuse to express a passion and it dies. Count ten before venting your anger and its occasion seems ridiculous. Whistling to keep up courage is no mere figure of speech. On the other hand, sit all day in a moping posture, sigh and reply to everything with a dismal voice, and your melancholy lingers. There is no more valuable precept in moral education than this, as all who have experience know: If we wish to conquer undesirable emotional tendencies in ourselves, we must assiduously, and in the first instance cold-bloodedly, go through the outward movements of those contrary dispositions which we prefer to cultivate. Smooth the brow, brighten the eye, contract the dorsal rather than the ventral aspect of the frame, and speak in a major key, and your heart must be frigid indeed if it does not gradually thaw."

Along the same lines Halleck says: "Actors have frequently testified to the fact that emotion will arise if they go through the appropriate muscular movements. In talking to a character on the stage, if they clinch the fists and frown, they often find themselves becoming really angry; if they start with counterfeit laughter, they find themselves growing cheerful. A German professor says that he cannot walk with a schoolgirl's mincing step and air without feeling frivolous."

The wise student will acquire a great control over his emotional nature if he will re-read and study the above statements and quotations until he has grasped their spirit and essence. In those few lines he is given a philosophy of self-control and self-mastery that will be worth much to him if he will but apply it in practice. Patience, perseverance, practice, and will are required, but the reward is great. Even to those who have not the persistency to apply this truth fully, there will be a partial reward if they will use it to the extent of restraining so far as possible any undue physical expression of undesirable emotional excitement.

Some writers seem to regard capacity for great emotional excitement and expression as a mark of a rich and full character or noble soul. This is far from being true. While it is a fact that the cultivation of certain emotions tends to create a noble character and a full life, it is equally true that the tendency to "gush" and indulge in hysterical or sentimental excesses is a mark of an ill-controlled nature and a weak, rather than strong, character. Moreover, it is a fact that excess in emotional excitement and expression tends toward the dissipation of the finer and nobler feelings which otherwise would seek an outlet in actual doing and practical action. In the language of the old Scotch engineer in the story, they are like the old locomotive which "spends sae much steam at the whustle that she hae nane left to gae by."

Emotional excitement and expression are largely dependent upon habit and indulgence, although there is a great difference, of course, in the emotional nature and tendencies of various persons. Emotions, like physical actions or intellectual processes, become habitual by repetition. And habit renders all physical or mental actions easy of repetition. Each time one manifests anger, the deeper the mental path is made, and the easier it is to travel that path the next time. In the same way each time that anger is conquered and inhibited, the easier will it be to restrain it the next time. In the same way desirable habits of emotion and expression may be formed.

Another point in the cultivation, training, and restraint of the emotions is that which has to do with the control of the ideas which we allow to come into the mind. Ideative habits may be formed—*are* formed, in fact, by the majority of persons. We may cultivate the habit of looking on the bright side of things; of looking for the best in those we meet; of expecting the best things instead of the worst. By resolutely refusing to give welcome to ideas calculated to arouse certain emotions, feelings, passions, desires, sentiments, or similar mental states, we may do much to prevent the arousing of the emotion itself.

Emotions usually are called forth by some idea, and if we shut out the idea we may prevent the emotional feeling from appearing. In this connection the universal rule of psychology may be applied: *A mental state may be inhibited or restrained by turning the attention to the opposite mental state.*

The control of the attention is really the control of every mental state. We may use the will in the direction of the control of the attention—the development and direction of voluntary attention—and thus actually control every phase of mental activity. The will is nearest to the ego, or central being of man, and the attention is the chief tool and instrument of the will. This fact cannot be repeated too often. If it is impressed upon the mind it will prove to be useful and valuable in many emergencies of mental life. He who controls his attention controls his mind, and in controlling his mind controls himself.

12

The Instinctive Emotions

MANY attempts to classify the emotions have been made by the psychologists, but the best authorities hold that beyond the purpose of ordinary convenience in considering the subject *any* classification is scientifically useless by reason of its incompleteness. As James cleverly puts it: "Any classification of the emotions is seen to be as true and as natural as any other, if it only serves some purpose." The difficulty attending the attempted classification arises from the fact that every emotion is more or less complex, and is made up of various feelings and shades of emotional excitement. Each emotion blends into others. Just as a few elements of matter may be grouped into hundreds of thousands of combinations, so the elements of feeling may be grouped into thousands of shades of emotion. It is said that the two elements of carbon and hydrogen form combinations resulting in five thousand varieties of material substance, "from anthracite to marsh gas, from black coke to colorless naphtha." The same thing may be said of the emotional combinations formed from two principal elements of feeling. Moreover, the close distinction between sensation and feeling on the one hand, and between feeling and emotion on the other, serves to further complicate the task.

For the purposes of our consideration, let us divide the emotions into five general classes, as follows: (1) Instinctive emotions, (2) social emotions, (3) religious emotions, (4) æsthetic emotions, (5) intellectual emotions. We shall now consider each of the above five classes in turn.

THE INSTINCTIVE EMOTIONS

Instinct is defined as "unconscious, involuntary, or unreasoning prompting to any action," or "the natural unreasoning impulse by which an animal is guided to the performance of any action, without thought of improving the method." An authority says: "Instinct is a natural impulse leading animals, even prior to all experience, to perform certain actions tending to the welfare of the individual or the perpetuation of the species, apparently without understanding the object at which they may be supposed to aim, or deliberating as to the best methods to employ. In many cases, as in the construction of the cells of the bee, there is a perfection about the result which reasoning man could not have equaled, except by an application of the higher mathematics to direct the operations carried out. Mr. Darwin considers that animals, in time past as now, have varied in their mental qualities, and that those variations are inherited. Instincts also vary slightly in a state of nature. This being so, natural selection can ultimately bring them to a high degree of perfection."

It was formerly the fashion to ascribe instinct in the lower animals, and in man, to something akin to "innate ideas" implanted in each species and thereafter continued by inheritance. But the application of the idea of evolution to the science of psychology has resulted in brushing away these old ideas. Today it holds that that which we call "instinct" is the result of gradual development in the course of evolution, the accumulated experience of the race being stored away in the race memory, each individual adding a little thereto by his acquired habits and experiences. Psychologists now hold that the lower forms of these race tendencies are closely akin to purely reflex actions, and the higher forms, which are known as "instinctive emotions," are phenomena of the subconscious mind resulting from race memory and race experience.

Clodd says: "Instinct is the higher form of reflex action. The salmon migrates from sea to river; the bird makes its nest or migrates from one zone to another by an unvarying route, even leaving its young behind to perish; the bee builds its six-sided cell; the spider spins its web; the chick breaks its way through the shell, balances itself, and picks up grains of corn; the newborn babe sucks its mother's breast—all in virtue of like acts on the part of their ancestors, which, arising in the needs of the creature, and gradually becoming automatic, have not varied during long ages, the tendency to repeat them being transmitted within the germ from which insect, fish, bird, and man have severally sprung."

Schneider says: "It is a fact that men, especially in childhood, fear to go into a dark cavern, or a gloomy wood. This feeling of fear arises, to be sure, partly from the fact that we easily suspect that dangerous beasts may lurk in these localities—a suspicion due to stories we have heard and read. But, on the other hand, it is quite sure that this fear at a certain perception is also directly inherited. Children who have been carefully guarded from all ghost stories are nevertheless terrified and cry if led into a dark place, especially if sounds are made there. Even an adult can easily observe that an uncomfortable timidity steals over him in a lonely wood at night, although he may have the fixed conviction that not the slightest danger is near. This feeling of fear occurs in many men even in their own houses after dark, although it is much stronger in a dark cavern or forest. The fact of such instinctive fear is easily explicable when we consider that our savage ancestors through immemorable generations were accustomed to meet with dangerous beasts in caverns, especially bears, and were for the most part attacked by such beasts during the night and in the woods, and that thus an inseparable association between the perceptions of darkness, caverns, woods, and fear took place, and was inherited."

James says: "Nothing is commoner than the remark that man differs from lower creatures by the almost total absence of instincts, and the assumption of their work in him by reason. * * * We may confidently say that however uncertain man's reactions upon his environment may sometimes seem in comparison with those of the lower mammals, the uncertainty is probably not due to their possession of any principles of action which he lacks. *On the contrary, man possesses all the impulses that they have, and a great many more besides.* * * * High places cause fear of a peculiarly sickening sort, though here again individuals differ. The utterly blind instinctive character of the motor impulses here is shown by the fact that they are almost always entirely unreasonable, but that reason is powerless to suppress them. * * * Certain ideas of supernatural agency, associated with real circumstances, produce a peculiar kind of horror. This horror is probably explicable as the result of a combination of simple horrors. To bring the ghostly terror to its maximum, many unusual elements of the dreadful must combine, such as loneliness, darkness, inexplicable sounds, especially of a dismal character, moving pictures half discerned (or, if discerned, of dreadful aspect), and a vertiginous baffling of the expectation. * * * In view of the fact that cadaveric, reptilian, and underground horrors play so specific and constant a part in many nightmares and forms of delirium, it seems not altogether unwise to ask whether these forms of dreadful circumstance may not at a former period have been more normal objects of the environment than now. The evolutionist ought to have no difficulty in explaining these terrors, and the scenery that provokes them, as relapses into the consciousness of the cave men, a consciousness usually overlaid in us by experiences of a more recent date."

Instinctive emotion manifests as an impulse arising from the dim recesses of the feeling or emotional nature—an incentive toward a dimly conscious end. It differs from the almost purely automatic nature of certain forms of reflex process, for its beginning is a feeling arising from the subconscious regions, which strives to excite an activity of conscious volition. The feeling is from the subconscious, but the activity is conscious. The end may not be perceived in consciousness, or at least is but dimly perceived, but the action leading to the end is in full consciousness. Instinct is seen to have its origin in the past experiences of the race, transmitted by heredity and preserved in the race memory. It has for its object the preservation of the individual and of the species. Its end is often something far removed in time from the moment, or the welfare of the species rather than that of the individual; for instance, the caterpillar providing for its future states, or the bird building its nest, or the bees building cells and providing honey for their successors, for very few bees live to partake of the honey which they have gathered and stored—they are animated by "the spirit of the hive."

The most elementary forms of the instinctive emotions are those which have to do with the preservation of the individual, his comfort, and personal physical welfare. This class of emotions comprises what are generally known as purely "selfish" feelings, having little or no concern for the welfare of others. In this class we find the emotional feelings which have to do with the satisfaction of hunger and thirst, the securing of comfortable quarters and warm clothing, and the spirit of combat and strife arising from the desire to obtain these. These elemental feelings had their birth early in the history of life, and indeed life itself depended very materially upon them for its preservation and continuance. It was necessary for the primitive living thing to be "selfish." When man appeared, only those survived who manifested these feelings strongly; the others were pushed to the wall and perished. Even in our civilization the man below the average in this class of feelings will find it difficult to survive.

13

The Passions

ARISING from the most elemental instinctive emotions, we find what may be termed "the passions." By the term "passion" is meant those strong feelings in which the elemental selfish instincts are manifested in relation to other persons, either in the phase of attraction or repulsion. In this class we find the elementary phases of love, and the feelings of hate, anger, jealousy, revenge, etc. This class of emotions usually manifests violently, as compared with the other emotions. The passions generally arise from self-preservation, race preservation and reproduction, self-interest, self-aggrandizement, etc., and may be regarded as a more complex phase of the elemental instinctive emotions. The elemental instinctive emotions of self-preservation and self-comfort cause the individual to experience and manifest the passional emotions of desire for combat, anger, hate, revenge, etc., while the instinctive emotions leading to reproduction and continuance of the race give rise to the passional emotions of sexual love, jealousy, etc. The desire to attract the other sex increases ambition, vanity, love of display, and other feelings.

It is only when this class of emotions blends with the higher emotions that the passions become purified and refined. But it must not be forgotten that these emotions were very necessary for the welfare of the race in the early stage of its evolution, and that they still play an active part in human life, under the greater or less restraint imposed by civilized society. Nor should it be forgotten that from these emotions have evolved the highest love of one human being for another. From instinctive sexual love and the "racial instinct" have developed the higher affection of man for woman, and woman for man, in all their beautiful manifestations—and the love of the parent for the child, and the love of the child for the parent. The first manifestation of altruism arises in the love of the living creature for its mate, and in the love of the parents for their offspring.

In certain forms of life where the association of the sexes is merely for the moment, and is not followed by protection, mutual aid, and companionship, there is found an absence of mutual affection of any kind, the only feeling being an elemental reproductive instinct bringing the male and female together for the moment—an almost purely reflex activity. In the same way, in the cases of certain animals (the rattlesnake, for instance) in which the young are able to protect themselves from birth, there is seen a total absence of parental affection or the return thereof. Human love between the sexes, in its higher and lower degrees, is a natural evolution from passional emotion of a low order, due to the growth of social, ethical, moral, and æsthetic emotion arising from the necessities of the increasing complexity and development of human life.

The simpler forms of passional emotion are almost entirely instinctive in their manifestation. Indeed, in many cases, there appears to be but little more than a high form of reflex nervous action. The following words of William James give us an interesting view of this fact of life: "The cat runs after the mouse, runs or shows fight before the dog, avoids falling from walls and trees, shuns fire and water, not because he has any notion either of life or of death or of self-preservation. He acts in each case separately and simply because he cannot help it; being so framed that when that particular running thing called a mouse appears in his field of vision, he *must* pursue; that when that particular barking and obstreperous thing called a dog appears there, he *must* retire if at a distance, and scratch if close by; that he *must* withdraw his feet from water, and his face from flame, etc. * * * Now, why do the various animals do what seem to us such strange things in the presence of such outlandish stimuli? Why does the hen, for instance, submit herself to the tedium of incubating such a fearfully uninteresting set of objects as a nestful of eggs, unless she have some sort of prophetic inkling of the result? The only answer is *ad hominem*. We can only interpret the instinct of brutes by what we know of instincts in ourselves. Why do men always lie down, when they can, on soft beds rather than on soft floors? Why do they sit around a stove on a cold day? Why, in a room, do they place themselves, ninety-nine times out of a hundred, with their faces toward its middle rather than to the wall? Why does the maiden interest the youth so much that everything about her seems more important and significant than anything else in the world? Nothing more can be said than that these are human ways, and that every creature likes its own ways, and takes to following them as a matter of course. Science may come and consider these ways, and find that most of them are useful. But it is not for the sake of their utility that they are followed, but because at the moment of following them we feel that it is the only appropriate and natural thing to do. Not one man in a million, when taking his dinner, ever thinks of its utility. He eats because the food tastes good, and makes him want more. If you should ask him *why* he wants to eat more of what tastes like that, instead of revering you as a philosopher he will probably laugh at you for a fool."

James continues: "It takes, in short, what Berkeley called a mind debauched by learning to carry the process of making the natural seem strange, so far as to ask the *why* of any instinctive human act. To the metaphysician alone can such questions arise as: Why do we smile when pleased and not scowl? Why are we unable to talk to a crowd as to a single friend? Why does a particular maiden turn our wits upside down? The common man can only say, '*Of course* we smile, *of course* our heart palpitates at the sight of the crowd, *of course* we love the maiden—that beautiful soul clad in that perfect form, so palpably and flagrantly made from all eternity to be loved!' And so, probably, does each animal feel about the particular things it tends to do in the presence of particular objects. They, too, are *a priori* syntheses. To the lion it is the lioness which is made to be loved; to the bear, the she bear. To the broody hen the notion would seem monstrous that there should be a creature in the world to whom a nestful of eggs was not the utterly fascinating, precious, and never-to-be-too-much-sat-upon object which it is to her. Thus we may be sure that however mysterious some animals' instincts may appear to us, our instincts will appear no less mysterious to them. And we may conclude that, to the animal which obeys it, every impulse and every step of that instinct shines with its own sufficient light, and seems at the moment the only externally right and proper thing to do. It may be done for its own sake exclusively."

One has very little need, as a rule, to develop the passional emotions. Instinct has taken pretty good care that we shall have our share of this class of feelings. But there is a need to train, restrain, govern, and control these emotions, for the conditions which brought about their original being have changed. Our social conventions require that we should subordinate these passional feelings, to some extent at least. Society insists that we must restrict our love impulses to certain limits and to certain quarters, and that we subdue our anger and hate, except toward the enemies of our land, the disturbers of public peace, and the menacers of the social conventions of our time and land. The public welfare requires that we inhibit our fighting impulses, except in cases of self-defense or war. Public policy requires that we keep our ambitions within reasonable limits, which limits change from time to time, of course. In short, society has stepped in and insisted that man, as a social being, must not only acquire a *social conscience* but must also develop sociable emotions and inhibit his unsociable ones. The evolution of man's nature has caused him unconsciously to modify his elemental, instinctive, passional emotions, and subordinate them to the dictates of social, ethical, moral, and æsthetic feelings and ideals, and to intellectual considerations. Even the original elemental instincts of the lower animals have been modified by reason of the social requirements of the pack, herd, or drove, until the modified instinct is now the ruling force.

The general principles of emotional control, restraint, and mastery, as given in a preceding chapter, are applicable to the particular class of emotions now under consideration here.

(1) By refraining from the physical expression, one may at least partially inhibit the emotion.

(2) By refusing to create the habit, one may more easily manifest control.

(3) By refusing to dwell upon the idea or mental picture of the exciting object, one may lessen the stimulus.

(4) By cultivating the opposite class of emotions, one may inhibit any class of feeling.

(5) And, finally, by acquiring a control of the attention, by means of the will, one has the reins firmly in hand, and may drive or hold back the steeds of passion as he wills.

The passions are like fiery horses, useful if well under control, but most dangerous if the control is lost. The ego is the driver, the will his hands, attention the reins, habit the bit, and the passions the horses. To drive the chariot of life under social conditions, the ego must have strong hands (will) to tighten or loosen the reins of attention. He must also employ a well designed and shaped bit of habit. Without strong hands, good reins, and well-adjusted bit, the fiery steeds of passion may gain control and, running away, dash the chariot and its driver over the precipice and on to the jagged rocks below.

14

The Social Emotions

AS man became a social animal he developed new traits of character, new habits of action, new ideals, new customs, and consequently new emotions. Emotions long entertained and long manifested by the race become more or less instinctive, and are passed along in the form of either (*a*) inherited stimulus akin to, but lesser in degree and force than, the more elemental emotions; or (*b*) of inherited *tendency* to manifest the acquired emotional feeling upon the presentation of sufficiently strong stimuli. Hence arises that which we have called "the social emotions."

Under the classification of "the social emotions" are those acquired tendencies of action and feeling of the race which are more or less altruistic, and are concerned with the welfare of others and one's duties and obligations toward society and our fellow men. In this class are found the emotions which impel us to perform what we consider or feel to be our duty toward our neighbors, and our obligations and duty toward the state, as expressed in its laws, the customs of men of our country, or the ideals of the community. In another phase it manifests as sympathy, fellow feeling, and "kindness" in general. In its first phase we find civic virtue, law-abiding inclination, honesty, "square dealing," and patriotism; in its second phase we find sympathy for others, charity, mutual aid, the alleviation of poverty and suffering, the erection of asylums for orphans and the aged, hospitals for the sick, and the formation of societies for general charitable work.

In many cases we find the social, ethical, and moral emotions closely allied with religious emotion, and by many these are supposed to be practically identical, but there is a vast difference in spite of their frequent association. For instance, we find many persons of high civic virtue, of exalted moral ideals, and manifesting ethical qualities of the most advanced type, who are lacking in the ordinary religious feelings. On the other hand, we too frequently find persons professing great religious zeal, and apparently experiencing the most intense religious emotional feeling, who are deficient in social, civic, ethical, and moral qualities, in the best sense of these terms. The aim of all religion worthy of the name, however, is to encourage ethical and moral as well as religious emotions.

We must here make the distinction between those manifesting the actions termed ethical and moral *because they feel that way,* and those who merely comply with the conventional requirements *because they fear the consequences* of their violation. The first class have the true social, ethical, and moral feelings, tastes, ideals, and inclinations; while the second manifest merely the elementary feelings of self-preservation and selfish prudence. The first class are "good" because they feel that way and find it natural to be so; while the others are "good" merely because they have to be or be punished by legal penalty or public opinion, loss of prestige, loss of financial support, etc.

The social, moral, and ethical emotions are believed to have arisen in the race by reason of the association of individuals in communities and the rise of the necessity for mutual aid and forbearance. Even many of the species of the lower animals have social, moral, or ethical codes of their own, based on the experience of the species or family, infractions of which they punish severely. In the same way sympathy and the altruistic feelings are supposed to have arisen. The community of interest and understanding in the tribe, family, or clan brought not only the feeling of natural defense and protection but also the finer, inner sympathetic feeling of the pains and sufferings of their associates. This, in the progress of the race, has developed into broader and more complex ideals and feelings.

Theology explains the moral feelings as resulting from conscience, which it holds to be a special faculty of the mind, or soul, divinely given. Science, while admitting the existence of the state of feelings which we call "conscience," denies its supernatural origin, and ascribes it to the result of evolution, heredity, experience, education, and suggestion. Conscience, according to science, is a compound of intellectual and emotional states. Conscience is not an invariable or infallible guide, but *depends entirely upon the heredity, education, experience, and environment of the individual.* It accompanies the moral and ethical codes of the race, which vary with time and with country. Actions which were thought right a century ago are condemned now; likewise, things condemned a century ago are thought right now. What is commended in Turkey is condemned in England, and vice versa. Moral tastes and ideals, like æsthetic ones, vary with time and country. There is no absolute code which has been always true, in all places. There is an evolution in the ideals of morals and ethics as in everything else, and "conscience" and the moral and ethical emotions accompany the changing ideals.

Many of the moral and ethical principles originally arose from necessity or utility, but have since developed into natural, spontaneous feeling on the part of the race. It is held that the race is rapidly developing a "social conscience" which will cause the wiping out of many social conditions which are now the disgrace of civilization. It is predicted that in time the race will look back upon the existence of poverty in our civilization as our generation now looks back upon the existence of slavery, imprisonment for debt, capital punishment for the theft of a loaf of bread, the killing of prisoners of war, etc. It is thought that, in time, wars of conquest will be deemed as utterly immoral as today is regarded the murder of a body of men by a band of pirates or bandits. In the same way the economic slavery of today will be seen as immoral as now seems the physical slavery of the past. In not far distant time it will seem incredible that society could have ever allowed one of its members to die of hunger in the streets, or of poverty and inattention in the sick room of the hovel. Not only will the ideals and feelings of ethical and moral responsibility change and evolve, but the feelings of personal sympathy will evolve in accordance therewith. At least such is the dream and prophecy of some of the world's greatest thinkers.

The social, ethical, and moral emotions may be developed by a study of the evolution and meaning of society on the one hand, and the perception of the condition of the lives of less fortunate individuals on the other. The first will awaken new ideas of the history and real meaning of social association and mutual intercourse, and will develop a new sense of responsibility, duty, and civic and social pride. The second will awaken understanding and sympathy, and a desire to do what one can to help those who are "the under dog," and also to bring about a better state of affairs in general. The study of history and civilization, of sociology and civics, will do much in the first direction. The study of human-kind, and its life problems and condition, will do the same in the second case. In both cases there will be awakened a new sense of "right and wrong"—a new conception of "ought and ought not"—regarding one's relations to the race, society, and his fellow beings.

Let no one deceive himself or herself by the smug assumption that the race has entirely emerged from barbarism and is now on the top wave of civilization. The truth, as known to all careful and conscientious thinkers, is that we are but *half* civilized, if, indeed, that much. Many of our customs and conventions are those of a half-barbarous people. Our ideals are low, our customs often vile. We lack not only high ideals but in many cases we show a lack of sanity in our social conventions. But evolution is moving us slowly ahead. A better day is dawning. The signs are in the air, to be seen by all thoughtful men. Civilization is climbing the ladder, aided by the evolution of the social, ethical, and moral emotions and the development of the intellect.

In connection with this phase of the emotions, we invite the student to consider the following excellent words of Professor Davidson in his "History of Greek Education": "It is not enough for a man to understand the conditions of rational life in his own time. He must likewise *love* these conditions and *hate* whatever leads to life of an opposite kind. This is only another way of saying that he must love the good and hate the evil; for the good is simply what conduces to rational or moral life, and the evil simply what leads away from it. It is perfectly obvious, as soon as it is pointed out, that all immoral life is due to a false distribution of affection, which again is often, though by no means always, due to a want of intellectual cultivation. He that attributes to anything a value greater or less than it really possesses, in the order of things, has already placed himself in a false relation to it, and will certainly, when he comes to act with reference to it, act immorally."

15

The Religious Emotions

BY "the religious emotions" is meant that class of emotional feeling arising from the faith and belief in, or consciousness of the presence of, supernatural beings, powers, entities, or forces. This form of emotion is regarded as distinct from the ethical and moral emotions, although frequently found in connection therewith. Likewise, it is independent of any special form of intellectual belief, for it is far more fundamental and often exists without creed, philosophy, or stated belief, the only manifestation in such cases being a "feeling" of the existence of supernatural beings, forces, and powers to which man has a relation and to which he owes obedience. To those who may think that this is too narrow a conception of religious emotion we refer the following definition of "religion" from the dictionaries: "The acts or feelings which result from the belief of a god, or gods, having superior control over matter, life, or destiny. Religion is subjective, designating the feelings and acts of men which relate to God; theology is objective, denoting the science which investigates the existence, laws, and attributes of God;" or (objectively) "the outer form and embodiment which the inward spirit of a true or a false devotion assumes," (subjectively) "the feeling of veneration with which the worshiper regards the Being he adores."

Darwin, in his "Descent of Man," says that the feeling of religious devotion is a highly complex one, consisting of love, complete submission to an exalted and mysterious superior, a strong sense of dependence, fear, reverence, gratitude, hope for the future, and perhaps other elements. He is of the opinion that no man can experience so complex an emotion until advanced in his intellectual and moral faculties to at least a moderately high level. The authorities generally agree with Darwin, although the more recent study of the history of religion has shown that religious feeling has a far more primitive origin than that indicated by Darwin.

It is true that the lower animals are not deemed capable of anything approaching religious feeling, unless there is a feeling approaching it in the attitude of the dog and horse and other domestic animals toward their masters. But man, as soon as he is able to attribute natural phenomena to a supernatural cause and power, manifests a crude religious feeling and emotion. He begins by believing in, fearing, and worshiping natural forces and objects, such as the sun, the moon, the wind, thunder and lightning, the ocean, rivers, mountains, etc. It is claimed that there is no natural object that has not been deified and worshiped by some people at some time in the history of the race. Later, man acquired the anthropomorphic conception of deities and created many gods in his own image, endowing them with his own attributes, qualities, and characteristics. The mental characteristics and morals of a people can always be ascertained by a knowledge of the average conception of deity held by them. Polytheism, or the belief in many gods, was succeeded by monotheism, or belief in one god.

Monotheism ranges from the crudest conception of a manlike god to the highest conception of a spiritual Being transcending all human qualities, attributes, or characteristics. Man began by believing in many god *things*, then in many god *persons*, then in a one god-person, then in one God who is a spirit, then in One Universal Spirit which is God. It is a far cry from the savage, manlike god of old to the conception of the Universal Spirit of the "God-drunken philosopher," Spinoza. The extreme of religious belief is that which holds that "there is nothing but God—all else is illusion," of pantheistic idealism. Buddhism (at least in its original form) discarded the idea of a Supreme Being, and held that Ultimate Reality is but Universal *Law*; hence the accusation that Buddhism is an "atheistic religion," although it is one of the world's greatest religions, having over 400,000,000 followers.

But the *beliefs* of the religious person may be considered as resulting from intellectual processes; his religious *feelings and emotions* arise from another part of his mental being. It is the testimony of the authorities of all religions that religious conviction is an inner experience rather than an intellectual conception. The emotional element is always active in religious manifestations everywhere. The purely intellectual religion is naught but a philosophy. Religion without feeling and emotion is an anomaly. In all true religion there exists a feeling of inner assurance and faith, love, awe, dependence, submission, reverence, gratitude, hope, and perhaps fear. The emotional element must always be present, not necessarily in the form of emotional excess, as in the case of revival hysteria or the dance of the whirling dervishes, but at least in the form of the calm, fervent feeling of "that peace which passeth understanding." When religion departs from the emotional phase it becomes merely a "school of philosophy," or an "ethical culture society."

The student must not lose sight of the uplifting influence of true religious emotion by reason of his knowledge of its lowly origin. Like the lotus, which has its roots in the slimy, filthy mud of the river, and its stem in the muddy, stagnant, and foul waters thereof, but its beautiful flower unfolded in the clear air and facing the sun, so is religious feeling responsible for some of the most beautiful and uplifting ideals and actions of the race. If its origin and history contain much that is not consistent with the highest ideals of the race today, it is not the fault of religion but of the race itself. Religion, like all else in the universal manifestation, is under the laws of evolution, growth, and development. What the religion of the future may be, we know not. But the prophets of the race are dreaming visions of a religion as much higher than that of today as the latter is higher than the crude fetishism of the savage.

The following quotation from John Fiske's "Through Nature to God" is appropriate in this place. Fiske says: "My aim is to show that 'that other influence,' that inward conviction, the craving for a final cause, the theistic assumption, is itself one of the master facts of the universe, and as much entitled to respect as any fact in physical nature can possibly be. The argument flashed upon me about ten years ago while reading Herbert Spencer's controversy with Frederic Harrison concerning the nature and reality of religion. Because Spencer derived historically the greater part of modern belief in an Unseen World from the savage's primeval world of dreams and ghosts, some of his critics maintained that logical consistency required him to dismiss the modern belief as utterly false; otherwise he would be guilty of seeking to evolve truth from falsehood. 'By no means,' replied Spencer. 'Contrariwise, the ultimate form of the religious consciousness is the final development of a consciousness which at the outset contained a germ of truth obscured by multitudinous errors.'" Fiske, in this connection, quotes the Tennysonian question:

"'Who forged that other influence,
That heat of inward evidence,
By which he doubts against the sense?'"

The religious emotions may be developed by allowing the mind to dwell upon the Power underlying the universe of fleeting, changing forms; by reading prose and poetry in which an appeal is made to the religious instinct; by listening to music which awakens the emotion of reverence and awe; and, finally, by meditating upon the inner spirit immanent in every living being. As an old Hindu sage once said: "There are many paths by which men arrive at a knowledge of the presence of God, but there is but one goal and destination."

16

The Æsthetic Emotions

BY "the æsthetic emotions" is meant those emotional feelings which are concerned with the perception of beauty or taste, and by reason of which we "like" or "dislike" certain perceptions of sensory impressions. In order to get a clearer idea, let us consider what is meant by "beauty" and "taste."

"Beauty" is defined as "that quality or assemblage of qualities in an object which gives the eye or the ear intense pleasure; or that characteristic in an object which gratifies the intellect or moral feeling." "Taste" (in this sense of the term) is defined as "nice perception, or the power of perceiving and relishing excellence in human performances; the power of appreciating the finer qualities of art; the faculty of discerning beauty, order, congruity, proportion, symmetry, or whatever constitutes excellence, particularly in the fine arts or literature; the faculty of the mind by which we both perceive and enjoy whatever is beautiful or sublime in the works of nature and art. The possession of taste insures grace and beauty in the works of an artist, and the avoidance of all that is low or mean. It is as often the result of an innate sense of beauty or propriety as of art education, and no genius can compensate for the want of it. * * * Tastes differ so much among individuals, nations, or in different ages and conditions of civilization that it is utterly impossible to set up a standard of taste applicable to all men and to all stages in the evolution of society."

The æsthetic sense, feeling, and emotion are products of the later stages of the evolution of the mind of man. Their roots, however, may be seen in the crude attempts at decoration and adornment in the savage, and still further back in the tendency of certain birds to adorn their nests or "bowers." Moreover, some sense of beauty must exist in the lower animals, which are influenced thereby in the selection of their mates, the bright plumage of the birds, and the coloring of the insects and higher animals evidencing the existence of at least a primitive æsthetic sense. Herbert Spencer says that one characteristic of the æsthetic feelings is that they are separated from the functions vitally requisite and necessary to sustain life, and it is not until the latter are reasonably well satisfied that the former begin to manifest in force.

The authorities hold that the basic element concerned in the manifestation of the æsthetic emotional feeling is the *sensory* element, which consists of the pleasure arising from the perception of objects of vision or hearing which are deemed beautiful. There is a certain nervous satisfaction which arises from the perception of the sensation of the sight of a beautiful thing, or of the hearing of beautiful sound. Just *why* certain sights prove agreeable and others disagreeable, or certain sounds pleasant and others unpleasant, is very difficult to determine. Association and habit may have something to do with the beauty of sight object, and there may be natural harmony of vibration in colors as there is in sound. In the case of sounds there is undoubtedly a natural harmony between the vibrations of certain notes of the scale and inharmony between others. Some have held that the secret of the enjoyment of music is found in the natural appreciation of rhythm, as rhythm is a cosmic manifestation evident in everything from great to small. But these theories do not account for the differences existing in the tastes regarding color and music manifested by different individuals, races, and classes of people.

Grant Allen says: "The vulgar are pleased with great masses of color, especially red, orange, and purple, which give their coarse, nervous organization the requisite stimulus. The refined, with nerves of less caliber, but greater discriminativeness, require delicate combinations of complementaries and prefer neutral tints to the glare of the primary hues. Children and savages love to dress in all the colors of the rainbow." In the same way persons of certain types of taste are pleased with "rag time" and cheap, rollicking songs or dances, while others shudder at these and find delight in the classic productions of the great composers.

There is also the *intellectual* element to be reckoned with in the æsthetic emotions. The intellect must discover the beauty in certain objects before the emotion is aroused by the perception. Halleck says: "Every time the mind discerns unity amid variety, order, rhythm, proportion, or symmetry, an æsthetic emotion arises. * * * The traveler with a trained intellect will see far more beauty than an ignorant one. In looking at a cathedral, a large part of the æsthetic enjoyment comes from tracing out the symmetry, from comparing part with part. Not until this process is complete will the full beauty of the structure as a whole be perceived. If the traveler knows something of mediæval architecture before starting on his European trip, he will see far more beauty.

The opposite of the æsthetic, which we call the ugly, is the unsymmetrical, the disorderly—that in which we can discover no rhythm, plan, or beauty."

The element of *associative suggestion* also enters into the manifestation of æsthetic emotional feeling. The mind accepts the suggestion of the beauty of certain styles of art, or the excellence of certain classes of music. There are fashions in art and music, as in clothes, and what is thought beautiful today may be deemed hideous tomorrow. This is not entirely due to the evolution of taste, for in many cases the old fashions are revived and again deemed beautiful. There is, moreover, the effect of the association of the object of emotion with certain events or persons. This association renders the thing popular, and therefore agreeable and beautiful for the time being. The suggestion in a story will often cause the beauty of a certain scene, or the harmony of a certain piece of music, to dawn upon thousands of persons. Some noted person sets the seal of approval upon a certain picture or musical composition and lo! the multitude calls it beautiful. It must not be supposed, however, that the crowd always counterfeits this sense of beauty and excellence which has been suggested to it. On the contrary, genuine æsthetic feeling often results from the discovery so made.

There is style and fashion in the use of words, resulting from fashion, which gives rise to æsthetic feelings regarding them. These feelings do not arise from the consideration of the nature of the object expressed by the word; of two words designating the same thing, one causes disgust and the other at least passive tolerance. For instance, in speaking of the sensible moisture which is emitted from the pores of the skin, we may use either of the respective terms "sweat" or "perspiration." Both mean the same thing, and have an equally respectable origin. But to many persons the word "sweat" causes unpleasant æsthetic emotion, while the word "perspiration" is accepted without remonstrance. Some persons abhor the term "victuals," while "viands" or "food" are accepted without protest. There is often an unpleasant, low, vulgar association connected with some words which accounts for the disfavor with which they are received, and which association is absent from the more "polite" terms employed to indicate the same thing. But in other cases there is nothing but the simple suggestion of fashion and style to account for the æsthetic acceptance or rejection.

It is possible that some psychologist of the future will establish the truth of the theory now tentatively advanced by a few investigators, namely, that taste and the sense of beauty depend almost entirely upon the element of suggestion, manifested as association, influence of authority, habit, fashion, imitation, etc.

It is known that the emotional nature is peculiarly liable to suggestion, and that tastes may be created or destroyed by repeated suggestion under the most favorable circumstances. It is thought likely that if we could trace back to its roots every emotion of taste, we would find it arising from some associative, suggestive influence connected with another and more elemental class of emotions.

Regarding the fact that there is no universal standard of taste or beauty, Halleck says: "It has been said that æsthetics cannot be treated in a scientific way because there is no standard of taste. *'De gustibus non est disputandum'* ('there is no disputing about tastes') is an old proverb. Of two equally intelligent persons, the one may like a certain book, the other dislike it. * * * While it is true that the standard of taste is a varying one within certain limits, it is no more so than that of morals. As men's nervous systems, education, and associations differ, we may scientifically conclude that their tastes must differ. The greater the uniformity in the factors the less does the product vary. On the other hand, within certain limits, the standard of æsthetics is relatively uniform. *It is fixed by the majority of intelligent people of any age and country.* To estimate the standard by which to judge of the correctness of language or of the literary taste of any era, we examine the conversations of the best speakers, the works of the standard writers."

The æsthetic emotions may be developed and cultivated by exercise and practice, and particularly by association and familiarity with beautiful things, and with those who have "good taste." Appreciation of beauty is more or less contagious, up to a certain point of development, at least, and if one wishes to recognize, understand, and appreciate beauty, he should go where beauty is, and where its votaries are gathered. The study of standard works of art, or objects of nature, or the best productions of the composers of music, will do much to develop and unfold one's higher æsthetic feelings and understanding.

It is claimed by some of the best authorities that to develop the finer and higher æsthetic feelings and understanding we must learn to find beauty and excellence in things removed from ourselves or our selfish interests. The narrow, selfish emotions kill the æsthetic feelings—the two cannot exist together. The person whose thoughts are centered on himself or herself very rarely finds beauty or excellence in works of art or music. Grant Allen well sums up the subject in the following words: "*Good taste is the progressive product of progressing fineness and discrimination in the nerves, educated attention, high and noble emotional constitution, and increasing intellectual faculties.*"

17

The Intellectual Emotions

BY "the intellectual emotions" is meant that class of emotional feeling resulting from the presence of objects of intellectual interest. This class of emotions depends for its satisfaction upon the exercise of the intellectual faculties, from the most simple to the most complex, and including perception, memory, imagination, reason, judgment, and all the logical faculties. Those who are accustomed to employing the mind through voluntary attention, particularly in the direction of creative ideation or constructive imagination, experience these emotions to a greater or less degree.

The exercise of perception, if we are skilled therein, gives us a pleasurable feeling, and if we succeed in making an interesting or important discovery by reason thereof, we experience a strong degree of emotional satisfaction. Likewise, we experience agreeable feelings when we are able to remember distinctly something which might well have been forgotten, or when we succeed in recalling something which had escaped our memory for the moment. In the same way the exercise of the imagination is a source of great pleasure in many cases in the direction of writing, planning, inventing, or other creative processes, or even in the building of air castles. The exercise of the logical faculties gives great pleasure to those in whom these faculties are well developed.

Halleck well says: "There was probably not a happier moment in Newton's life than when he had succeeded in demonstrating that the same power which caused the apple to fall held the moon and the planets in their orbits. When Watts discovered that steam might be harnessed like a horse, when an inventor succeeds in perfecting a labor-lightening device, whenever an obscurity is cleared away, the reason for a thing understood, and a baffling instance brought under a general law, intellectual emotion results."

The pleasurable feelings we experience upon the reading of a good book, or the discovery of real poetry, are forms of intellectual emotion. The same class of emotional feeling is aroused when we witness a good play. Among other instances of this class we mention the perception of clever work of any kind, intricate machinery, ingenious devices, helpful improvements, or other works of man which indicate the existence of thought and inventive ability in the designer or builder. To appreciate mental work of this kind we must bring a mind developed along the same or similar lines. It has well been said that before one can take away anything from a book he must bring something to it. It takes mentality to recognize and appreciate mentality or the work of mentality.

The study of scientific subjects is a source of great pleasure to those who are inclined to such pursuits. To the scientific mind the study of the latest work on the favorite branch gives a joy which nothing else is capable of arousing. To the philosopher the works of other philosophers of the same school give intense satisfaction.

It is claimed that the sense of humor and wit is an intellectual emotion, for it depends upon the detection of the ludicrous features of a happening. Certain psychologists have held that the distinctive element of humor is the feeling attendant upon the perception of incongruity; while that of wit is the feeling of superiority on the part of the witty person, and the corresponding chagrin of the object of his wit. It would seem, however, that the appreciation of wit must depend upon the intellectual perception of cleverness of expression and the pleasure resulting from the discovery thereof, and that the feeling of humor is aroused principally by reason of the incongruous element; the feeling of self-satisfaction as contrasted with the discomfiture of the other person belongs to the more selfish emotions. An authority says: "Humor is a mental faculty which tends to discover incongruous resemblances between things which essentially differ, or essential differences between things put forth as the same, the result being internal mirth or an outburst of laughter. Wit does so likewise, but the two are different. Humor has deep human sympathy, and loves men while raising a laugh against their weaknesses. Wit is deficient in sympathy, and there is often a sting in its ridicule. Somewhat contemptuous of mankind, it has not the patience to study them thoroughly, but must content itself with noting superficial resemblances or differences. Humor is patient and keenly observant, and penetrates beneath the surface; while, therefore, the sallies of wit are often one-sided and unfair, those of humor are, as a rule, just and wise."

The development and cultivation of the intellectual emotions depend, of course, upon education, training, exercise, and practice. The cultivation of the intellect (which has been referred to, in part, in the previous parts of this book, and which will be again considered in the chapters devoted to the intellect) results in the development and cultivation of the emotions accompanying intellectual effort. In a general way, however, it may be said that the reading of the best works of fiction, science, and philosophy will bring out in time the best form of intellectual enjoyment and feeling. The highest gives the best—that is the rule. The present chapter should be read and studied in connection with those devoted to the intellect.

BLENDED EMOTIONS

As we have said at the beginning of our consideration of the subject of the emotions, the majority of emotions are composed of several feelings, and tend to blend and combine emotional elements. For instance, the emotion of sexual love certainly has its origin in the instinctive feelings of the race, and its motive element is that of passion. But passion is far from being all there is in human sexual love. Above the plane of passion is found the social emotion of companionship, protection, and care; the desire for the welfare of the loved one; the mingling of the love of the parent with that of the mate. Human love manifests many of the altruistic emotions during its course. The welfare of the loved one becomes the chief concern of life, often stronger even than self-preservation. The joy of the loved one becomes the greatest joy, far surpassing the more selfish forms of happiness. Then come the æsthetic feelings, which find satisfaction in the two "liking the same things," sympathy and community of feeling being the connecting link. The several ideals of the two combining, there is produced an idealistic union, which is often called "spiritual harmony." Finally, there is found the blending of the intellectual emotions, in which harmony there exists one of the highest forms of pleasure satisfaction between two persons of opposite sexes. It is said that the more things that a man and woman "like" in common, the closer will be their "liking" for each other. "I love you because you love the things I love," is no rare thought and expression.

So it is seen that though born in elemental instinct and passion, human sexual love is something far different in its flowering. And yet without its root it would not be, and cannot be. This is an excellent example of the complex nature of the most common emotions. It may be used as a typical illustration. What is true of it is also true, in a way and in a degree, of every other form of emotion. Therefore in studying a particular emotion, be not too quick to cry, "It is this; it is that!" but rather seek to say, "It is composed of this and that, of this and that!" Few, if any, emotions are simple; the majority are very complex. Hence the difficulty of satisfactory classification, and the danger of dogmatic definition.

18

The Role of the Emotions

THE average person greatly underestimates the part played by the emotional nature in the mental activities of the individual. He is inclined to the opinion that, with the exception of the occasional manifestation of some strong emotional feeling, the majority of persons go through life using only the reasoning and reflective faculties in deciding the problems of life and guiding the mental course of action. There can be no greater mistake concerning the mental activities. So far from being subordinate to the intellect, the emotional nature in the majority of cases dominates the reasoning faculties. There are but very few persons who are able to detach themselves, even in a small degree, from the feelings, and to decide questions cold-bloodedly by pure reason or intellectual effort. Moreover, there are but few persons whose wills are guided by pure reason; the feelings supply the motive for the majority of acts of will. The intellect, even when used, is generally employed to better carry out the dictates of feeling and desire. Much of our reasoning is performed in order to justify our feelings, or to find proofs for the position dictated by our desires, feelings, sympathies, prejudices, or sentiments. It has been said that "men seek not reasons but *excuses for their actions.*"

Moreover, in the elementary processes of the intellect the emotions play an important part. We have seen that attention largely follows interest, and interest results from feeling. Therefore our attention, and that which arises from it, is dependent largely upon the feelings. Thus feeling asserts its power in guarding the very outer gate of knowledge, and determines largely what shall or shall not enter therein. It is one of the constantly-appearing paradoxes of psychology, that while feelings have originally arisen from attention, it is equally true that attention depends largely upon the interest resulting from the feelings. This is readily admitted in the case of involuntary attention, which always goes out toward objects of interest and feeling, but is likewise true of even voluntary attention, which we direct to something of greater or more nearly ultimate interest than the things of lesser or more immediate interest.

Sully says: "By an act of will I may resolve to turn my attention to something—say a passage in a book. But if, after the preliminary process of adjustment of the mental eye the object opens up no interesting phase, all the willing in the world will not produce a calm, settled state of concentration. The will introduces mind and object; it cannot force an attachment between them. No compulsion of attention ever succeeded in making a young child cordially embrace and appropriate, by an act of concentration, an unsuitable and therefore uninteresting object. We thus see that even voluntary interest is not removed from the sway of interest. What the will *does* is to determine *the kind of interest* that shall prevail at the moment."

Again, we may see that memory is largely dependent upon interest in re-cording and recalling its impressions. We remember and recall most easily that which most greatly interests us. In proportion to the lack of interest in a thing do we find difficulty in remembering or recalling it. This is equally true of the imagination, for it refuses to dwell upon that which is *not* interesting. Even in the reasoning processes we find the will balking at uninteresting subjects, but galloping along, pushing before it the rolling chair of interesting intellectual application.

Our judgments are affected by our feelings. It is much easier to approve of the actions of some person we like, or whose views accord with our own, than of an individual whose personality and views are distasteful to us. It is very difficult to prevent prejudice, for or against, from influencing our judgments. It is also true that we "find that for which we look" in things and persons, and that which we expect and look for is often dependent upon our feelings. If we dislike a person or thing we are usually able to perceive no end of undesirable things in him or it; while if we are favorably inclined we easily find many admirable qualities in the same person or thing. A little change in our feeling often results in the formation of an entirely new set of judgments regarding a person or thing.

Halleck well says: "On the one hand the emotions are favorable to intel-lectual action, since they supply the interest one feels in study. One may feel intensely concerning a certain subject and be all the better student. Hence the emotions are not, as was formerly thought, entirely hostile to intellectual action. Emotion often quickens the perception, burns things indelibly into the memory, and doubles the rapidity of thought. On the other hand strong feel-ings often vitiate every operation of the intellect. They cause us to see only what we wish to, to remember only what interests our narrow feeling at the time, and to reason from selfish data only. * * * Emotion puts the magnifying end of the telescope to our intellectual eyes where our own interests are concerned, the minimizing end when we are looking at the interest of others. * * * *Thought is deflected when it passes through an emotional medium, just as a sunbeam is when it strikes water.*"

As for the will, the best authorities hold that it is almost if not entirely dependent upon desire for its motive force. As desire is an outgrowth and development of feeling and emotion, it is seen that even the will depends upon feeling for its inciting motives and its direction. We shall consider this point at greater detail in the chapters devoted to the activities of the will.

We would remind you again, at this point, of the great triangle of the mind, the emotional, ideative, and volitional activities—feeling, thinking, and willing—and their constant reaction upon each other and absolute interdependence. We find that our feelings arise from previous willing and ideation, and are aroused by ideas and repressed by will; again we see that our ideas are largely dependent upon the interest supplied by our feelings, and that our judgments are influenced by the emotive side of our mental life, the will also having its part to play in the matter. We also see that the will is called into activity by the feelings, and often guided or restrained by our thoughts, the will, indeed, being considered as moved entirely by our feelings and ideas. Thus is the trinity of mental forces seen ever in mutual relation—constant action and reaction ever existing between them.

19

The Emotions and Happiness

"HAPPINESS" has been defined by an authority as "the pleasurable emotion arising from the gratification of all desires; the enjoyment of pleasure without pain." Another has said that "happiness is the state in which all desires are satisfied." But these definitions have been attacked. It is held by many that a state of the absolute *satisfaction* of desire would not be happiness, for happiness consists largely in pleasurable anticipation and imaginings which disappear upon the realization of the desire. It is held that absolute satisfaction would be a negative state. Paley expressed a better idea when he said that "any condition may be denominated 'happy' in which the amount or aggregate of pleasure exceeds that of pain, and the degree of happiness depends upon the quantity of this excess."

Some have held that an existing contrast between pain and pleasure (the balance being in favor of the latter) is necessary to establish happiness. Be this as it may, it is admitted by all that one's happiness or unhappiness depends entirely upon one's emotional nature and the degree of the satisfaction thereof. And it is generally admitted that to be happy is the great aim and object of the life of the majority of persons—if, indeed, not of *every* person—the happiness, of course, depending upon the quality and degree of the emotions forming the person's emotional nature. Thus it is seen that we are dependent upon the emotional side of our mental life in this as in nearly everything else making life worthwhile.

Theologians have often sought to point out that happiness is not the goal of life and living, but human nature has always insisted that happiness is the greatest end, and philosophy has generally supported it. But wisdom shows that happiness is not always dependent upon the pleasure of the moment, for the sacrifice of immediate pleasure frequently results in a much greater happiness in the future. In the same way an immediate disagreeable task often gains for us a greater satisfaction in the future. Likewise, it is frequently greater happiness to sacrifice a personal pleasure for the happiness of others than it would be to enjoy the pleasure of the moment at the expense of the pain of the other. There is often a far greater pleasure resulting from an altruistic action of self-sacrifice than in the performance of the selfish, egoistic act. But, as the subtle reasoner may insist, the result is the same—the ultimate happiness and satisfaction of the self. This conclusion does not rob the altruistic act of its virtue, however, for the person who finds his greatest pleasure in giving pleasure to others is to be congratulated—as is the community which shelters him.

There is no virtue in pain, suffering, sacrifice, or unhappiness *for its own sake*. This illusion of asceticism is vanishing from the human mind. Sacrifice on the part of the individual is valuable and valid only when it results in higher present or future happiness for the individual or someone else. There is no virtue in pain, physical or mental, except as a step to a greater good for ourselves or others. Pain at the best is merely nature's alarm and warning of "not this way." It is also held that pain serves to bring out pleasure by contrast, and is therefore valuable in this way. Be this as it may, no normal individual deliberately seeks ultimate pain in preference to ultimate happiness; the greatest ultimate happiness to one's self and to those he loves is the normal and natural goal of the normal person. But the concept of "those he loves," in many cases, includes the race as well as the immediate family.

Wisdom shows the individual that the greatest happiness comes to him who controls and restrains many of his feelings. Dissipation results in pain and unhappiness ultimately. The doctrine of thoughtless indulgence is unphilosophical and is contradicted by the experience of the race. Moreover, wisdom shows that the highest happiness comes not from the indulgence of the physical feelings alone, or to excess, but rather from the cultivation, development, and manifestation of the higher feelings—the social, æsthetic, and intellectual emotions. The higher pleasures of life, literature, art, music, science, invention, constructive imagination, etc., yield a satisfaction and happiness keener and more enduring than can possibly the lower forms of feeling. But the human being must not despise any part of his emotional being. Everything has its uses, which are good; and its abuses, which are bad. Every part of one's being, mental and physical, is well to use; but no part is well used if it uses the individual instead of being itself used.

A recent writer has held that the end and aim of life should not be the pursuit of happiness, but rather the building of character. The obvious answer is that the two are identical in spirit, for to the man who appreciates the value of character, its attainment is the greatest happiness; the wise teach that the greatest happiness comes to him who is possessed of a well-rounded, developed character. Another writer has said that "the aim of life should be self-improvement, with a due regard to the interest of others." This is but saying that the greatest happiness to the wise man lies in this course. Any one who is wise enough, or great enough, to make these ends the aim and goal of life will find the greatest happiness therefrom. Arnold Bennett advances as a good working philosophy of life: "cheerfulness, kindliness, and rectitude." Can anyone doubt that this course would bring great ultimate happiness?

Happiness consists in that which "contents the spirit," and the latter depends entirely upon the character of the feelings and emotions entertained by one, as weighed in the balance of reason, and as passed upon by judgment and the sense of right action. The greatest degree of happiness, or at least the greatest ratio of pleasure over pain, is obtained by a careful and intelligent cultivation of the feeling side of one's being in connection with the cultivation of the intellect and the mastery of the will. To be able to bring the capacity for enjoyment to its highest; to be able to intelligently choose that which will bring the greatest ultimate happiness in accordance with right action; and, finally, to be able to use the will in the direction of holding fast to that which is good and rejecting that which is bad—this is the power of creating happiness. The feelings, the intellect, and the will—here, as ever—combine to manifest the result.

Finally, it must be remembered that all human happiness consists in part of the ability to bear pain—to suffer. There must be the dash of Stoicism in the wise Epicurean. One must learn to pluck from pain, suffering, and unhappiness the secret drop of honey which lies at its heart, and which consists in the knowledge of the meaning and use of pain and the means whereby it may be transmuted into knowledge and experience, from which later happiness may be distilled. To profit by pain, to transmute suffering into joy, to transform present unhappiness into a future greater happiness—this is the privilege of the philosopher.

The mental states and activities known as "desire" are a direct development of the feeling and emotional phase of the mind and form the motive power of the will. Desire, in fact, may be said to be composed of feeling on one side and will on the other. But the influence of the intellect or reasoning faculties has a most important part to play in the evolution of feeling into desire, and in the consequent action of the will by the presentation and weighing of conflicting desires. Therefore, the logical place for the consideration of the activities of the intellect is at this point—between emotion and will. Accordingly, we shall leave the subject of feeling and emotion for the present, to be taken up again in connection with the subject of *desire*, after we have considered the intellectual processes of the mind. But, as has been indicated, we shall see the presence and influence of the feelings and emotions even in the activities of the intellect.

20

The Intellect

THE class of mental states or processes grouped together under the name of "intellectual processes," forms the second great division of the mental states, the two others being "feeling" and "will," respectively.

"Intellect" has been defined as follows: "The part or faculty of the human mind by which it knows, as distinguished from the power to feel and to will; the thinking faculty; the understanding;" also as "that faculty of the human mind by which it receives or comprehends the ideas communicated to it by the senses or the perception, or other means, as distinguished from the power to feel and to will; the power or faculty to perceive objects in their relations; the power to judge and comprehend; also the capacity for higher forms of knowledge, as distinguished from the power to perceive and imagine."

In the preceding chapters we have seen that the individual is able to experience sensations in consciousness, and that he is able to *perceive* them mentally, the latter being the first step in intellectual activity. We have also seen that he is able to reproduce the perception by means of memory and imagination, and that by means of the latter he is able to re-combine and rearrange the objects of perception. We have also seen that he has what are known as "feelings," which depend upon his previous experience and that of his progenitors. So far the mind has been considered merely as a receiving and reproducing instrument, with the added attachment of the re-combining power of the imagination. Up to this point the mind may be compared to the phonographic cylinder, with an attachment capable of re-combining its recorded impressions. The impressions are received and perceived, are stored away, are reproduced, and by the use of the imagination are re-combined.

Up to this point the mind is seen to be more or less of an automatic, instinctive faculty. It may be traced from the purely reflex activity of the lowest forms of life up through the lower animals, step by step, until a very high degree of mental power is perceived in animals like the horse, dog, or elephant. But there is something lacking. There is missing that peculiar power of thinking in symbols and abstract conceptions which distinguishes the human race and which is closely bound up with the faculty of language or expressing thoughts in words. The comparatively high mental process of the lower animals is dwarfed by the human faculty of "thinking." And *thinking* is the manifestation of the intellect.

What is it to *think*? Strange to say, very few persons can answer this question correctly at first. They find themselves inclined to answer the inquiry in the words of the child: "Why, to think is to *think*!" Let us see if we can make it plain. The dictionary definition is a little too technical to be of much use to the beginner, but here it is: "To employ any of the intellectual powers except that of simple perception through the senses." But what are the "intellectual powers" so employed, and how are they employed? Let us see.

Stating the matter plainly in common terms, we may say that "thinking" is the mental process of (1) comparing our perceptions of things with each other, noting the points of likeness and of difference; (2) classifying them according to the ascertained likeness or difference, and thus tying them up in mental bundles with each set of "things of a kind" in its own bundle; (3) forming the abstract, symbolic mental idea (concept) of each class of things, so grouped, which we may afterward use as we use figures in mathematical calculations; (4) using these concepts in order to form *inferences*, that is, to reason from the known to the unknown, and to form judgments regarding things; (5) comparing these judgments and deducing higher judgments from them; and so on.

Without thinking, man would be dependent upon each particular experience for his knowledge, except so far as memory and imagination could instinctively aid him. By thought processes he is enabled to infer that if certain things be true of one of a certain kind of things, the same thing may be expected from others of the same class. As he is able to note points of likeness or difference, he is able to form clearer and truer inferences. In addition, he is able to apply his constructive imagination to the rearrangement and recombination of things whose nature he has discovered, and thus progress along the line of material achievement as well as of knowledge. It must be remembered, however, that the intellect depends entirely for its material upon the perception, which in turn receives its raw material from the senses. The intellect merely groups together the material of perception, makes inferences, draws conclusions from, and forms conclusions regarding, them, and in the case of constructive imagination recombines them in effective forms and arrangement. The intellect is the last in order in the course of mental evolution. It appears last in order in the mind of the child, but it often persists in old age after the feelings have grown dim and the memory weak.

CONCEPTS

What is known as the "concept" is the first fruit of the elemental processes of thought. The various images of outside objects are sensed, then perceived, and then grouped according to their likenesses and differences, and the result is the production of concepts. It is difficult to define a concept so as to convey any meaning to the beginner. For instance, the dictionaries give the definition as "an abstract, general conception, idea, or notion formed in the mind." Not very clear this, is it? Perhaps we can understand it better if we say that the terms dog, cat, man, horse, house, etc., each expresses a concept. Every term expresses a concept; every general name of a thing or quality is a term applied to the concept. We shall see this a little clearer as we proceed.

We form a concept in this way: (1) We *perceive* a number of things; (2) then we notice certain *qualities* possessed by things—certain properties, attributes, or characteristics which make the thing what it is; (3) then we *compare* these qualities of the thing with the qualities of other things and see that there is a likeness in some cases, in various degrees, and a difference in other cases, in various degrees; (4) then we *generalize* or *classify* the perceived things according to their ascertained likenesses and differences; (5) then we form a *general idea* or *concept* embodying each class of thing; and, finally, we give to the concept a *term*, or *name*, which is its symbol.

The concept is a *general idea* of a class of things; the *term* is the expression of that general idea. The concept is the idea of a class of things; the term is the *label* affixed to the thing. To illustrate this last distinction, let us take the concept and term of "bird," for instance. By perception, comparison, and classification of the qualities of living things we have arrived at the conclusion that there exists a great general class the qualities of which may be stated thus: "Warm-blooded, feathered, winged, oviparous, vertebrate." To this general class of quality-possessing animals we apply the English term "bird." The name is merely a symbol. In German the term is *vogel*; in Latin, *avis*; but in each and every case the *general idea* or *concept* above stated, *i.e.*, "warm-blooded, feathered, winged, oviparous, vertebrate," is meant. If anything is found having all of those particular qualities, then we know it must be what we call a "bird." And everything that we call a "bird" must have those qualities. The term "bird" is the symbol for that particular combination of qualities existing in a thing.

There is a difference between a mental image of the imagination and a concept. The mental image must always be of a *particular* thing, while the concept is always an idea of a *general class* of things which cannot be clearly pictured in the mind. For instance, the imagination may form the mental picture of any known bird, or even of an imaginary bird, but that bird always will be a distinct, *particular* bird. Try to form a mental picture of the general class of birds—how will you do it? Do you realize the difficulty? First, such an image would have to include the characteristics of the large birds, such as the eagle, ostrich, and condor; and of the small birds, such as the wren and humming bird. It must be a composite of the shape of all birds, from the ostrich, swan, eagle, crane, down to the sparrow, swallow, and humming bird. It must picture the particular qualities of birds of prey, water birds, and domestic fowls, as well as the grain eaters. It must exhibit all the colors found in bird life, from the brightest reds and greens down to the sober grays and browns. A little thought will show that a clear mental image of such a concept is impossible. What the most of us do, when we think of "bird," is to picture a vague, flying shape of dull color; but when we stop to think that the term must also include the waddling duck and the scratching barnyard chicken, we see that our mental image is faulty. The trouble is that the term "bird" really means "all-bird," and we cannot picture an "all-bird" from the very nature of the case. Our terms, therefore, are like mathematical figures, or algebraic symbols, which we use for ease, speed, and clearness of thinking.

The trouble does not end here. Concepts not only include the general idea of *things*, but also the general idea of the *qualities of things*. Thus sweetness, hardness, courage, and energy are concepts, but we cannot form a mental image of them by themselves. We may picture a sweet *thing*, but not sweetness itself. So you see that a concept is a purely abstract mental idea—a symbol— akin to the figures 1, 2, 3, etc., and used in the same way. They *stand* for general classes of things. A "term" is the verbal and written expression of the general idea or concept. The student is requested to fix these distinctions in his mind, so as to render further understanding of them easy.

21

Conception

THE process of conception has been well defined by Gordy as "that act of mind by which it forms an idea of a class; or that act of the mind that enables us to use general names intelligently." He adds: "It is, of course, understood that I am using the word 'class' to denote an indefinite number of individuals that resemble each other in certain particulars."

PERCEPTION

The first step in conception, as we have seen, is that of perception. It is readily perceived that the character of our intellectual processes depends materially upon the variety, clearness, and accuracy of our perceptions. Therefore, again, we would refer our students to the chapter in which we have stated the importance of clear perception.

MEMORY

The future steps of conception depend materially upon the clearness of the memory, as we can classify objects only by remembering their qualities beyond the immediate moment of actual, original perception. Therefore, the memory should be strengthened for this as well as other objects.

ABSTRACTION

The second step in conception is that of the mental abstraction of qualities from the observed thing. That is, we must perceive and then mentally *set aside* the observed qualities of the thing. For instance, man first perceived the existence of certain qualities in things. He found that a certain number of things possessed some of these qualities in common, while others possessed other qualities in the same way, and thus arose classification from comparison. But both comparison and classification are possible only by abstraction, or *the perception of the quality as a "thing"*; thus, the abstraction of the idea of the quality of *sweetness* from the idea of sugar. Sweetness is a *quality* rather than a thing itself. It is something possessed by sugar which helps to make sugar what it is.

Color, shape, size, mental qualities, habits of action—these are some of the qualities first observed in things and abstracted from them in thought. Redness, sweetness, hardness, softness, largeness, smallness, fragrance, swiftness, slowness, fierceness, gentleness, warmness, coldness, etc.—these are abstracted qualities of things. Of course these qualities are really never divorced from things, but the mind divorces them in order to make thinking easier. An authority says: "Animals are incapable of making abstractions, and that is the reason why they cannot develop formal thought. * * * Abstract thought is identical with rational thought, which is the characteristic feature of the thought of speaking beings. This is the reason why abstract thought is upon earth the exclusive property of man, and why brutes are incapable of abstract thought. The process of naming is the mechanism of abstraction, for names establish the mental independence of the objects named."

The processes of abstraction depend upon attention—concentrated attention. Attention directed to the qualities of a thing tends to abstract the qualities in thought from the thing itself. Mill says: "Abstraction is primarily the result of attention." Hamilton says: "Attention and abstraction are only the same process viewed in different relations." Cultivation of the power of abstraction means principally cultivation of attention. Any mental activity which tends toward *analysis* or separation of a thing into its parts, qualities, or elements will serve to cultivate and develop the power of abstraction.

The habit of converting *qualities* into concepts is acquired by *transforming adjective terms into their corresponding noun terms*. For instance, a piece of colored candy possesses the *qualities* of being round, hard, red, sweet, etc. Transforming these adjective qualities into noun terms we have the *concepts* of roundness, hardness, redness, and sweetness, respectively.

COMPARISON

The third step in conception is that of *comparison*, in which the qualities of several things are compared or examined for likenesses and differences. We find many qualities in which the several things differ, and a few in which there is a likeness. Classes are formed from resemblances or likenesses, while individuals are separated from apparent classes by detection of differences. Finally, it is found that separate things, while having many points of difference which indicate their individuality, nevertheless have a few points of likeness which indicate that they belong to the same general family or class. The detection of likenesses and differences in the qualities of various things is an important mental process. Many of the higher thought processes depend largely upon the ability to compare things properly. The development of attention and perception tends to develop the power of comparison.

CLASSIFICATION or GENERALIZATION

The fourth step in conception is that of classification or generalization, whereby we place individual things in a mental bundle or class, and then this bundle in company with other bundles into a higher class, and so on. Thus we group all the individual small birds having certain characteristics into a species, then several related species into a larger family, and this into a still larger, until finally we group all the bird families into the great family which we call "birds" and of which the simple term "bird" expresses the general concept.

Jevons says: "We classify things together whenever we observe that they are like each other in any respect, and therefore think of them together. In classifying a collection of objects, we do not merely put together into groups those which resemble each other, but we also divide each class into smaller ones in which the resemblance is more complete. Thus the class of *white substances* may be divided into those which are solid, and those which are fluid, so that we get the two minor classes of solid-white and fluid-white substances. It is desirable to have names by which to show that one class is contained in another, and, accordingly, we call the class which is divided into two or more smaller ones the *genus*, and the smaller ones into which it is divided, the *species*."

Every *species* is a small family of the individuals composing it, and at the same time is an individual species of the genus just above it; the *genus*, in turn, is a family of several species, and at the same time an individual genus in the greater family or genus above it.

The student may familiarize himself with the idea of generalization by considering himself as an individual, John Smith. John represents that unit of generalization. The next step is to combine John with the other Smiths of his immediate family. Then this family may be grouped with his near blood relations, and so on, until finally all the related Smiths, near and remote, are grouped together in a great Smith family.

Or, in the same way, the family group may be enlarged until it takes in all the white people in a county, then all the white people in the state, then all in the United States; then all the white races, then all the white and other light-skinned races, then all mankind. Then, if one is inclined, the process may be continued until it embraces every living creature from moneron to man. Reversing the process, living creatures may be divided and subdivided until all mankind is seen to stand as a class. Then the race of man may be divided into sub-races according to color; then the white race may be subdivided into Americans and non-Americans. Then the Americans may be divided into inhabitants of the several states, or into Indianans and non-Indianans; then into the inhabitants of the several counties of Indiana, and thus the Posey Countians are reached. Then the Posey County people are divided into Smiths and non-Smiths; then the Smith family into its constituent family groups, and then into the smaller families, and so on, until the classification reaches one particular John Smith, who at last is found to be an individual—in a class by himself. This is the story of the ascending and descending processes of generalization.

22

Classes of Concepts

IN the preceding chapter we have seen the process of conception—of the forming of concepts. *The idea of a general class of things or qualities is a concept.* Each concept contains the qualities which are *common to all* the individuals composing the class, but not those qualities which pertain only to the minor classes or the individuals. For instance, the concept of "bird" will necessarily include the common qualities of warm-bloodedness, featheredness, wingedness, oviparousness, and vertebratedness. But it will *not* include color, special shape, size, or special features or characteristics of the subfamilies or individuals composing the great class. The class comprises the individuals and subclasses composing it; the concept includes the general and common qualities which *all* in the class possess. A *percept* is the mental image of a particular thing; a *concept* is the mental idea of the general qualities of a class of things. A percept arises from the perception of a sensation; a concept is a purely mental, abstract creation, whose only existence is in the world of ideas and which has no corresponding individual object in the world of sense.

There are two general classes of concepts, namely: (1) concrete concepts, in which the common qualities of a class of things are combined into one conceptual idea, such as "bird," of which we have spoken; (2) abstract concepts, in which is combined the idea of some *quality* common to a number of things, such as "sweetness" or "redness." Jevons's well-known rule for terms is an aid in remembering this classification: *"A concrete term is the name of a thing; an abstract term is the name of a quality of a thing."*

It is a peculiar fact and rule of concrete concepts that (1) the larger the class of things embraced in a concept, the smaller are its general qualities; and (2) the larger the number of general qualities included in a concept, the smaller the number of individuals embraced by it. For instance, the term "bird" embraces a great number of individuals—all the birds that are in existence, in fact, but it has but few general qualities, as we have seen. On the contrary, the concept "stork" has a much larger number of general qualities, but embraces far fewer individuals. Finally, the individual is reached, and we find that it has more qualities than any class can have; but it is composed of the smallest possible number of individuals, one. The secret is this: No two individuals can have as many qualities *in common* as each has individually, unless they are precisely alike, which is impossible in nature.

IMPERFECT CONCEPTS

It is said that outside of strictly scientific definitions very few persons agree in their concepts of the same thing. Each has his or her own concept of the particular thing which he or she expresses by the same term. A number of persons asked to define a common term like "love," "religion," "faith," "belief," etc., will give such a variety of answers as to cause wonderment. As Green says: "My idea or image is mine alone—the reward of careless observation if imperfect; of attentive, careful, and varied observation if correct. Between mine and yours a great gulf is fixed. No man can pass from mine to yours, or from yours to mine. Neither in any proper sense of the term can mine be conveyed to you. Words do not convey thoughts; they are not vehicles of thoughts in any true sense of that term. A word is simply a common symbol which each associates with his own idea or image."

The reason of the difference in the concepts of several persons is that very few of our concepts are nearly perfect; the majority of them are quite imperfect and incomplete. Jevons gives us an idea of this in his remarks on classification: "Things may seem to be very much like each other which are not so. Whales, porpoises, seals, and several other animals live in the sea exactly like a fish; they have a similar shape and are usually classed among fish. People are said to go whale fishing. Yet these animals are not really fish at all, but are much more like dogs and horses and other quadrupeds than they are like fish. They cannot live entirely under water and breathe the air contained in the water like fish, but they have to come to the surface at intervals to take breath. Similarly, we must not class bats with birds because they fly about, although they have what would be called wings; these wings are not like those of birds, and, in truth, bats are much more like rats and mice than they are like birds. Botanists used at one time to classify plants according to their size, as trees, shrubs, or herbs, but we now know that a great tree is often more similar in character to a tiny herb than it is to other great trees. A daisy has little resemblance to a great Scotch thistle; yet the botanist regards them as very similar. The lofty growing bamboo is a kind of grass, and the sugar cane also belongs to the same class with wheat and oats."

It is a matter of importance that clear concepts should be formed regarding at least the familiar things of life. The list of clear concepts should be added to from time to time by study, investigation, and examination. The dictionary should be consulted frequently, and a term studied until one has a clear meaning of the concept the term seeks to express. A good encyclopedia (not necessarily an expensive one, in these days of cheap editions) will also prove very useful in this respect. As Halleck says: "It must be borne in mind that most of our concepts are subject to change during our entire life; that at first they are made only in a tentative way; that experience may show us, at any time, that they have been erroneously formed, that we have abstracted too little or too much, made the class too wide or too narrow, or that here a quality must be added or there one taken away."

It is a good practice to make a memorandum of anything of which you may hear, but of which you know nothing, and then later to make a brief but thorough investigation of that thing, by means of the dictionary and encyclopedia, and of whatever good works may be obtained on the subject, not leaving it until you feel that you have obtained at least a *clear idea* of what the thing really *means*. A half hour each evening devoted to exercise of this kind will result in a wonderful increase of general information. We have heard of a man who made a practice of reading a short article in the encyclopedia every evening, giving preference to subjects generally classed as familiar. In a year he made a noticeable advance in general knowledge as well as habits of thought. In five years he was looked upon by his associates as a man of a remarkably large field of general information and of more than ordinary intelligence, which verdict was a just one. As a rule we waste far more time on worthless fiction than we are willing to devote to a little self-improvement of this kind. We shrink at the idea of a general course of instructive reading, little realizing that we can take our study in small installments and at a very little cost in time or labor.

Our concepts form the material which our intellect uses in its reasoning processes. No matter how good a reasoner one may be, unless he has a good supply of general information about the things of which he is reasoning, he will not make much real headway. We must begin at the bottom and build a firm foundation upon which the intellectual structure may be erected. This foundation is composed of *facts*. These facts are represented by our clear and correct concepts.

23

Judgments

WE have seen the several steps of the mental process whereby simple sensations are transformed into percepts and then into concepts or general ideas. The formation of the concept is considered as the first great step in thinking. The second great step in thinking is that of the formation of the "judgment." The definition of "judgment," as the term is used in logic; is "the comparing together in the mind of two ideas of things, and determining whether they agree or disagree with each other, or that one of them does or does not belong to the other. Judgment is, therefore, (*a*) affirmative or (*b*) negative, as (*a*) 'Snow is white,' or (*b*) 'All white men are not Europeans.'"

What in logic is called a "proposition" is the expression in words of a logical judgment. Hyslop defined the term "proposition" as follows: "Any affirmation or denial of an agreement between two conceptions." For instance, we compare the concepts "sparrow" and "bird" and find that there is an agreement, and that the former belongs to the latter; this mental process is a *judgment*. We then announce the judgment in the *proposition*: "The sparrow is a bird." In the same way we compare the concepts "bat" and "bird," find that there is a disagreement, and form the judgment that neither belongs to the other, which we express in the proposition: "The bat is not a bird." Or we may form the judgment that "sweetness" is a quality of "sugar," which we express in the proposition: "Sugar is sweet." Likewise, we may form the judgment which results in the proposition: "Vinegar is not sweet."

While the process of judgment is generally considered as constituting the second great step of thinking, coming after the formation of the concept, and consisting of the comparing of concepts, it must be remembered that the act of judging is far more elementary than this, for it is found still farther back in the history of thought processes. By that peculiar law of paradox which we find everywhere operative in mind processes, the same process of forming judgments which is used in comparing concepts also has been used in forming the same concepts in the stage of comparison. In fact, the result of all comparison, high or low, must be *a judgment*.

Halleck says: "Judgment is necessary in forming concepts. When we decide that a quality is or is not common to a class, we are really judging. This is another evidence of the complexity and unified action of the mind."

Brooks says: "The power of judgment is of great value in its products. It is involved in or accompanies every act of the intellect, and thus lies at the foundation of all intellectual activity. It operates directly in every act of the understanding, and even aids the other faculties of the mind in completing their activities and products. * * * Strictly speaking, every intelligent act of the mind is accompanied with a judgment. To know is to discriminate and, therefore, to judge. Every sensation or cognition involves a knowledge and so a judgment that it exists. The mind cannot think at all without judging; to think is to judge. Even in forming the notions which judgment compares, the mind judges. Every notion or concept implies a previous act of judgment to form it; in forming a concept we compare the common attributes before we unite them, and comparison is judgment. It is thus true that 'Every concept is a contracted judgment; every judgment an expanded concept.'"

It is needless to say that as judgments lie at the base of our thinking, and also appear in every part of its higher structure, the importance of correct judgment in thought cannot be overestimated. But it is often very difficult to form correct judgment even regarding the most familiar things around us. Halleck says: "In actual life things present themselves to us with their qualities disguised or obscured by other conflicting qualities. Men had for ages seen burning substances and had formed a concept of them. A certain hard, black, stony substance had often been noticed, and a concept had been formed of it. This concept was imperfect; but it is very seldom that we meet with perfect, sharply-defined concepts in actual life. So it happened that for ages the concept of burning substance was never linked by judgment to the concept of stone coal. The combustible quality in the coal was overshadowed by its stony attributes. 'Of course stone will not burn,' people said. One cannot tell how long the development of mankind was retarded for that very reason. England would not today be manufacturing products for the rest of the world had not someone judged coal to be a combustible substance. * * * Judgment is ever silently working and comparing things that to past ages seemed dissimilar; and it is constantly abstracting and leaving out of the field of view those qualities which have simply served to obscure the point at issue."

Gordy says: "The credulity of children is proverbial; but if we get our facts at first hand, if we study 'the living, learning, playing child,' we shall see that he is quite as remarkable for incredulity as for credulity. The explanation is simple: *He tends to believe the first suggestion that comes into his mind, no matter from what source*; and since his belief is not the result of any rational process, he cannot be made to disbelieve it in any rational way. Hence it is that he is very credulous about any matter about which he has no ideas; but let the idea once get possession of his mind, and he is quite as remarkable for incredulity as before for credulity. * * * If we study the larger child—the man with a child's mind, an uneducated man—we shall have the same truth forced upon us. If the beliefs of men were due to processes of reasoning, where they have not reasoned they would not believe. But do we find it so? Is it not true that the men who have the most positive opinions on the largest variety of subjects—so far as they have ever heard of them—are precisely those who have the least right to them? Socrates, we remember, was counted the wisest man in Athens because he alone resisted his natural tendency to believe in the absence of evidence; he alone would not delude himself with the conceit of knowledge without the reality; and it would scarcely be too much to say that the intellectual strength of men is in direct proportion to the number of things they are absolutely certain of. * * * I do not, of course, mean to intimate that we should have no opinions about matters that we have not personally investigated. We take, and ought to take, the opinion of some men about law, and others about medicine, and others about particular sciences, and so on. But we should clearly realize the difference between holding an opinion on trust and holding it as the result of our own investigations."

Brooks says: "It should be one of the leading objects of the culture of young people to lead them to acquire the habit of forming judgments. They should not only be led to see things but to have opinions about things. They should be trained to see things in their relations and to put these relations into definite propositions. Their ideas of objects should be worked up into thoughts concerning the objects. Those methods of teaching are best which tend to excite a thoughtful habit of mind that notices the similitudes and diversities of objects and endeavors to read the thoughts which they embody and of which they are the symbols."

The study of logic, geometry, and the natural sciences is recommended for exercise of the faculty of judgment and the development thereof. The study and practice of even the lower branches of mathematics are also helpful in this direction. The game of checkers or chess is recommended by many authorities. Some have advocated the practice of solving enigmas, problems, rebuses, etc., as giving exercise to this faculty of the mind. The cultivation of the "Why?"

attitude of mind, and the answering of one's own mental questions, is also helpful, if not carried to excess. "Doubting Thomas" is not always a term of reproach in these days of scientific habits of thought, and "the man from Missouri" has many warm admirers.

24

Primary Laws of Thought

IN connection with this subject we herewith call the attention of the student to the well-known Primary Laws of Thought which have been recognized as valid from the time of the ancient Greek logicians. These laws are self-evident, and are uncontradictable. They are axiomatic. Jevons says of them: "Students are seldom able to see at first their full meaning and importance. All arguments may be explained when these self-evident laws are granted; and it is not too much to say that the whole of logic will be plain to those who will constantly use these laws as their key." Here are the Three Primary Laws of Thought:

I. *Law of Identity.* "Whatever is, *is.*"

II. *Law of Contradiction.* "Nothing can both be and not be."

III. *Law of Excluded Middle.* "Everything must either be or not be; there is no middle course."

I. The first of these laws, called "*The Law of Identity,*" informs us that a thing is always itself, no matter under what guise or form it is perceived or may present itself. An animal is always a bird if it possesses the general characteristics of a "bird," no matter whether it exhibits the minor characteristics of an eagle, a wren, a stork, or a humming bird. In the same way a whale is a mammal because it possesses the general characteristics of a mammal notwithstanding that it swims in the water like a fish. Also, sweetness is always sweetness, whether manifested in sugar, honey, flowers, or products of coal tar. If a thing *is* that thing, then it *is,* and it cannot be logically claimed that it *is not.*

II. The second of these laws, called "*The Law of Contradiction,*" informs us that the same quality or class cannot be both affirmed and denied of a thing at the same time and place. A sparrow cannot be said to be both "bird" and "not bird" at the same time. Neither can sugar be said to be "sweet" and "not sweet" at the same time. A piece of iron may be "hot" at one end and "not hot" at another, but it cannot be both "hot" and "not hot" at the same place at the same time.

III. The third of these laws, called "*The Law of Excluded Middle*," informs us that a given quality or class *must* be affirmed or denied to *everything* at any given time and place. Everything either must be of a certain class or not, must possess a certain quality or not, at a given time or place. There is no other alternative or middle course. It is axiomatic that any statement *must* either be or not be true of a certain other thing at any certain time and place; there is no escape from this. Anything *either* must be "black" or "not black," a bird or not a bird, alive or not alive, at any certain time or place. There is nothing else that it can be; it cannot both be and not be at the same time and place, as we have seen; therefore, it must either be or not be that which is asserted of it. The judgment must decide which alternative; but it has only two possible choices.

But the student must not confuse opposite qualities or things with "not-ness." A thing may be "black" or "not black," but it need not be white to be "not black," for blue is likewise "not black" just as it is "not white." The neglect of this fact frequently causes error. We must always affirm either the existence or non-existence of a quality in a thing; but this is far different from affirming or denying the existence of the opposite quality. Thus a thing may be "not hard" and yet it does not follow that it is "soft"; it may be *neither* hard nor soft.

FALLACIOUS APPLICATION

There exists what are known as "fallacies" of application of these primary laws. A fallacy is an unsound argument or conclusion. For instance, because a particular man is found to be a liar, it is fallacious to assume that "*all* men are liars," for lying is a particular quality of the individual man, and not a general quality of the family of men. In the same way because a stork has long legs and a long bill, it does not follow that all birds must have these characteristics simply because the stork is a bird. *It is fallacious to extend an individual quality to a class.* But it is sound judgment to assume that a class quality must be possessed by all individuals in that class. It is a far different proposition which asserts that "*some* birds are black," from that which asserts that "*all* birds are black." The same rule, of course, is true regarding negative propositions.

Another fallacy is that which assumes that because the affirmative or negative proposition has not been, or cannot be, proved, it follows that the opposite proposition must be true. The true judgment is simply "not proven."

Another fallacious judgment is that which is based on attributing absolute quality to that which is but relative or comparative. For instance, the terms "hot" and "cold" are relative and comparative, and simply denote one's relative opinion regarding a fixed and certain degree of temperature. The *certain* thing is the degree of temperature, say 75 degrees Fahrenheit; of this we may logically claim that it *is* or *is not* true at a certain time or place. It either *is* 75 degrees Fahrenheit or it *is not*. But to one man this may seem *warm* and to another *cold*; both are right in their judgments, so far as their own relative feelings are concerned. But neither can claim absolutely that it is *warm* or *cold*. Therefore, it is a fallacy to ascribe absolute quality to a relative one. The *absolute fact* comes under the Law of Excluded Middle, but a personal opinion is not an absolute fact.

There are other fallacies which will be considered in other chapters of this book, under their appropriate heading.

25

Reasoning

REASONING, the third great step in thinking, may be said to consist of ascertaining new truths from old ones, new judgments from old ones, unknown facts from known ones; in short, of proceeding logically from the known to the unknown, using the known as the foundation for the unknown which is sought to be known. Gordy gives us the following excellent definition of the term: "Reasoning is the act of going from the known to the unknown through other beliefs; of basing judgment upon judgments; reaching beliefs through beliefs." Reasoning, then, is seen to be a process of building a structure of judgments, one resting upon the other, the topmost point being the final judgment, but the whole constituting an edifice of judgment. This may be seen more clearly when the various forms of reasoning are considered.

IMMEDIATE REASONING

The simplest form of reasoning is that known as "immediate reasoning," by which is meant reasoning by directly comparing two judgments without the intervention of the third judgment, which is found in the more formal classes of reasoning. This form of reasoning depends largely upon the application of the Three Primary Laws of Thought, to which we have referred in a previous chapter.

It will be seen that *if* (*a*) a thing is always itself, then (*b*) all that is included in it must partake of its nature. Thus, the bird family has certain class characteristics, therefore by immediate reasoning we know that *any* member of that family must possess those class characteristics, whatever particular characteristics it may have in addition. And we likewise know that we cannot attribute the *particular* characteristics, as a matter of course, to the other members of the class. Thus, though all sparrows are birds, it is not true that all birds are sparrows. "All biscuits are bread; but all bread is not biscuit."

In the same way we know that a thing cannot be bird and mammal at the same time, for the mammals form a not-bird family. And, likewise, we know that everything *must* be either bird or not bird, but that being not bird does not mean being a mammal, for there are many other not-bird things than mammals. In this form of reasoning distinction is always made between the *universal* or general class, which is expressed by the word *all*, and the *particular* or individual, which is expressed by the word "some." Many persons fail to note this difference in their reasoning, and fallaciously reason, for instance, that because *some* swans are white, *all* swans must be so, which is a far different thing from reasoning that if *all* is so and so, then *some* must be so and so. Those who are interested in this subject are referred to some elementary text-book on logic, as the detailed consideration is too technical for consideration here.

REASONING BY ANALOGY

Reasoning by analogy is an elementary form of reasoning, and is the particular kind of reasoning employed by the majority of persons in ordinary thought. It is based upon the unconscious recognition by the human mind of the principle which is expressed by Jevons as: "*If two or more things resemble each other in many points, they will probably resemble each other in more points.*" The same authority says: "Reasoning by analogy differs only in degree from that kind of reasoning called '*generalization.*' When *many things* resemble each other in a *few properties*, we argue about them by generalization. When a *few things* resemble each other in *many properties*, it is a case of analogy."

While this form of reason is frequently employed with more or less satisfactory results, it is always open to a large percentage of error. Thus, persons have been poisoned by toadstools by reason of false analogous reasoning that because mushrooms are edible, then toadstools, which resemble them, must also be fit for food; or, in the same way, because certain berries resemble other edible berries they must likewise be good food. As Brooks says: "To infer that because John Smith has a red nose and is also a drunkard, then Henry Jones, who also has a red nose, is also a drunkard, would be dangerous inference. Conclusions of this kind drawn from analogy are frequently dangerous." Halleck says: "Many false analogies are manufactured, and it is excellent thought training to expose them. The majority of people think so little that they swallow these false analogies just as newly-fledged robins swallow small stones dropped into their mouths."

Jevons, one of the best authorities on the subject, says: "There is no way in which we can really assure ourselves that we are arguing safely by analogy. The only rule that can be given is this: That the more closely two things resemble each other, the more likely it is that they are the same in other respects, especially in points closely connected with those observed. In order to be clear about our conclusions, we ought, in fact, never to rest satisfied with mere analogy, but ought to try to discover the general laws governing the case. * * * We find that reasoning by analogy is not to be depended upon, unless we make such an inquiry into the causes and laws of the things in question that we really employ inductive and deductive reasoning."

HIGHER FORMS OF REASONING

The two higher forms of reasoning are known, respectively, as (1) inductive reasoning, or inference from particular facts to general laws; and (2) deductive reasoning, or inference from general truths to particular truths. While the class distinction is made for the purpose of clear consideration, it must not be forgotten that the two forms of reasoning are generally found in combination. Thus, in inductive reasoning many steps are taken by the aid of deductive reasoning; and, likewise, before we can reason deductively from general truths to particular ones we must have discovered the general truths by inductive reasoning from particular facts. Thus there is a unity in all reasoning processes as there is in all mental operations. Inductive reasoning is a *synthetical* process; deductive reasoning, an *analytical* one. In the first we combine and build up, in the latter we dissect and separate.

26

Inductive Reasoning

INDUCTIVE reasoning is based upon the axiom: "*What is true of the many is true of the whole.*" This axiom is based upon man's belief in the uniformity of nature. Inductive reasoning is a mental ladder by which we climb from particular facts to general laws, but the ladder rests upon the belief that the universe is governed by law.

The steps in inductive reasoning are as follows:

I. Observation, investigation, and examination of particular facts or things. If we wish to know the general characteristics of the bird family, we must first examine a sufficient number of birds of many kinds so as to discover the comparatively few general characteristics possessed by *all* of the bird family, as distinct from the particular characteristics possessed by only *some* of that family. The greater the number of individuals examined, the narrower becomes our list of the general qualities common to *all*. In the same way we must examine many kinds of flowers before we come to the few general qualities common to all flowers, which we combine in the general concept of "flower." The same, of course, is true regarding the discovery of general laws from particular facts. We examine the facts and then work toward a general law which will explain them. For instance, the Law of Gravitation was discovered by the observation and investigation of the fact that all objects are attracted to the earth; further investigation revealed the fact that all material objects are attracted to each other; then the general law was discovered, or, rather, the hypothesis was advanced, was found to explain the facts, and was verified by further experiments and observation.

II. The second step in inductive reasoning is the making of an hypothesis. An hypothesis is a proposition or principle assumed as a *possible* explanation for a set or class of facts. It is regarded as a "working theory," which must be examined and tested in connection with the facts before it is finally accepted. For instance, after the observation that a number of magnets attracted steel, it was found reasonable to advance the hypothesis that "all magnets attract steel." In the same way was advanced the hypothesis that "all birds are warm-blooded, winged, feathered, oviparous vertebrates." Subsequent observation and experiment established the hypothesis regarding the magnet, and regarding the general qualities of the bird family. If a single magnet had been found which did not attract steel, then the hypothesis would have fallen. If a single bird had been discovered which was not warm-blooded, then that quality would have been stricken from the list of the necessary characteristics of all birds.

A theory is merely a hypothesis which has been verified or established by continued and repeated observation, investigation, and experiment.

Hypotheses and theories arise very frequently from the subconscious assimilation of a number of particular facts and the consequent flashing of a "great guess," or "sacred suspicion of the truth," into the conscious field of attention. The scientific imagination plays an important part in this process. There is, of course, a world of difference between a "blind guess" based upon insufficient data and a "scientific guess" resulting from the accumulation of a vast store of careful and accurate information. As Brooks says: "The forming of a hypothesis requires a suggestive mind, a lively fancy, a philosophic imagination that catches a glimpse of the idea through the form or sees the law standing behind the fact." But accepted theories, in the majority of cases, arise only by testing out and rejecting many promising hypotheses and finally settling upon the one which best answers all the requirements and best explains the facts. As an authority says: "To try wrong guesses is with most persons the only way to hit upon right ones."

III. Testing the hypothesis by deductive reasoning is the third step in inductive reasoning. This test is made by applying the hypothetical principle to particular facts or things; that is, to follow out mentally the hypothetical principle to its logical conclusion. This may be done in this way: "If *so and so* is correct, then it follows that *thus and so* is true," etc. If the conclusion agrees with reason, then the test is deemed satisfactory so far as it has gone. But if the result proves to be a logical absurdity or inconsistent with natural facts, then the hypothesis is discredited.

IV. Practical verification of the hypothesis is the fourth step in inductive reasoning. This step consists of the actual comparison of observed facts with the "logical conclusions" arising from applying deductive reasoning to the general principle assumed as a premise. The greater number of facts agreeing with the conclusions arising from the premise of the hypothesis, the greater is deemed the "probability" of the latter. The authorities generally assume a hypothesis to be *verified* when it accounts for *all* the facts which properly are related to it. Some extremists contend, however, that before a hypothesis may be considered as absolutely verified, it must not only account for all the associated facts but that also there must be no other possible hypothesis to account for the same facts. The "facts" referred to in this connection may be either (1) observed phenomena, or (2) the conclusions of deductive reasoning arising from the assumption of the hypothesis, or (3) the agreement between the observed facts and the logical conclusions. The last combination is generally regarded as the most logical. The verification of a hypothesis must be "an all-around one," and there must be an agreement between the observed facts and the logical conclusions in the case—the hypothesis must "fit" the facts, and the facts must "fit" the hypothesis. The "facts" are the glass slipper of the Cinderella legend—the several sisters of Cinderella were discarded hypotheses, the slipper and the sisters not "fitting." When Cinderella's foot was found to be the one foot upon which the glass slipper fitted, then the Cinderella hypothesis was considered to have been proved—the glass slipper was hers and the prince claimed his bride.

27

Deductive Reasoning

WE have seen in the preceding chapter that from particular facts we reason inductively to general principles or truths. We have also seen that one of the steps of inductive reasoning is the testing of the hypothesis by deductive reasoning. We shall now also see that the results of inductive reasoning are used as premises or bases for deductive reasoning. These two forms of reasoning are opposites and yet complementary to each other; they are in a sense independent and yet are interdependent. Brooks says: "The two methods of reasoning are the reverse of each other. One goes from particulars to generals; the other from generals to particulars. One is a process of analysis; the other is a process of synthesis. One rises from facts to laws; the other descends from laws to facts. Each is independent of the other, and each is a valid and essential method of inference."

Halleck well expresses the spirit of deductive reasoning as follows: "After induction has classified certain phenomena and thus given us a major premise, we may proceed deductively to apply the inference to any new specimen that can be shown to belong to that class. Induction hands over to deduction a ready-made premise. Deduction takes that as a fact, making no inquiry regarding its truth. Only after general laws have been laid down, after objects have been classified, after major premises have been formed, can deduction be employed."

Deductive reasoning proceeds from general principles to particular facts. It is a descending process, analytical in its nature. It rests upon the fundamental axiomatic basis that *whatever is true of the whole is true of its parts,* or *whatever is true of the universal is true of the particulars.*

The process of deductive reasoning may be stated briefly as follows: (1) A general principle of a class is stated as a *major premise*; (2) a particular thing is stated as belonging to that general class, this statement being the *minor premise*;

therefore (3) the general class principle is held to apply to the particular thing, this last statement being the *conclusion*. (*A "premise" is "a proposition assumed to be true."*)

The following gives us an illustration of the above process:

I. (*Major premise*)—A bird is a warm-blooded, feathered, winged, oviparous vertebrate.

II. (*Minor premise*)—The sparrow is a bird; therefore

III. (*Conclusion*)—The sparrow is a warm-blooded, feathered, winged, oviparous vertebrate.

Or, again:

I. (*Major premise*)—Rattlesnakes frequently bite when enraged, and their bite is poisonous.

II. (*Minor premise*)—This snake before me is a rattlesnake; therefore

III. (*Conclusion*)—This snake before me may bite when enraged, and its bite will be poisonous.

The average person may be inclined to object that he is not conscious of going through this complicated process when he reasons about sparrows or rattlesnakes. But he *does*, nevertheless. He is not conscious of the steps, because mental habit has accustomed him to the process, and it is performed more or less automatically. But these three steps manifest in all processes of deductive reasoning, even the simplest. The average person is like the character in the French play who was surprised to learn that he had "been talking prose for forty years without knowing it." Jevons says that the majority of persons are equally surprised when they find out that they have been using logical forms, more or less correctly, without having realized it. He says: "A large number even of educated persons have no clear idea of what logic is. Yet, in a certain way, every one must have been a logician since he began to speak."

There are many technical rules and principles of logic which we cannot attempt to consider here. There are, however, a few elementary principles of correct reasoning which should have a place here. What is known as a "syllogism" is the expression in words of the various parts of the complete process of reasoning or argument. Whately defines it as follows: "A syllogism is an argument expressed in strict logical form so that its conclusiveness is manifest from the structure of the expression alone, without any regard to the meaning of the term." In short, *if* the two premises are accepted as correct, it follows that there can be only one true logical conclusion resulting therefrom. In abstract or theoretical reasoning the word "*if*" is assumed to precede each of the two premises, the "therefore" before the conclusion resulting from the "if," of course. The following are the general rules governing the syllogism:

I. Every syllogism must consist of three, and no more than three, propositions, namely (1) the major premise, (2) the minor premise, and (3) the conclusion.

II. The conclusion must naturally follow from the premises, otherwise the syllogism is invalid and constitutes a fallacy or sophism.

III. One premise, at least, must be affirmative.

IV. If one premise is negative, the conclusion must be negative.

V. One premise, at least, must be universal or general.

VI. If one premise is particular, the conclusion also must be particular.

The last two rules (V. and VI.) contain the essential principles of all the rules regarding syllogisms, and any syllogism which breaks them will be found also to break other rules, some of which are not stated here for the reason that they are too technical. These two rules may be tested by constructing syllogisms in violation of their principles. The reason for them is as follows: (Rule V.) Because "from two particular premises no conclusion can be drawn," as, for instance: (1) Some men are mortal; (2) John is a man. We cannot reason from this either that John *is* or *is not* mortal. The major premise should read "*all* men." (Rule VI.) Because "a universal conclusion can be drawn only from two universal premises," an example being needless here, as the conclusion is so obvious.

CULTIVATION OF REASONING FACULTIES

There is no royal road to the cultivation of the reasoning faculties. There is but the old familiar rule: Practice, exercise, use. Nevertheless there are certain studies which tend to develop the faculties in question. The study of arithmetic, especially mental arithmetic, tends to develop correct habits of reasoning from one truth to another—from cause to effect. Better still is the study of geometry; and best of all, of course, is the study of logic and the practice of working out its problems and examples. The study of philosophy and psychology also is useful in this way. Many lawyers and teachers have drilled themselves in geometry solely for the purpose of developing their logical reasoning powers.

Brooks says: "So valuable is geometry as a discipline that many lawyers and others review their geometry every year in order to keep the mind drilled to logical habits of thinking. * * * The study of logic will aid in the development of the power of deductive reasoning. It does this, first, by showing the method by which we reason. To know how we reason, to see the laws which govern the reasoning process, to analyze the syllogism and see its conformity to the laws of thought, is not only an exercise of reasoning but gives that knowledge of the process that will be both a stimulus and a guide to thought. No one can trace the principles and processes of thought without receiving thereby an impetus to thought. In the second place, the study of logic is probably even more valuable because it gives practice in deductive thinking. This, perhaps, is its principal value, since the mind reasons instinctively without knowing how it reasons. One can think without the knowledge of the science of thinking just as one can use language correctly without a knowledge of grammar; yet as the study of grammar improves one's speech, so the study of logic can but improve one's thought."

In the opinion of the writer hereof, one of the best though simple methods of cultivating the faculties of reasoning is to acquaint one's self thoroughly with the more common *fallacies* or forms of false reasoning—so thoroughly that not only is the false reasoning detected at once but also the *reason* of its falsity is readily understood. To understand the wrong ways of reasoning is to be on guard against them. By guarding against them we tend to eliminate them from our thought processes. If we eliminate the false we have the true left in its place. Therefore we recommend the weeding of the logical garden of the common fallacies, to the end that the flowers of pure reason may flourish in their stead. Accordingly, we think it well to call your attention in the next chapter to the more common fallacies, and the reason of their falsity.

28

Fallacious Reasoning

A FALLACY is defined as "an unsound argument or mode of arguing which, while appearing to be decisive of a question, is in reality not so; or a fallacious statement or proposition in which the error is not readily apparent. When a fallacy is used to deceive others, it is called 'sophistry,'" It is important that the student should understand the nature of the fallacy and understand its most common forms. As Jevons says: "In learning how to do right it is always desirable to be informed as to the ways in which we are likely to go wrong. In describing to a man the road which he should follow, we ought to tell him not only the turnings which he is to take but also the turnings which he is to avoid. Similarly, it is a useful part of logic which teaches us the ways and turnings by which people most commonly go astray in reasoning."

In presenting the following brief statement regarding the more common forms of fallacy, we omit so far as possible the technical details which belong to text-books on logic.

FALLACIES

I. *True Collective but False Particular*—An example of this fallacy is found in the argument that because the French race, collectively, are excitable, therefore a particular Frenchman must be excitable. Or that because the Jewish race, collectively, are good business people, therefore the particular Jew must be a good business man. This is as fallacious as arguing that because a man may drown in the ocean he should avoid the bath, basin, or cup of water. There is a vast difference between the whole of a thing and its separate parts. Nitric acid and glycerin, separately, are not explosive, but, combined, they form nitro-glycerin, a most dangerous and powerful explosive. Reversing this form of illustration, we remind you of the old saying: "Salt is a good thing; but one doesn't want to be put in pickle."

II. *Irrelevant Conclusion*—This fallacy consists in introducing in the conclusion matter not contained in the premises, or in the confusing of the issue. For instance: (1) All men are sinful; (2) John Smith is a man; therefore (3) John Smith is a horse thief. This may sound absurd, but many arguments are as fallacious as this, and for the same reason. Or another and more subtle form: (1) All thieves are liars; (2) John Smith is a liar; therefore (3) John Smith is a thief. The first example arises from the introduction of new matter, and the last from the confusion of the issue.

III. *False Cause*—This fallacy consists in attributing cause to a thing which is merely coincident with, or precedent to, the effect. For instance: (1) The cock crows just before or at the moment of sunrise; therefore (2) the cock-crowing is the cause of the sunrise. Or, again: (1) Bad crops followed the election of a Whig president; therefore (2) the Whig party is the cause of the bad crops. Or, again: (1) Where civilization is the highest, there we find the greatest number of high hats; therefore (2) high hats are the cause of civilization.

IV. *Circular Reasoning*—In this form of fallacy the person reasoning or arguing endeavors to explain or prove a thing by itself or its own terms. For instance: (1) The Whig party is honest because it advocates honest principles; (2) the Whig principles are honest because they are advocated by an honest party. A common form of this fallacy in its phase of sophistry is the use of synonyms in such a manner that they seem to express more than the original conception, whereas they are really but other terms for the same thing. An historic example of circular reasoning is the following: (1) The Church of England is the true Church, because it was established by God; (2) it must have been established by God, because it is the true Church. This form of sophistry is most effective when employed in long arguments in which it is difficult to detect it.

V. *Begging the Question*—This fallacy arises from the use of a false premise, or at least of a premise the truth of which is not admitted by the opponent. It may be stated, simply, as "*the unwarranted assumption of a premise, generally the major premise.*" Many persons in public life argue in this way. They boldly assert an unwarranted premise, and then proceed to argue logically from it. The result is confusing to the average person, for, the steps of the reasoning being logical, it seems as if the argument is sound, the fact of the unwarranted premise being overlooked. The person using this form of sophistry proceeds on Aaron Burr's theory of truth being "that which is boldly asserted and plausibly maintained."

Bulwer makes one of his characters mention a particularly atrocious form of this fallacy (although an amusing one) in the following words: "Whenever you are about to utter something astonishingly false, always begin with: 'It is an acknowledged fact,' etc. Sir Robert Filmer was a master of this manner of writing. Thus with what a solemn face that great man attempted to cheat. He would say: *'It is a truth undeniable* that there cannot be any multitude of men whatsoever, either great or small, etc., but that in the same multitude there is one man among them *that in nature hath a right to be King of all the rest—as being the next heir of Adam!'* "

Look carefully for the major premise of propositions advanced in argument, spoken or written. Be sure that the person making the proposition is not "begging the question" by *the unwarranted assumption of the premise.*

GENERAL RULE OF INFERENCE

Hyslop says concerning valid inferences and fallacious ones: "We cannot infer *anything* we please from any premises we please. We must conform to certain definite rules or principles. Any violation of them will be a fallacy. There are two simple rules which should not be violated: (1) *The subject-matter in the conclusion should be of the same general kind as in the premises*; (2) *the facts constituting the premises must be accepted and must not be fictitious.*" A close observance of these rules will result in the detection and avoidance of the principal forms of fallacious reasoning and sophistry.

SOPHISTICAL ARGUMENTS

There are a number of tricky practices resorted to by persons in argument, that are fallacious in intent and result, which we do not consider here in detail as they scarcely belong to the particular subject of this book. A brief mention, however, may be permitted in the interest of general information. Here are the principal ones:

(1) Arguing that a proposition is correct because the opponent cannot prove the contrary. The fallacy is seen when we realize that the statement, "The

moon is made of green cheese," is not proved because we cannot prove the contrary. No amount of failure to *disprove* a proposition really *proves* it; and no amount of failure to *prove* a proposition really *disproves* it. As a general rule, the burden of proof rests upon the person stating the proposition, and his opponent is not called upon to disprove it or else have it considered proved. The old cry of "You cannot *prove* that it is *not* so" is based upon a fallacious conception.

(2) Abuse of the opponent, his party, or his cause. This is no real argument or reasoning. It is akin to proving a point by beating the opponent over the head.

(3) Arguing that an opponent does not live up to his principles is no argument against the principles he advocates. A man may advocate the principle of temperance and yet drink to excess. This simply proves that he preaches better than he practices; but the truth of the principle of temperance is not affected in any way thereby. The proof of this is that he may change his practices; and it cannot be held that the change of his personal habits improves or changes the nature of the principle.

(4) Argument of authority is not based on logic. Authority is valuable when really worthy, and merely as corroboration or adding weight; but it is not logical argument. The *reasons* of the authority alone constitute a real argument. The abuse of this form of argument is shown, in the above reference to "begging the question," in the quotation from Bulwer.

(5) Appeal to prejudice or public opinion is not a valid argument, for public opinion is frequently wrong and prejudice is often unwarranted. And, at the best, they "have nothing to do with the case" from the standpoint of logic. The abuse of testimony and claimed evidence is also worthy of examination, but we cannot go into the subject here.

FALLACIES OF PREJUDICE

But perhaps the most dangerous of all fallacies in the search for truth on the part of the most of us are those which arise from the following:

(1) The tendency to reason from what we feel and wish to be true, rather than from the actual facts of the case, which causes us unconsciously to assume the mental attitude of "if the facts agree with our likes and pet theories, all is well; if they do not, so much the worse for the facts."

(2) The tendency in all of us to perceive only the facts that agree with our theories and to ignore the others. We find that for which we seek, and overlook that which does not interest us. Our discoveries follow our interest, and our interest follows our desires and beliefs.

The intelligent man or woman realizes these tendencies of human nature and endeavors to avoid them in his or her own reasoning, but is keenly conscious of them in the arguments and reasoning of others. A failure to observe and guard one's self against these tendencies results in bigotry, intolerance, narrowness, and intellectual astigmatism.

29

The Will

THE activities of the will comprise the third great class of mental processes. Psychologists always have differed greatly in their conception of just what constitutes these activities. Even today it is difficult to obtain a dictionary definition of the will that agrees with the best opinion on the subject. The dictionaries adhere to the old classification and conception which regarded the will as "that faculty of the mind or soul by which it chooses or decides." But with the growth of the idea that the will acts according to the strongest motive, and that the motive is supplied by the average struck between the desires of the moment, under the supervision of the intellect, the conception of will as the choosing and deciding faculty is passing from favor. In the place of the older conception has come the newer one which holds that the will is primarily concerned with *action*.

It is difficult to place the will in the category of mental processes. But it is generally agreed that it abides in the very center of the mental being, and is closely associated with what is called the ego, or self. The will seems to have at least three general phases, viz.: (1) The phase of desire, (2) the phase of deliberation or choice, and (3) the phase of expression in action. In order to understand the will, it is necessary to consider each of these three phases of its activities.

(1) DESIRE

The first phase of will, which is called "desire," is in itself somewhat complex. On its lower side it touches, and, in fact, blends into, feeling and emotion. Its center consists of a state of *tension*, akin to that of a coiled spring or a cat crouching ready for a spring. On its higher side it touches, penetrates, and blends into the other phases of the will which we have mentioned.

Desire is defined as "a feeling, emotion, or excitement of the mind directed toward the attainment, enjoyment, or possession of some object from which pleasure, profit, or gratification is expected." Halleck gives us the following excellent conception of the moving spirit of desire: "*Desire has for its object something which will bring pleasure or get rid of pain, immediate or remote, for the individual or for some one in whom he is interested. Aversion, or a striving away from something, is merely the negative aspect of desire.*"

In Halleck's statement, above quoted, we have the explanation of the part played by the intellect in the activities of will. The intellect is able to perceive the relations between present action and future results, and is able to point the way toward the suppression of some desires in order that other and better ones may be manifested. It also serves its purposes in regulating the "striking of the average" between conflicting desires. Without the intervention of the intellect, the temporary desire of the moment would invariably be acted upon without regard to future results or consequences to one's self and others. It also serves to point out the course of action calculated to give the most satisfactory expression of the desire.

While it is a fact that the action of will depends almost entirely upon the motive force of desire, it is likewise true that desire may be created, regulated, suppressed, and even killed by the action of the will. The will, by giving or refusing attention to a certain class of desires, may either cause them to grow and wax strong, or else die and fade away. It must be remembered, however, that this use of the will itself springs from another set of desires or feelings.

Desire is aroused by feelings or emotions rising from the subconscious planes of the mind and seeking expression and manifestation. We have considered the nature of the feelings and emotions in previous chapters, which should be read in connection with the present one. It should be remembered that the feeling or emotional side of desire arises from either inherited race memories existing as instincts, or from the memory of the past experiences of the individual. In some cases the feeling first manifests in a vague unrest caused by subconscious promptings and excitement. Then the imagination pictures the object of the feeling, or certain memory images connected with it, and the desire thus manifests on the plane of consciousness.

The entrance of the desire feeling into consciousness is accompanied by that peculiar *tension* which marks the second phase of desire. This tension, when sufficiently strong, passes into the third phase of desire, or that in which desire blends into will action. Desire in this stage makes a demand upon will for expression and action. From mere feeling, and tension of feeling, it becomes *a call to action*. But before expression and action are given to it, the second phase of will must manifest at least for a moment; this second phase is that known as deliberation, or the weighing and balancing of desires.

(2) DELIBERATION

The second phase of will, known as deliberation, is more than the purely intellectual process which the term would indicate. The intellect plays an important part, it is true, but there is also an almost instinctive and automatic *weighing and balancing of desires*. There is seldom only one desire presenting its claims upon the will at any particular moment. It is true that occasionally there arises an emotional desire of such dominant power and strength that it crowds out every other claimant at the bar of deliberation. But such instances are rare, and as a rule there are a host of rival claimants, each insisting upon its rights in the matter at issue. In the man of weak or undeveloped and untrained intellect, the struggle is usually little more than a brief combat between several desires, in which *the strongest at the moment wins*. But with the development of intellect new factors arise and new forces are felt. Moreover, the more complex one's emotional nature, and the greater the development of the higher forms of feeling, the more intense is the struggle of deliberation or the fight of the desires.

We see, in Halleck's definition, that desire has not only the object of "bringing pleasure or getting rid of pain" for the individual, but that the additional element of the welfare of "some one in whom he is interested" is added, which element is often the deciding factor. This element, of course, arises from the development and cultivation of one's emotional nature. In the same way we also see that it is not merely the *immediate* welfare of one's self or those in whom one is interested that speaks before the bar, but also the more *remote* welfare. This consideration of future welfare depends upon the intellect and cultivated imagination under its control. Moreover, the trained intellect is able to discover possible greater satisfaction in some course of action other than in the one prompted by the clamoring desire of the moment. This explains why the judgment and action of an intelligent man, as a rule, are far different from those of the unintelligent one; and also why a man of culture tends toward different action from that of the uncultured; and likewise, why the man of broad sympathies and high ideals acts in a different way from one of the opposite type. But the principle is ever the same—the feelings manifest in desire, the greatest ultimate satisfaction apparent at the moment is sought, and the strongest set of desires wins the day.

Halleck's comment on this point is interesting. He says: "Desire is not always proportional to the idea of one's own selfish pleasure. Many persons, after forming an idea of the vast amount of earthly distress, desire to relieve it, and the desire goes out in action, as the benevolent societies in every city testify. Here the individual pleasure is none the less, but it is secondary, coming from the pleasure of others. The desire of the *near* often raises a stronger desire than the *remote*. A child frequently prefers a thing immediately if it is only one tenth as good as something he might have a year hence. A student often desires more the leisure of today than the success of future years. Though admonished to study, he wastes his time and thus loses incomparably greater future pleasure when he is tossed to the rear in the struggle for existence."

The result of this weighing and balancing of the desire is, or should be, *decision and choice*, which then passes into action. But many persons seem unable to "make up their own mind," and require a push or urge from without before they will act. Others decide, without proper use of the intellect, upon what they call "impulse," but which is merely impatience. Some are like the fabled donkey which starved to death when placed at an equal distance between two equally attractive haystacks and was unable to decide towards which to move. Others follow the example of Jeppe, in the comedy, who, when given a coin with which to buy a piece of soap for his wife, stood on the corner deliberating whether to obey orders or to buy a drink with the money. He wants the drink, but realizes that his wife will beat him if he returns without the soap. "My stomach says drink; my back says soap," says Jeppe. "But," finally he remarks, "is not a man's stomach more to him than his back? Yes, says I."

The final decision depends upon the striking a balance between the desires—the weighing of desire for and desire against—desire for this and desire for something else. The strength of the several desires depends upon nearness and present interest arising from attention, as applied to the feelings and emotions arising from heredity, environment, experience, and education, which constitute character; and also upon the degree of intellectual clearness and power in forming correct judgments between the desires.

It must be remembered, however, that the intellect appears not as an opponent of the principle of the satisfaction of desire, but merely as an instrument of the ego in determining which course of action will result in the greatest ultimate satisfaction, direct or indirect, present or future. For, *at the last, every individual acts so as to bring himself the greatest satisfaction, immediate or future, direct or indirect, either personal or through the welfare of others, as this may appear to him at the particular moment of deliberation.* We always act in the direction of that which will greater "content our spirit." This will be found to be the spirit of all decisions, although the motive is often hidden and difficult to find even by the individual himself, many of the strongest motives having their origin in the subconscious planes of mentality.

(3) ACTION

The third and final phase of will is that known as action—the act of volition by which the desire-idea is expressed in physical or mental activity. The old conception of the will held that the decisive phase of the will was its characteristic and final phase, ignoring the fact that the very essence or spirit of will is bound up with *action*. Even those familiar with the newer conception frequently assume that the act of decision is the final phase of will, ignoring the fact that we frequently *decide* to do a thing and yet may never carry out the intention and decision. The act of willing is not complete unless action is expressed. There must be the manifestation of the motor element or phase of will, else the will process is incomplete.

A weakness of this last phase of will affects the entire will and renders its processes ineffective. The world is filled with persons who are able to *decide* what is best to do, and what should be done, but who never actually *act* upon the decision. The few persons who promptly follow up the decision with vigorous action are those who accomplish the world's work. Without the full manifestation of this third phase of will the other two phases are useless.

TYPES OF WILL

So far we have considered merely the highest type of will—that which is accompanied by conscious deliberation, in which the intellect takes an active part. In this process, not only do the conflicting feelings push themselves forward with opposing claims for recognition, but the intellect is active in examining the case and offering valuable testimony as to the comparative merits of the various claimants and the effect of certain courses of action upon the individual. There are, however, several lower forms of will manifestation which we should briefly consider in passing.

Reflex Action—The will is moved to action by the reflex activities of the nervous system which have been mentioned in the earlier chapters of this book. In this general type we find unconscious reflex action, such as that manifested when a sleeper is touched and moves away, or when the frog's leg twitches when the nerve end is excited. We also find conscious reflex action, such as that manifested by the winking of the eye, or the performance of habitual physical motion, such as the movement in walking, operating the sewing machine or typewriter, playing the piano, etc.

Impulsive Action—The will is often moved to action by a dim idea or faint perception of purpose or impulse. The action is almost instinctive, although there is a vague perception of purpose. For instance, we feel an impulse to turn toward the source of a strange sound or sight, or other source of interest or curiosity. Or we may feel an impulse arising from the subconscious plane of our mind, causing a dimly-conscious idea of movement or action to relieve the tension. For instance, one may feel a desire to exercise, or to seek fresh air or green fields, although he had not been thinking of these things at the time.

These impulses arise from a subconscious feeling of fatigue or desire for change, which, added to a fleeting idea, produces the impulse. Unless an impulse is inhibited by the will activities inspired by other desires, habits, ideas, or ideals, we act upon it in precisely the same way that a young child or animal does. Hoffding says of this type of action: "The psychological condition of the impulse is, that with the momentary feeling and sensation should be combined a more or less clear idea of something which may augment the pleasure or diminish the pain of the moment."

Instinctive Action—The will is frequently moved to action by an instinctive stimulus. This form of will activity closely resembles the last-mentioned form, and often it is impossible to distinguish between the two. The activities of the bee in building its comb and storing its honey, the work of the silkworm and caterpillar in building their resting places, are examples of this form of action. Indeed, even the building of the nest of the bird may be so classed. In these cases there is an intelligent action toward a definite end, but the animal is unconscious of that end. The experiences of the remote ancestors of these creatures recorded their impressions upon the subconscious mind of the species, and they are transmitted in some way to all of that species. The nervous system of every living thing is a record cylinder of the experiences of its early ancestors, and these cylinders tend to reproduce these impressions upon appropriate occasions. In preceding chapters we have shown that even man is under the influence of instinct to a greater extent than he imagines himself to be.

30

Will-Training

IT is of the utmost importance that the individual develop, cultivate, and train his will so as to bring it under the influence of the higher part of his mental and moral being. While the will is used most effectively in developing and training the intellect and building character, it itself must be trained by itself to habitually come under the guidance of the intellect and under the influence of that which we call character.

The influence of the trained will upon the several mental faculties is most marked. There are no faculties which may not be cultivated by the will. The first and great task of the will in this direction is the control and direction of the attention. The will determines the kind of interest that shall prevail at the moment, and the kind of interest largely determines the character of the man, his tastes, his feelings, his thoughts, his acts. Gordy says: "Cooperating with a pre-existing influence, the will can make a weaker one prevail over a stronger. * * * It determines which of pre-existing influences shall have control over the mind."

Moreover, concentrated and continued attention depends entirely upon the exercise of the will. As Gordy says: "If the will relaxes its hold upon the activities of the mind, the attention is liable to be carried away by any one of the thousands of ideas that the laws of association are constantly bringing into our minds."

Even in the matter of mental images the will asserts its sway, and the imagination may be trained to be the obedient servant of the developed will. Regarding the influence of the will upon character, Davidson says: "It is not enough for a man to understand correctly and love duly the conditions of moral life in his own time; he must, still further, be willing and able to fulfill these conditions. And he certainly cannot do this unless his will is trained to perfect freedom, so that it responds, with the utmost readiness, to the suggestions of

his discriminating intelligence and the movements of his chastened affections."
Halleck says: "We gradually make our characters by separate acts of will, just
as a blacksmith by repeated blows beats out a horseshoe or an anchor from a
shapeless mass of iron. A finished anchor or horseshoe was never the product
of a single blow."

TRAINING THE WILL

Perhaps the best way to train the will is to *use* it intelligently, and with a purpose. The training of any faculty of the mind is at the same time a training of
the will. The attention being so closely allied to the will, it follows that a careful
training of attention will result in a strengthening of the will. The training of the
emotional side of one's nature also brings results in the strengthening of the will.

Halleck gives his students excellent advice regarding the training of the
will. It would be hard to find anything better along these lines than the following from his pen: "Nothing schools the will, and renders it ready for effort
in this complex world, better than accustoming it to face disagreeable things.
Professor James advises all to do something occasionally for no other reason
than that they would rather not do it, if it is nothing more than giving up a
seat in a street car. He likens such effort to the insurance that a man pays on
his house. He has something that he can fall back on in time of trouble. A
will schooled in this way is always ready to respond, no matter how great the
emergency. While another would be crying over spilled milk, the possessor of
such a will has already found another cow. * * * The only way to secure such
a will is to practice doing disagreeable things. There are daily opportunities.
* * * A man who had declared his aversion to what he deemed the dry facts of
political economy was one day found knitting his brow over a chapter of John
Stuart Mill. When a friend expressed surprise, the man replied: 'I am playing
the schoolmaster with myself. I am reading this because I dislike it.' Such a
man has the elements of success in him. * * * On the other hand, the one who
habitually avoids disagreeable action is training his will to be of no use to him
at a time when supreme effort is demanded. Such a will can never elbow its way
to the front in life."

HABITS

Habits are the beaten track over which the will travels. The beaten path of habit
is the line of least resistance to the will. One who would train his will must
needs pay attention to providing it with the proper mental paths over which to

travel. The rule for the creation of habits is simply this: *Travel over the mental path as often as possible.* The rule for breaking undesirable habits is this: *Cultivate the opposite habit.* In these two rules is expressed the gist of what has been written on the subject.

Professor William James has left to the world some invaluable advice regarding the cultivation of right habits. He bases his rules upon those of Professor Bain, elaborates these, and adds some equally good ones. We herewith quote freely from both James and Bain on this subject; it is the best ever written regarding habit building.

I. "In the acquisition of a new habit, or the leaving off of an old one, launch yourself with as strong and decided an initiative as possible. This will give your new beginning such a momentum that the temptation to break down will not occur as soon as it otherwise might; and every day during which a breakdown is postponed adds to the chances of it not occurring at all."—*James.*

II. "Never suffer an exception to occur till the new habit is securely rooted in your life. Every lapse is like the letting fall of a ball of string which one is carefully winding up—a single slip undoes more than a great many turns will wind again."—*James.* "It is necessary, above all things, in such a situation, never to lose a battle. Every gain on the wrong side undoes the effect of many conquests on the right. The essential precaution is so to regulate the two opposing powers that the one may have a series of uninterrupted successes, until repetition has fortified it to such a degree as to enable it to cope with the opposition, under any circumstances."—*Bain.*

III. "Seize the very first possible opportunity to act on every resolution you make, and on every emotional prompting you may experience in the direction of the habits you aspire to gain. It is not in the moment of their forming, but in the moment of their producing *motor effects*, that resolves and aspirations communicate their new 'set' to the brain."—*James.* "The actual presence of the practical opportunity alone furnishes the fulcrum upon which the lever can rest, by which the moral will may multiply its strength and raise itself aloft. He who has no solid ground to press against will never get beyond the stage of empty gesture making."—*Bain.*

IV. "Keep the faculty alive in you by a little gratuitous exercise every day. That is, be systematically ascetic or heroic in little, unnecessary points;

do every day something for no other reason than that you would rather not do it, so that when the hour of dire need draws nigh, it may find you not unnerved and untrained to stand the test. * * * The man who has daily inured himself to habits of concentrated attention, energetic volition, and self-denial in unnecessary things will stand like a tower when everything rocks around him, and when his softer fellow mortals are winnowed like chaff in the blast."—*James.*

31

Will-Tonic

IN addition to the general rules for developing and training the will given in the preceding chapter, we ask you to tone up and strengthen the will by the inspiration to be derived from the words of some of the world's great thinkers and doers. In these words there is such a vital statement of the recognition, realization, and manifestation of that something within, which we call "will," that it is a dull soul, indeed, which is not inspired by the contagion of the idea. These expressions are the milestones on the Path of Attainment, placed by those who have preceded us on the journey. We submit these quotations without comment; they speak for themselves.

WORDS OF THE WISE

"They can who think they can. Character is a perfectly educated will."

"Nothing can resist the will of a man who knows what is true and wills what is good."

"In all difficulties advance and will, for within you is a power, a living force, which the more you trust and learn to use will annihilate the opposition of matter."

"The star of the unconquered will, It rises in my breast,
Serene and resolute and still, And calm and self-possessed.

So nigh is grandeur to our dust, So near is God to man,
When duty whispers low, 'Thou must!' The youth replies, 'I can!'"

"The longer I live, the more certain I am that the great difference between men, between the feeble and the powerful, the great and the insignificant, is energy—invincible determination—a purpose once fixed, and then death or victory. That quality will do anything that can be done in this world, and no talents, no circumstances, no opportunities will make a two-legged creature a man without it."—*Buxton.*

"It masters time, it conquers space;
It cows that boastful trickster, Chance,
And bids the tyrant Circumstance
Uncrown, and fill a servant's place.

"The Human Will, that forcer unseen,
The offspring of a deathless Soul,
Can hew a way to any goal,
Through walls of granite intervene."

"Resolve is what makes a man manifest; not puny resolve, not crude determinations, not errant purpose, but that strong and indefatigable will which treads down difficulties and danger as a boy treads down the heaving frost lands of winter, which kindles his eye and brain with a proud pulse beat toward the unattainable. Will makes men giants."—*Donald G. Mitchell.*

"There is no chance, no destiny, no fate
Can circumvent, or hinder, or control
The firm resolve of a determined soul.
Gifts count for nothing, will alone is great;
All things give way before it soon or late.

What obstacle can stay the mighty force
Of the sea-seeking river in its course,
Or cause the ascending orb of day to wait?
Each well-born soul must win what it deserves.

Let the fools prate of luck.

The fortunate is he whose earnest purpose never swerves,
Whose slightest action, or inaction serves,
The one great aim.
Why, even death itself stands still
And waits an hour sometimes
For such a will."

—*Ella Wheeler Wilcox.*

"I have brought myself by long meditation to the conviction that a human being with a settled purpose must accomplish it, and that nothing can resist a will which will stake even existence upon its fulfillment."—*Lord Beaconsfield.*

"A passionate desire and an unwearied will can perform impossibilities, or what may seem to be such to the cold and feeble."—*Sir John Simpson.*

"It is wonderful how even the casualties of life seem to bow to a spirit that will not bow to them, and yield to subserve a design which they may, in their first apparent tendency, threaten to frustrate. When a firm, decisive spirit is recognized, it is curious to see how the space clears around a man and leaves him room and freedom."—*John Foster.*

"The great thing about General Grant is cool persistency of purpose. He is not easily excited, and he has got the grip of a bulldog. When he once gets his teeth in, nothing can shake him off."—*Abraham Lincoln.*

"I am bigger than anything that can happen to me. All these things are outside my door, *and I've got the key.* * * * Man was meant to be, and ought to be, stronger and more than anything that can happen to him. Circumstances, 'Fate,' 'Luck,' are all outside; and if he cannot change them, he can always *beat* them."—*Charles F. Lummis.*

"The truest wisdom is a resolute determination." "Impossible is a word found only in the dictionary of fools." "Circumstances! I *make* circumstances!" —*Napoleon.*

"He who fails only half wills."—*Suwarrow.*

"That which the easiest becomes a habit in us is the will. Learn, then, to will strongly and decisively; thus fix your floating life, and leave it no longer to be carried hither and thither, like a withered leaf, by every wind that blows."

"Man owes his growth chiefly to that active striving of the will—that encounter which we call effort—and it is astonishing to find how often results apparently impracticable are thus made possible. * * * It is will—force of purpose—that enables a man to do or be whatever he sets his mind upon being or doing."

"A strong, defiant purpose is many-handed and lays hold of whatever is near that can serve it; it has a magnetic purpose that draws to itself whatever is kindred. * * * Let it be your first study to teach the world that you are not wood and straw; that there is some iron in you."—*Munger.*

"It's *dogged* as does it."—*Yorkshire Proverb.*

"One talent with a will behind it will accomplish more than ten without it, as a thimbleful of powder in a rifle, the bore of whose barrel will give it direction, will do greater execution than a carload burned in the open air."
—*O.S. Marden.*

"Will may not endow man with talents or capacities; but it does one very important matter—it enables him to make the best, the very best, of his powers."
—*Fothergill.*

"Tender-handed stroke a nettle, And it stings you for your pains.
Grasp it like a man of mettle, And it soft as down remains."

"Don't flinch; don't foul; but hit the line hard."—*Roosevelt.*

"The more difficulties one has to encounter, within and without, the more significant and the higher in inspiration his life will be."

THE KEYNOTE

I Can!

"I Can and I Will"—The recognition—Equal to any task—A feeling of calm confidence—An abiding sense of power, reserve force and security—The Something within—The triple key to the door of attainment—The vibrations of Success.

"I Can and I Will!!!" Have you ever said these words to yourself with a firm conviction that you were speaking the truth—with the strong feeling that needed no other proof. If so, you then felt within you a thrill which seemed to cause every atom of your being to vibrate in harmony with some note in the grand scale of Life, sounded by the Real Self. You caught a momentary glimpse of the Inner Light—heard a stray note of the Song of the Soul—were conscious for the moment of YOURSELF. And in that moment of ecstasy you knew that untold power and possibilities were yours. You felt that you were in touch with all Strength, Power, Knowledge, Happiness and Peace. You felt that you were equal to any task—capable of executing any undertaking. For the moment there was no Fear in the world for you. All the Universe seemed to vibrate in the same key with your thought. For the moment you Recognized the Truth.

But alas, the spirit of doubt, distrust, fear and unfaith called you again to Earth—and the vision faded. And yet, the remembrance of the sight—the echo of the sound—the remnant of the new-found strength—is with you still. You still find that memory to be a stimulus to great efforts—a comforting thought in times of weakness and trial. You have been able to accomplish much by the aid of the lingering vibrations of the mighty thought.

In times of great peril—grave perplexities—life and death struggles, a feeling of calm confidence and strength often comes to us, and we are borne on by a power *of* us and *in* us (and yet in everything else, too) that seems to lift us off our feet and sweep us on to safety—to peace—to rest. We are possessed of an abiding sense of power, reserve force and security. When extraordinary conditions confront us—when our bodies seem paralyzed—our minds stupefied—our willpower gone, we are often made conscious of the existence of the Real Self, and it answers our involuntary demand, and comes to rescue with the cheering cry: "I AM HERE!"

Many of us have made use of this inner strength without realizing it. One day we were sorely distressed and made the demand, and lo! it was answered. We knew not from whence came this new-found strength, but we were conscious of the uplift, and felt more confidence in ourselves. The next time we *confidently* demanded the aid, and again we were answered. We acquired that which we call confidence and faith in ourselves, and were carried over many a dark place and started on the road to Success. Our repeated success caused us to think and speak of our "luck," and we grew to believe that we had a "star," and took chances and risks that others would not dream of. We dared. We made some apparent failures, but we soon came to know them as only lessons leading to *ultimate* success. The "I Can and I Will" feeling carried us over rough places safely, and we got to simply *know* that we would "get there" in the end.

And so we went on and on, knowing that if we advanced three steps and slipped back two, we were still one step ahead. We had confidence, because we *knew* that "things would come our way" in the end. And so long as we held this attitude, we *did* succeed, and it was only when we lost heart at some unexpected slip—only when, after having attained success, we became dazed and frightened, and began to fear that our "luck might turn" and that we would lose all of our accumulations—it was only *then*, I say—that our star waned.

Talk with any successful man, and, if truthful, he will admit having felt, from the time of his first success, that he had some sort of "pull" with Fate—some "lucky star"—some special Providence operating in his behalf. He grew to *expect* results—to have confidence in things turning out right—to have faith in *something* of which he knew not the nature—and he was not disappointed. Things seemed to work in his favor—not always just in the way he expected, sometimes in an entirely different way—matters seemed somehow to straighten themselves out in the end—so long as he kept his "nerve." He did not know the source of his strength, but he believed in it and trusted it just the same.

Let us wake up and recognize this Something Within—let us begin to understand this "I Can and I Will" feeling—let us cherish it if we have it, and cultivate it if we have it not. Do you know that we are young giants who have not discovered our own strength? Are you not aware that there are powers latent within us, pressing forth for development and unfoldment? Do you not know that earnest desire, faith and calm demand will bring to us that which we require—will place at our hand the tools with which we are to work out our destiny—will guide us in the proper use of the tools—will make us grow? Do you not know that Desire, Faith and Work is the triple key to the doors of Attainment? There are possibilities before us, awaiting our coming, of which we have never dreamed. Let us assert ourselves—take up the key—unlock the doors—and enter our kingdom.

To accomplish, we must be possessed of earnest desire—must be as confident of ultimate success as we are of the rising of tomorrow's sun—we must have Faith. And we must work out the end with the tools and instruments that will present themselves day by day. We will find that Desire, Confidence, Faith and Work will not only brush aside the obstacles from our path, but will also begin to assert that wonderful force, as yet so little understood—the Law of Attraction—which will draw to us that which is conducive to our success, be it ideas, people, things, yes, even *circumstances*. Oh, ye of little Faith, why do you not see these things?

The world is looking for these "I Can and I Will" people—it has places ready for them—the supply does not begin to equal the demand. Pluck up courage ye unfortunate ones—ye doubters—ye "I Can't" people! Begin the fight by abolishing Fear from your minds. Then start to climb the ladder of Attainment, shouting "I CAN AND I WILL" with all your might, drowning out the sound of the "buts," "ifs," "supposings," "you can'ts" and "aren't you afraids" of your wet-blanket friends at the foot of the ladder. Do not bother about the upper rounds of the ladder—you will reach them in time—but give your whole attention to the round just ahead of you, and when you have gained a firm footing on that, then look at the next one. One round at a time, remember, and *give your entire attention to each step*. Climb with Desire, Confidence and Faith inspiring each step, and the task will become a pleasure. You will be conscious of some mighty force attracting you upward and onward as you progress. And don't try to pull some other fellow off the ladder—there's room enough for both of you—be kind, be kind.

If you fail to feel the "I Can and I Will" vibrations within you, start in to-day, and *say* "I Can and I Will"—THINK "I Can and I Will"—ACT "I Can and I Will," and get the vibrations started in motion. Remember that as the one note of the violin, if constantly sounded, will cause the mighty bridge to vibrate in unison so will one positive thought, held constantly, manifest itself both in yourself, others and things. So begin sounding the note today—this very moment. Sound it constantly. Send forth a clear, glad, joyous note—a note of Faith—a note of coming Victory. Sound it over and over again, and soon you will become conscious that the vibrations have commenced, and that the mighty structure of your being is quivering and vibrating to the keynote: "I CAN AND I WILL."

THE ART OF
LOGICAL
THINKING
OR
THE LAWS OF
REASONING

Contents

1

Reasoning

"Reasoning" is defined as: "The act, process or art of exercising the faculty of reason; the act or faculty of employing reason in argument; argumentation, ratiocination; reasoning power; disputation, discussion, argumentation." Stewart says: "The word reason itself is far from being precise in its meaning. In common and popular discourse it denotes that power by which we distinguish truth from falsehood, and right from wrong, and by which we are enabled to combine means for the attainment of particular ends."

By the employment of the reasoning faculties of the mind we compare objects presented to the mind as percepts or concepts, taking up the "raw materials" of thought and weaving them into more complex and elaborate mental fabrics which we call abstract and general ideas of truth. Brooks says: "It is the thinking power of the mind; the faculty which gives us what has been called thought-knowledge, in distinction from sense-knowledge. It may be regarded as the mental architect among the faculties; it transforms the material furnished by the senses . . . into new products, and thus builds up the temples of science and philosophy." The last-mentioned authority adds: "Its products are twofold, ideas and thoughts. An idea is a mental product which when expressed in words does not give a proposition; a thought is a mental product which embraces the relation of two or more ideas. The ideas of the understanding are of two general classes; abstract ideas and general ideas. The thoughts are also of two general classes; those pertaining to contingent truth and those pertaining to necessary truth. In contingent truth, we have facts, or immediate judgments, and general truths including laws and causes, derived from particular facts; in necessary truth we have axioms, or self-evident truths, and the truths derived from them by reasoning, called theorems."

In inviting you to consider the processes of reasoning, we are irresistibly reminded of the old story of one of Moliere's plays in which one of the characters expresses surprise on learning that he "had been talking prose for forty years without knowing it." As Jevons says in mentioning this: "Ninety-nine people out of a hundred might be equally surprised on hearing that they had been converting propositions, syllogizing, falling into paralogisms, framing hypotheses and making classifications with genera and species. If asked whether they were logicians, they would probably answer, No! They would be partly right; for I believe that a large number even of educated persons have no clear idea of what logic is. Yet, in a certain way, every one must have been a logician since he began to speak."

So, in asking you to consider the processes of reasoning we are not assuming that you never have reasoned—on the contrary we are fully aware that you in connection with every other person, have reasoned all your mature life. That is not the question. While everyone reasons, the fact is equally true that the majority of persons reason incorrectly. Many persons reason along lines far from correct and scientific, and suffer therefor and thereby. Some writers have claimed that the majority of persons are incapable of even fairly correct reasoning, pointing to the absurd ideas entertained by the masses of people as a proof of the statement. These writers are probably a little radical in their views and statements, but one is often struck with wonder at the evidences of incapacity for interpreting facts and impressions on the part of the general public. The masses of people accept the most absurd ideas as truth, providing they are gravely asserted by someone claiming authority. The most illogical ideas are accepted without dispute or examination, providing they are stated solemnly and authoritatively. Particularly in the respective fields of religion and politics do we find this blind acceptance of illogical ideas by the multitude. Mere assertion by the leaders seems sufficient for the multitude of followers to acquiesce.

In order to reason correctly it is not merely necessary to have a good intellect. An athlete may have the proper proportions, good framework, and symmetrical muscles, but he cannot expect to cope with others of his kind unless he has learned to develop those muscles and to use them to the best advantage. And, in the same way, the man who wishes to reason correctly must develop his intellectual faculties and must also learn the art of using them to the best advantage. Otherwise he will waste his mental energy and will be placed at a disadvantage when confronted with a trained logician in argument or debate. One who has witnessed a debate or argument between two men equally strong intellectually, one of whom is a trained logician and the other lacking this advantage, will never forget the impression produced upon him by the unequal struggle. The conflict is like that of a powerful wrestler, untrained in the little tricks and turns of the science, in the various principles of applying force in a certain way at a certain time, at a certain place, with a trained and experienced wrestler. Or of a conflict between a muscular giant untrained in the art of boxing, when confronted with a trained and experienced exponent of "the manly art." The result of any such conflict is assured in advance. Therefore, everyone should refuse to rest content without a knowledge of the art of reasoning correctly, for otherwise he places himself under a heavy handicap in the race for success, and allows others, perhaps less well-equipped mentally, to have a decided advantage over him.

Jevons says in this connection: "To be a good logician is, however, far more valuable than to be a good athlete; because logic teaches us to reason well, and reasoning gives us knowledge, and knowledge, as Lord Bacon said, is power. As athletes, men cannot for a moment compare with horses or tigers or monkeys. Yet, with the power of knowledge, men tame horses and shoot tigers and despise monkeys. The weakest framework with the most logical mind will conquer in the end, because it is easy to foresee the future, to calculate the result of actions, to avoid mistakes which might be fatal, and to discover the means of doing things which seemed impossible. If such little creatures as ants had better brains than men, they would either destroy men or make them into slaves. It is true that we cannot use our eyes and ears without getting some kind of knowledge, and the brute animals can do the same. But what gives power is the deeper knowledge called Science. People may see, and hear, and feel all their lives without really learning the nature of things they see. But reason is the mind's eye, and enables us to see why things are, and when and how events may be made to happen or not to happen. The logician endeavors to learn exactly what this reason is which makes the power of men. We all, as I have said, must reason well or ill, but logic is the science of reasoning and enables us to distinguish between the good reasoning which leads to truth, and the bad reasoning which every day betrays people into error and misfortune."

In this volume we hope to be able to point out the methods and principles of correctly using the reasoning faculties of the mind, in a plain, simple manner, devoid of useless technicalities and academic discussion. We shall adhere, in the main, to the principles established by the best of the authorities of the old school of psychology, blending the same with those advanced by the best authorities of the New Psychology. No attempt to make of this book a school text-book shall be made, for our sole object and aim is to bring this important subject before the general public composed of people who have neither the time nor inclination to indulge in technical discussion nor academic hairsplitting, but who desire to understand the underlying working principles of the Laws of Reasoning.

2

The Process of Reasoning

The processes of Reasoning may be said to comprise four general stages or steps, as follows:

I. Abstraction, by which is meant the process of drawing off and setting aside from an object, person or thing, a quality or attribute, and making of it a distinct object of thought. For instance, if I perceive in a lion the quality of strength, and am able to think of this quality abstractly and independently of the animal—if the term strength has an actual mental meaning to me, independent of the lion—then I have abstracted that quality; the thinking thereof is an act of abstraction; and the thought-idea itself is an abstract idea. Some writers hold that these abstract ideas are realities, and "not mere figments of fancy." As Brooks says: "The rose dies, but my idea of its color and fragrance remains." Other authorities regard Abstraction as but an act of attention concentrated upon but the particular quality to the exclusion of others, and that the abstract idea has no existence apart from the general idea of the object in which it is included. Sir William Hamilton says: "We can rivet our attention on some particular mode of a thing, as its smell, its color, its figure, its size, etc., and abstract it from the others. This may be called Modal Abstraction. The abstraction we have now been considering is performed on individual objects, and is consequently particular. There is nothing necessarily connected with generalization in abstraction; generalization is indeed dependent on abstraction, which it supposes; but abstraction does not involve generalization."

II. Generalization, by which is meant the process of forming Concepts or General Ideas. It acts in the direction of apprehending the common qualities of objects, persons and things, and combining and uniting them into a single notion or conception which will comprehend and include them all. A General Idea or Concept differs from a particular idea in that it includes within itself the qualities of the particular and other particulars, and accordingly may be applied to any one of these particulars as well as to the general class. For instance, one may have a particular idea of some particular horse, which applies only to that particular horse. He may also have a General Idea of horse, in the generic or class sense, which idea applies not only to the general class of horse but also to each and every horse which is included in that class. The expression of Generalization or Conception is called a Concept.

III. Judgment, by which is meant the process of comparing two objects, persons or things, one with another, and thus perceiving their agreement or disagreement. Thus we may compare the two concepts horse and animal, and perceiving a certain agreement between them we form the judgment that: "A horse is an animal"; or comparing horse and cow, and perceiving their disagreement, we form the judgment: "A horse is not a cow." The expression of a judgment is called a Proposition.

IV. Reasoning, by which is meant the process of comparing two objects, persons or things, through their relation to a third object, person or thing. Thus we may reason (a) that all mammals are animals; (b) that a horse is a mammal; (c) that, therefore, a horse is an animal; the result of the reasoning being the statement that: "A horse is an animal." The most fundamental principle of reasoning, therefore, consists in the comparing of two objects of thought through and by means of their relation to a third object. The natural form of expression of this process of Reasoning is called a Syllogism.

It will be seen that these four processes of reasoning necessitate the employment of the processes of Analysis and Synthesis, respectively. Analysis means a separating of an object of thought into its constituent parts, qualities or relations. Synthesis means the combining of the qualities, parts or relations of an object of thought into a composite whole. These two processes are found in all processes of Reasoning. Abstraction is principally analytic; Generalization or Conception chiefly synthetic; Judgment is either or both analytic or synthetic; Reasoning is either a synthesis of particulars in Induction, or an evolution of the particular from the general in Deduction.

There are two great classes of Reasoning; viz., (1) Inductive Reasoning, or the inference of general truths from particular truths; and (2) Deductive Reasoning, or the inference of particular truths from general truths.

Inductive Reasoning proceeds by discovering a general truth from particular truths. For instance, from the particular truths that individual men die we discover the general truth that "All men must die"; or from observing that in all observed instances ice melts at a certain temperature, we may infer that "All ice melts at a certain temperature." Inductive Reasoning proceeds from the known to the unknown. It is essentially a synthetic process. It seeks to discover general laws from particular facts.

Deductive Reasoning proceeds by discovering particular truths from general truths. Thus we reason that as all men die, John Smith, being a man, must die; or, that as all ice melts at a certain temperature, it follows that the particular piece of ice under consideration will melt at that certain temperature. Deductive Reasoning is therefore seen to be essentially an analytical process.

Mills says of Inductive Reasoning: "The inductive method of the ancients consisted in ascribing the character of general truths to all propositions which are true in all the instances of which we have knowledge. Bacon exposed the insufficiency of this method, and physical investigation has now far outgrown the Baconian conception. . . . Induction, then, is that operation by which we infer that what we know to be true in a particular case or cases, will be true in all cases which resemble the former in certain assignable respects. In other words, induction is the process by which we conclude that what is true of certain individuals of a class is true of the whole class, or that what is true at certain times will be true in similar circumstances at all times."

Regarding Deductive Reasoning, a writer says: "Deductive Reasoning is that process of reasoning by which we arrive at the necessary consequences, starting from admitted or established premises." Brooks says: "The general truths from which we reason to particulars are derived from several distinct sources. Some are intuitive, as the axioms of mathematics or logic. Some of them are derived from induction. . . . Some of them are merely hypothetical, as in the investigation of the physical sciences. Many of the hypotheses and theories of the physical sciences are used as general truth for deductive reasoning; as the theory of gravitation, the theory of light; etc. Reasoning from the theory of universal gravitation, Leverrier discovered the position of a new planet in the heavens before it had been discovered by human eyes."

Halleck points out the interdependence of Inductive and Deductive Reasoning in the following words: "Man has to find out through his own experience, or that of others, the major premises from which he argues or draws his conclusions. By induction we examine what seems to us a sufficient number of individual cases. We then conclude that the rest of these cases, which we have not examined, will obey the same general laws. . . . The premise, 'All cows chew the cud,' was laid down after a certain number of cows had been examined. If we were to see a cow twenty years hence, we should expect that she chewed her cud. . . . After Induction has classified certain phenomena and thus given us a major premise, we proceed deductively to apply the inference to any new specimen that can be shown to belong to that class."

The several steps of Deductive Reasoning shall now be considered in turn as we proceed.

3

The Concept

In considering the process of thinking, we must classify the several steps or stages of thought that we may examine each in detail for the purpose of comprehending them combined as a whole. In actual thinking these several steps or stages are not clearly separated in consciousness, so that each stands out clear and distinct from the preceding and succeeding steps or stages, but, on the contrary, they blend and shade into each other so that it is often difficult to draw a clear dividing line. The first step or stage in the process of thinking is that which is called a concept.

A concept is a mental representation of anything. Prof. Wm. James says: "The function by which we mark off, discriminate, draw a line around, and identify a numerically distinct subject of discourse is called conception." There are five stages or steps in each concept, as follows:

I. Presentation. Before a concept may be formed there must first be a presentation of the material from which the concept is to be formed. If we wish to form the concept, animal, we must first have perceived an animal, probably several kinds of animals—horses, dogs, cats, cows, pigs, lions, tigers, etc. We must also have received impressions from the sight of these animals which may be reproduced by the memory—represented to the mind. In order that we may have a full concept of animal we should have perceived every kind of animal, for otherwise there would be some elements of the full concept lacking. Accordingly it is practically impossible to have a full concept of anything. The greater the opportunities for perception the greater will be the opportunity for conception. In other books of this series we have spoken of the value and importance of the attention and of clear and full perception. Without an active employment of the attention, it is impossible to receive a clear perception of anything; and unless the perception has been clear, it is impossible for the mind to form a clear concept of the thing perceived. As Sir Wm. Hamilton has said: "An act of attention, that is an act of concentration, seems thus necessary to every exertion of consciousness, as a certain contraction of the pupil is requisite to every exertion of vision. . . . Attention, then, is to consciousness what the contraction of the pupil is to sight, or to the eye of the mind what the microscope or telescope is to the bodily eye. . . . It constitutes the half of all intellectual power." And Sir B. Brodie said: "It is attention, much more than in the abstract power of reasoning, which constitutes the vast difference which exists between minds of different individuals." And as Dr. Beattie says: "The force with which anything strikes the mind is generally in proportion to the degree of attention bestowed upon it."

II. Comparison. Following the stage of Presentation is the stage of Comparison. We separate our general concept of animal into a number of sub-concepts, or concepts of various kinds of animals. We compare the pig with the goat, the cow with the horse, in fact each animal with all other animals known to us. By this process we distinguish the points of resemblance and the points of difference. We perceive that the wolf resembles the dog to a considerable degree; that it has some points of resemblance to the fox; and a still less distinct resemblance to the bear; also that it differs materially from the horse, the cow or the elephant. We also learn that there are various kinds of wolves, all bearing a great resemblance to each other, and yet having marked points of difference. The closer we observe the various individuals among the wolves, the more points of difference do we find. The faculty of Comparison evidences itself in inductive reasoning; ability and disposition to analyze, classify, compare, etc. Fowler says that those in whom it is largely developed "Reason clearly and correctly from conclusions and scientific facts up to the laws which govern them; discern the known from the unknown; detect error by its incongruity with facts; have an excellent talent for comparing, explaining, expounding, criticising, exposing, etc." Prof. William James says: "Any personal or practical interest in the results to be obtained by distinguishing, makes one's wits amazingly sharp to detect differences. And long training and practice in distinguishing has the same effect as personal interest. Both of these agencies give to small amounts of objective difference the same effectiveness upon the mind that, under other circumstances, only large ones would make."

III. Abstraction. Following the stage of Comparison is that of Abstraction. The term "Abstraction" as used in psychology means: "The act or process of separating from the numerous qualities inherent in any object, the particular one which we wish to make the subject of observation and reflection. Or, the act of withdrawing the consciousness from a number of objects with a view to concentrate it on some particular one. The negative act of which Attention is the positive." To abstract is "to separate or set apart." In the process of Abstraction in our consideration of animals, after having recognized the various points of difference and resemblance between the various species and individuals, we proceed to consider some special quality of animals, and, in doing so, we abstract, set aside, or separate the particular quality which we wish to consider. If we wish to consider the size of animals, we abstract the quality of size from the other qualities, and consider animals with reference to size alone. Thus we consider the various degrees of size of the various animals, classifying them accordingly. In the same way we may abstract the quality of shape, color or habits, respectively, setting aside this quality for special observation and classification. If we wish to study, examine or consider certain qualities in a thing we abstract that particular quality from the other qualities of the thing; or we abstract the other qualities until nothing is left but the particular quality under consideration. In examining or considering a class or number of things, we first abstract the qualities possessed in common by the class or number of things; and also abstract or set aside the qualities not common to them.

For instance; in considering classes of animals, we abstract the combined quality of milk-giving and pouch-possessing which is possessed in common by a number of animals; then we group these several animals in a class which we name the Marsupialia, of which the opossum and kangaroo are members. In these animals the young are brought forth in an imperfect condition, undeveloped in size and condition, and are then kept in the pouch and nourished until they are able to care for themselves. Likewise, we may abstract the idea of the placenta, the appendage which connects the young unborn animal with the mother, and by means of which the foetus is nourished. The animals distinguished by this quality are grouped together as the Placental Mammals. The Placental Mammals are divided into various groups, by an Abstraction of qualities or class resemblance or difference, as follows: The Edentata, or toothless creatures, such as the sloths, ant-eaters, armadillos, etc.; the Sirenia, so-named from their fancied resemblance to the fabled "sirens," among which class are the sea-cows, manatees, dugongs, etc.; the Cetacea, or whale family, which although fish-like in appearance, are really mammals, giving birth to living young which they nourish with breast-milk, among which are the whales, porpoises, dolphins, etc.; the Ungulata, or hoofed animals, such as the horse, the tapir, the rhinoceros, the swine, the hippopotamus, the camel, the deer, the sheep, the cow, etc.; the Hyracoidea, having teeth resembling both the hoofed animals and the gnawing animals, of which the coney or rock-rabbit is the principal example; the Proboscidea, or trunked animals, which family is represented by the various families of elephants; the Carnivora, or flesh-eaters, represented by various sub-families and species; the Rodentia, or gnawers; the Insectivora, or insect feeders; the Cheiroptera, or finger-winged; the Lemuroidea, or lemurs, having the general appearance of the monkey, but also the long bushy tail of the fox; the Primates, including the monkeys, baboons, man-apes, gibbons, gorillas, chimpanzees, orang-outangs and Man.

In all of these cases you will see that each class or general family possesses a certain common quality which gives it its classification, and which quality is the subject of the Abstraction in considering the particular group of animals. Further and closer Abstraction divides these classes into sub-classes; for instance, the family or class of the Carnivora, or flesh-eaters, may be divided by further Abstraction into the classes of seals, bears, weasels, wolves, dogs, lions, tigers, leopards, etc. In this process, we must first make the more general Abstraction of the wolf and similar animals into the dog-family; and the lion, tiger and similar forms into the cat-family.

Halleck says of Abstraction: "In the process of Abstraction, we draw our attention away from a mass of confusing details, unimportant at the time, and attend only to qualities common to the class. Abstraction is little else than centering the power of attention on some qualities to the exclusion of others."

IV. Generalization. Arising from the stage of Abstraction is the stage of Generalization. Generalization is: "The act or process of generalizing or making general; bringing several objects agreeing in some point under a common or general name, head or class; an extending from particulars to generals; reducing or arranging in a genus; bringing a particular fact or series of facts into a relation with a wider circle of facts." As Bolingbroke says: "The mind, therefore, makes its utmost endeavors to generalize its ideas, beginning early with such as are most familiar and coming in time to those which are less so." Under the head of Abstraction we have seen that through Abstraction we may Generalize the various species into the various families, and thus, in turn, into the various sub-families. Following the same process we may narrow down the sub-families into species composed of various individuals; or into greater and still greater families or groups. Generalization is really the act of Classification, or forming into classes all things having certain qualities or properties in common. The corollary is that all things in a certain generalized class must possess the particular quality or property common to the class. Thus we know that all animals in the class of the Carnivora must eat flesh; and that all Mammals possess breasts from which they feed their young. As Halleck says: "We put all objects having like qualities into a certain genus, or class. When the objects are in that class, we know that certain qualities will have a general application to them all."

V. Denomination. Following closely upon the step of Generalization or Classification, is the step of Denomination. By Denomination we mean "the act of naming or designating by a name." A name is the symbol by which we think of a familiar thing without the necessity for making a distinct mental image upon each occasion of thought. Or, it may be considered as akin to a label affixed to a thing. As in the case of the algebraic symbols, a, b, c, x, and y, by the use of which we are able to make intricate calculations easily and rapidly, so may we use these word symbols much more readily than we could the lengthy descriptions or even the mental images of the thing symbolized. It is much easier for us to think "horse" than it would be to think the full definition of that animal, or to think of it by recalling a mental picture of the horse each time we wished to think of it. Or, it is much better for us to be able to glance at a label on a package or bottle than to examine the contents in detail. As Hobbes says: "A word taken at pleasure to serve for a mark, which may raise in our minds a thought like to some thought we had before, and which being pronounced to others, may be to them a sign of what thought the speaker had or had not, before in his mind." Mill says: "A name is a word (or set of words) serving the double purpose of a mark to recall to ourselves the likeness of a former thought and as a sign to make it known to others." Some philosophers regard names as symbols of our ideas of things, rather than of the things themselves; others regard them as symbols of the things themselves. It will be seen that the value of a name depends materially upon the correct meaning and understanding regarding it possessed by the person using it.

4

The Use of Concepts

Having observed the several steps or stages of a concept, let us now consider the use and misuse of the latter. At first glance it would appear difficult to misuse a concept, but a little consideration will show that people very commonly fall into error regarding their concepts.

For instance, a child perceives a horse, a cow or a sheep and hears its elders apply the term "animal" to it. This term is perfectly correct, although symbolizing only a very general classification or generalization. But, the child knowing nothing of the more limited and detailed classification begins to generalize regarding the animal. To it, accordingly, an "animal" is identical with the dog or the cow, the sheep or the horse, as the case may be, and when the term is used the child thinks that all animals are similar to the particular animal seen. Later on, when it hears the term "animal" applied to a totally different looking creature, it thinks that a mistake has been made and a state of confusion occurs. Or, even when a term is applied within narrower limits, the same trouble occurs. The child may hear the term "dog" applied to a mastiff, and it accordingly forms a concept of dog identical with the qualities and attributes of the mastiff. Later, hearing the same term applied to a toy-terrier, it becomes indignant and cries out that the latter is no "dog" but is something entirely different. It is not until the child becomes acquainted with the fact that there are many kinds of creatures in the general category of "dog" that the latter term becomes fully understood and its appropriate concept is intelligently formed. Thus we see the importance of the step of Presentation.

In the same way the child might imagine that because some particular "man" had red hair and long whiskers, all men were red-haired and long-whiskered. Such a child would always form the concept of "man" as a creature possessed of the personal qualities just mentioned. As a writer once said, readers of current French literature might imagine that all Englishmen were short, dumpy, red-cheeked and irascible, and that all Englishwomen had great teeth and enormous feet; also that readers of English literature might imagine that all Frenchmen were like monkeys, and all Frenchwomen were sad coquettes. In the same way many American young people believe that all Englishmen say "Don't you know" and all Englishwomen constantly ejaculate: "Fancy!" Also that every Englishman wears a monocle. In the same way, the young English person, from reading the cheap novels of his own country, might well form the concept of all Americans as long-legged, chin-whiskered and big-nosed, saying "Waal, I want to know," "I reckon," and "Du tell," while they tilted themselves back in a chair with their feet on the mantelpiece. The concept of a Western man, entertained by the average Eastern person who has never traveled further West than Buffalo, is equally amusing. In the same way, we have known Western people who formed a concept of Boston people as partaking of a steady and continuous diet of baked beans and studiously reading Browning and Emerson between these meals.

Halleck says: "A certain Norwegian child ten years old had the quality white firmly imbedded in his concept man. Happening one day to see a negro for the first time, the child refused to call him a man until the negro's other qualities compelled the child to revise his concept and to eliminate whiteness. If that child should ever see an Indian or a Chinaman, the concept would undergo still further revision. A girl of six, reared with an intemperate father and brothers, had the quality of drunkenness firmly fixed in her concept of man. A certain boy kept, until the age of eleven, trustworthiness in his concept of man. Another boy, until late in his teens thought that man was a creature who did wrong not from determination but from ignorance, that any man would change his course to the right path if he could but understand that he was going wrong. Happening one day to hear of a wealthy man who was neglecting to provide comforts for his aged mother in her last sickness, the boy concluded that the man did not know his mother's condition. When he informed the man, the boy was told to mind his own business. The same day he heard of some politicians who had intentionally cheated the city in letting a contract and he immediately revised his concept. It must be borne in mind that most of our concepts are subject to change during our entire life; that at first they are made only in a tentative way; that experience may show us, at any time, that they have been erroneously formed, that we have, abstracted too little or too much, made this class too wide or too narrow, or that here a quality must be added or there one taken away."

Let us now consider the mental processes involved in the formation and use of a concept. We have first, as we have seen, the presentation of the crude material from which the concept must be formed. Our attention being attracted to or directed toward an object, we notice its qualities and properties. Then we begin a process of comparison of the object perceived or of our perception of it. We compare the object with other objects or ideas in our mind, noting similarities and differences and thereby leading towards classification with similar objects and opposed dissimilar ones. The greater the range of other objects previously perceived, the greater will be the number of relations established between the new object or idea and others. As we advance in experience and knowledge, the web of related objects and ideas becomes more intricate and complex. The relations attaching to the child's concept of horse is very much simpler than the concept of the experienced adult. Then we pass on to the step of analysis, in which we separate the qualities of the object and consider them in detail. The act of abstraction is an analytical process. Then we pass on to the step of synthesis, in which we unite the materials gathered by comparison and analysis, and thus form a general idea or concept regarding the object. In this process we combine the various qualities discerned by comparison and analysis, and grouping them together as in a bundle, we tie them together with the string of synthesis and thus have a true general conception. Thus from the first general conception of horse as a simple thing, we notice first that the animal has certain qualities lacking in other things and certain others similar to other things; then we analyze the various qualities of the horse, recognized through comparison, until we have a clear and distinct idea of the various parts, qualities and properties of the horse; then we synthesize, and joining together these various conceptions of the said qualities, we at last form a clear general concept of the horse as he is, with all his qualities. Of course, if we later discover other qualities attached to the horse, we add these to our general synthesized concept—our concept of horse is enlarged.

Of course these various steps in the formation and use of a concept are not realized as distinct acts in the consciousness, for the processes are largely instinctive and subconscious, particularly in the case of the experienced individual. The subconscious, or habit mind, usually attends to these details for us, except in instances in which we deliberately apply the will to the task, as in cases of close study, in which we take the process from the region of the involuntary and place it in the voluntary category. So closely related and blended are these various steps of the process, that some authorities have disputed vigorously upon the question as to which of the two steps, comparison or analysis, precedes the other. Some have claimed that analysis must precede comparison, else how could one compare without having first analyzed the things to be compared. Others hold that comparison must precede analysis, else how could one note a quality unless he had his attention drawn to it by its resemblance to or difference from qualities in other objects. The truth seems to lie between the two ideas, for in some cases there seems to be a perception of some similarity or difference before any analysis or abstraction takes place; while in others there seems to be an analysis or abstraction before comparison is possible. In this book we have followed the arrangement favored by the latest authorities, but the question is still an open one to many minds.

As we have seen, the general concept once having been formed, the mind proceeds to classify the concept with others having general qualities in common. And, likewise, it proceeds to generalize from the classification, assuming certain qualities in certain classes. Then we proceed to make still further generalizations and classifications on an ascending and widening scale, including seeming resemblances less marked, until finally we embrace the object with other objects in as large a class as possible as well as in as close and limited a sub-class as possible. As Brooks says: "Generalization is an ascending process. The broader concept is regarded as higher than the narrower concept; a concept is considered higher than a percept; a general idea stands above a particular idea. We thus go up from particulars to generals; from percepts to concepts; from lower concepts to higher concepts. Beginning down with particular objects, we rise from them to the general idea of their class. Having formed a number of lower classes, we compare them as we did individuals and generalize them into higher classes. We perform the same process with these higher classes, and thus proceed until we are at last arrested in the highest class, Being. Having reached the pinnacle of generalization, we may descend the ladder by reversing the process through which we ascend."

From this process of generalization, or synthesis, we create from our simple concepts our general concepts. Some of the older authorities distinguished between these two classes by terming the former "conceptions," and reserving the term "concepts" for the general concepts. Brooks says of this: "The products of generalization are general ideas called concepts. We have already discussed the method of forming conceptions and now consider the nature of the concept itself. . . . A concept is a general idea. It is a general notion which has in it all that is common to its own class. It is a general scheme which embraces all the individuals of the class while it resembles in all respects none of its class. Thus my conception of a quadruped has in it all four-footed animals, but it does not correspond in all respects to any particular animals; my conception of a triangle embraces all triangles, but does not agree in details with any particular triangle. The general conception cannot be made to fit exactly any particular object, but it teems with many particulars. These points may be illustrated with the concepts horse, bird, color, animal, etc."

So we may begin to perceive the distinction and difference between a concept and a mental image. This distinction, and the fact that a concept cannot be imaged, is generally difficult for the beginner. It is important that one should have a clear and distinct understanding regarding this point, and so we shall consider it further in the following chapter.

5

Concepts and Images

As we have said, a concept cannot be imaged—cannot be used as the subject of a mental image. This statement is perplexing to the student who has been accustomed to the idea that every conception of the mind is capable of being reproduced in the form of a mental image. But the apparently paradoxical statement is seen as quite simple when a little consideration is given to it.

For instance, you have a distinct general concept of animal. You know what you mean when you say or think, animal. You recognize an animal when you see one and you understand what is meant when another uses the word in conversation. But you cannot form a mental image of the concept, animal. Why? Because any mental image you might form would be either a picture of some particular animal or else a composite of the qualities of several animals. Your concept is too broad and general to allow of a composite picture of all animals. And, in truth, your concept is not a picture of anything that actually exists in one particular, but an abstract idea embracing the qualities of all animals. It is like the algebraic x—a symbol for something that exists, but not the thing itself.

As Brooks says: "A concept cannot be represented by a concrete image. This is evident from its being general rather than particular. If its color, size or shape is fixed by an image, it is no longer general but particular." And Halleck says: "It is impossible to image anything without giving that image individual marks. The best mental images are so definite that a picture could be painted from them. A being might come under the class man and have a snub nose, blonde hair, scanty eyebrows, and no scar on his face. The presence of one of these individual peculiarities in the concept man would destroy it. If we form an image of an apple, it must be either of a yellow, red, green, or russet apple, either as large as a pippin or as small as a crab-apple. A boy was asked what he thought of when 'apple' was mentioned. He replied that he thought of 'a big, dark-red, apple with a bad spot on one side, near the top.' That boy could image distinctly, but his power of forming concepts was still in its infancy."

So we see that while a mental image must picture the particular and individual qualities, properties and appearances of some particular unit of a class, a concept can and must contain only the class qualities—that is, the qualities belonging to the entire class. The general concept is as has been said "a general idea . . . a general notion which has in it all that is common to its own class." And it follows that a "general idea" of this kind cannot be pictured. A picture must be of some particular thing, while a concept is something above and higher than particular things. We may picture a man, but we cannot picture Man the concept of the race. A concept is not a reproduction of the image of a thing, but on the contrary is an idea of a class of things. We trust that the student will consider this point until he arrives at a clear understanding of the distinction, and the reason thereof.

But, while a concept is incapable of being pictured mentally as an image, it is true that some particular representative of a class may be held in the mind or imagination as an idealized object, as a general representative of the class, when we speak or think of the general term or concept, providing that its real relation to the concept is recognized. These idealized objects, however, are not concepts—they are percepts reproduced by the memory. It is important, however, to all who wish to convey their thought plainly, that they be able to convert their concepts into idealized representative objects. Otherwise, they tend to become too idealistic and abstract for common comprehension. As Halleck well says: "We should in all cases be ready to translate our concepts, when occasion requires, into the images of those individuals which the concept represents. A concept means nothing except in reference to certain individuals. Without them it could never have had existence and they are entitled to representation. A man who cannot translate his concepts into definite images of the proper objects, is fitted neither to teach, preach, nor practice any profession. . . . There was, not long ago, a man very fond of talking about fruit in the abstract; but he failed to recognize an individual cranberry when it was placed before him. A humorist remarked that a certain metaphysician had such a love for abstractions, and such an intense dislike for concrete things, as to refuse to eat a concrete peach when placed before him."

In the beginning many students are perplexed regarding the difference between a percept and a concept. The distinction is simple when properly considered. A percept is: "the object of an act of perception; that which is perceived." A concept is: "a mental representation." Brooks makes the following distinction: "A percept is the mental product of a real thing; a concept is a mere idea or notion of the common attributes of things. A percept represents some particular object; a concept is not particular, but general. A percept can be described by particulars; a concept can be described only by generals. The former can usually be represented by an image, the latter cannot be imagined, it can only be thought." Thus one is able to image the percept of a particular horse which has been perceived; but he is unable to image correctly the concept of horse as a class or generic term.

In connection with this distinction between perception and conception, we may as well consider the subject of apperception, a term favored by many modern psychologists, although others steadfastly decline to recognize its necessity or meaning and refuse to employ it. Apperception may be defined as: "perception accompanied by comprehension; perception accompanied by recognition." The thing perceived is held to be comprehended or recognized— that is, perceived in a new sense, by reason of certain previously acquired ideas in the mind. Halleck explains it as: "the perception of things in relation to the ideas which we already possess." It follows that all individuals possessed of equally active organs of perception, and equally active attention, will perceive the same thing in the same way and in the same degree. But the apperception of each individual will differ and vary according to his previous experience and training, temperament and taste, habit and custom. For instance, the familiar story of the boy who climbed a tree and watched the passers-by, noting their comments. The first passer-by noticing the tree, says aloud: "That would make a good stick of timber." "Good morning, Mr. Carpenter," said the boy. The next man said: "That tree has fine bark." "Good morning, Mr. Tanner," said the boy. Another said, "I bet there's a squirrel's nest up in that tree." "Good morning, Mr. Hunter," said the boy.

The woman sees in a bird something pretty and "cunning." The hunter sees in it something to kill. The ornithologist sees it as something of a certain genus and species, and perhaps also as something appropriate for his collection. The farmer perceives it to be something destructive of either insects or crops. A thief sees a jail as something to be dreaded; an ordinary citizen, something useful for confining objectionable people; a policeman, something in the line of his business. And so on, the apperception differing upon the previous experience of the individual. In the same way the scientist sees in an animal or rock many qualities of which the ordinary person is ignorant. Our training, experience, prejudices, etc., affect our apperception.

And so, we see that in a measure our concepts are determined not only by our simple perceptions, but also materially by our apperceptions. We conceive things not only as they are apparent to our senses, but also as colored and influenced by our previous impressions and ideas. For this reason we find widely varying concepts of the same things among different individuals. Only an absolute mind could form an absolute concept.

6

<hr>

Terms

In logic the words concept and term are practically identical, but in the popular usage of the terms there is a distinct difference. This difference is warranted, if we depart from the theoretical phase of logic, for the word concept really denotes an idea in the mind, while the word term really denotes a word or name of an idea or concept—the symbol of the latter. In a previous chapter we have seen that Denomination, or "the act of naming or designating by a name" is the final step or stage in forming a concept. And it is a fact that the majority of the words in the languages of civilized people denote general ideas or concepts. As Brooks says: "To give each individual or particular idea a name peculiar to itself would be impracticable and indeed impossible; the mind would soon become overwhelmed with its burden of names. Nearly all the ordinary words of our language are general rather than particular. The individuals distinguished by particular names, excepting persons and places, are comparatively few. Most objects are named only by common nouns; nearly all of our verbs express general actions; our adjectives denote common qualities, and our adverbs designate classes of actions and qualities. There are very few words in the language, besides the names of persons and places, that do not express general ideas."

In logic the word term is employed to denote any word or words which constitute a concept. The word concept is employed strictly in the sense of a subject of thought, without reference to the words symbolizing it. The concept, or subject of thought, is the important element or fact and the term denoting it is merely a convenient symbol of expression. It must be remembered that a term does not necessarily consists of but a single word, for often many words are employed to denote the concept, sometimes even an entire clause or phrase being found necessary for the current term. For the purpose of the consideration of the subjects to be treated upon in this book, we may agree that: A term is the outward symbol of a concept; and that: The concept is the idea expressed by the term.

There are three general parts or phases of Deductive Logic, namely: Terms, Propositions and Syllogisms. Therefore, in considering Terms we are entering into a consideration of the first phase of Deductive Logic. Unless we have a correct understanding of Terms, we cannot expect to understand the succeeding stages of Deductive Reasoning. As Jevons says: "When we join terms together we make a Proposition; when we join Propositions together, we make an argument or piece of reasoning. . . . We should generally get nothing but nonsense if we were to put together any terms and any propositions and to suppose that we were reasoning. To produce a good argument we must be careful to obey certain rules, which it is the purpose of Logic to make known. But, in order to understand the matter perfectly, we ought first to learn exactly what a term is, and how many kinds of terms there may be; we have next to learn the nature of a proposition and the different kinds of propositions. Afterwards we shall learn how one proposition may by reasoning be drawn from other propositions in the kind of argument called the syllogism."

Now, having seen that terms are the outward symbols or expression of concepts, and are the names of things which we join together in a proposition, let us proceed to consider the different kinds of terms, following the classifications adopted by the authorities.

A term may contain any number of nouns, substantive or adjective or it may contain but a single noun. Thus in, "Tigers are ferocious," the first term is the single substantive "tigers"; the second term is the single adjective "ferocious." And in the proposition, "The King of England is the Emperor of India," there are two terms, each composed of two nouns, "King of England" being the first term and "Emperor of India" being the second term. The proposition, "The library of the British Museum is the greatest collection of books in the world," contains fifteen words but only two terms; the first term being "The library of the British Museum," in which are two substantives, one adjective, two definite articles and one preposition; the second term being, "the greatest collection of books in the world," which contains three substantives, one adjective, two articles, and two prepositions. The above illustration is supplied by Jevons, who adds: "A logical term, then, may consist of any number of nouns, substantive or adjective, with the articles, prepositions and conjunctions required to join them together; still it is only one term if it points out, or makes us think of a single object, or collection, or class of objects." (A substantive, is: "the part of speech which expresses something that exists, either material or immaterial.")

The first classification of terms divides them into two general classes, viz., (1) Singular Terms; and (2) General Terms.

A Singular Term is a term denoting a single object, person or thing. Although denoting only a single object, person or thing, it may be composed of several words; or it may be composed of but one word as in the case of a proper name, etc. The following are Singular Terms, because they are terms denoting but a single object, person or thing: "Europe; Minnesota; Socrates; Shakespeare; the first man; the highest good; the first cause; the King of England; the British Museum; the Commissioner of Public Works; the main street of the City of New York." It will be noted that in all of the examples given, the Singular Term denotes a particular something, a specific thing, a something of which there is but one, and that one possesses particularity and individuality. As Hyslop says: "Oneness of kind is not the only or distinctive feature of Singular Terms, but individuality, or singularity, as representing a concrete individual whole."

A General Term is a term which applies, in the same sense, to each and every individual object, person or thing in a number of objects, persons or things of the same kind, or to the entire class composed of such objects persons or things of the same kind. For instance, "horse; man; biped; mammal; trees; figures; grain of sand; matter," etc. Hyslop says, regarding General Terms: "In these instances the terms denote more than one object, and apply to all of the same kind. Their meaning is important in the interpretation of what are called universal propositions."

Another general classification of Terms divides them into two respective classes, as follows: (1) Collective Terms; and (2) Distributive Terms. Hyslop says of this classification: "This division is based upon the distinction between aggregate wholes of the same kind and class terms. It partly coincides with the division into Singular and General Terms, the latter always being distributive."

A Collective Term is one which denotes an aggregate or collected whole of objects, persons or things of the same or similar kind, which collective whole is considered as an individual, although composed of a totality of separate individual objects, persons or things. Thus the following terms: "regiment; congregation; army; family; crowd; nation; company; battalion; class; congress; parliament; convention;" etc. are Collective Terms, because they denote collective, aggregate or composite wholes, considered as an individual.

A Distributive Term is a term which denotes each and every individual object, person or thing in a given class. For example, are the terms: "man; quadruped; biped; mammal; book; diamond; tree." As Hyslop says: "General terms are always distributive." Also: "It is important also to keep clear the distinction between class wholes and collective wholes. . . . They are often confused so as to call a term denoting a class a Collective Term."

Another general classification of Terms divides them into the following two respective classes; (1) Concrete Terms; and (2) Abstract Terms.

A Concrete Term is a term denoting either a definite object, person or thing which is subject to perception and experience, and may be considered as actually existent concretely, as for instance: horse; man; mountain; dollar; knife; table; etc., or else an attribute thought of and used solely as an attribute, as for instance: "beautiful, wise, noble, virtuous, good," etc.

An Abstract Term is a term denoting the attribute, quality or property considered as apart from the object, person or thing and as having an abstract existence, as for instance: "beauty; wisdom; nobility; goodness; virtue," etc. As we have seen elsewhere, these qualities have no real existence in themselves, but are known and thought of only in connection with concrete objects, persons and things. Thus we cannot know "Beauty," but may know beautiful things; we cannot know "Virtue," but we may know virtuous people, etc.

An attribute or quality is concrete when expressed as an adjective; and abstract when expressed as a noun; as for instance, "beautiful" and "beauty," respectively, or "virtuous" and "virtue," respectively. The distinction may be summed up as follows: A Concrete Term is the name of a thing or of a quality of a thing expressed as an adjective and as merely a quality; while an Abstract Term is the name of a quality of a thing, expressed as a noun and as a "thing" in itself.

Certain terms may be used as either Concrete Terms or as Abstract Terms, and certain authorities have seen fit to classify them as Mixed Terms, as for instance the terms: "government; religion; philosophy;" etc.

Another general classification of Terms divides them into two respective classes as follows: (1) Positive Terms; and (2) Negative Terms.

A Positive Term is a term which denotes its own qualities, as for instance: "good, human, large, square, black, strong," etc. These terms indicate the presence of the quality denoted by the term itself.

A Negative Term is a term denoting the absence of a quality, as for instance: "inhuman, inorganic, unwell, unpleasant, non-conducive," etc. These terms deny the presence of certain qualities, rather than asserting the presence of an opposite quality. They are essentially negative in nature and in form. Jevons says: "We may usually know a Negative Term by its beginning with one of the little syllables un-, in-, a-, an-, non-, or by its ending with -less." Hyslop says: "The usual symbols of Negative Terms are in, un, less, dis, a, or an, anti, mis, and sometimes de, and non and not." Jevons adds: "If the English language were a perfect one, every term ought to have a Negative Term exactly corresponding to it, so that all adjectives and nouns would be in pairs. Just as convenient has its negative inconvenient; metallic, non-metallic; logical, illogical; and so on; so blue should have its negative, non-blue; literary, non-literary; paper, non-paper. But many of these Negative Terms would be seldom or never used, and if we happen to want them, we can make them for the occasion by putting not-, or non-, before the Positive Term. Accordingly, we find in the dictionary only those Negative Terms which are much employed."

The last named authority also says: "Sometimes the same word may seem to have two or even more distinct negatives. There is much difference between undressed and not-dressed, that is 'not in evening dress.' Both seem to be negatives of 'dressed,' but this is because the word has two distinct meanings."

Some authorities insist upon closer and further classification, as for instance, in the case of what they call a Privative Term, denoting the absence of qualities once possessed by the object, person or thing, as: "deaf, dead, blind, dark," etc. Hyslop says that these terms "are Positive in form and Negative in matter or meaning." Also in the case of what they call a Nego-positive Term, denoting "the presence of a positive quality expressed in a negative manner," as: disagreeable, inhuman, invaluable, etc. These last mentioned classes however are regarded by some as the result of "carrying too far" the tendency toward classification, and the two general classes, Positive and Negative, are thought sufficient for the purpose of the general student. The same objection applies to a classification occasionally made i.e., that which is called an Infinitated Term, denoting a term the intent of which is to place in a distinct category every object, person or thing other than that expressed in the corresponding Positive Term. The intent of the term is to place the positive idea in one class, and all else into a separate one. Examples of this class of terms are found in: "not-I, not-animal, not-tree, unmoral," etc. Hyslop says of these terms: "They are not always, if ever, recognized as rhetorically elegant, but are valuable often to make clear the really negative, or infinitatively negative nature of the idea in mind."

Another general classification of Terms divides them into two respective classes, as follows: (1) Absolute Terms; and (2) Relative Terms.

An Absolute Term is a term denoting the presence of qualities intrinsic to the object, and not depending upon any relation to any other object, as for instance: "man; book; horse; gun;" etc. These terms may be related to many other terms, but are not necessarily related to any other.

A Relative Term is a term denoting certain necessary relations to other terms, as for instance: "father; son; mother; daughter; teacher; pupil; master;

servant;" etc. Thus it is impossible to think of "child" except in relation to "parent," or vice versa. The one term implies the existence of its related term.

Hyslop says of the above classification: "Relative Terms suggest the thought of other individuals with the relation involved as a part of the term's meaning, while Absolute Terms suggest only the qualities in the subject without a relation to others being necessarily involved."

Some authorities also classify terms as higher and lower; also as broad and narrow. This classification is meant to indicate the content and extent of the term. For instance, when we classify, we begin with the individuals which we then group into a small class. These classes we then group into a larger class, according to their resemblances. These larger classes then go to form a part of still larger classes, and so on. As these classes advance they form broader terms; and as we retreat from the general class into the less general and more particular, the term becomes narrower. By some, the broader term which includes the narrower is called the higher term, and the narrower are called the lower terms. Thus animal would be a higher and broader term than dog, cat or tiger because it includes the latter. Brooks says: "Since a concept is formed by the union of the common attributes of individuals, it thus embraces both attributes and individuals. The attributes of a concept constitute what is called its content; the individuals it embraces constitute its extent."

Accordingly, the feature of including objects in a concept or term is called its extension; while the feature of including attributes or qualities is called its intension. It follows as a natural consequence that the greater the extension of a term, the less its intension; the greater its intension, the less its extension. We will understand this more clearly when we consider that the more individuals contained in a term, the fewer common properties or qualities it can contain; and the more common properties, the fewer individuals. As Brooks says: "The concept man has more extension than poet, orator or statesman, since it embraces more individuals; and less intension, since we must lay aside the distinctive attributes of poet, orator and statesman in order to unite them in a common class man." In the same way the general term animal is quite extended for it includes a large number of individual varieties of very different and varied characteristics and qualities; as for instance, the lion, camel, dog, oyster, elephant, snail, worm, snake, etc. Accordingly its intension must be small for it can include only the qualities common to all animals, which are very few indeed. The definition of the term shows how small is its intension, as: "Animal. An organic being, rising above a vegetable in various respects, especially in possessing sensibility, will and the power of voluntary motion." Another narrows the intension still further when he defines animal as: "a creature which possesses, or has possessed, life." Halleck says: "Animal is very narrow in intension, very broad in extension. There are few qualities common to all animals, but there is a vast number of animals. To give the full meaning of the term in extension, we should have to name every animal, from the microscopic infusoria to the tiger, from the angleworm to the whale. When we decrease the extension to one species of animal, horse, the individuals are fewer, the qualities more numerous."

The importance of forming clear and distinct concepts and of grouping, classifying and generalizing these into larger and broader concepts and terms is recognized by all authorities and is generally regarded as forming the real basis of all constructive thought. As Brooks says: "Generalization lies at the basis of language: only as man can form general conceptions is it possible for him to form a language. . . . Nearly all the ordinary words in our language are general rather than particular. . . . This power of generalization lies also at the basis of science. Had we no power of forming general ideas, each particular object would be a study by itself, and we should thus never pass beyond the very alphabet of knowledge. Judgments, except in the simplest form, would be impossible; and it is difficult to see how even the simplest form of the syllogism could be constructed. No general conclusion could be drawn from particulars, nor particular conclusions from generals; and thus neither inductive nor deductive reasoning would be possible. The classifications of science could not be made; and knowledge would end at the very threshold of science."

7

The Meaning of Terms

Every term has its meaning, or content, as some authorities prefer to call it. The word or words of which the term is composed are merely vocal sounds, serving as a symbol for the real meaning of the term, which meaning exists only in the mind of the person understanding it. To one not understanding the meaning of the term, the latter is but as a meaningless sound, but to one understanding it the sound awakens mental associations and representation and thus serves its purpose as a symbol of thought.

Each concrete general term has two meanings, (1) the actual concrete thing, person or object to which the term is applied; and (2) the qualities, attributes or properties of those objects, persons or things in consequence of which the term is applied. For instance, in the case of the concrete term book, the first meaning consists of the general idea of the thing which we think of as a book, and the second meaning consists of the various qualities which go to make that thing a book, as the printed pages, the binding, the form, the cover, etc. Not only is that particular thing a book, but every other thing having the same or similar properties also must be a book. And so, whenever I call a thing a book it must possess the said qualities. And, whenever I combine the ideas of these qualities in thought, I must think of a book. As Jevons says: "In reality, every ordinary general term has a double meaning: it means the things to which it is applied, . . . it also means, in a totally different way, the qualities and peculiarities implied as being in the things. Logicians say that the number of things to which a term applies is the extension of the term; while the number of qualities or peculiarities implied is the intension."

The extension and intension of terms has been referred to in the previous chapter. The general classification of the degrees of extension of a general term is expressed by the two terms, Genus and Species, respectively. The classification of the character of the intension of a term is expressed by the term, Difference, Property and Accident, respectively.

Genus is a term indicating: "a class of objects containing several species; a class more extensive than a species; a universal which is predicable of several things of different species."

Species is a term denoting: "a smaller class of objects than a genus, and of two or more of which a genus is composed; a predicable that expresses the whole essence of its subject in so far as any common term can express it."

An authority says: "The names species and genus are merely relative and the same common term may, in one case, be the species which is predicated of an individual, and in another case the individual of which a species is predicated. Thus the individual, George, belongs to the logical species Man, while Man is an individual of the logical species Animal." Jevons says: "It is desirable to have names by which to show that one class is contained in another, and accordingly we call the class which is divided into two or more smaller ones, the genus, and the smaller ones into which it is divided, the species." Animal is a genus of which man is a species; while man, in turn, is a genus of which Caucasian is a species; and Caucasian, in turn, becomes a genus of which Socrates becomes a species. The student must avoid confusing the logical meaning of the terms genus and species with the use of the same terms in Natural History. Each class is a "genus" to the class below it in extension; and each class is a "species" to the class above it in extension. At the lowest extreme of the scale we reach what is called the infima species, which cannot be further subdivided, as for instance "Socrates"—this lowest species must always be an individual object, person or thing. At the highest extreme of the scale we reach what is summum genus, or highest genus, which is never a species of anything, for there is no class higher than it, as for instance, "being, existence, reality, truth, the absolute, the infinite, the ultimate," etc. Hyslop says: "In reality there is but one summum genus, while there may be an indefinite number of infimae species. All intermediate terms between these extremes are sometimes called subalterns, as being either genera or species, according to the relation in which they are viewed."

Passing on to the classification of the character of the intension of terms, we find:

Difference, a term denoting: "The mark or marks by which the species is distinguished from the rest of the genus; the specific characteristic." Thus the color of the skin is a difference between the Negro and the Caucasian; the number of feet the difference between the biped and the quadruped; the form and shape of leaves the difference between the oak and the elm trees, etc. Hyslop says: "Whatever distinguishes one object from another can be called the differentia. It is some characteristic in addition to the common qualities and determines the species or individual under the genus."

Property, a term denoting: "A peculiar quality of anything; that which is inherent in or naturally essential to anything." Thus a property is a distinguishing mark of a class. Thus black skin is a property of the Negro race; four feet a property of quadrupeds; a certain form of leaf a property of the oak tree. Thus a difference between two species may be a property of one of the species.

Accident, a term denoting: "Any quality or circumstance which may or may not belong to a class, accidentally as it were; or, whatever does not really constitute an essential part of an object, person or thing." As, for instance, the redness of a rose, for a rose might part with its redness and still be a rose—the color is the accident of the rose. Or, a brick may be white and still be a brick, although the majority of bricks are red—the redness or whiteness of the brick are its accidents and not its essential properties. Whately says: "Accidents in Logic are of two kinds—separable and inseparable. If walking be the accident of a particular man, it is a separable one, for he would not cease to be that man though he stood still; while, on the contrary, if Spaniard is the accident connected with him, it is an inseparable one, since he never can cease to be, ethnologically considered, what he was born."

Arising from the classification of the meaning or content of terms, we find the process termed "Definition."

Definition is a term denoting: "An explanation of a word or term." In Logic the term is used to denote the process of analysis in which the properties and differences of a term are clearly stated. There are of course several kinds of definitions. For instance, there is what is called a Real Definition, which Whately defines as: "A definition which explains the nature of the thing by a particular name." There is also what is called a Physical Definition, which is: "A definition made by enumerating such parts as are actually separable, such as the hull, masts, etc., of a ship." Also a Logical Definition, which is: "A definition consisting of the genus and the difference. Thus if a planet be defined as 'a wandering star,' star is the genus, and wandering points out the difference between a planet and an ordinary star." An Accidental Definition is: "A definition of the accidental qualities of a thing." An Essential Definition is: "a definition of the essential properties and differences of an object, person or thing."

Crabbe discriminates between a Definition and an Explanation, as follows: "A definition is correct or precise; an explanation is general or ample. The definition of a word defines or limits the extent of its signification; it is the rule for the scholar in the use of any word; the explanation of a word may include both definition and illustration; the former admits of no more words than will include the leading features in the meaning of any term; the latter admits of an unlimited scope for diffuseness on the part of the explainer."

Hyslop gives the following excellent explanation of the Logical Definition, which as he states is the proper meaning of the term in Logic. He states:

"The rules which regulate Logical Definition are as follows:

1. A definition should state the essential attributes of the species defined.

2. A definition must not contain the name of word defined. Otherwise the definition is called a circulus in definiendo.

3. The definition must be exactly equivalent to the species defined.

4. A definition should not be expressed in obscure, figurative, or ambiguous language.

5. A definition must not be negative when it can be affirmative."

A correct definition necessarily requires the manifestation of the two respective processes of Analysis and Synthesis.

Analysis is a term denoting: "The separation of anything into its constituent elements, qualities, properties and attributes." It is seen at once that in order to correctly define an object, person or thing, it is first necessary to analyze the latter in order to perceive its essential and accidental properties or differences. Unless the qualities, properties and attributes are clearly and fully perceived, we cannot properly define the object itself.

Synthesis is a term denoting: "The act of joining or putting two or more things together; in Logic: the method by composition, in opposition to the method of resolution or analysis." In stating a definition we must necessarily join together the various essential qualities, properties and attributes, which we have discovered by the process of analysis; and the synthesized combination, considered as a whole, is the definition of the object expressed by the term.

8

Judgments

The first step in the process of reasoning is that of Conception or the forming of Concepts. The second step is that of Judgment, or the process of perceiving the agreement or disagreement of two conceptions.

Judgment in Logic is defined as: "The comparing together in the mind of two notions, concepts or ideas, which are the objects of apprehension, whether complex or incomplex, and pronouncing that they agree or disagree with each other, or that one of them belongs or does not belong to the other. Judgment is therefore affirmative or negative."

When we have in our mind two concepts, we are likely to compare them one with the other, and to thus arrive at a conclusion regarding their agreement or disagreement. This process of comparison and decision is what, in Logic, is called Judgment.

In every act of Judgment there must be at least two concepts to be examined and compared. This comparison must lead to a Judgment regarding their agreement or disagreement. For instance, we have the two concepts, horse and animal. We examine and compare the two concepts, and find that there is an agreement between them. We find that the concept horse is included in the higher concept of animal and therefore, we assert that: "The horse is an animal." This is a statement of agreement and is, therefore, a Positive Judgment. We then compare the concepts horse and cow and find a disagreement between them, which we express in the statement of the Judgment that: "The horse is not a cow." This Judgment, stating a disagreement is what is called a Negative Judgment.

In the above illustration of the comparison between the concepts horse and animal we find that the second concept animal is broader than the first, horse, so broad in fact that it includes the latter. The terms are not equal, for we cannot say, in truth, that "an animal is the horse." We may, however, include a part of the broader conception with the narrower and say: "some animals are horses." Sometimes both concepts are of equal rank, as when we state that: "Man is a rational animal."

In the process of Judgment there is always the necessity of the choice between the Positive and the Negative. When we compare the concepts horse and animal, we must of necessity decide either that the horse is an animal, or else that it is not an animal.

The importance of the process of Judgment is ably stated by Halleck, as follows: "Were isolated concepts possible, they would be of very little use. Isolated facts are of no more service than unspun wool. We might have a concept of a certain class of three-leaved ivy, as we might also of poisons. Unless judgment linked these two concepts and decided that this species of ivy is poisonous, we might take hold of it and be poisoned. We might have a concept of bread and also one of meat, fruit and vegetables. If we also had a concept of food, unrelated to these, we should starve to death, for we should not think of them as foods. A vessel, supposing itself to be far out at sea, signaled another vessel that the crew were dying of thirst. That crew certainly had a concept of drinkable things and also of water. To the surprise of the first, the second vessel signaled back, 'Draw from the sea and drink. You are at the mouth of the Amazon.' The thirsty crew had not joined the concept drinkable to the concept of water over the ship's side. A man having taken an overdose of laudanum, his wife lost much valuable time in sending out for antidotes, because certain of her concepts had not been connected by judgment. She had good concepts of coffee and of mustard; she also knew that an antidote to opium was needed; but she had never linked these concepts and judged that coffee and mustard were antidotes to opium. The moment she formed that judgment she was a wiser woman for her knowledge was related and usable. . . . Judgment is the power revolutionizing the world. The revolution is slow because nature's forces are so complex, so hard to be reduced to their simplest forms and so disguised and neutralized by the presence of other forces. . . . Fortunately judgment is ever silently working and comparing things that, to past ages, have seemed dissimilar; and it is continually abstracting and leaving out of the field of view those qualities which have simply served to obscure the point at issue."

Judgment may be both analytic or synthetic in its processes; and it may be neither. When we compare a narrow concept with a broader one, as a part with a whole, the process is synthetic or an act of combination. When we compare a part of a concept with another concept, the process is analytic. When we compare concepts equal in rank or extent, the process is neither synthetic nor analytic. Thus in the statement that: "A horse is an animal," the judgment is synthetic; in the statement that: "some animals are horses," the judgment is analytic; in the statement that: "a man is a rational animal," the judgment is neither analytic nor synthetic.

Brooks says: "In one sense all judgments are synthetic. A judgment consists of the union of two ideas and this uniting is a process of synthesis. This, however, is a superficial view of the process. Such a synthesis is a mere mechanical synthesis; below this is a thought-process which is sometimes analytic, sometimes synthetic and sometimes neither analytic nor synthetic."

The same authority states: "The act of mind described is what is known as logical judgment. Strictly speaking, however, every intelligent act of the mind is accompanied with a judgment. To know is to discriminate and, therefore, to judge. Every sensation or cognition involves a knowledge and so a judgment that it exists. The mind cannot think at all without judging; to think is to judge. Even in forming the notions which judgment compares, the mind judges. Every notion or concept implies a previous act of judgment to form it: in forming a concept, we compare the common attributes before we unite them; and comparison is judgment. It is thus true that 'Every concept is a contracted judgment; every judgment an expanded concept.' This kind of judgment, by which we affirm the existence of states of consciousness, discriminate qualities, distinguish percepts and form concepts, is called primitive or psychological judgment."

In Logical Judgment there are two aspects; i.e., Judgment by Extension and Judgment by Intension. When we compare the two concepts horse and animal we find that the concept horse is contained in the concept animal and the judgment that "a horse is an animal" may be considered as a Judgment by Extension. In the same comparison we see that the concept horse contains the quality of animality, and in attributing this quality to the horse, we may also say "the horse is an animal," which judgment may be considered as a Judgment by Intension. Brooks says: "Both views of Judgment are correct; the mind may reach its judgment either by extension or by intension. The method by extension is usually the more natural."

When a Judgment is expressed in words it is called a Proposition. There is some confusion regarding the two terms, some holding that a Judgment and a proposition are identical, and that the term "proposition" may be properly used to indicate the judgment itself. But the authorities who seek for clearness of expression and thought now generally hold that: "A Proposition is a Judgment expressed in words." In the next chapter, in which we consider Propositions, we shall enter into a more extended consideration of the subject of Judgments as expressed in Propositions, which consideration we omit at this point in order to avoid repetition. Just as the respective subjects of Concepts and Terms necessarily blend into each other, so do the respective subjects of Judgments and Propositions. In each case, too, there is the element of the mental process on the one hand and the verbal expression of it on the other hand. It will be well to keep this fact in mind.

9

Propositions

We have seen that the first step of Deductive Reasoning is that which we call Concepts. The second step is that which we call Propositions.

In Logic, a Proposition is: "A sentence, or part of a sentence, affirming or denying a connection between the terms; limited to express assertions rather than extended to questions and commands." Hyslop defines a Proposition as: "any affirmation or denial of an agreement between two conceptions."

Examples of Propositions are found in the following sentences: "The rose is a flower"; "a horse is an animal"; "Chicago is a city"; all of which are affirmations of agreement between the two terms involved; also in: "A horse is not a zebra"; "pinks are not roses"; "the whale is not a fish"; etc., which are denials of agreement between the terms.

The Parts of a Proposition are: (1) the Subject, or that of which something is affirmed or denied; (2) the Predicate, or the something which is affirmed or denied regarding the Subject; and (3) the Copula, or the verb serving as a link between the Subject and the Predicate.

In the Proposition: "Man is an animal," the term man is the Subject; the term an animal is the Predicate; and the word is, is the Copula. The Copula is always some form of the verb to be, in the present tense indicative, in an affirmative Proposition; and the same with the negative particle affixed, in a negative Proposition. The Copula is not always directly expressed by the word is or is not, etc., but is instead expressed in some phrase which implies them. For instance, we say "he runs," which implies "he is running." In the same way, it may appear at times as if the Predicate was missing, as in: "God is," by which is meant "God is existing." In some cases, the Proposition is inverted, the Predicate appearing first in order, and the Subject last, as in: "Blessed are the peacemakers;"

or "Strong is Truth." In such cases judgment must be used in determining the matter, in accordance with the character and meaning of the terms.

An Affirmative Proposition is one in which the Predicate is affirmed to agree with the Subject. A Negative Proposition is one in which the agreement of the Predicate and Subject is denied. Examples of both of these classes have been given in this chapter.

Another classification of Propositions divides them in three classes, as follows (1) Categorical; (2) Hypothetical; (3) Disjunctive.

A Categorical Proposition is one in which the affirmation or denial is made without reservation or qualification, as for instance: "Man is an animal," "the rose is a flower," etc. The fact asserted may not be true, but the statement is made positively as a statement of reality.

A Hypothetical Proposition is one in which the affirmation or denial is made to depend upon certain conditions, circumstances or suppositions, as for instance: "If the water is boiling-hot, it will scald," or "if the powder be damp, it will not explode," etc. Jevons says: "Hypothetical Propositions may generally be recognized by containing the little word 'if;' but it is doubtful whether they really differ much from the ordinary propositions. . . . We may easily say that 'boiling water will scald,' and 'damp gunpowder will not explode,' thus avoiding the use of the word 'if.'"

A Disjunctive Proposition is one "implying or asserting an alternative," and usually containing the conjunction "or," sometimes together with "either," as for instance: "Lightning is sheet or forked"; "Arches are either round or pointed"; "Angles are either obtuse, right angled or acute."

Another classification of Propositions divides them in two classes as follows: (1) Universal; (2) Particular.

A Universal Proposition is one in which the whole quantity of the Subject is involved in the assertion or denial of the Predicate. For instance: "All men are liars," by which is affirmed that all of the entire race of men are in the category of liars, not some men but all the men that are in existence. In the same way the Proposition: "No men are immortal" is Universal, for it is a universal denial.

A Particular Proposition is one in which the affirmation or denial of the Predicate involves only a part or portion of the whole of the Subject, as for instance: "Some men are atheists," or "Some women are not vain," in which cases the affirmation or denial does not involve all or the whole of the Subject. Other examples are: "A few men," etc.; "many people," etc.; "certain books," etc.; "most people," etc.

Hyslop says: "The signs of the Universal Proposition, when formally expressed, are all, every, each, any, and whole or words with equivalent import."

The signs of Particular Propositions are also certain adjectives of quantity, such as some, certain, a few, many, most or such others as denote at least a part of a class.

The subject of the Distribution of Terms in Propositions is considered very important by Logicians, and as Hyslop says: "has much importance in determining the legitimacy, or at least the intelligibility, of our reasoning and the assurance that it will be accepted by others." Some authorities favor the term, "Qualification of the Terms of Propositions," but the established usage favors the term "Distribution."

The definition of the Logical term, "Distribution," is: "The distinguishing of a universal whole into its several kinds of species; the employment of a term to its fullest extent; the application of a term to its fullest extent, so as to include all significations or applications." A Term of a Proposition is distributed when it is employed in its fullest sense; that is to say, when it is employed so as to apply to each and every object, person or thing included under it. Thus in the proposition, "All horses are animals," the term horses is distributed; and in the proposition, "Some horses are thoroughbreds," the term horses is not distributed. Both of these examples relate to the distribution of the subject of the proposition. But the predicate of a proposition also may or may not be distributed. For instance, in the proposition, "All horses are animals," the predicate, animals, is not distributed, that is, not used in its fullest sense, for all animals are not horses—there are some animals which are not horses and, therefore, the predicate, animals, not being used in its fullest sense is said to be "not distributed." The proposition really means: "All horses are some animals."

There is however another point to be remembered in the consideration of Distribution of Terms of Propositions, which Brooks expresses as follows: "Distribution generally shows itself in the form of the expression, but sometimes it may be determined by the thought. Thus if we say, 'Men are mortal,' we mean all men, and the term men is distributed. But if we say 'Books are necessary to a library,' we mean, not 'all books' but 'some books.' The test of distribution is whether the term applies to 'each and every.' Thus when we say 'men are mortal,' it is true of each and every man that he is mortal."

The Rules of Distribution of the Terms of Proposition are as follows:

1. All universals distribute the subject.

2. All particulars do not distribute the subject.

3. All negatives distribute the predicate.

4. All affirmatives do not distribute the predicate.

The above rules are based upon logical reasoning. The reason for the first two rules is quite obvious, for when the subject is universal, it follows that the whole subject is involved; when the subject is particular it follows that only a part of the subject is involved. In the case of the third rule, it will be seen that in every negative proposition the whole of the predicate must be denied the subject, as for instance, when we say: "Some animals are not horses," the whole class of horses is cut off from the subject, and is thus distributed. In the case of the fourth rule, we may readily see that in the affirmative proposition the whole of the predicate is not denied the subject, as for instance, when we say that: "Horses are animals," we do not mean that horses are all the animals, but that they are merely a part or portion of the class animal—therefore, the predicate, animals, is not distributed.

In addition to the forms of Propositions given there is another class of Propositions known as Definitive or Substitutive Propositions, in which the Subject and the Predicate are exactly alike in extent and rank. For instance, in the proposition, "A triangle is a polygon of three sides" the two terms are interchangeable; that is, may be substituted for each other. Hence the term "substitutive." The term "definitive" arises from the fact that the respective terms of this kind of a proposition necessarily define each other. All logical definitions are expressed in this last mentioned form of proposition, for in such cases the subject and the predicate are precisely equal to each other.

10

Immediate Reasoning

In the process of Judgment we must compare two concepts and ascertain their agreement of disagreement. In the process of Reasoning we follow a similar method and compare two judgments, the result of such comparison being the deduction of a third judgment.

The simplest form of reasoning is that known as Immediate Reasoning, by which is meant the deduction of one proposition from another which implies it. Some have defined it as: "reasoning without a middle term." In this form of reasoning only one proposition is required for the premise, and from that premise the conclusion is deduced directly and without the necessity of comparison with any other term of proposition.

The two principal methods employed in this form of Reasoning are; (1) Opposition; (2) Conversion.

Opposition exists between propositions having the same subject and predicate, but differing in quality or quantity, or both. The Laws of Opposition are as follows:

I. (1) If the universal is true, the particular is true. (2) If the particular is false, the universal is false. (3) If the universal is false, nothing follows. (4) If the particular is true, nothing follows.

II. (1) If one of two contraries is true, the other is false. (2) If one of two contraries is false, nothing can be inferred. (3) Contraries are never both true, but both may be false.

III. (1) If one of two sub-contraries is false, the other is true. (2) If one of two sub-contraries is true, nothing can be inferred concerning the other. (3) Sub-contraries can never be both false, but both may be true.

IV. (1) If one of two contradictories is true, the other is false. (2) If one of two contradictories is false, the other is true. (3) Contradictories can never be both true or both false, but always one is true and the other is false.

In order to comprehend the above laws, the student should familiarize himself with the following arrangement, adopted by logicians as a convenience:

{UNIVERSAL {AFFIRMATIVE (A)
{   {NEGATIVE   (E)
PROPOSITIONS {
{   {AFFIRMATIVE (I)
{PARTICULAR {NEGATIVE   (O)

Examples of the above: Universal Affirmative (A): "All men are mortal;" Universal Negative (E): "No man is mortal;" Particular Affirmative (I): "Some men are mortal;" Particular Negative (O): "Some men are not mortal."

The following examples of abstract propositions are often used by logicians as tending toward a clearer conception than examples such as given above:

(A) "All A is B."

(I) "Some A is B."

(E) "No A is B."

(O) "Some A is not B."

These four forms of propositions bear certain logical relations to each other, as follows:

A and E are styled contraries. I and O are sub-contraries; A and I and also E and O are called subalterns; A and O and also I and E are styled contradictories.

A close study of these relations, and the symbols expressing them, is necessary for a clear comprehension of the Laws of Opposition stated a little further back, as well as the principles of Conversion which we shall mention a little further on. The following chart, called the Square of Opposition, is also employed by logicians to illustrate the relations between the four classes of propositions:

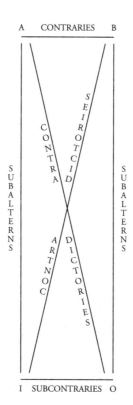

Conversion is the process of immediate reasoning by which we infer from a given proposition another proposition having the predicate of the original for its subject and the subject of the original for its predicate; or stated in a few words: Conversion is the transposition of the subject and predicate of a proposition. As Brooks states it: "Propositions or judgments are converted when the subject and predicate change places in such a manner that the resulting judgment is an inference from the given judgment." The new proposition, resulting from the operation or Conversion, is called the Converse; the original proposition is called the Convertend.

The Law of Conversion is that: "No term must be distributed in the Converse that is not distributed in the Convertend." This arises from the obvious fact that nothing should be affirmed in the derived proposition than there is in the original proposition.

There are three kinds of Conversion; viz: (1) Simple Conversion; (2) Conversion by Limitation; (3) Conversion by Contraposition.

In Simple Conversion there is no change in either quality or quantity. In Conversion by Limitation the quality is changed from universal to particular. In Conversion by Negation the quality is changed but not the quantity. Referring to the classification tables and symbols given in the preceding pages of this chapter, we may now proceed to consider the application of these methods of Conversion to each of the four kinds of propositions; as follows:

The Universal Affirmative (symbol A) proposition is converted by Limitation, or by a change of quality from universal to particular. The predicate not being "distributed" in the convertend, we must not distribute it in the converse by saying "all." Thus in this case we must convert the proposition, "all men are mortal" (A), into "some mortals are men" (I).

The Universal Negative (symbol E) is converted by Simple Conversion, in which there is no change in either quality or quantity. For since both terms of "E" are distributed, they may both be distributed in the converse without violating the law of conversion. Thus "No man is mortal" is converted into: "No mortals are men." "E" is converted into "E."

The Particular Affirmative (symbol I) is also converted by Simple Conversion in which there is no change in either quality or quantity. For since neither term is distributed in "I," neither term may be distributed in the converse, and the latter must remain "I." For instance; the proposition: "Some men are mortal" is converted into the proposition, "Some mortals are men."

The Particular Negative (symbol O) is converted by Conversion by Negation, in which the quality is changed but not the quantity. Thus in converting the proposition: "Some men are not mortal," we must not say "some mortals are not men," for in so doing we would distribute men in the predicate, where it is not distributed in the convertend. Avoiding this, we transfer the negative particle from the copula to the predicate so that the convertend becomes "I" which is converted by Simple Conversion. Thus we transfer "Some men are not mortal" into "Some men are not-mortal" from which we easily convert (by Simple Conversion) the proposition: "Some not-mortals are men."

It will be well for students, at this point, to consider the three following Fundamental Laws of Thought as laid down by the authorities, which are as follows:

The Law of Identity, which states that: "The same quality or thing is always the same quality or thing, no matter how different the conditions in which it occurs."

The Law of Contradiction, which states that: "No thing can at the same time and place both be and not be."

The Law of Excluded Middle, which states that: "Everything must either be or not be; there is no other alternative or middle course."

Of these laws, Prof. Jevons, a noted authority, says: "Students are seldom able to see at first their full meaning and importance. All arguments may be explained when these self-evident laws are granted; and it is not too much to say that the whole of logic will be plain to those who will constantly use these laws as the key."

11

Inductive Reasoning

Inductive Reasoning, as we have said, is the process of discovering general truth from particular truths, or inferring general laws from particular facts. Thus, from the experience of the individual and the race regarding the particular truth that each and every man under observation has been observed to die sooner or later, it is inferred that all men die, and hence, the induction of the general truth that "All men must die." Or, as from experience we know that the various kinds of metals expand when subjected to heat, we infer that all metals are subject to this law, and that consequently we may arrive by inductive reasoning at the conclusion that: "All metals expand when subjected to heat." It will be noticed that the conclusion arrived at in this way by Inductive Reasoning forms the fundamental premise in the process of Deductive Reasoning. As we have seen elsewhere, the two processes, Inductive and Deductive Reasoning, respectively are interdependent—resting upon one another.

Jevons says of Inductive Reasoning: "In Deductive Reasoning we inquire how we may gather the truth contained in some propositions called Premises, and put into another proposition called the Conclusion. We have not yet undertaken to find out how we can learn what propositions really are true, but only what propositions are true when other ones are true. All the acts of reasoning yet considered would be called deductive because we deduce, or lead down the truth from premises to conclusion. It is an exceedingly important thing to understand deductive inference correctly, but it might seem to be still more important to understand inductive inference, by which we gather the truth of general propositions from facts observed as happening in the world around us." Halleck says: "Man has to find out through his own experience, or that of others, the major premises from which he argues or draws his conclusions. By induction we examine what seems to us a sufficient number of individual cases. We then conclude that the rest of these cases, which we have not examined, will obey the same general law. . . . Only after general laws have been laid down, after objects have been classified, after major premises have been formed, can deduction be employed."

Strange as may now appear, it is a fact that until a comparatively recent period in the history of man, it was held by philosophers that the only way to arrive at all knowledge was by means of Deductive Reasoning, by the use of the Syllogism. The influence of Aristotle was great and men preferred to pursue artificial and complicated methods of Deductive Reasoning, rather than to reach the truth by obtaining the facts from Nature herself, at first hand, and then inferring general principle from the facts so gathered. The rise of modern scientific methods of reasoning, along the lines of Inductive Inference, dates from about 1225-1300. Roger Bacon was one of the first to teach that we must arrive at scientific truth by a process of observation and experimentation on the natural objects to be found on all sides. He made many discoveries by following this process. He was ably seconded by Galileo who lived some three hundred years later, and who also taught that many great general truths might be gained by careful observation and intelligent inference. Lord Francis Bacon, who lived about the same time as Galileo, presented in his Novum Organum many excellent observations and facts regarding the process of Inductive Reasoning and scientific thought. As Jevons says: "Inductive logic inquires by what manner of reasoning we can gather the laws of nature from the facts and events observed. Such reasoning is called induction, or inductive inquiry, and, as it has actually been practiced by all the great discoverers in science, it consists in four steps."

The Four Steps in Inductive Reasoning, as stated by Jevons, are as follows:

First Step—Preliminary observation

Second Step—The making of hypotheses

Third Step—Deductive reasoning

Fourth Step—Verification

It will be seen that the process of Inductive Reasoning is essentially a synthetic process, because it operates in the direction of combining and uniting particular facts or truths into general truths or laws which comprehend, embrace and include them all. As Brooks says: "The particular facts are united by the mind into the general law; the general law embraces the particular facts and binds them together into a unity of principle and thought. Induction is thus a process of thought from the parts to the whole—a synthetic process." It will also be seen that the process of Inductive Reasoning is essentially an ascending process, because it ascends from particular facts to general laws; particular truths to universal truths; from the lower to the higher, the narrower to the broader, the smaller to the greater.

Brooks says of Inductive Reasoning: "The relation of induction to deduction will be clearly seen. Induction and Deduction are the converse, the opposites of each other. Deduction derives a particular truth from a general truth; Induction derives a general truth from particular truths. This antithesis appears in every particular. Deduction goes from generals to particulars; Induction goes from particulars to generals. Deduction is an analytic process; Induction is a synthetic process. Deduction is a descending process—it goes from the higher truth to the lower truth; Induction is an ascending process—it goes from the lower truth to the higher. They differ also in that Deduction may be applied to necessary truths, while Induction is mainly restricted to contingent truths." Hyslop says: "There have been several ways of defining this process. It has been usual to contrast it with Deduction. Now, deduction is often said to be reasoning from general to particular truths, from the containing to the contained truth, or from cause to effect. Induction, therefore, by contrast is defined as reasoning from the particular to the general, from the contained to the containing, or from effect to cause. Sometimes induction is said to be reasoning from the known to the unknown. This would make deduction, by contrast, reasoning from the unknown to the known, which is absurd. The former ways of representing it are much the better. But there is still a better way of comparing them. Deduction is reasoning in which the conclusion is contained in the premises. This is a ground for its certitude and we commit a fallacy whenever we go beyond the premises as shown by the laws of the distribution of terms. In contrast with this, then, we may call inductive reasoning the process by which we go beyond the premises in the conclusion. . . . The process here is to start from given facts and to infer some other probable facts more general or connected with them. In this we see the process of going beyond the premises. There are, of course, certain conditions which regulate the legitimacy of the procedure, just as there are conditions determining deduction. They are that the conclusion shall represent the same general kind as the premises, with a possibility of accidental differences. But it goes beyond the premises in so far as known facts are concerned."

The following example may give you a clearer idea of the processes of Inductive Reasoning:

First Step. Preliminary Observation. Example: We notice that all the particular magnets which have come under our observation attract iron. Our mental record of the phenomena may be stated as: "A, B, C, D, E, F, G, etc., and also X, Y, and Z, all of which are magnets, in all observed instances, and at all observed times, attract iron."

Second Step. The Making of Hypotheses. Example: Upon the basis of the observations and experiments, as above stated, and applying the axiom of Inductive Reasoning, that: "What is true of the many, is true of the whole," we feel justified in forming a hypothesis or inference of a general law or truth, applying the facts of the particulars to the general, whole or universal, thus: "All magnets attract iron."

Third Step. Deductive Reasoning. Example: Picking up a magnet regarding which we have had no experience and upon which we have made no experiments, we reason by the syllogism, as follows: (1) All magnets attract iron; (2) This thing is a magnet; therefore (3) This thing will attract iron. In this we apply the axiom of Deductive Reasoning:

"Whatever is true of the whole is true of the parts."

Fourth Step. Verification. Example: We then proceed to test the hypothesis upon the particular magnet, so as to ascertain whether or not it agrees with the particular facts. If the magnet does not attract iron we know that either our hypothesis is wrong and that some magnets do not attract iron; or else that our judgment regarding that particular "thing" being a magnet is at fault and that it is not a magnet. In either case, further examination, observation and experiment is necessary. In case the particular magnet does attract iron, we feel that we have verified our hypothesis and our judgment.

12

Reasoning by Induction

The term "Induction," in its logical usage, is defined as follows: "(a) The process of investigating and collecting facts; and (b) the deducing of an inference from these facts; also (c) sometimes loosely used in the sense of an inference from observed facts." Mill says: "Induction, then, is that operation of the mind, by which we infer that what we know to be true in a particular case or cases, will be true in all cases which resemble the former in certain assignable respects. In other words, Induction is the process by which we conclude that what is true of certain individuals of a class, is true of the whole class, or that what is true at certain times will be true in similar circumstances at all times."

The Basis of Induction is the axiom that: "What is true of the many is true of the whole." Esser, a well known authority, states this axiom in rather more complicated form, as follows: "That which belongs or does not belong to many things of the same kind, belongs or does not belong to all things of the same kind."

This basic axiom of Induction rests upon the conviction that Nature's laws and manifestations are regular, orderly and uniform. If we assume that Nature does not manifest these qualities, then the axiom must fall, and all inductive reason must be fallacious. As Brooks well says: "Induction has been compared to a ladder upon which we ascend from facts to laws. This ladder cannot stand unless it has something to rest upon; and this something is our faith in the constancy of Nature's laws." Some authorities have held that this perception of the uniformity of Nature's laws is in the nature of an intuitive truth, or an inherent law of our intelligence. Others hold that it is in itself an inductive truth, arrived at by experience and observation at a very early age. We are held to have noticed the uniformity in natural phenomena, and almost instinctively infer that this uniformity is continuous and universal.

The authorities assume the existence of two kinds of Induction, namely:

(1) Perfect Induction; and (2) Imperfect Induction. Other, but similar, terms are employed by different authorities to designate these two classes.

Perfect Induction necessitates a knowledge of all the particulars forming a class; that is, all the individual objects, persons, things or facts comprising a class must be known and enumerated in this form of Induction. For instance, if we knew positively all of Brown's children, and that their names were John, Peter, Mark, Luke, Charles, William, Mary and Susan, respectively; and that each and every one of them were freckled and had red hair; then, in that case, instead of simply generalizing and stating that: "John, Peter, Mark, Luke, Charles, William, Mary and Susan, who are all of Brown's children, are freckled and have red hair," we would save words, and state the inductive conclusion: "All Brown's children are freckled and have red hair." It will be noticed that in this case we include in the process only what is stated in the premise itself, and we do not extend our inductive process beyond the actual data upon which it is based. This form of Induction is sometimes called "Logical Induction," because the inference is a logical necessity, without the possibility of error or exception. By some authorities it is held not to be Induction at all, in the strict sense, but little more than a simplified form of enumeration. In actual practice it is seldom available, for it is almost impossible for us to know all the particulars in inferring a general law or truth. In view of this difficulty, we fall back upon the more practical form of induction known as:

Imperfect Induction, or as it is sometimes called "Practical Induction," by which is meant the inductive process of reasoning in which we assume that the particulars or facts actually known to us correctly represent those which are not actually known, and hence the whole class to which they belong. In this process it will be seen that the conclusion extends beyond the data upon which it is based. In this form of Induction we must actually employ the principle of the axiom: "What is true of the many is true of the whole"—that is, must assume it to be a fact, not because we know it by actual experience, but because we infer it from the axiom which also agrees with past experience. The conclusion arrived at may not always be true in its fullest sense, as in the case of the conclusion of Perfect Induction, but is the result of an inference based upon a principle which gives us a reasonable right to assume its truth in absence of better knowledge.

In considering the actual steps in the process of Inductive Reasoning we can do no better than to follow the classification of Jevons, mentioned in the preceding chapter, the same being simple and readily comprehended, and therefore preferable in this case to the more technical classification favored by some other authorities. Let us now consider these four steps.

First Step. Preliminary observation. It follows that without the experience of oneself or of others in the direction of observing and remembering particular facts, objects, persons and things, we cannot hope to acquire the preliminary facts for the generalization and inductive inference necessary in Inductive Reasoning. It is necessary for us to form a variety of clear Concepts or ideas of facts, objects, persons and things, before we may hope to generalize from these particulars. In the chapters of this book devoted to the consideration of Concepts, we may see the fundamental importance of the formation and acquirement of correct Concepts. Concepts are the fundamental material for correct reasoning. In order to produce a perfect finished product, we must have perfect materials, and a sufficient quantity of them. The greater the knowledge one possesses of the facts and objects of the outside world, the better able is he to reason therefrom. Concepts are the raw material which must feed the machinery of reasoning, and from which the final product of perfected thought is produced. As Halleck says: "There must first be a presentation of materials. Suppose that we wish to form the concept fruit. We must first perceive the different kinds of fruit—cherry, pear, quince, plum, currant, apple, fig, orange, etc. Before we can take the next step, we must be able to form distinct and accurate images of the various kinds of fruit. If the concept is to be absolutely accurate, not one kind of fruit must be overlooked. Practically this is impossible; but many kinds should be examined. Where perception is inaccurate and stinted, the products of thought cannot be trustworthy. No building is firm if reared on insecure foundations."

In the process of Preliminary Observation, we find that there are two ways of obtaining a knowledge of the facts and things around us. These two ways are as follows:

I. By Simple Observation, or the perception of the happenings which are manifested without our interference. In this way we perceive the motion of the tides; the movement of the planets; the phenomena of the weather; the passing of animals, etc.

II. By the Observation of Experiment, or the perception of happenings in which we interfere with things and then observe the result. An experiment is: "A trial, proof, or test of anything; an act, operation, or process designed to discover some unknown truth, principle or effect, or to test some received or reputed truth or principle." Hobbes says: "To have had many experiments is what we call experience." Jevons says: "Experimentation is observation with something more; namely, regulation of the things whose behavior is to be observed. The advantages of experiment over mere observation are of two kinds. In the first place, we shall generally know much more certainly and accurately with what we are dealing, when we make experiments than when we simply observe natural events. . . . It is a further advantage of artificial experiments, that they enable us to discover entirely new substances and to learn their properties. . . . It would be a mistake to suppose that the making of an experiment is inductive reasoning, and gives us without further trouble the laws of nature. Experiments only give us the facts upon which we may afterward reason. . . . Experiments then merely give facts, and it is only by careful reasoning that we can learn when the same facts will be observed again. The general rule is that the same causes will produce the same effects. Whatever happens in one case will happen in all like cases, provided that they are really like, and not merely apparently so. . . . When we have by repeated experiments tried the effect which all the surrounding things might have on the result, we can then reason with much confidence as to similar results in similar circumstances. . . . In order that we may, from our observations and experiments, learn the law of nature and become able to foresee the future, we must perform the process of generalization. To generalize is to draw a general law from particular cases, and to infer that what we see to be true of a few things is true of the whole genus or class to which these things belong. It requires much judgment and skill to generalize correctly, because everything depends upon the number and character of the instances about which we reason."

Having seen that the first step in Inductive Reasoning is Preliminary Observation, let us now consider the next steps in which we may see what we do with the facts and ideas which we have acquired by this Observation and Experiment.

13

Theory and Hypotheses

Following Jevons' classification, we find that the Second Step in Inductive Reasoning is that called "The Making of Hypotheses."

A Hypothesis is: "A supposition, proposition or principle assumed or taken for granted in order to draw a conclusion or inference in proof of the point or question; a proposition assumed or taken for granted, though not proved, for the purpose of deducing proof of a point in question." It will be seen that a Hypothesis is merely held to be possibly or probably true, and not certainly true; it is in the nature of a working assumption, whose truth must be tested by observed facts. The assumption may apply either to the cause of things, or to the laws which govern things. Akin to a hypothesis, and by many people confused in meaning with the latter, is what is called a Theory.

A Theory is: "A verified hypothesis; a hypothesis which has been established as, apparently, the true one." An authority says "Theory is a stronger word than hypothesis. A theory is founded on principles which have been established on independent evidence. A hypothesis merely assumes the operation of a cause which would account for the phenomena, but has not evidence that such cause was actually at work. Metaphysically, a theory is nothing but a hypothesis supported by a large amount of probable evidence." Brooks says: "When a hypothesis is shown to explain all the facts that are known, these facts being varied and extensive, it is said to be verified, and becomes a theory. Thus we have the theory of universal gravitation, the Copernican theory of the solar system, the undulatory theory of light, etc., all of which were originally mere hypotheses. This is the manner in which the term is usually employed in the inductive philosophy; though it must be admitted that it is not always used in this strict sense. Discarded hypotheses are often referred to as theories; and that which is actually a theory is sometimes called a hypothesis."

The steps by which we build up a hypothesis are numerous and varied. In the first place we may erect a hypothesis by the methods of what we have described as Perfect Induction, or Logical Induction. In this case we proceed by simple generalization or simple enumeration. The example of the freckled, red-haired children of Brown, mentioned in a previous chapter, explains this method. It requires the examination and knowledge of every object or fact of which the statement or hypothesis is made. Hamilton states that it is the only induction which is absolutely necessitated by the laws of thought. It does not extend further than the plane of experience. It is akin to mathematical reasoning.

Far more important is the process by which hypotheses are erected by means of inferences from Imperfect Induction, by which we reason from the known to the unknown, transcending experience, and making true inductive inferences from the axiom of Inductive Reasoning. This process involves the subject of Causes. Jevons says: "The cause of an event is that antecedent, or set of antecedents, from which the event always follows. People often make much difficulty about understanding what the cause of an event means, but it really means nothing beyond the things that must exist before in order that the event shall happen afterward."

Causes are often obscure and difficult to determine. The following five difficulties are likely to arise: I. The cause may be out of our experience, and is therefore not to be understood; II. Causes often act conjointly, so that it is difficult to discover the one predominant cause by reason of its associated causes; III. Often the presence of a counteracting, or modifying cause may confuse us; IV. Often a certain effect may be caused by either of several possible causes; V. That which appears as a cause of a certain effect may be but a co-effect of an original cause.

Mill formulated several tests for ascertaining the causal agency in particular cases, in view of the above-stated difficulties. These tests are as follows: (1) The Method of Agreement; (2) The Method of Difference; (3) The Method of Residues; and (4) The Method of Concomitant Variations. The following definitions of these various tests are given by Atwater as follows:

Method of Agreement: "If, whenever a given object or agency is present without counteracting forces, a given effect is produced, there is a strong evidence that the object or agency is the cause of the effect."

Method of Difference: "If, when the supposed cause is present the effect is present, and when the supposed cause is absent the effect is wanting, there being in neither case any other agents present to effect the result, we may reasonably infer that the supposed cause is the real one."

Method of Residue: "When in any phenomena we find a result remaining after the effects of all known causes are estimated, we may attribute it to a residual agent not yet reckoned."

Method of Concomitant Variations: "When a variation in a given antecedent is accompanied by a variation of a given consequent, they are in some manner related as cause and effect."

Atwater adds: "Whenever either of these criteria is found free from conflicting evidence, and especially when several of them concur, the evidence is clear that the cases observed are fair representatives of the whole class, and warrant a valid inductive conclusion."

Jevons gives us the following valuable rules:

I. "Whenever we can alter the quantity of the things experimented on, we can apply a rule for discovering which are causes and which are effects, as follows: We must vary the quantity of one thing, making it at one time greater and at another time less, and if we observe any other thing which varies just at the same times, it will in all probability be an effect."

II. "When things vary regularly and frequently, there is a simple rule, by following which we can judge whether changes are connected together as causes and effects, as follows: Those things which change in exactly equal times are in all likelihood connected together."

III. "It is very difficult to explain how it is that we can ever reason from one thing to a class of things by generalization, when we cannot be sure that the things resemble each other in the important points. . . . Upon what grounds do we argue? We have to get a general law from particular facts. This can only be done by going through all the steps of inductive reasoning. Having made certain observations, we must frame hypotheses as to the circumstances, or laws from which they proceed. Then we must reason deductively; and after verifying the deductions in as many cases as possible, we shall know how far we can trust similar deductions concerning future events. . . . It is difficult to judge when we may, and when we may not, safely infer from some things to others in this simple way, without making a complete theory of the matter. The only rule that can be given to assist us is that if things resemble each other in a few properties only, we must observe many instances before inferring that these properties will always be joined together in other cases."

14

Making and Testing Hypotheses

The older philosophers and logicians were often at a loss how to reasonably account for the origin of hypotheses. It will be seen, after giving the matter a little thought, that the actual formation of the hypothesis is more than a mere grouping together or synthesis of facts or ideas—there is another mental process which actually evolves the hypothesis or theory—which gives a possible reason. What is this mental process? Let us consider the matter. Brooks well says: "The hypotheses of science originate in what is called anticipation. They are not the result of a mere synthesis of facts, for no combination of facts can give the law or cause. We do not see the law; we see the facts and the mind thinks the law. By the power of anticipation, the mind often leaps from a few facts to the cause which produces them or the law which governs them. Many hypotheses were but a happy intuition of the mind. They were the result of what La Place calls 'a great guess,' or what Plato so beautifully designates as 'a sacred suspicion of truth.' The forming of hypotheses requires a suggestive mind, a lively fancy, a philosophic imagination, that catches a glimpse of the idea through the form, or sees the law standing behind the fact."

The student of The New Psychology sees in the mental operation of the forming of the hypothesis—"the mind thinking the law"—but an instance of the operation of the activities of the Subconscious Mind, or even the Super-conscious Mind. (See the volume on the Subconscious Mind in this series.) Not only does this hypothesis give the explanation which the old psychology has failed to do, but it agrees with the ideas of others on the subject as stated in the above quotation from Brooks; and moreover agrees with many recorded instances of the formation of great hypotheses. Sir Wm. Hamilton discovered the very important mathematical law of quaternions while walking one day in the Dublin Observatory. He had pondered long on the subject, but without result. But, finally, on that eventful day he suddenly "felt the galvanic circle of

thought" close, and the result was the realization of the fundamental mathematical relations of the problem. Berthelot, the founder of Synthetic Chemistry,
has testified that the celebrated experiments which led to his remarkable discoveries were seldom the result of carefully followed lines of conscious thought or
pure reasoning processes; but, instead, came to him "of their own accord," so
to speak, "as from a clear sky." In these and many other similar instances, the
mental operation was undoubtedly purely subjective and subconscious. Dr. Hud-
son has claimed that the "Subjective Mind" cannot reason inductively, and that
its operations are purely and distinctly deductive, but the testimony of many
eminent scientists, inventors and philosophers is directly to the contrary.

In this connection the following quotation from Thomson is interesting:
"The system of anatomy which has immortalized the name of Oken is the
consequence of a flash of anticipation which glanced through his mind when
he picked up in a chance walk the skull of a deer, bleached and disintegrated
by the weather, and exclaimed after a glance, 'It is part of a vertebral column!'
When Newton saw the apple fall, the anticipatory question flashed through his
mind, 'Why do not the heavenly bodies fall like this apple?' In neither case had
accident any important share; Newton and Oken were prepared by the deepest
previous study to seize upon the unimportant fact offered to them, and to show
how important it might become; and if the apple and the deer-skull had been
wanting, some other falling body, or some other skull, would have touched the
string so ready to vibrate. But in each case there was a great step of anticipation;
Oken thought he saw a type of the whole skeleton in a single vertebra, while
Newton conceived at once that the whole universe was full of bodies tending
to fall. . . . The discovery of Goethe, which did for the vegetable kingdom what
Oken did for the animal, that the parts of a plant are to be regarded as meta-
morphosed leaves, is an apparent exception to the necessity of discipline for
invention, since it was the discovery of a poet in a region to which he seemed
to have paid no especial or laborious attention. But Goethe was himself most
anxious to rest the basis of this discovery upon his observation rather than his
imagination, and doubtless with good reason. . . . As with other great discoveries, hints had been given already, though not pursued, both of Goethe's and
Oken's principles. Goethe left his to be followed up by others, and but for his
great fame, perhaps his name would never have been connected with it. Oken
had amassed all the materials necessary for the establishment of his theory; he
was able at once to discover and conquer the new territory."

It must not be supposed, however, that all hypotheses flashing into the field
of consciousness from the Subconsciousness, are necessarily true or correct. On
the contrary many of them are incorrect, or at least only partially correct. The

Subconsciousness is not infallible or omniscient—it merely produces results according to the material furnished it. But even these faulty hypotheses are often of value in the later formation of a correct one. As Whewell says: "To try wrong guesses is with most persons the only way to hit upon right ones." Kepler is said to have erected at least twenty hypotheses regarding the shape of the earth's orbit before he finally evolved the correct one. As Brooks says: "Even incorrect hypotheses may be of use in scientific research, since they may lead to more correct suppositions." The supposition of the circular motions of the heavenly bodies around the earth as a center, which lead to the conception of epicycles, etc., and at last to the true theory is an illustration of this. So the 'theory of phlogiston' in chemistry, made many facts intelligible, before the true one of 'oxidation' superseded it. And so, as Thomson says, "with the theory that 'Nature abhors a vacuum,' which served to bring together so many cognate facts not previously considered as related. Even an incorrect conception of this kind has its place in science, so long as it is applicable to the facts; when facts occur which it cannot explain, we either correct it or replace it with a new one. The pathway of science, some one remarks, is strewn with the remains of discarded hypotheses."

Halleck says regarding the danger of hasty inference: "Men must constantly employ imperfect induction in order to advance; but great dangers attend inductive inferences made from too narrow experience. A child has experience with one or two dogs at his home. Because of their gentleness, he argues that all dogs are gentle. He does not, perhaps, find out the contrary until he has been severely bitten. His induction was too hasty. He had not tested a sufficiently large number of dogs to form such a conclusion. From one or two experiences with a large crop in a certain latitude, a farmer may argue that the crop will generally be profitable, whereas it may not again prove so for years. A man may have trusted a number of people and found them honest. He concludes that people as a rule are honest, trusts a certain dishonest man, and is ruined. The older people grow, the more cautious they generally become in forming inductive conclusions. Many instances are noted and compared; but even the wisest sometimes make mistakes. It once was a generally accepted fact that all swans were white. Nobody had ever seen a dark swan, and the inference that all swans were white was regarded as certainly true. Black swans were, however, found in Australia."

Brooks says regarding the probability of hypotheses: "The probability of a hypothesis is in proportion to the number of facts and phenomena it will explain. The larger the number of facts and phenomena that it will satisfactorily account for, the greater our faith in the correctness of our supposition. . . . If there is more than one hypothesis in respect to the facts under consideration, that one which accounts for the greatest number of facts is the most probable. . . . In order to verify a hypothesis it must be shown that it will account for all the facts and phenomena. If these facts are numerous and varied, and the subject is so thoroughly investigated that it is quite certain that no important class of facts has been overlooked, the supposition is regarded as true, and the hypothesis is said to be verified. Thus the hypothesis of the 'daily rotation' of the earth on its axis to account for the succession of day and night is accepted as absolutely true. This is the view taken by Dr. Whewell and many other thinkers in respect to the verification of a hypothesis. Some writers, however, as Mill and his school, maintain that in order to verify a hypothesis, we must show not only that it explains all the facts and phenomena, but that there is no other possible hypothesis which will account for them. . . . The former view of verification is regarded as the correct one. By the latter view, it is evident that a hypothesis could never be verified."

Jevons says: "In the fourth step (verification), we proceed to compare these deductions with the facts already collected, or when necessary and practicable, we make new observations and plan new experiments, so as to find out whether the hypothesis agrees with nature. If we meet with several distinct disagreements between our deductions and our observations, it will become likely that the hypothesis is wrong, and we must then invent a new one. In order to produce agreement it will sometimes be enough to change the hypothesis in a small degree. When we get hold of a hypothesis which seems to give results agreeing with a few facts, we must not at once assume that it is certainly correct. We must go on making other deductions from it under various circumstances, and, whenever it is possible, we ought to verify these results, that is, compare them with facts observed through the senses. When a hypothesis is shown in this way to be true in a great many of its results, especially when it enables us to predict what we should never otherwise have believed or discovered, it becomes certain that the hypothesis itself is a true one. . . . Sometimes it will happen that two or even three quite different hypotheses all seem to agree with certain facts, so that we are puzzled which to select. . . . When there are thus two hypotheses, one as good as the other, we need to discover some fact or thing which will agree with one hypothesis and not with the other, because this immediately enables us to decide that the former hypothesis is true and the latter false."

In the above statements regarding the verification of hypotheses we see references made to the testing of the latter upon the "facts" of the case. These facts may be either the observed phenomena or facts apparent to the perception, or else facts obtained by deductive reasoning. The latter may be said to be facts which are held to be true if the hypothesis be true. Thus if we erect the hypothesis that "All men are mortal," we may reason deductively that it will follow that each and every thing that is a man must die sooner or later. Then we test our hypotheses upon each and every man whom we may subject to observation and experiment. If we find a single man who does not die, then the test disproves our hypotheses; if on the contrary all men (the "facts" in the case) prove to be mortal, then is our hypotheses proven or established. The deductive reasoning in this case is as follows: "If so-and-so is true regarding such-and-such a class; and if this particular thing belongs to that class; then it will follow that so-and-so is true regarding this particular thing." This argument is expressed in what is called a Hypothetical Proposition (see Chapter 9), the consideration of which forms a part of the general subject of Deductive Reasoning. Therefore as Jevons has said, "Deductive Reasoning is the Third Step in Inductive Reasoning, and precedes Verification," which we have already considered. Halleck says: "After Induction has classified certain phenomena and thus given us a major premise, we may proceed deductively to apply the inference to any new specimen that can be shown to belong to that class. Induction hands over to deduction a ready-made major premise. . . . Deduction takes that as a fact, making no inquiry about its truth. . . . Only after general laws have been laid down, after objects have been classified, after major premises have been formed, can deduction be employed."

In view of the above facts, we shall now proceed to a consideration of that great class of Reasoning known under the term—Deductive Reasoning.

15

Deductive Reasoning

We have seen that there are two great classes of reasoning, known respectively, as (1) Inductive Reasoning, or the discovery of general truth from particular truths; and (2) Deductive Reasoning, or the discovery of particular truths from general truths.

As we have said, Deductive Reasoning is the process of discovering particular truths from a general truth. Thus from the general truth embodied in the proposition "All horses are animals," when it is considered in connection with the secondary proposition that "Dobbin is a horse," we are able to deduce the particular truth that: "Dobbin is an animal." Or, in the following case we deduce a particular truth from a general truth, as follows: "All mushrooms are good to eat; this fungus is a mushroom; therefore, this fungus is good to eat." A deductive argument is expressed in a deductive syllogism.

Jevons says regarding the last stated illustration: "Here are three sentences which state three different facts; but when we know the two first facts, we learn or gather the third fact from the other two. When we thus learn one fact from other facts, we infer or reason, and we do this in the mind. Reasoning thus enables us to ascertain the nature of a thing without actual trial. If we always needed to taste a thing before we could know whether it was good to eat or not, cases of poisoning would be alarmingly frequent. But the appearance and peculiarities of a mushroom may be safely learned by the eye or the nose, and reasoning upon this information and the fact already well known, that mushrooms are good to eat, we arrive without any danger or trouble at the conclusion that the particular fungus before us is good to eat. To reason, then, is to get some knowledge from other knowledge."

The student will recognize that Deductive Reasoning is essentially an analytic process, because it operates in the direction of analyzing a universal or general truth into its particulars—into the particular parts which are included within it—and asserting of them that "what is true of the general is true of the particular." Thus in the general truth that "All men are mortal," we see included the particular truth that "John Smith is mortal"—John Smith having been discovered to be a man. We deduce the particular truth about John Smith from the general truth about "all men." We analyze "all men" and find John Smith to be one of its particular parts. Therefore, "Deduction is an inference from the whole to its parts; that is, an analytic process."

The student will also recognize that Deductive Reasoning is essentially a descending process, because it operates in the direction of a descent from the universal to the particular; from the higher to the lower; from the broader to the narrower. As Brooks says: "Deduction descends from higher truths to lower truths, from laws to facts, from causes to phenomena, etc. Given the law, we can by deduction descend to the facts that fall under the law, even if we have never before seen the facts; and so from the cause we may pass down to observed and even unknown phenomena."

The general truths which are used as the basis of Deductive Reasoning are discovered in several ways. The majority arise from Inductive Reasoning, based upon experience, observation and experiment. For instance in the examples given above, we could not truthfully assert our belief that: "All horses are animals" unless we had previously studied both the horse and animals in general. Nor without this study could we state that "Dobbin is a horse." Nor could we, without previous study, experience and experiment truthfully assert that: "All mushrooms are good to eat;" or that "this fungus is a mushroom;" and that "therefore, this fungus is good to eat." Even as it is, we must be sure that the fungus really is a mushroom, else we run a risk of poisoning ourselves. General truths of this kind are not intuitive, by any means, but are based upon our own experience or the experience of others.

There is a class of general truths which are called intuitive by some authorities. Halleck says of these: "Some psychologists claim that we have knowledge obtained neither through induction nor deduction; that we recognize certain truths the moment we perceive certain objects, without any process of inference. Under the head of intuitive knowledge are classified such cases as the following: We perceive an object and immediately know that it is a time relation, as existing now and then. We are said to have an intuitive concept of time. When we are told that the whole is greater than a part; that things equal to the same thing are equal to each other; that a straight line cannot enclose space, we immediately, or intuitively, recognize the truth of these statements. Attempts at proof do not make us feel surer of their truth. . . . We say that it is self-evident, or that we know the fact intuitively. The axioms of mathematics and logic are said to be intuitive."

Another class of authorities, however, deny the nature of intuitive knowledge of truth, or intuitive truths. They claim that all our ideas arise from sensation and reflection, and that what we call "intuition" is merely the result of sensation and reflection reproduced by memory or heredity. They hold that the intuitions of animals and men are simply the representation of experiences of the race, or individual, arising from the impressions stored away in the subconsciousness of the individual. Halleck states regarding this: "This school likens intuition to instinct. It grants that the young duck knows water instinctively, plunges into it, and swims without learning. These psychologists believe that there was a time when this was not the case with the progenitors of the duck. They had to gain this knowledge slowly through experience. Those that learned the proper aquatic lesson survived and transmitted this knowledge through a modified structure, to their progeny. Those that failed in the lesson perished in the struggle for existence. . . . This school claims that the intuition of cause and effect arose in the same way. Generations of human beings have seen the cause invariably joined to the effect; hence, through inseparable association came the recognition of their necessary sequence. The tendency to regard all phenomena in these relations was with steadily increasing force transmitted by the laws of heredity to posterity, until the recognition of the relationship has become an intuition."

Another class of general truths is merely hypothetical. Hypothetical means "Founded on or including a hypothesis or supposition; assumed or taken for granted, though not proved, for the purpose of deducing proofs of a point in question." The hypotheses and theories of physical science are used as general truths for deductive reasoning. Hypothetical general truths are in the nature of premises assumed in order to proceed with the process of Deductive Reasoning, and without which such reasoning would be impossible. They are, however, as a rule not mere assumptions, but are rather in the nature of assumptions rendered plausible by experience, experiment and Inductive Reasoning. The Law of Gravitation may be considered hypothetical, and yet it is the result of Inductive Reasoning based upon a vast multitude of facts and phenomena.

The Primary Basis of Deductive Reasoning may be said to rest upon the logical axiom, which has come down to us from the ancients, and which is stated as follows: "Whatever is true of the whole is true of its parts." Or, as later authorities have expressed it: "Whatever is true of the general is true of the particular." This axiom is the basis upon which we build our Deductive Reasoning. It furnishes us with the validity of the deductive inference or argument. If we are challenged for proof of the statement that "This fungus is good to eat," we are able to answer that we are justified in making the statement by the self-evident proposition, or axiom, that "Whatever is true of the general is true of the particular." If the general "mushroom" is good to eat, then the particular, "this fungus" being a mushroom, must also be good to eat. All horses (general) being animals, then according to the axiom, Dobbin (particular horse) must also be an animal.

This axiom has been stated in various terms other than those stated above. For instance: "Whatever may be affirmed or denied of the whole, may be denied or affirmed of the parts;" which form is evidently derived from that used by Hamilton who said: "What belongs, or does not belong, to the containing whole, belongs or does not belong, to each of the contained parts." Aristotle formulated his celebrated Dictum as follows: "Whatever can be predicated affirmatively or negatively of any class or term distributed, can be predicated in like manner of all and singular the classes or individuals contained under it."

There is another form of Deductive Reasoning, that is a form based upon another axiom than that of: "Whatever is true of the whole is true of the parts." This form of reasoning is sometimes called Mathematical Reasoning, because it is the form of reasoning employed in mathematics. Its axiom is stated as follows: "Things which are equal to the same thing, are equal to one another." It will be seen that this is the principle employed in mathematics. Thus: "x equals y; and y equals 5; therefore, x equals 5." Or stated in logical terms: "A equals B; B equals C; therefore, A equals C." Thus it is seen that this form of reasoning, as well as the ordinary form of Deductive Reasoning, is strictly mediate, that is, made through the medium of a third thing, or "two things being compared through their relation to a third."

Brooks states: "The real reason for the certainty of mathematical reasoning may be stated as follows: First, its ideas are definite, necessary, and exact conceptions of quantity. Second, its definitions, as the description of these ideas are necessary, exact, and indisputable truths. Third, the axioms from which we derive conclusions by comparison are all self-evident and necessary truths. Comparing these exact ideas by the necessary laws of inference, the result must be absolutely true. Or, stated in another way, using these definitions and axioms as the premises of a syllogism, the conclusion follows inevitably. There is no place or opportunity for error to creep in to mar or vitiate our derived truths."

In conclusion, we wish to call your attention to a passage from Jevons which is worthy of consideration and recollection. Jevons says: "There is a simple rule which will enable us to test the truth of a great many arguments, even of many which do not come under any of the rules commonly given in books on logic. This rule is that whatever is true of one term is true of any term which is stated to be the same in meaning as that term. In other words, we may always substitute one term for another if we know that they refer to exactly the same thing. There is no doubt that a horse is some animal, and therefore the head of a horse is the head of some animal. This argument cannot be brought under the rules of the syllogism, because it contains four distinct logical terms in two propositions; namely, horse, some animal; head of horse, head of some animal. But it easily comes under the rule which I have given, because we have simply to put 'some animal' instead of 'a horse.' A great many arguments may be explained in this way. Gold is a metal; therefore a piece of gold is a piece of metal."

The same eminent authority says: "When we examine carefully enough the way in which we reason, it will be found in every case to consist in putting one thing or term in place of another, to which we know it to have an exact resemblance in some respect. We use the likeness as a kind of bridge, which leads us from a knowledge of one thing to a knowledge of another; thus the true principle of reasoning may be called the substitution of similars, or the passing from like to like. We infer the character of one thing from the character of something which acts as a go-between, or third term. When we are certain there is an exact likeness, our inference is certain; when we only believe that there probably is, or guess that there is, then our inferences are only probable, not certain."

16

The Syllogism

The third and highest phase or step in reasoning—the step which follows after those styled Conception and Judgment—is generally known by the general term "Reasoning," which term, however, is used to include the two precedent steps as well as the final step itself. This step or process consists of the comparing of two objects, persons or things, through their relation to a third object, person or thing. As, for instance, we reason (a) that all mammals are animals; (b) that a horse is a mammal; and (c) that, therefore, a horse is an animal. The most fundamental principle of this step or reasoning consists in the comparing of two objects of thought through and by means of their relation to a third object. The natural form of expression of this process of reasoning is called a "Syllogism."

The process of reasoning which gives rise to the expression of the argument in the form of a Syllogism must be understood if one wishes to form a clear conception of the Syllogism. The process itself is very simple when plainly stated, although the beginner is sometimes puzzled by the complicated definitions and statements of the authorities. Let us suppose that we have three objects, A, B and C, respectively. We wish to compare C and B, but fail to establish a relation between them at first. We however are able to establish a relation between A and B; and between C and A. We thus have the two propositions (1) "A equals B; and (2) C equals A." The next step is that of inferring that "if A equals B, and C equals A, then it must follow, logically, that C equals B." This process is that of indirect or mediate comparison, rather than immediate. C and B are not compared directly or immediately, but indirectly and through the medium of A. A is thus said to mediate between B and C.

This process of reasoning embraces three ideas or objects of thought, in their expression of propositions. It comprises the fundamental or elemental form of reasoning. As Brooks says: "The simplest movement of the reasoning process is the comparing of two objects through their relation to a third." The result of this process is an argument expressed in what is called a Syllogism. Whately says that: "A Syllogism is an argument expressed in strict logical form so that its conclusiveness is manifest from the structure of the expression alone, without any regard to the meaning of the terms." Brooks says: "All reasoning can be and naturally is expressed in the form of the syllogism. It applies to both inductive and deductive reasoning, and is the form in which these processes are presented. Its importance as an instrument of thought requires that it receive special notice."

In order that the nature and use of the Syllogism may be clearly understood, we can do no better than to at once present for your consideration the well-known "Rules of the Syllogism," an understanding of which carries with it a perfect comprehension of the Syllogism itself.

The Rules of the Syllogism state that in order for a Syllogism to be a perfect Syllogism, it is necessary:

I. That there should be three, and no more than three, Propositions. These three propositions are: (1) the Conclusion, or thing to be proved; and (2 and 3) the Premises, or the means of proving the Conclusion, and which are called the Major Premise and Minor Premise, respectively. We may understand this more clearly if we will examine the following example:

Major Premise: "Man is mortal;" (or "A is B").
Minor Premise: "Socrates is a man;" (or "C is A"). Therefore:
Conclusion: "Socrates is mortal" (or "C is B").

It will be seen that the above Syllogism, whether expressed in words or symbols, is logically valid, because the conclusion must logically follow the premises. And, in this case, the premises being true, it must follow that the conclusion is true. Whately says: "A Syllogism is said to be valid when the conclusion logically follows from the premises; if the conclusion does not so follow, the Syllogism is invalid and constitutes a Fallacy, if the error deceives the reasoner himself; but if it is advanced with the idea of deceiving others it constitutes a Sophism."

The reason for Rule I is that only three propositions—a Major Premise, a Minor Premise, and a Conclusion—are needed to form a Syllogism. If we have more than three propositions, then we must have more than two premises from which to draw one conclusion. The presence of more than two premises would result in the formation of two or more Syllogisms, or else in the failure to form a Syllogism.

II. That there should be three and no more than three Terms. These Terms are (1) The Predicate of the Conclusion; (2) the Subject of the Conclusion; and (3) the Middle Term which must occur in both premises, being the connecting link in bringing the two other Terms together in the Conclusion.

The Predicate of the Conclusion is called the Major Term, because it is the greatest in extension compared with its fellow terms. The Subject of the Conclusion is called the Minor Term because it is the smallest in extension compared with its fellow terms. The Major and Minor Terms are called the Extremes. The Middle Term operates between the two Extremes.

The Major Term and the Middle Term must appear in the Major Premise.

The Minor Term and the Middle Term must appear in the Minor Premise.

The Minor Term and the Major Term must appear in the Conclusion.

Thus we see that The Major Term must be the Predicate of the Conclusion; the Minor Term the Subject of the Conclusion; the Middle Term may be the Subject or Predicate of either of the premises, but must always be found once in both premises.

The following example will show this arrangement more clearly:

In the Syllogism: "Man is mortal; Socrates is a man; therefore Socrates is mortal," we have the following arrangement: "Mortal," the Major Term; "Socrates," the Minor Term; and "Man," the Middle Term; as follows:

Major Premise: "Man" (middle term) is mortal (major term).

Minor Premise: "Socrates" (minor term) is a man (major term).

Conclusion: "Socrates" (minor term) is mortal (major term).

The reason for the rule that there shall be "only three" terms is that reasoning consists in comparing two terms with each other through the medium of a third term. There must be three terms; if there are more than three terms, we form two syllogisms instead of one.

III. That one premise, at least, must be affirmative. This, because "from two negative propositions nothing can be inferred." A negative proposition asserts that two things differ, and if we have two propositions so asserting difference, we can infer nothing from them. If our Syllogism stated that: (1) "Man is not mortal;" and (2) that "Socrates is not a man;" we could form no Conclusion, either that Socrates was or was not mortal. There would be no logical connection between the two premises, and therefore no Conclusion could be deduced therefrom. Therefore, at least one premise must be affirmative.

IV. If one premise is negative, the conclusion must be negative. This because "if one term agrees and another disagrees with a third term, they must disagree with each other." Thus if our Syllogism stated that: (1) "Man is not mortal;" and (2) that: "Socrates is a man;" we must announce the Negative Conclusion that: (3) "Socrates is not mortal."

V. That the Middle Term must be distributed; (that is, taken universally) in at least one premise. This "because, otherwise, the Major Term may be compared with one part of the Middle Term, and the Minor Term with another part of the latter; and there will be actually no common Middle Term, and consequently no common ground for an inference." The violation of this rule causes what is commonly known as "The Undistributed Middle," a celebrated Fallacy condemned by the logicians. In the Syllogism mentioned as an example in this chapter, the proposition "Man is mortal," really means "All men," that is, Man in his universal sense. Literally the proposition is "All men are mortal," from which it is seen that Socrates being "a man" (or some of all men) must partake of the quality of the universal Man. If the Syllogism, instead, read: "Some men are mortal," it would not follow that Socrates must be mortal—he might or might not be so. Another form of this fallacy is shown in the statement that (1) White is a color; (2) Black is a color; hence (3) Black must be White. The two premises really mean "White is some color; Black is some color;" and not that either is "all colors." Another example is: "Men are bipeds; birds are bipeds; hence, men are birds." In this example "bipeds" is not distributed as "all bipeds" but is simply not-distributed as "some bipeds." These syllogisms, therefore, not being according to rule, must fail. They are not true syllogisms, and constitute fallacies.

To be "distributed," the Middle Term must be the Subject of a Universal Proposition, or the Predicate of a Negative Proposition; to be "undistributed" it must be the Subject of a Particular Proposition, or the Predicate of an Affirmative Proposition. (See chapter on Propositions.)

VI. That an extreme, if undistributed in a Premise, may not be distributed in the Conclusion. This because it would be illogical and unreasonable to assert more in the conclusion than we find in the premises. It would be most illogical to argue that: (1) "All horses are animals; (2) no man is a horse; therefore (3) no man is an animal." The conclusion would be invalid, because the term animal is distributed in the conclusion, (being the predicate of a negative proposition) while it is not distributed in the premise (being the predicate of an affirmative proposition).

As we have said before, any Syllogism which violates any of the above six syllogisms is invalid and a fallacy.

There are two additional rules which may be called derivative. Any syllogism which violates either of these two derivative rules, also violates one or more of the first six rules as given above in detail.

The Two Derivative Rules of the Syllogism are as follows:

VII. That one Premise at least must be Universal. This because "from two particular premises no conclusion can be drawn."

VIII. That if one premise is Particular, the Conclusion must be particular also. This because only a universal conclusion can be drawn from two universal premises.

The principles involved in these two Derivative Rules may be tested by stating Syllogisms violating them. They contain the essence of the other rules, and every syllogism which breaks them will be found to also break one or more of the other rules given.

17

Varieties of Syllogisms

The authorities in Logic hold that with the four kinds of propositions grouped in every possible order of arrangement, it is possible to form nineteen different kinds of valid arguments, which are called the nineteen moods of the syllogism. These are classified by division into what are called the four figures, each of which figures may be known by the position of the middle term in the premises. Logicians have arranged elaborate and curious tables constructed to show what kinds of propositions when joined in a particular order of arrangement will make sound and valid syllogisms. We shall not set forth these tables here, as they are too technical for a popular presentation of the subject before us, and because they are not necessary to the student who will thoroughly familiarize himself with the above stated Laws of the Syllogism and who will therefore be able to determine in every case whether any given argument is a correct syllogism, or otherwise.

In many instances of ordinary thought and expression the complete syllogistic form is omitted, or not stated at full length. It is common usage to omit one premise of a syllogism, in ordinary expression, the missing premise being inferred by the speaker and hearer. A syllogism with one premise unexpressed is sometimes called an Enthymene, the term meaning "in the mind." For instance, the following: "We are a free people, therefore we are happy," the major premise "All free people are happy" being omitted or unexpressed. Also in "Poets are imaginative, therefore Byron was imaginative," the minor premise "Byron was a poet" is omitted or unexpressed. Jevons says regarding this phase of the subject: "Thus in the Sermon on the Mount, the verses known as the Beatitudes consist each of one premise and a conclusion, and the conclusion is put first. 'Blessed are the merciful: for they shall obtain mercy.' The subject and the predicate of the conclusion are here inverted, so that the proposition is really 'The merciful are blessed.' It is evidently understood that 'All who shall obtain mercy are blessed,' so that the syllogism, when stated at full length, becomes: 'All who shall obtain mercy are blessed; All who are merciful shall obtain mercy; Therefore, all who are merciful are blessed.' This is a perfectly good syllogism."

Whenever we find any of the words: "because, for, therefore, since," or similar terms, we may know that there is an argument, and usually a syllogism.

We have seen that there are three special kinds of Propositions, namely, (1) Categorical Propositions, or propositions in which the affirmation or denial is made without reservation or qualification; (2) Hypothetical Propositions, in which the affirmation or denial is made to depend upon certain conditions, circumstances, or suppositions; and (3) Disjunctive Propositions, in which is implied or asserted an alternative.

The forms of reasoning based upon these three several classes of propositions bear the same names as the latter. And, accordingly the respective syllogisms expressing these forms of reasoning also bear the class name or term. Thus, a Categorical Syllogism is one containing only categorical propositions; a Hypothetical Syllogism is one containing one or more hypothetical propositions; a Disjunctive Syllogism is one containing a disjunctive proposition in the major premise.

Categorical Syllogisms, which are far more common than the other two kinds, have been considered in the previous chapter, and the majority of the examples of syllogisms given in this book are of this kind. In a Categorical Syllogism the statement or denial is made positively, and without reservation or qualification, and the reasoning thereupon partakes of the same positive character. In propositions or syllogisms of this kind it is asserted or assumed that the premise is true and correct, and, if the reasoning be logically correct it must follow that the conclusion is correct, and the new proposition springing therefrom must likewise be Categorical in its nature.

Hypothetical Syllogisms, on the contrary, have as one or more of their premises a hypothetical proposition which affirms or asserts something provided, or "if," something else be true. Hyslop says of this: "Often we wish first to bring out, if only conditionally, the truth upon which a proposition rests, so as to see if the connection between this conclusion and the major premise be admitted. The whole question will then depend upon the matter of treating the minor premise. This has the advantage of getting the major premise admitted without the formal procedure of proof, and the minor premise is usually more easily proved than the major. Consequently, one is made to see more clearly the force of the argument or reasoning by removing the question of the material truth of the major premise and concentrating attention upon the relation between the conclusion and its conditions, so that we know clearly what we have first to deny if we do not wish to accept it."

By joining a hypothetical proposition with an ordinary proposition we create a Hypothetical Proposition. For instance: "If York contains a cathedral it is a city; York does contain a cathedral; therefore, York is a city." Or: "If dogs have four feet, they are quadrupeds; dogs do have four feet; therefore dogs are quadrupeds." The Hypothetical Syllogism may be either affirmative or negative; that is, its hypothetical proposition may either hypothetically affirm or hypothetically deny. The part of the premise of a Hypothetical Syllogism which conditions or questions (and which usually contains the little word "if") is called the Antecedent. The major premise is the one usually thus conditioned. The other part of the conditioned proposition, and which part states what will happen or is true under the conditional circumstances, is called the Consequent. Thus, in one of the above examples: "If dogs have four feet" is the Antecedent; and the remainder of the proposition: "they are quadrupeds" is the Consequent. The Antecedent is indicated by the presence of some conditional term as: if, supposing, granted that, provided that, although, had, were, etc., the general sense and meaning of such terms being that of the little word "if." The Consequent has no special indicating term.

Jevons gives the following clear and simple Rules regarding the Hypothetical Syllogism:

I. "If the Antecedent be affirmed, the consequent may be affirmed. If the Consequent be denied, the Antecedent may be denied."

II. "Avoid the fallacy of affirming the consequent, or denying the antecedent. This is a fallacy because of the fact that the conditional statement made in the major premise may not be the only one determining the consequent." The following is an example of "Affirming the Consequent:" "If it is raining, the sky is overclouded; the sky is overclouded; therefore, it is raining." In truth, the sky may be overclouded, and still it may not be raining. The fallacy is still more apparent when expressed in symbols, as follows: "If A is B, C is D; C is D; therefore, A is B." The fallacy of denying the Antecedent is shown by the following example: "If Radium were cheap it would be useful; Radium is not cheap; therefore Radium is not useful." Or, expressed in symbols: "If A is B, C is D; A is not B; therefore C is not D." In truth Radium may be useful although not cheap. Jevons gives the following examples of these fallacies: "If a man is a good teacher, he thoroughly understands his subject; but John Jones thoroughly understands his subject; therefore, he is a good teacher." Also, "If snow is mixed with salt it melts; the snow on the ground is not mixed with salt; therefore it does not melt."

Jevons says: "To affirm the consequent and then to infer that we can affirm the antecedent, is as bad as breaking the third rule of the syllogism, and allowing an undistributed middle term. . . . To deny the antecedent is really to break the fourth rule of the syllogism, and to take a term as distributed in the conclusion which was not so in the premises."

Hypothetical Syllogisms may usually be easily reduced to or converted into Categorical Syllogisms. As Jevons says: "In reality, hypothetical propositions and syllogisms are not different from those which we have more fully considered. It is all a matter of the convenience of stating the propositions." For instance, instead of saying: "If Radium were cheap, it would be useful," we may say "Cheap Radium would be useful;" or instead of saying: "If glass is thin, it breaks easily," we may say "Thin glass breaks easily." Hyslop gives the following Rule for Conversion in such cases: "Regard the antecedent of the hypothetical proposition as the subject of the categorical, and the consequent of the hypothetical proposition as the predicate of the categorical. In some cases this change is a very simple one; in others it can be effected only by a circumlocution."

The third class of syllogisms, known as The Disjunctive Syllogism, is the exception to the law which holds that all good syllogisms must fit in and come under the Rules of the Syllogism, as stated in the preceding chapter. Not only does it refuse to obey these Rules, but it fails to resemble the ordinary syllogism in many ways. As Jevons says: "It would be a great mistake to suppose that all good logical arguments must obey the rules of the syllogism, which we have been considering. Only those arguments which connect two terms together by means of a middle term, and are therefore syllogisms, need obey these rules. A great many of the arguments which we daily use are of this nature; but there are a great many other kinds of arguments, some of which have never been understood by logicians until recent years. One important kind of argument is known as the Disjunctive Syllogism, though it does not obey the rules of the syllogism, or in any way resemble syllogisms."

The Disjunctive Syllogism is one having a disjunctive proposition in its major premise. The disjunctive proposition also appears in the conclusion when the disjunction in the major premise happens to contain more than two terms. A disjunctive proposition, we have seen, is one which possesses alternative predicates for the subject in which the conjunction "or" (sometimes accompanied by "either") appears. As for instance: "Lightning is sheet or forked"; or, "Arches are either round or pointed;" or, "Angles are either obtuse, or right angled, or acute." The different things joined together by "or" are called Alternatives, the term indicating that we may choose between the things, and that if one will not answer our purpose we may take the other, or one of the others if there be more than one other.

The Rule regarding the Use of Disjunctive Syllogisms is that: "If one or more alternatives be denied, the rest may still be affirmed." Thus if we say that "A is B or C," or that "A is either B or C," we may deny the B but still affirm the C. Some authorities also hold that "If we affirm one alternative, we must deny the remainder," but this view is vigorously disputed by other authorities. It would seem to be a valid rule in cases where the term "either" appears as: "A is either B or C," because there seems to be an implication that one or the other alone can be true. But in cases like: "A is B or C," there may be a possibility of both being true. Jevons takes this latter view, giving as an example the proposition: "A Magistrate is a Justice-of-the-Peace, a Mayor, or a Stipendiary Magistrate," but it does not follow that one who is a Justice-of-the-Peace may not be at the same time a Mayor. He states: "After affirming one alternative we can only deny the others if there be such a difference between them that they could not be true at the same time." It would seem that both contentions are at the same time true, the example given by Jevons illustrating his contention, and the proposition "The prisoner is either guilty or innocent" illustrating the contentions of the other side.

A Dilemma is a conditional syllogism whose Major Premise presents some sort of alternative. Whately defines it as: "A conditional syllogism with two or more antecedents in the major, and a disjunctive minor." There being two mutually exclusive propositions in the Major Premise, the reasoner is compelled to admit one or the other, and is then caught between "the two horns of the dilemma."

18

Reasoning by Analogy

What is called Reasoning by Analogy is one of the most elementary forms of reasoning, and the one which the majority of us most frequently employ. It is a primitive form of hasty generalization evidencing in the natural expectation that "things will happen as they have happened before in like circumstances." The term as used in logic has been defined as "Resemblance of relations; Resemblances of any kind on which an argument falling short of induction may be founded." Brooks says: "Analogy is that process of thought by which we infer that if two things resemble each other in one or more particulars, they will resemble each other in some other particular."

Jevons states the Rule for Reasoning by Analogy, as follows: "If two or more things resemble each other in many points, they will probably resemble each other also in more points." Others have stated the same principle as follows: "When one thing resembles another in known particulars, it will resemble it also in the unknown;" and "If two things agree in several particulars, they will also agree in other particulars."

There is a difference between generalization by induction, and by analogy. In inductive generalization the rule is: "What is true of the many is true of all"; while the rule of analogy is: "things that have some things in common have other things in common." As Jevons aptly remarks: "Reasoning by Analogy differs only in degree from that kind of reasoning called 'Generalization.' When many things resemble each other in a few properties, we argue about them by Generalization. When a few things resemble each other in many properties, it is a case of analogy." Illustrating Analogy, we may say that if in A we find the qualities, attributes or properties called a, b, c, d, e, f, g, respectively, and if we find that in B the qualities, etc., called a, b, c, d, e, respectively, are present, then we may reason by analogy that the qualities f and g must also belong to B.

Brooks says of this form of reasoning: "This principle is in constant application in ordinary life and in science. A physician, in visiting a patient, says this disease corresponds in several particulars with typhoid fever, hence it will correspond in all particulars, and is typhoid fever. So, when the geologist discovers a fossil animal with large, strong, blunt claws, he infers that it procured its food by scratching or burrowing in the earth. It was by analogy that Dr. Buckland constructed an animal from a few fossil bones, and when subsequently the bones of the entire animal were discovered, his construction was found to be correct." Halleck says: "In argument or reasoning we are much aided by the habit of searching for hidden resemblances. . . . The detection of such a relation cultivates thought. If we are to succeed in argument, we must develop what some call a sixth sense of such relations. . . . The study of poetry may be made very serviceable in detecting analogies and cultivating the reasoning powers. When the poet brings clearly to mind the change due to death, using as an illustration the caterpillar body transformed into the butterfly spirit, moving with winged ease over flowering meadows, he is cultivating our apprehension of relations, none the less valuable because they are beautiful."

But the student must be on guard against the deceptive conclusions sometimes arising from Reasoning by Analogy. As Jevons says: "In many cases Reasoning by Analogy is found to be a very uncertain guide. In some cases unfortunate mistakes are made. Children are sometimes killed by gathering and eating poisonous berries, wrongly inferring that they can be eaten, because other berries, of a somewhat similar appearance, have been found agreeable and harmless. Poisonous toadstools are occasionally mistaken for mushrooms, especially by people not accustomed to gathering them. In Norway mushrooms are seldom seen, and are not eaten; but when I once found a few there and had them cooked at an inn, I was amused by the people of the inn, who went and collected toadstools and wanted me to eat them also. This was clearly a case of mistaken reasoning by analogy. Even brute animals reason in the same way in some degree. The beaten dog fears every stick, and there are few dogs which will not run away when you pretend to pick up a stone, even if there be no stone to pick up." Halleck says: "Many false analogies are manufactured, and it is excellent thought training to expose them. The majority of people think so little that they swallow these false analogies just as newly fledged robins swallow small stones dropped into their open mouths. . . . This tendency to think as others do must be resisted somewhere along the line, or there can be no progress." Brooks says: "The argument from Analogy is plausible, but often deceptive. Thus to infer that since American swans are white, the Australian swan is white, gives a false conclusion, for it is really black. So to infer that because John Smith has a red nose and is a drunkard, then Henry Jones who also has a red nose is also a drunkard, would be a dangerous inference. . . . Conclusions of this kind drawn from analogy are frequently fallacious."

Regarding the Rule for Reasoning from Analogy, Jevons says: "There is no way in which we can really assure ourselves that we are arguing safely by analogy. The only rule that can be given is this; that the more closely two things resemble each other, the more likely it is that they are the same in other respects, especially in points closely connected with those observed. . . . In order to be clear about our conclusions, we ought in fact never to rest satisfied with mere analogy, but ought to try to discover the general laws governing the case. In analogy we seem to reason from one fact to another fact without troubling ourselves either with deduction or induction. But it is only by a kind of guess that we do so; it is not really conclusive reasoning. We ought properly to ascertain what general laws of nature are shown to exist by the facts observed, and then infer what will happen according to these laws. . . . We find that reasoning by analogy is not to be depended upon, unless we make such an inquiry into the causes and laws of the things in question, that we really employ inductive and deductive reasoning."

Along the same lines, Brooks says: "The inference from analogy, like that from induction, should be used with caution. Its conclusion must not be regarded as certain, but merely as reaching a high degree of probability. The inference from a part to a part, no more than from a part to the whole, is attended with any rational necessity. To attain certainty, we must show that the principles which lie at the root of the process are either necessary laws of thought or necessary laws of nature; both of which are impossible. Hence analogy can pretend to only a high degree of probability. It may even reach a large degree of certainty, but it never reaches necessity. We must, therefore, be careful not to accept any inference from analogy as true until it is proved to be true by actual observation and experiment, or by such an application of induction as to remove all reasonable doubt."

19

Fallacies

A Fallacy is: "An unsound argument or mode of arguing, which, while appearing to be decisive of a question, is in reality not so; an argument or proposition apparently sound, but really fallacious; a fallacious statement or proposition, in which the error is not apparent, and which is therefore likely to mislead or deceive; sophistry."

In Deductive Reasoning, we meet with two classes of Fallacies; namely, (1) Fallacious Premise; and (2) Fallacious Conclusion. We shall now consider each of these in turn.

Fallacious Premise is in effect an unwarranted assumption of premises. One of the most common forms of this kind of Fallacy is known as "Begging the Question," the principle of which is the assumption of a fundamental premise which is not conceded; the unwarrantable assumption of that which is to be proved; or the assumption of that by which it is to be proved, without proving it. Its most common form is that of boldly stating some unproven fact, authoritatively and positively, and then proceeding to use the statement as the major premise of the argument, proceeding logically from that point. The hearer perceiving the argument proceeding logically often fails to remember that the premise has been merely assumed, without warrant and without proof and omitting the hypothetical "if." One may proceed to argue logically from the premise that "The moon is made of green cheese," but the whole argument is invalid and fallacious because of the fact that the person making it has "begged the question" upon an unwarranted premise. Hyslop gives a good example of this form of fallacy in the case of the proposition "Church and State should be united." Proof being demanded the advocate proceeds to "beg the question" as follows: "Good institutions should be united; Church and State are good institutions; therefore, Church and State should be united." The proposition that "Good institutions should be united" is fallacious, being merely assumed and not proven. The proposition sounds reasonable, and few will feel disposed to dispute it at first, but a little consideration will show that while some good institutions may well be united, it is not a general truth that all should be so.

"Begging the Question" also often arises from giving a name to a thing, and then assuming that we have explained the thing. This is a very frequent practice with many people—they try to explain by merely applying names. An example of this kind is had in the case of the person who tried to explain why one could see through a pane of glass by saying "because it is transparent." Or when one explains that the reason a certain substance breaks easily is "because it is brittle." Moliere makes the father of a dumb girl ask why his daughter is dumb. The physician answers: "Nothing is more easy than to explain it; it comes from her having lost the power of speech." "Yes, yes," objects the father, "but the cause, if you please, why she has lost the power of speech." The physician gravely replies: "All our best authors will tell you that it is the impeding of the action of the tongue."

Jevons says: "The most frequent way, perhaps, in which we commit this kind of fallacy is to employ names which imply that we disapprove of something, and then argue that because it is such and such, it must be condemned. When two sportsmen fall out in some manner relating to the subject of game, one will, in all probability, argue that the act of the other was 'unsportsmanlike,' and therefore should not have been done. Here is to all appearance a correct syllogism:

"No unsportsmanlike act should be done; John Robinson's act was unsportsmanlike: Therefore, John Robinson's act should not have been done.

"This is quite correct in form; but it is evidently the mere semblance of an argument. 'Unsportsmanlike' means what a sportsman should not do. The point to be argued was whether the act fell within the customary definition of what was unsportsmanlike."

Arising from "Begging the Question," and in fact a class of the latter, is what is called "Reasoning in a Circle." In this form of fallacy one assumes as proof of a proposition the proposition itself; or, uses the conclusion to prove the premise. For instance: "This man is a rascal because he is a rogue; and he is a rogue because he is a rascal." Or, "It is warm because it is summer; and it is summer because it is warm." Or "He never drinks to excess, because he is never intemperate in drinking."

Brooks says: "Thus to argue that a party is good because it advocates good measures, and that certain measures are good because they are advocated by so excellent a party, is to reason in a circle. So when persons argue that their church is the true one, because it was established by God, and then argue that since it is the true church it must have been founded by God, they fall into this fallacy. To argue that 'the will is determined by the strongest motive' and to define the strongest motive as 'that which influences the will,' is to revolve in a circle of thought and prove nothing. Plato commits this error when he argues the immortality of the soul from its simplicity, and afterwards attempts to prove its simplicity from its immortality." It needs care to avoid this error, for it is surprising how easily one falls into it. Hyslop says: "The fallacy of Reasoning in a Circle occurs mostly in long arguments where it can be committed without ready detection. . . . When it occurs in a long discourse it may be committed without easy discovery. It is likely to be occasioned by the use of synonyms which are taken to express more than the conception involved when they do not." What is called a Vicious Circle is caused when the conclusion of one syllogism is used for a proposition in another syllogism, which in its turn comes to be used as a basis for the first or original syllogism.

Fallacious Conclusion is in effect an unwarranted or irrelevant assumption of a logical conclusion. There are many forms of this fallacy among which are the following:

Shifting ground, which consists in the pretence of proving one thing while in reality merely a similar or related thing is being proved. In this class is the argument that because a man is profane he must necessarily be dishonest; or that because a man denies the inspiration of the Scriptures he must be an atheist.

Fallacious Questioning, in which two or more related questions are asked, and the answer of one is then applied to the other. For instance: "You assert that the more civilized a community, the more silk-hats are to be found in it?" "Yes." "Then, you state that silk-hats are the promoters and cause of civilization in a community?" A question of this kind is often so arranged that an answer either in the affirmative or the negative will lead to a false or fallacious inference. For instance, the question once asked a respectable citizen on the witness stand: "Have you stopped beating your mother?" An answer of either "Yes" or "No," was out of the question, for it would have placed the witness in a false position, for he had never beaten his mother, nor been accused of the same.

Partial Proof, in which the proof of a partial or related fact is used to infer a proof of the whole fact or a related one. For instance, it is fallacious to argue that a man has been guilty of drunkenness by merely proving that he was seen entering a saloon.

Appeal to Public Opinion, in which the prejudices of the public are appealed to rather than its judgment or reason. In politics and theological argument this fallacy is frequent. It is no argument, and is reprehensible.

Appeal to Authority, or Reverence, in which the reverence and respect of the public for certain persons is used to influence their feelings in place of their judgment or reason. For instance: "Washington thought so-and-so, and therefore it must be right;" or "It is foolish to affirm that Aristotle erred;" or "It has been believed by men for two thousand years, that, etc;" or "What our fathers believed must be true." Appeals of this kind may have their proper place, but they are fallacies nevertheless, and not real argument.

Appeal to Profession, in which an appeal is made to practices, principles or professions of the opponent, rather than to reason or judgment. Thus we may argue that a certain philosophy or religion cannot be sound or good, because certain people who hold it are not consistent, or not worthy, moral or sober. This argument is often used effectively against an opponent, and is valid against him personally. But it is no valid argument against his philosophy or belief, because he may act in violation of them, or he may change his practices and still adhere to his beliefs—the two are not joined.

Appeal to General Belief, in which an appeal is made to general or universal belief, although the same may be unsupported by proof. This is quite common, but is no real argument. The common opinion may be erroneous, as history proves. A few centuries ago this argument could have been used in favor of the earth being flat, etc. A half-century ago it was used against Darwin. Today it is being used against other new ideas. It is a fallacy by its very nature.

Appeal to Ignorance, in which an appeal is made to the ignorance of the opponent that his conviction may follow from his inability to prove the contrary. It is virtually no argument that: "So-and-so must be true, because you cannot prove that it is not." As Brooks says: "To argue that there is no material world, because we cannot explain how the mind knows it to exist, is the celebrated fallacy of Hume in philosophy. The fact that we cannot find a needle in a haystack is no proof that it is not there."

Introduction of New Matter, also called Non Sequitur, in which matter is introduced into the conclusion that is not in the premises. Hyslop gives the following example of it: "All men are rational; Socrates is a man; therefore, Socrates is noble." De Morgan gives the following more complex example: "Episcopacy is of Scripture origin; The Church of England is the only Episcopal church in England; therefore, the church established is the church that ought to be supported."

Other fallacies, resembling in some respects those above mentioned, are as follows:

Fallacy of Ambiguous Terms, in which different meanings of the same word are used to produce the fallacious argument. As Jevons says: "A word with two distinct meanings is really two words."

Confusion between Collective and General Meanings of a Term, of which Jevons says: "It would be obviously absurd to argue that because all the books in the British Museum Library are sure to give information about King Alfred, therefore any particular book will be sure to give it. By 'all the books in the British Museum Library,' we mean all taken together. There are many other cases where the confusion is not so evident, and where great numbers of people are unable to see the exact difference."

Arguing from the Collective to the General, in which the fallacy consists of arguing that because something is true of the whole of a group of things, therefore it is true of any of those things. Jevons says: "All the soldiers in a regiment may be able to capture a town, but it is absurd to suppose that therefore every soldier in the regiment could capture the town single handed. White sheep eat a great deal more than black sheep; but that is because there are so many more of them."

Uncertain Meaning of a Sentence, from which confusion arises and fallacious argument may spring. Jevons says: "There is a humorous way of proving that a cat must have three tails: Because a cat has one tail more than no cat; and no cat has two tails; therefore, any cat has three tails." Here the fallacy rests upon a punning interpretation of "no."

Proving the Wrong Conclusion, in which the attempt to confuse conclusions is made, with the result that some people will imagine that the case is established. Jevons says: "This was the device of the Irishman, who was charged with theft on the evidence of three witnesses, who had seen him do it; he proposed to call thirty witnesses who had not seen him do it. Equally logical was the defense of the man who was called a materialist, and who replied, 'I am not a materialist; I am a barber.'"

Fallacy of Unsuccessful Argument, in which is attempted the illogical conclusion that because a certain argument has failed the opposite conclusion is proven. This fallacy is quite common, especially in cases of juries. One side fails to prove certain contentions, and the jury leaps to the conclusion that the opposite contention must be correct. This is clearly fallacious, for there is always the possibility of a third explanation. In the case of a claim of alibi juries are apt to fall into this fallacy. The failure of the attempt to establish an alibi is often held to be in the nature of proof of the guilt of the accused. Old trial lawyers assert that a failure to establish a claimed alibi tends to injure the chance of the accused more than direct evidence against him. Yet, as all logical reasoners will see, there is no logical validity in any such inference. As Jevons has well said: "No number of failures in attempting to prove a proposition really disprove it."

At the end of each failure the case simply stands in the same position as before the attempt; i.e., "not proven."

All Violations of the Rules of the Syllogism constitute fallacies, as may be seen by forming a syllogism in violation of one or more of the rules.

The logicians, particularly those of ancient times, took great pains to discover and name new variations of fallacies, many of which were hair-splitting in nature, and not worthy of being considered seriously. Some of those which we have enumerated may possibly be open to the same criticism, but we have omitted many of the worst offenders against practical common sense. An understanding of the fundamental Laws of Reasoning is sufficient to expose and unmask all fallacies, and such understanding is far more valuable than the memorizing of the names of hair-splitting fallacies which would not deceive a child.

In addition to the above stated fallacies of Deductive Reasoning, there are other fallacies which are met with in Inductive Reasoning. Let us briefly consider them.

Hasty and False Generalization is a common fallacy of this class. Persons sometimes see certain qualities in a few individuals of a class, and mistakenly infer that all the individuals in that class must possess these same qualities. Travelers frequently commit this fallacy. Englishmen visiting the United States for a few weeks have been known to publish books upon their return home making the most ridiculous generalizations regarding the American people, their assertions being based upon the observation of a few scattered individuals, often not at all representative. Americans traveling abroad commit similar errors. A flying trip through a country does not afford the proper opportunity for correct generalization. As Brooks says: "No hypothesis should be accepted as true until the facts are so numerous that there can be no doubt of its being proved."

Fallacies of Observation result from incorrect methods of observation among which may be mentioned the following: (1) Careless Observation, or inexact perception and conception; (2) Partial Observation, in which one observes only a part of the thing or fact, omitting the remainder, and thus forming an incomplete and imperfect concept of the thing or fact; (3) Neglect of Exceptions and Contradictory Facts, in which the exceptions and contradictory facts are ignored, thereby giving undue importance to the observed facts; (4) Assumption of Facts which are not real facts, or the assumption of the truth of things which are untrue; (5) Confusing of Inferences with Facts, which is most unwarrantable.

Fallacies of Mistaken Cause result from the assumption of a thing as a cause, when it is not so, of which the following are familiar examples: Substituting the Antecedent for the Cause, which consists in assuming a mere antecedent thing for a cause of another thing. Thus one might assume that the crowing of the cock was the cause of daybreak, because it preceded it; or that a comet was the cause of the plague which followed its appearance; or in the actual case in which a child reasoned that doctors caused deaths, because observation had shown that they always visited persons before they died; or that crops failed because a President of a certain political party had been inaugurated a few months before. Some fallacies of everyday reasoning are quite as illogical as those just mentioned. Substituting the Symptom for the Cause, which consists in assuming as a cause some mere symptom, sign or incident of the real cause. To assume that the pimples of measles were the cause of the disease, would be to commit a fallacy of this kind. We have mentioned elsewhere the fallacy which would assume silk-hats to be the cause of Civilization, instead of being a mere incident of the latter. Politicians are fond of assuming certain incidents or signs of a period, as being the causes of the prosperity, culture and advancement of the period, or the reverse. One might argue, with equal force, that automobiles were the causes of national prosperity, pointing to the fact that the more automobiles to be seen the better the times. Or, that straw hats produced hot weather, for similar reasons.

The Fallacy of Analogy consists in assuming a resemblance or identity, where none exists. We have spoken of this in another chapter. Brooks says, also: "It is a fallacy to carry an analogy too far; as to infer from the parable of the praying of the importunate woman that God resembles the unjust judge."

In conclusion, we would call your attention to the following words from Jevons, in which he expresses the gist of the matter: "It is impossible too often to remind people that, on the one hand, all correct reasoning consists in substituting like things for like things, and inferring that what is true of one will be true of all which are similar to it in the points of resemblance concerned in the matter. On the other hand, all incorrect reasoning consists in putting one thing for another where there is not the requisite likeness. It is the purpose of the rules of deductive and inductive logic to enable us to judge as far as possible when we are thus rightly or wrongly reasoning from some things to others."

THE SECRET OF THE "I AM"

The Ego—The physical plane—The mental plane—The new plane of consciousness—The Real Self—The "I"—The Temple of the Living Spirit—Development of the "I Am" consciousness—The Higher Reason.

"Lord of a thousand worlds am I,
And I reign since time began;
And Night and Day in cyclic sway,
Shall pass while their deeds I scan.
Yet time shall cease, ere I find release,
For I am the Soul of Man."
—CHARLES H. ORR.

Many of us are accustomed to thinking of ourselves on the physical plane alone. When we think of the Ego—the "I" of ourselves, we picture it as a human body with organs ranging from the finest—the brain, down to those of coarser atomic structure. To one living on this plane of consciousness the body is the *real* self, and the Mind but an appendage to the body. Such a man speaks of "my mind" or "my soul," as he speaks of "my hat," "my coat," "my shoes"—as things belonging to him, which he uses, but which are not *him*. To him the Body is the real man—the Mind something useful to the body—the Spirit a nebulous hypothetical something of which he has but a hazy idea and no consciousness. He lives on the physical plane alone.

Others picture their "I" as Intellect or Mind, having control of the body and its organs, and having its abode in the brain, or brains, of the human being. To these people the Intellect is the Real Self, in fact to many of this class the Intellect is elevated to the position of God, and they bow down to and worship it. They realize the subjection of the body to the Mind, and are aware of the wonderful power of the latter over the particular body under its control; the bodies of others; the minds of others. To them the Intellect is the highest self, identical with the Spirit. They are conscious of the wonderful workings of the mind, but are conscious of nothing higher. To some of them death seems to end all, their idea of mind being that it is a product of the brain. Others feel that somehow, somewhere, their Intellect will maintain its existence, but it is merely a *belief* or hope, based upon the words of others who have claimed authority to speak. They have no consciousness of pre-existence or future existence—no perception of that REAL SELF which *knows* itself to be Eternal.

A third class have so far progressed along the Path of Life that they have crossed the borders of a new plane of consciousness. They are in a strange land—they see no familiar landmarks—they do not recognize the country that lies before them. Their friends, whom they have left just a few feet behind across the border, do not seem to realize the difference the short distance has made to those who have traveled it, and therefore doubt the prospect seen from the new point of view. Those who have crossed the border find that they have acquired a *consciousness* of a real Existence. The "I" consciousness has passed beyond the Intellectual plane and is able to look back to that plane and the one still further back, the Physical plane. "I" recognizes the value of both Mind and Body, but regards them both as but instruments, tools or servants, with which to work. "I" feels that it has existed from the beginning (if beginning there was) and will exist until the end (if end there be). "I" feels a keen pleasure in mere existence—in the NOW. "I" knows itself to be a part of the WHOLE THING—knows that the UNIVERSE is its home. "I" knows itself to be a tiny drop of Spirit from the Great Spirit Ocean; a ray from the Supreme Sun; a particle of the Divine Being, encased in a material body, using that body and a force called Mind, with which to manifest itself. "I" does not at present *understand* all things—far from it. It has not as yet been able to bring its tools to that degree of perfection. It merely *knows* that it IS, and has ALWAYS BEEN, and ALWAYS WILL BE. "I" allows Intellect to indulge in speculations, but contents itself with the knowledge that it IS—it frets not itself with the problems of the past or future, but lives in the NOW, and knows itself to be a part of the WHOLE. "I" knows that it cannot be destroyed or injured—that it exists in accordance with Law (and that Law is Good) and asks no further light at this time, knowing that in its progress through matter, discarding sheath after sheath, more *knowing* will surely come. It says trustfully and confidently, to the Absolute: "Thy Will be Done."

Knowing itself to be immortal, "I" has no fear of the death of the body—one body is as good as another to it—it is willing to lay aside the body as it does a coat, when it has outworn or outgrown it. Knowing itself to be impregnable to harm, "I" has no Fearthought—it fears nothing. Knowing that the Law is working for development (always for ultimate good) "I" is not disturbed by the cares, troubles and sorrows of Life—it knows them for what they are. The body may be in pain, the mind may be burdened with sorrow, but "I," *knowing*, smiles.

"I" knows itself to be One with the "I" of all living creatures, and knowing this cannot manifest Hate, Fear, Envy, Jealousy—it cannot Despise or Condemn. These and other feelings of the old life drop from the person like a discarded mantle when "I" mounts its throne. "I" recognizes that others may not have progressed so far on the path as itself, but knows them to be but fellow travelers on the same road, who are doing the best they know how, considering their stage of the journey. "I" recognizes Ignorance—not Evil. "I" has but one feeling toward Mankind and the whole living world—LOVE. Aye, Love and Comradeship for even the *last man*, for it knows that that last man cannot be left out of the great scheme of Life.

"I" knows that it has traveled a long road leading to its present position, and that all Life is traveling the same. "I" looks back and sees others covered with the mire and dust of the road, far back on the Path, but knowing that it has traveled the same stage of the journey—been covered with the same mire and mud—it cannot condemn. "I" knows that it is but on the threshold of the new consciousness—the borderland of the Cosmic Knowing—and that far beyond lie regions of marvelous beauty which will in turn be traveled, and then on and on, increasing in strength and knowing-power each day. "I" sees endless phases of existence opening up to the vision—it cannot at this time *understand*, but it knows of the existence of the Law, and is content. "I" has the courage of Intelligent Faith, and presses forward cheerfully to the Divine Adventure. All this—and more.

To the man or woman who understands, the task of self-development becomes a labor of love—an exalted task rather than the mere selfish striving after power. As the sculptor saw in the block of marble the form of the angel, and was impelled to cut away the surrounding material in order to liberate the angelic form—so may we, seeing the God-like form within us, strive to liberate it. That inner form is the real self—the "I." If you have never realized this truth, relax body and mind and indulge in a little introspection; turn your gaze inward; listen to the voice of the Spirit. You will be conscious of a faint recognition of the Something Within striving to make itself manifest to your understanding—asking for the proper tools with which to work. Listen, listen in The Silence! Day by day the Voice will grow plainer—day by day the Light will grow brighter—your own is coming to you, at last. O, joy unspeakable! O tears! O laughter! After long ages you are coming in sight of the Promised Land.

Know yourself O Man! Know that you have within you the Divine Spark, to which both body and mind are but servants. Know that your body is the Temple of the Living Spirit and respect it as such. Know that your Intellect is but the instrument of the manifestation of the Spirit—the "I."

Do not crawl on your belly like a worm; do not humble yourself in the dust and call upon heaven to witness what a despicable creature you are; do not call yourself a miserable sinner worthy only of eternal damnation. No! a thousand times No! Rise to your feet; raise your head; face the skies; throw back your shoulders; fill your lungs with Nature's ozone. Then say to yourself: "I AM."

Man has acquired a wonderful power when he can *understandingly* say: "I AM a part of the Eternal Life Principle; I AM created in the Divine Image; I AM filled with the Divine Breath of Life; Nothing can hurt ME, for I AM ETERNAL."

The first requisite for the acquirement of an understanding of the Law is the recognition of the existence and the power of the Real Self—the "I." The more complete the recognition the greater the power. Special directions for the acquirement of this faculty of recognition cannot be given. It must be grown into and felt, rather than reasoned out by the Intellect. You will not be long in doubt as to whether or not you are on the right track; if you are right you will begin to realize it at once. You will have glimpses of it, and then it may slip away from you for a while, but fear not, you cannot escape it in the end.

You will feel that your body is but as a garment which whilst covering you temporarily is not YOU. You will feel that you are separate and apart from your body, although for a time living in it. You will feel that you could as well live in some other body, and still retain your sense of individuality. You will realize then even your mind is not You, but is merely the instrument through which You manifest yourself, and which being imperfect prevents the complete expression of the Spirit. In short, when you say, or think, "I AM," you are conscious of the existence of your *real* self, and feel the growth of a new sense of power within you. This recognition of the self may be faint, but encourage it and it will grow, and whilst growing will manifest itself to your mind by impressing upon the latter the knowledge of the proper plan for further development. It is another example of "to him that hath shall be given."

This mere calling of their attention to the fact will awaken the first glimmer of recognition in some; others will find it necessary to reflect upon the idea and awaken to a recognition of the Truth more slowly. Some will not *feel* the Truth.

To such I say: The time is not yet ripe for your recognition of this great Truth, but the seed is planted and the plant will appear in time. This may seem like the veriest nonsense to you now, but the time will come when you will admit its literal correctness. You will find that a desire has been created that will cause a mental unrest until more light is received. As Walt Whitman says: "My words will itch in your ears till you understand them." As Emerson says: "You cannot escape from your good." To those who feel the first indications of the awakening of the Spirit, I say: Carry the thought with you and it will unfold like the lotus, naturally and gradually; the truth once recognized cannot be lost, and there is no standing still in nature.

What has been said is but a faint hint of a mighty Truth, which nestles in the bosom of the esoteric teachings of all religions—in the philosophies of the Orient and of ancient Greece. You will find it in the songs of the poets—in the writings of the mystics. The advanced science of this age touches it without recognizing it fully. It is not a thing that can well be conveyed by words—it is not easily comprehended by purely intellectual processes—it must be *felt* and lived out by those who are ready for it—those for whom the time has come. It has been known to the Few throughout all ages and in all times. All races have known it. It has been handed down from teacher to pupil from the earliest days. It is that Truth which Edward Carpenter refers to when he says:

"O, let not the flame die out! Cherished age after age in its dark caverns, in its holy temples cherished. Fed by pure ministers of love—let not the flame die out."

It is difficult to convey even a hint of this Truth to any but those who are prepared to receive it. To others it will seem to be arrant folly. As Emerson says: "Every man's words, who speaks from that life, must sound vain to those who do not dwell in the same thought on their own part. I dare not speak for it. My words do not carry its august sense; they fall short and cold. Only itself can inspire whom it will * * * * Yet I desire even by profane words, if sacred I may not use, to indicate the heaven of this deity, and to report what hints I have collected of the transcendent simplicity and energy of the Highest Law."

If you prefer to try to solve the Problem of Life—the Riddle of the Universe—by scientific investigation, by exact reasoning, formal thought, mathematical demonstration—by all means follow this method. You will be taught the lesson of the power and the limitations of the human intellect. And after you have traveled round and round the circle of thought and find that you are but covering the same ground over and over again—after you have run into the intellectual *cul de sac*, the blind alley of Logic—after you have beaten your wings against the cage of the Unknowable and fall exhausted and bruised—after you have done all these things and have learned your lesson—then listen to the voice within, see the tiny flame which burns steadily and cannot be extinguished, feel the pressure of the Something Within *and let it unfold*. You will then begin to understand that as the mind of Man developed by slow stages from mere sensation to simple consciousness; from simple consciousness to self-consciousness (in its lower and higher degrees) so is there a consciousness, higher than we have heretofore imagined, in store for Man, which is even now beginning to manifest itself. You may then understand that there may be an Intelligent Faith which *knows*, not simply believes. These and other lessons you will learn in time. And when you have reached the stage where you *feel* the promptings of the Higher Reason, and live in accordance therewith, you will say with Carpenter:

"Lo! the healing power descending from within, calming the enfevered mind, spreading peace among the grieving nerves. Lo! the eternal saviour, the sought after of all the world, dwelling hidden (to be disclosed) within each * * * * O joy insuperable."

DYNAMIC
THOUGHT
OR
THE LAW OF
VIBRANT
ENERGY

"I am attacked by two very opposite sects—the Scientists and the Know-Nothings; both laugh at me, calling me the 'Frogs' Dancing Master,' but I know that I have discovered one of the greatest Forces in Nature."

—GALVINI.

"A fire-mist and a planet, A crystal and a cell,
A jelly-fish and a saurian,
And caves where the cave-men dwell; Then a sense of law and beauty,
And a face turned from the clod,—Some call it Evolution,
And others call it God."
"Like tides on a crescent sea-beach, When the moon is new and thin,
Into our hearts high yearnings Come welling and surging in,—
Come from the mystic ocean Whose rim no foot has trod,—
Some of us call it Longing, And others call it God."

—W. H. CARRUTH.

Contents

Foreword

This is a queer book. It is a marriage of the Ancient Occult Teachings to the latest and most advanced conceptions of Modern Science—an odd union, for the parties thereto are of entirely different temperaments. The marriage might be expected to result disastrously, were it not for the fact that a connecting link has been found that gives them a bond of common interest. No two people may truly love each other, unless they also love something in common—the more they love in common, the greater will be their love for each other. And, let us trust that this will prove true in this marriage of Occultism and Science, celebrated in this book.

The Occultists usually get at the "facts" first, but they manage to evolve such outrageous theories to explain the facts, that the world will have none of their wares, and turns to Science for something "reasonable." Science, proceeding along different lines, at first denies these "facts" of the Occultists, not finding them accounted for by any of her existing theories; but, later on, when the "facts" have been finally thrust under her eyes, after repeated attempts and failures, she says, "Oh, yes, of course!" and proceeds to evolve a new theory, welding it with other scientific hypotheses, and after attaching a new label thereto, she proudly exhibits the thing as "the latest discovery of Modern Science"—and smiles indulgently, or indignantly, when the theory of the old Occultists is mentioned, saying,

"Quite a different thing, we assure you!" And yet, in all justice, be it said, Science usually proceeds to find much better "proofs" to fit the "facts" of Occultism, than did the Occultists themselves. The Occultist "sees things," but is a poor hand at "proofs"—while the Scientist is great on "proofs," but so often, and so long, fails to see many things patent to the Occultist who is able to "look within" himself, but who is then unable to positively and scientifically "prove" the facts. This is easily explained—the Occultist's information comes from "within," while the Scientists comes from without—and "proofs" belong to the "without" side of Mentation. And this is why the Occultists so often make such a bungle regarding "proofs" and the Scientist fails to see "facts" that are staring the Occultist in the face.

The whole history of Occultism and Science proves the above. Take the phenomenon called "Mesmerism" for instance—it was an old story with the Occultists, who had been for years aware of it, theoretically and practically. Mesmer brought it into general prominence, and Science laughed at it and at Mesmer's "fluid" theory, and called him a charlatan and imposter. Years afterwards, Braid, an English surgeon, discovered that some of the facts of "Mesmerism" were true, and he announced his discovery in a scientific manner, and lo! his views were accepted, and the thing was called "Hypnotism," poor old Mesmer being forgotten, because of his theory. Then, after a number of years, certain other aspects of the phenomenon were discovered, and scientifically re-labelled "Suggestion," and the re-naming was supposed to "explain" the entire subject, the learned ones now saying, "Pooh, 'tis nothing but 'Suggestion,' as if *that* explained the matter. But so far, they have only accepted certain phases of this form of Dynamic Thought—for that is what it is, and there are many other phases of which they do not dream.

And the same is true of the Occult Teaching that there is "Life in Everything—the Universe is Alive." For years, this idea was hooted at, and we had learned scientific discourses upon "dead Matter," "inert substance," etc. But, only within the past decade—yes, within the last five years, has Science discovered that there was Life in Everything, and that even in the Atom of mineral and chemical substance, there was to be found evidence of Mind. And Science is beginning to plume itself on its "recent discovery," and to account for it by a new theory, which is "quite a different thing, we assure you," from the old Occult Theory.

And the same will prove true in the case of the Occult Teaching of an Universal Mind, or Cosmic Mind. Science and Philosophy have long laughed at this, but even now their foremost investigators have come to the borders of a new country, and are gasping in amazement at what they see beyond its borders—they are now talking about "Life and Mind in the Ether"—and before long they will discard their paradoxical, absurd, hypothetical Ether, and say, "We are bathed in an Ocean of Mind"—only they will insist that this "Ocean of Mind" is, somehow, a "secretion of Matter"—something oozing out from the pores of Matter, perhaps.

But Science is doing valuable work in the direction of investigation and experiment, and in this way is *proving the principal occult teachings* in a way impossible to the Occultists themselves.

So, you see that both Occultism and Science have their own work to do—and neither can do the work of the other. Just now Science is coquetting with the question of "Thought Transmission," etc., at which she has for so long sneered and laughed. By and by she will accept the facts, and then proceed to prove them by a series of careful and conclusive experiments, and will then announce the result, solemnly, as "a triumph of Science."

And so, in this book you will find a marriage of the old Occult Teachings and Modern Scientific Researches and Investigation. And the two are bound together with that bond forged by the writer of the book—heated in the oven of his mind, and hammered into shape with his "untrained" thought—a crude, clumsy thing, but it serves its purpose—a thing called "*The Theory of Dynamic Thought.*"

And so, this is what this Theory is—a "*tie that binds.*" How you will like it depends upon yourself. For himself, the writer does not hesitate to say that he is pleased with his handiwork, rude, and clumsy though it may be. He believes that he has made a thing that will stand wear and tear, and that though it be not beautifully finished, it "will serve," and "be useful." And that is the main thing, after all. And, then, perhaps, some may see beauty in the very crudeness of the thing—may see that it bears the loving mark of the hammer that beat it into shape—may recognize that over it has passed the caress of the hand that made it—and in that seeing there may come the recognition of a beauty that is beyond "prettiness."

William Walker Atkinson.
Los Angeles, California, February 16, 1906.

1

"In the Beginning"

This book will deal with Life. It holds that Life is Universal—that it is inherent in, and manifests (in different degrees) in every part, particle, phase, aspect, condition, place, or relationship, in the World of Things that we call the Universe. It holds that Life manifests in two aspects or forms, which are generally found by us in connection and co-operation with each other, but which are both, probably, an expression of some One Thing higher than either. These two aspects or forms, which together go to make up or produce that which we know as "Life," are known as (1) Substance or Matter; and (2) Mind. In this book the term "Substance" is used in preference to "Matter," owing to the fact that the term "Matter" has become closely identified with certain ideas of the Materialistic school of thought, and has generally been regarded by the public in the light of "dead matter," whereas this book holds that all Substance is Alive. The term "Mind" is used in the sense of "Mind, *as we know it*," rather than as "Mind, *as it is*"—or, as "The Cosmic Mind." In some places the term "Mind-principle" is used to convey the idea of "a portion of the Great Principle of Mind, of which that which we call 'Mind' is but a small and but partially expressed portion." These terms are explained and illustrated as we proceed. The aspect of "Energy or Force" is not treated as a separate aspect or form of Life, in this book, for the reason that it is regarded as merely a manifestation of Mind, as will appear as we proceed. We have much to say regarding Motion, but the writer has tried to explain and prove that, at the last, all Motion results from Mental Action, and that all Force and Energy is Vital—Mental Force and Energy.

This book is not intended to run along metaphysical or theological lines— its field is different. And so, while it recognizes the importance of these branches of human thought, still, it finds that its own particular field is sufficient to engross its entire attention, for the moment, and, consequently the aforesaid subjects shall not be touched upon except incidentally, in connection with the subject matter of the book. This being the case, there will be no discussion of the "origin of Life"—the question of "creation"—the problems of theology and metaphysics—the riddle of the "Why and Wherefore" of Life and the Universe. The writer has his own opinions upon these questions, but feels that this is not the place in which to air the same. For the purposes of the book, he prefers to leave every reader to his own favorite views and conceptions regarding these great subjects, feeling that the views regarding Life, Mind, Motion and Substance, that are advanced in this book, may be accepted by any intelligent reader, without prejudice to his, or her, accepted religious or philosophical views.

The writer sees that this something called "Life" exists—he finds it in evidence everywhere. And he sees it always in its aspects of Substance and Mind. And he feels justified in regarding "Life" as always existing in, and manifesting in these aspects—always in conjunction—at least, Life "as we know it."

And he finds certain apparent Laws of Life in operation in the Universe to which all Life, in all of its aspects, is apparently amenable. And he feels justified in considering these Laws constant, and invariable, and unchangeable so long as the Universe, as it now is, exists.

And with the above views in mind, this book will proceed to a consideration of its subject, without attempting to peer behind the veil separating the Universe from its Causer—Life from its Source.

But in justice to reader, subject and writer, the latter has thought it well to state that he *does* recognize, not only the veil, but That-which-is-behind-the-Veil. To proceed without this statement would be unfair and misleading. The writer wishes to be understood positively upon this point, even though the declaration may bring forth the derisive jeer of those who feel that they "have outgrown" this conception; or else the calm, superior, pitying smile of those who feel that the Universe is its own Cause and Effect. By "Universe," the writer means "The whole body of Things" (Webster). His declaration means that he believes in "That-which-is-above-Things"

The writer prefers not to attempt to "define" That which he calls "The Infinite." The word "Infinite" means "without limit in time, space, power, capacity, knowledge or excellence" (Webster). And to "define" is to "limit"; "mark the limits of"; "mark the end of," etc. The term "define," as applied to "The Infinite," is ridiculous—an absurd paradox. The writer echoes Spinoza's statement: "To define God is to deny Him." And so there shall be no attempt at definition or limitation.

But the human mind, in considering the subject, is bound by its own laws to think of "The Infinite" as Real, and actually being and existent, if it thinks of It at all. And if it thinks of It as "Infinite," it *must*, by its own laws, think of It as Causeless; Eternal; Absolute; Everywhere-present; All-Powerful; All-Wise.

The human mind is *compelled* to so consider The Infinite, if it think of It at all. But even in so thinking of It as "being" these things, it is doing something like "defining" or "limiting" It, for The Infinite must not only "be" those things, but it must "be" so much more, that "those things" are but as a grain of dust on the desert as compared to the real "Being" of The Infinite. For the "things" mentioned are but "finite" or "defined" things—things possessed by the Finite Things—and, at the best can be but symbols of the attributes or qualities of The Infinite; even the words "attributes" or "qualities'" being an absurdity as applied to The Infinite. This view, also, *must* be reported by the human reason, if it thinks about the matter at all.

The final report of the human reason regarding this matter is that it is insoluble and unthinkable to that reason, in its final analysis. This because the human reason is compelled to use terms, concepts, etc., derived from its experience with finite things, and therefore has no tools, measurements, or other appliances with which to "think," of The Infinite. All that it can do is to report that it finds that it has limits itself, and that it finds beyond those limits That which it cannot define, but which it is justified in considering as Infinite, and superior to all finite conceptions, such as Time, Space, Causation and Thought. (The idea of Thought being finite, equally with Time, Space and Causation, is not common, but the writer is compelled to place it in that category, because it is clearly under the laws of Time, Space, and Cause and Effect, and must be considered as "finite." The "knowledge" possessed by The Infinite must be something far transcending that which we know as the result of "mental operations," or "thinking.")

Certain fundamental truths seem to have been impressed upon the human intellect, and the reason is compelled to report in accordance therewith. But an analysis of these fundamental truths is futile, and the attempt only leads one into wild speculations. The only advantage that comes from the attempt is the strengthening of mental muscle of those who are able to stand the strain of the exercise; and the fact that by such attempt we are made aware that we do *not* know, and *cannot* know, by reasons of the nature of the Intellect, and are thus prevented from harboring absurd and childish theories about the Unknowable. To know that we do not know, and cannot know, is the next best thing to actually knowing.

The writer does not wish to be understood, that the limits of the human reason are unalterably fixed. On the contrary, he believes that additional fundamental portions of Truth are super-imposed upon the mind of the race from time to time. And he believes, yes, *knows,* that there are regions of the mind that give reports higher than those conveyed through the Intellect. And he believes that there are phases of knowledge in store for Man that will raise him as much higher than his present position, as that present position is superior to that of the earthworm. And he believes that there Beings in existence today, on planes of Life as yet undreamed of by the average man, who far transcend Man in power, wisdom and nature. He believes that Man is merely just entering into his kingdom, and does not realize the grandeur of that which is his Divine Inheritance.

It will be as well to mention here that the classification of Mind with the aspects of Life, in conjunction with Substance, and Motion, does not mean that the Ego or Man is a material thing. The writer believes that the Ego is a transcendent Being, partaking in some wonderful way of the essence of The Infinite—that it is a Soul—Immortal. He believes that as Paul says, "We are all children of God, but what we shall be does not as yet appear." These matters shall not be discussed in this book, but the writer wishes to make himself clear, in order to prevent misunderstanding. Again, in this respect, he must "fly in the face of Materialism."

But, although the writer expresses his belief in the existence of The Infinite, and bases his philosophy upon that basis, he does not wish to insist upon the identification of his conception with that of any other particular conception of the Source of Life. Nor does he insist upon names, or terms, in connection with the conception. He has used the term, "The Infinite," because it seems to be broader than any other of which he could think, but he uses it merely as a name for the Un-Nameable. So, if the reader prefers, he, or she, may use the terms: "God"; "Deity"; "First Cause"; "Principle"; "Unknowable"; "Infinite and Eternal Energy"; "The Thing-in-Itself"; "The Absolute"; or any of the other countless terms used by Man in his attempt to name the Un-Nameable—to describe the Un-Describable—to define the Un-Definable.

And all may retain their ideas, or lack of ideas, regarding the relation of The Infinite to their own particular religious views, or lack of views. The philosophy of this book need not disturb a man's religious belief—nor does it insist upon the man holding any special religious belief. Those are matters entirely for the exercise of the man's own reason and conscience. And they may retain their own pet philosophy regarding the origin, purposes or plan of the production and existence of the Universe—this book shall not meddle with their metaphysics or philosophy. What is herein offered may be assimilated with the fundamental ideas of nearly every form of religious or philosophical belief, it being in the nature of an Addition rather than a Subtraction, or Division. Its philosophy is Constructive rather than Destructive.

2

Things as They Are

In our last chapter we considered the Source-of-All-Things, which we called The Infinite. In this chapter we shall consider the All-Things itself, which men call The Universe. Note that the word Universe is derived from the Latin word "*Unus*," meaning "One," and "*Versor*," meaning "to turn," the combined word meaning, literally, "One that turns, or moves." The Latin words indicate a close meaning, namely, One thing in motion, turning its several aspects, and assuming many changes of appearance.

The writer does not intend touching upon theories of the origin of the Universe, nor of its purpose, or of any design in its production or management, nor of its possible or probable end. These questions do not belong to our subject, and then again, as was said in the last chapter, speculation regarding it is devoid of results, and leads one to quicksands and bogs of mental reasoning, from which it is difficult to extract oneself.

The answer to the Riddle of the Universe rests with The Infinite. But it is different with the case of the manifested Universe that is evidenced by our senses. Science is a different thing from metaphysics, and its process and mode of work, are along different lines. And, much knowledge of Things may be obtained from a consideration of it—remembering always, that its knowledge is confined to Things, and not to That-which-is-back-of-Things. And, so let us consider the Universe of Things.

Material Science has held that the Universe is composed of two principles, (1) Matter; (2) Energy or Force. Some hold that these two principles really are aspects of the same thing, and that there is really but one Principle, one aspect of which is shape, form, etc., and called Matter; the other a quality manifesting in Motion, which quality is called Force. Others, the most radical, hold that there is nothing but Matter, and that Force and Energy is but a "quality," or "power," inherent in Matter. Others hold that Force is the "real thing" and Matter but a form of Force. All branches hold to the idea that Matter and Energy are always found together, and cannot be thought of separately. Matter and Force are held to be Eternal, and Infinite, it following that there can be no addition to, or subtraction from either; all apparent loss and gain, creation and destruction being but change of form or mode. God is declared unnecessary, and the Universe is held to operate according to certain Laws of Matter or Force (either or both) which are unchangeable and immutable—eternal and always valid. Mind and Thought are held to be products of properties of Matter or Force (one or both), secreted, evolved, or produced in the Brain. The Soul is relegated to the waste heap, and discarded as useless in the new philosophy. *Moleschott* said, "Thought is a motion of Matter"; and *Holbach*, that "Matter enjoys the power of thinking." "Natural Laws" are held to be sufficient for the explanation of all phenomena, although ignoring the fact that the reason has never before formed the conception of a "law," without thinking it necessary to think of a "law-maker," or a power to enforce and administer the law. However, the philosophers hold that it is no more difficult to think of such a law than to try to form an idea of Space or Eternity, both of which are unthinkable to the human reason, but both of which are admitted as self-evident facts.

But notwithstanding this somewhat crude and "raw" reasoning, Material Science has accomplished a wonderful work in the world, and has brought to light facts of inestimable value to Man in mastering the material world, and in forming correct ideas of the solution of material difficulties. The facts of Material Science enables the world to cheerfully overlook its theories. And even the theories are rapidly undergoing a change, and, as we have stated, some of the most advanced scientists are rapidly reaching the position of the Occultists and mystics, bringing with them a mass of facts to back them up, to exhibit to the Occultists who dealt with principles rather than with details, or material facts, so far as fundamental theories were concerned. Each is boring his way through the mountain tunnel of the Unknown, and both will meet in the centre, their lines meeting each other without a variation. But the Occultists will call the tunnel-centre Mind, and the scientists will call it Matter, but both will be speaking of the same thing. And the Causer of the mountain will probably know that they both are right.

But, we are speaking of the new school of advanced Material Science now—not of the old conservative "All is Matter" people, who have been left behind. The new school speaks of Substance now, instead of Matter, and ascribes to "Substance" the properties of Matter, Energy, and something that they call

Sensation, by which they mean Mind in a crude form, and from which they say Mind and "Soul" evolved.

This new school of Scientists are very different from their predecessors—they are less "hide-bound," and far from being so "cock-sure" They are seeing Matter melting into Energy, and giving signs of Sensation, and they are beginning to feel that, after all, there must be a Thing-in-Itself, that is the real basis of, or "real thing" in Substance. There is heard very little among them about "dead matter"; "blind force"; or of the "mechanical theory" of Life and the Universe. Instead of it being a big machine, operated under mechanical laws, with Life as the steam, the Universe is beginning to be regarded as somehow filled with Life, and Science is finding new examples of Life in unexpected quarters, and the "dead matter" area is being narrowed.

Men who have followed the advances made by recent Science are holding their breaths in awe and earnest expectation—and those who are pushing the inquiries and investigations to the furthest extent are showing by their eager faces and trembling hands that they feel that they are very close to the border line separating the old Materialism from a New Science that will give Thought and Philosophy a new impetus and a new platform. Such men are feeling that they are seeing the old Matter melting away into something else—the old theories are falling apart under the light of new discoveries—and these men feel that they are penetrating a new and hitherto unexplored region of the Unknown. May success be theirs, for they are now on the right road to Truth.

In the following chapters we shall see frequent references to "Science"—and when we use the word we shall know it means this new school of Scientists, rather than the older school that is now being superceded. There is no conflict between True Occultism and True Science, notwithstanding their directly opposite theories and ideals—they are merely looking at the Truth from different viewpoints—at different sides of the same shield. A better day is coming, when they shall work together, instead of in opposition. There should be no partisanship in the search for Truth.

Things have worked this way: Occultism would enunciate a theory or principle—but would not attempt to prove it by material facts, for it had not gathered the facts, having found the principle within the mind, rather than without. Then, after laughing at the occult theory or principle, Science would search diligently for material facts to prove an opposite theory, and in so doing would unearth new facts that would support the Occultists contention. Then Science would discard its old theory (that is, the younger men would—the old ones, never) and proceed to proclaim a new theory or principle, under a new name, and backed up with a mass of facts and experiments that would create a new school with many enthusiastic followers. The old claim of the Occultists would then be forgotten or else go unrecognized under its old name; or disguised by the fantastic and *bizarre* coverings which some so-called Occultists had draped around the original Truth.

But, so long as Truth is being uncovered, what matters it who does the work, or by what name he calls his school. The movement is ever forward, and upward—what matter the banner under which the armies move?

In this book the writer will advance a very different theory of the Universe of All-Things from that of Modern Science, although he feels that his theory may easily be reconciled with the most advanced views of that school.

In the first place, as he has stated in the first chapter, he does not hold that the Universe, as we know it, is self-sufficient, but he recognizes a Something back of all phenomena and appearances, which Something he calls "The Infinite."

And he differs very materially from the views of those who claim that Mind is but a property, or quality, or something proceeding from Matter or Force, or Matter-Force, or Force-Matter—according to the views of the respective schools. He takes an entirely different and opposite position.

He holds that all that we call Matter (or Substance) and Mind (*as we know it*) are but aspects of something infinitely higher, and which may be called the "Cosmic Mind." He holds that *what we call* "Mind" is but a partial manifestation of the Cosmic Mind. And that Substance or Matter is but a cruder or grosser form of that which we call Mind, and which has been manifested in order to give Mind a Body through which to operate. But this view he merely states in passing, for he makes no attempt to demonstrate or prove the same, his idea being that it forms a different part of the general subject than the phase of "Dynamic Thought," to the consideration of which this book is devoted.

He also differs very materially from the Materialistic school in his conception of Force or Energy. Instead of regarding Force as a distinct principle, and as something of which Mind is but a form, he walks boldly out into the arena of Scientific Thought, and throwing down his gauntlet, proclaims his theory that "There is no such thing as Force apart from Life and Mind"—"All Force and Energy is the product of Life and Mind—all Force, Energy and Motion result from Vital-Mental Action—all Force, Energy and Motion is Vital-Mental Force, Energy and Motion."—"The Mind abiding in and permeating all Substance, not only has the power to Think, but also the power to Act, and to manifest Force and Energy, which are its inherent and essential properties."

He also takes the position that Mind is in and about and around Everything. And that "Everything is Alive and Thinking." And that there is no such things as "Dead-Matter," or "Blind-Force," but that all Substance, even to the tiniest Particle, is permeated with Life and Mind, and that all Force and Motion is caused and manifested by Mind.

He holds that all forms of Force, Energy and Motion, from the Attraction of the Particles of Matter, and their movements in response thereto, up to the Attraction of Gravitation, and the response of the Worlds, and Suns, and Stars, and Planets, thereto—are forms of Mental Energy and Force, and Action. And that from the tiniest atom, or particle, to the greatest Sun—all obey this Great Action of Mind—this Great Force of Mind—this Great Energy of Mind—this Great Power of Mind.

And upon this rock—this rock of Truth, he believes it to be—he takes his stand, and announces his belief, and bids all-comers take notice of what he believes to be a germ-thought that will grow, develop, and increase so that it will eventually permeate all Scientific Thought as the years roll along. He calls this theory "The Theory of Dynamic Thought."

3

The Universality of Life and Mind

The writer has deemed it advisable to preface his consideration of "Mind" in itself, as well as of Substance and Motion, with two chapters, the purpose of which will be to demonstrate that Mind, in some form or degree, is to be found in connection with all Things—and that Everything has Life—and that Mind is an accompaniment of all Life. To many the term "Mind" means only the "thinking quality" of man, or perhaps of the lower animals; and "Life" the property only of such organic creatures. For that reason it has been deemed advisable to point out that Life and Mind are found even in the lowest forms of substance—even in the inorganic world.

In this chapter and from now on, the writer shall use the term "*the* Mind," etc., to indicate the particular mental principle of the creature or thing—the bit of Mind that is segregated from the rest, and which each person thinks of as "mine," just as he thinks of "my" body, as distinguished from the universal supply of Substance. The term "Mind" will be used in its Universal sense.

And, the writer intends to use Elmer Gates' term, "*Mentation*," in the sense of "effort; action; or effect; in or of, the Mind"—in short, "mental process." The word is useful and when one has learned to use it, he will prefer it to the more complicated terms. Remember, then, please—"Mentation" means "Mental Process." Mentation includes that which we call "Thought," as well as some more elementary forms of mental process that we are not in the habit of dignifying by the term, Thought, which latter we usually reserve for mental process of a higher order.

So, then, "Mind" is the something of which one's particular Mind is composed; "The Mind" is that something possessed by one, by and through which he "thinks"; "Mentation" is mental process; and "Thought" is an advanced kind of Mentation. At least, the said words will be so employed in this book, from now on.

In this chapter, you are asked to consider the fact that Life is Universal—that Everything is Alive. And, that Mind and Mentation is an attribute of Life, and that, consequently, Everything has Mind, and is able to express a degree of Mentation.

Forms of Life, as we know them, are always seen as possessing two aspects, *viz.*, (1) Body (Substance); and (2) Mentation (Mind). The two aspects are always found in combination.

There may be living creatures who occupy bodies of so fine a form of Substance as to be invisible to the human senses—but their bodies would be "Substance" just as much as is the "body" of the granite rock. And, in order to "think," these beings would need to have a material something corresponding to the brain, though it be finer in quality than the rarest gas, vapor, or electric wave. No body, without Mentation; no Mentation without a body. This last is the invariable law of the world of Things. And naught but The Infinite—That-which-is-above-Things—can be exempt from that law.

In order to grasp the idea of the Universality of Mind, let us go back to the elementary forms of Things, and, step by step, see how Mentation manifests itself in every point on the scale from mineral to man—using "bodies ranging from the hardest rock to that finest form of known Substance—the Brain of Man. As Mind advances in the scale of evolution it creates its own working instrument—the body (including the brain) and shapes, and moulds it to admit of the fullest possible expression of Mentation possible at that stage. Mind is the moulder—body (and brain) that which is moulded. And Inclination, Desire, and Will, are the motive powers leading to gradual Unfoldment, the impelling cause being the craving for Satisfaction.

We shall make our journey backward—and ignoring Beings higher in the scale, we shall start with Man. Leaving out of the consideration, for the moment, the fact of the existence of the "Ego," or "Spirit" of Man, which is higher than Body or Mind—and considering "the Mind of Man," rather than the Man himself—we have our starting point on the downward journey of investigation. We need not devote much attention to the consideration of the Mind of Man, at this stage, although we shall have much to do with it, later on.

But we may undertake a brief consideration of the descending degrees of Mentation as manifested by Man, as we pass down the scale in the human family, considering in turn, the Newtons, Shakespeares, Emersons, Edisons, and their brothers in intellect, in the fields of mathematics, literature, music, art, invention, science, statesmanship, business, skilled workmanship, etc., respectively. From these high levels we pass down, gradually, through the strata of men of but a slightly lower degree of intellect—down through the strata of the "average man"—down through the strata of the ignorant man—down through the strata of the lowest type of our own race and time—down through the strata of the barbarian, then on to the savage, then on to the Digger Indian, the Bushman. What a difference from highest to lowest—a being from another world would doubt that they were all of the same family.

Then we pass rapidly through the various strata of the lower animal kingdom—from the comparatively high degree of Mentation of the horse, the dog, the elephant, etc., down through the descending scale of the mammals, the degree of Mentation becoming less marked at each step of the journey.

Then on through the bird kingdom. Then through the world of reptiles. Then through the family of fishes. Then through the millions of forms of insect life, including those wonderful creatures, the ant and the bee. Then on through the shell-fish family. Then on through the community of sponges, polyps, and other low forms of life. Then on to the vast empire of the microscopic creatures, whose name is legion. Then on to the plant life, the highest of which have "sensitive cells" that resemble brains and nerves—descending by stages to the lower plant life. Then still lower to the world of bacteria, microbes, and infusoria— the groups of cells with a common life—the monera—the single cell. The mind that has followed us in this descent of life, from the highest form to the cell-like "thing" merely "existing" in the slime at the bottom of the ocean, has acquired a sense of awe and sublimity not dreamed of by "the man on the street."

The degrees of Mentation in the lower animal kingdom are well known to all of us, therefore, we need not devote much time to their consideration at this time. Although the degree of Mentation in some of the lowly forms of animal life are scarcely above that of the plant life (in fact, are inferior to that of the highest plants), still we have accustomed ourselves to the use of the word "Mind" in connection with even the lowest animals, while we hesitate to apply the word to the plants.

It is true that some of us do not like to think of the lower animals "reasoning," so we use the word "Instinct" to denote the degree of Mentation of the lower animal. The writer does not object to the word; in fact, he shall use it for the sake of distinguishing between the several mental states. But, remember, "Instinct" is but a term used to denote a lesser form of "Reason"—and the "Instinct" of the horse or dog is a fine thing when we consider the "Reason" of the Bushman or Digger Indian. However, we shall not quarrel about words. Both "Reason" and "Instinct" mean degrees or forms of "Mentation," the word we are using. The lower forms of animal life exhibit Mentation along the lines of sex-action, feeling and taste. Then by degrees come smell, hearing and sight. And then something very like "reasoning" in the case of the dog, elephant, horse, etc. Mentation is everywhere in the animal kingdom, in some degree. No doubt about Life and Mentation, there.

But what about Mentation and Life in the plant life! All of you admit that there is "Life" there—but about Mentation, well; let us see! Some of you draw the line at the word "Mind" in connection with plants, although you freely admit the existence of "Life" there. Well, remember our axiom—"no Life without Mentation," Let us try to apply it.

A moment's reflection will give you instances of Mentation among the plants. Science has called it "Appetency," rather than admit "Mind," the word "Appetency" being defined as "an instinctive tendency on the part of iow forms of organic life to perform certain acts necessary for their well-being—such as to select and absorb such particles of matter as serve to support and nourish them." Well, that looks like a degree of Mentation, doesn't it? Many young animals evidence little or nothing more than "Appetency" in suckling. We shall adopt the word "Appetency" to designate the Mentation in plant-life. Remember this, please.

Anyone who has raised trees or plants has noticed the instinctive efforts of the plant to reach the water and sunlight. Potatoes in dark cellars have been known to send forth shoots twenty feet in length in order to reach an opening in the wall. Plants have been known to bend over during the night and dip their leaves in a pot of water several inches away. The tendrils of climbing plants seek for the stake or support, and find it, too, although it has been changed daily. The tendril will retwine itself, after it has been untwisted and bent in another direction. The tips of the roots of the tree are said to show a sensitiveness almost akin to that of the limb of an animal, and evidently possess something akin to nerve matter.

Duhamel placed some beans in a cylinder of moist earth. When they began to sprout, he turned the cylinder around quarter way of its circumference; then a little more the next day; and so on, a little each day, until the cylinder had described a complete revolution—had been turned completely around.

Then the beans were taken from the earth, and lo! the roots and sprouts formed a complete spiral. With every turn of the cylinder the roots and sprouts had changed their position and direction—the roots striving to grow "downward," and the sprouts striving to grow "upward"—until the spiral had formed. Akin to this is the boy's trick of uprooting a sprouting seed, and replanting it upside down, in which case the sprouts begin to turn a semicircle until it is able to grow straight up to the surface of the earth, while the roots describe a semicircle until they can grow downward once more.

And so on, story after story of "Appetency" or Mentation in plants might be told, until we reach the insect-catching species, when even the most conservative observer is forced to admit that: "Well, it does *almost* seem like thinking, doesn't it?" Any lover of plants, flowers or trees, and who has been able to study them at first hand, does not need much argument to prove that plant-life exhibits traces of Mentation, some of it pretty far advanced, too. Some lovers of plants go so far as to claim that one must "love" plants before they will succeed in growing them, and that the plants feel and respond to the feeling. But the writer does not insist upon this, but merely mentions it in passing.

Before leaving the subject of Mentation in plants, the writer is tempted to steal a little more space and tell you that plants do more than receive sensations of light and moisture. They exhibit rudimentary taste as well. Haeckel relates an interesting story of an insect-catching plant. He states that while it will bend its leaves when any solid body (excepting a raindrop) touches its surface, still it will secrete its acrid digestive fluid only when that object happens to be nitrogenous (meat or cheese). The plant is able to distinguish its meat diet (its food being insectivorous), and while it will supply its gastric juice for meat and cheese, as well as for the insect, it will not do so for other solids to which it is indifferent. He also mentions the fact that roots of trees and plants are able to taste the different qualities of soil, and will avoid poor soil and plunge into the richer parts of the earth. The sexual organism and life of plants also affords a great field for study to the student hunting for evidences of "life" and Mentation" in that kingdom.

The motion or circulation of the sap in trees and plants was formerly considered to be due to capillary attraction and purely "mechanical laws," but recent scientific experiments have shown it to be a vital action—an evidence of life and Mentation—the experiments having proven that if the cell-substance of the plant was poisoned or paralyzed, the circulation of sap immediately ceased, although the "mechanical principles" had not been interfered with in the least.

And now on to the mineral kingdom, "What," you may cry, "Mind and Mentation in the mineral and chemical world—surely not?" Yes, even in these low planes may be found traces of mental action. There is Life everywhere—even there. And where there is Life there is Mind. Away back among the chemical principles, and the minerals we may go in our search for Life and Mind—they cannot escape us—even there!

4

Life and Mind Among the Atoms

To the majority of persons the title of this chapter would seem an absurdity. Not to speak of Inorganic "Mind," the idea of "Life" in the Inorganic World would seem a ridiculous paradox to the "man on the street" who thinks of Substance as "dead," lifeless and inert. And, to tell the truth, even Science has held this view until a comparatively recent period, laughing to scorn the old Occult Teaching that the Universe is Alive, and capable of Thinking. But the recent discoveries of modern Science has changed all this, and we no longer hear Science speaking of "dead Matter" or "blind Force"—it recognizes that these terms are meaningless, and that the dreams of the old Occultists are coming true. Science confronts a live and thinking Universe. She is dazzled by the sight, and would shade her eyes, fearing to see that which she feels must present itself to her vision when her eyes become accustomed to the sight.

But a few daring minds among the scientific investigators are dreaming wonderful dreams today, and they tell us in broken tones of the wonderful visions that are passing before their sight.

They dare not tell it all, for they fear the ridicule of their fellows. Their visions are of Life—Universal Life. In its investigations of the Material, Science has penetrated so far into the recesses of Things that its most advanced thinkers and investigators now find themselves standing in the presence of the Immaterial. Science today is proclaiming the new doctrine—that is the same as the "old" doctrine of the Occultists—the doctrine of "Life Everywhere"— Life even in the hardest rock!

Before entering into our consideration of the evidence of Mentation in the Inorganic world, let us accustom ourselves to the idea of "something like Life" being found there. It will be better for us to approach the subject by easy stages. Where there is Life there must be Mind—so let us first look for evidences of Life.

The "man on the street" would require something more tangible than scientific explanations of "sensation," "attraction," etc. What can we offer him as an illustration? Let us see!

Suppose we call the attention of "the man" to the fact that metals get tired after considerable work without periods of rest. Science calls this the "fatigue of elasticity." When the metals are given rest, they recuperate and regain their former elasticity and health. "The man" may remember that his razor acts this way occasionally—and if he talks the matter over with his barber, his suspicions will be verified.

Then, if he consults a musician friend, he will be informed that tuning-forks also become tired, and lose their vibrating quality, until they are given a rest. Then his machinist friend will tell him that machinery in factories must be given a rest, occasionally, else it will begin to disintegrate and "die." Machinery will go on a strike for a rest, if it is overworked.

Then metals contract disease. Science informs us that zinc and tin have been infected, and the infection has spread from sheet to sheet crumbling the metal into powder—the spread of the infection resembling the spread of a plague among animals or plant-life. Science has experimented with copper and iron, and has found that these metals may be poisoned with chemicals, and will remain in a weakened condition until antidotes are administered. Window-glass workers declare that there is such a thing as "glass-disease," that will ruin fine stained glass windows unless the infected panes are removed. The "glass-disease" starts with one pane, and spreads gradually to the entire window, and from there to other windows. Metallurgists have found that when metallic ores are put under certain forms of pressure, they seem to lose strength, and become weak until the pressure is removed.

Do these things mean anything to the "Man of the Street?" Another step in the consideration of Life in the Inorganic world, is the realization of the fact that, after all, there is but the very finest line separating the higher forms of Mineral "life," from the lower forms of vegetable life, or the life of those "Things" which we may call either plants or animals. The "Life-line" is being pushed further back every day, by scientific investigation, and the "living" thing of today was the "inanimate" thing of yesterday. We hear much talk in the newspapers about some scientist, or another, "discovering life," or "creating life," in some "inanimate substance," Bless your hearts, you who are alarmed by these reports—no one can "create" life in anything, for it already exists there. The "discovery" is simply the realization of this fact.

Science, by means of the microscope, has brought to light forms of "living things," resembling in appearance the fine dust of inorganic minerals. These low forms of life exhibit but the simplest vital processes, the same very closely resembling chemical processes, although just a shade higher in the scale. Living creatures have been found which could be dried and laid aside like dust for several years, and then revived by being immersed in water, when they would resume their vital process as if they had been awakened from a sleep. Forms of life, called "Baccilli" have been discovered that can pass through degrees of heat and cold that can be expressed only by vague symbols or figures, the heat and cold being so intense that the unscientific mind cannot imagine it.

In appearance the "Diatoms" resemble the chemical crystals. These "Diatoms" are minute one-celled living "Things," having a hard but thin siliceous covering or shell, of extreme delicacy. They are what are known as "microscopic" creatures—that is, visible only through the microscope. Some of them are so small that it would take a thousand or more to cover the head of a pin. But, remember this—the microscope reveals them as "living creatures" performing vital functions. They are found in the deep waters of the ocean. To the naked eye they appear like fine sand or "dirt," but under the most powerful microscope, they are seen to comprise many species and varieties, exhibiting many peculiar shapes and forms—in fact, they have been called "living geometrical forms," their shapes and appearances almost exactly resembling those of the chemical and mineral crystals.

Science informs us that these and similar microscopic creatures, number thousands of families or species—and it is thought that the varieties of microscopic creatures outnumber the varieties of creatures visible to the unaided sight. And, remember, that there is probably a still greater world of "submicroscopic" creatures, that is a world invisible even when the most powerful microscope is used. Who knows what wonders are to be found there—what forms of creatures live, and move and have their being there.

In passing by the subject of the resemblance between the outward forms of living things and the crystals, it is interesting to note how the crystals of frost and ice resemble the forms of leaves, branches, flowers, foliage, etc.—the pane of glass covered with these frosty forms, resembles a garden. The disk of saltpeter, under the effect of polarized light, very closely resembles the form of the orchid.

Recent scientific experiments have shown that certain metallic salts, when subjected to a galvanic current, group themselves around one of the poles of the battery, and assume a mushroom-like shape and appearance. At first, they seem to be transparent, but gradually they assume color, the top becoming a bright red, with the under-side showing a pale rose color, the stem being of a pale straw color. The discoverers of these peculiar forms, called them by the German equivalent for "inorganic mushrooms," but even this term seems scarcely worthy of them, for they even show a trace of something like organs. Under the microscope they are seen to have fine canals or vein-like channels running through their stems, from top to base. And through these "veins" the "thing" absorbed fresh material and actually "grew" like low forms of fungus-life. Were these things merely minerals or chemical substances, or were they low forms of organic life? The lines between the Inorganic and the Organic are being wiped out rapidly. The Supreme Power that *caused* Life to Be, caused it to All, and did not divide Its manifestations into Dead-Things and Live-Things, but breathed into all the Breath of Life. And the more clearly we see the actual evidence of this, the greater does that Supreme Power seem to us.

A very low form of living creatures called the Monera, is held by Science to be the one of the strands of the connecting link between the organic and inorganic worlds. The Monera are the lowest and simplest form (at least so far known) of organic life. They may be said to be "organic" creatures *without organs*—being but little more than simple cells—tiny globules of plasm, surrounded by a thin membrane—their sole vital function being the absorption of nourishment through the pores of their covering (just as a piece of chalk would absorb water) and the consequent conversion of the nourishment into material for growth, the whole process resembling chemical action. The Monera reproduce their kind simply by cleavage or separation of the substance of the mother cell into two, and so on, being little more than the "growth" of crystals. The Monera are everywhere recognized, without question, as "living creatures," but they exhibit merely a trace more of life than do certain forms of crystals.

The difficulty in considering crystals as "living things" is partially due to the outward form and substance, so different from the form and substance of the higher "living things." But we have seen that the Diatoms took on shapes of crystals, and that the outer shell or covering was similar to silicia, a mineral, the inner substance being but a tiny speck of plasm, similar to that of the substance of a plant cell. And then we may look to the tiny bit of chalk dust which was once the skeleton-form of a living creature The same is true of coral. In the very low forms of life, the skeleton, or form, is the thing most apparent, the plasm of "living substance" being still smaller, and less apparent. And yet, the skeleton, or shell, was formed by the vital processes of the creature, and was a part of its "body," just as is the skeleton or bony structure of the higher animals. And, in the same sense it is "living substance," And, remember, that there is but little difference between these "bodies" of the low forms of life, and the bodies of crystals. And the chemical constituents of its plasmic inner body is but slightly different from that of the crystals. And its nature and vital process are by a shade higher in the scale than those of the crystals.

You may ask why we have said so much of Crystals. The reason is just this—Science has begun to think of Crystals as semi-living things, and its most advanced investigators and thinkers go further and assert that "the Crystals are alive—Crystallization is an evidence of life process."

Crystals arrange themselves in well-known and well-defined shapes, direction and order of formation being observed implicitly. Each crystal follows the laws and habits of its kind, just as do plants and animals. Its lines of crystallization are mathematically perfect, and according to the laws of its being. Not only this, but some substances have a range of six or seven different forms of crystal-forms possible to them. In some cases a chemical element assumes one form of crystallization when it manifests as one mineral, and a second form when it manifests in another form—in each case however, it manifests along well-known and recognized courses of action, movement, and shapes.

Crystals may be "killed" by a strong electrical discharge—that is, they are so affected that they disintegrate, their atoms separating to form new combinations, just as is the case with the "bodies" of higher forms of life. Some scientists have gone so far as to claim that they had discovered something akin to rudimentary sex-action in certain crystals, resembling the sex-process of the lowest plant-life. But this has not, as yet, been positively established, although it seems probable and reasonable. A recent writer in one of the magazines has said, "Crystallization, as we are to learn now, is not a mere mechanical grouping of dead atoms. It is a birth." This may seem mere "scientific poetry" until the process of crystallization is carefully studied, when it will be seen to give evidence, not only of something like vital and mental action, but also something very much like reproductive functioning of the lower forms of "life." There is an "assimilation" of material to build up the crystal in the first place, just as an animal assimilates matter to build up its shell—or a tree to form its bark. The "form" of the crystal is truly its "body," and behind and *in that body there is "something at work" that is not the body, but which is forming it*. And, later on, that crystal increases in size, and then begins to separate into two, throwing off a smaller crystal, identical in form with the parent crystal. This manner of reproduction is almost identical with the process of reproduction in the lower forms of "life," which consist merely of a like separation of the parent form into two, and the throwing off of the offspring.

The principal difference between the growth of crystals and of the Monera, is that the Crystals grow by absorbing fresh matter and attaching it to their outer surface, while the Monera grow by absorbing fresh material and growing outwardly, from within. But this may be accounted for by the difference in the density of their bodies, the Crystal being very solid, while the Monera is like a thin jelly. If the Crystal had a soft interior, it could grow like the Monera or Diatom, *but then it would be a Diatom.*

The process of crystallization is accountable only by the theory that in the crystal there exists something like life and Mentation. There is something more than mere "mechanical motion," or blind chance at work here. Does not the process of crystallization look like rudimentary purposive action! It may be said that it is movement and action in accordance with some established "Law of Nature"—granted, but is not that also true of the physical processes and growth of higher forms of life? Is the forming of the Crystal-form to be considered as a "mechanical effect" and the forming of the "shell" of the Monera to be considered a "mental and vital action'" If so, wherefore?

The point is that Crystals act as if they are "alive," and capable of assimilation, growth, and reproduction, in a manner and degree differing but very slightly from corresponding functioning of the lower forms of "life." Verily the Crystals are "alive"—and if alive they must have at least a trace of "Mind." Does it not appear that they exhibit something very like both? Quoting from a recent writer, let us notice that: "Recent investigations in the new department of science, which has been termed 'plasmology,' show in crystals phenomena which are absolutely analogous to vital phenomena—so much so that photographs of certain forms produced in the changes of crystals appear to be almost exact duplicates of those in the various lower forms of microbes. The question has been raised as to whether the microbe is no more alive than the crystal, or the latter equally endowed with life as is the former."

And now another step, in our search for Life. Remember, that the hardest rocks are composed of crystals of certain kinds. And, if the higher crystals have Life, then it is only fair to suppose that the lower and cruder forms are likewise endowed, even if in a still lower degree. And if all crystals are endowed with Life, then the most solid rocks, being composed of aggregations of crystals must be masses of Inorganic Life—and consequently, of Inorganic Mind. A Crystal, according to Webster, is "the regular form, bounded by plane surfaces, which a substance tends to assume in solidifying, through the inherent powers of cohesive attraction."

That definition of Webster tells the whole story, and we see that a "Crystal" is merely a "regular form" of a "Substance," which the substance "tends to assume in solidifying"—that is in re-assuming a solid form after being in a liquid or melted state, and that is just what all the rocks of the earth did when they emerged from the melted state in which they existed in the early days of the world's history. And this "tendency" that caused them to solidify, and assume certain crystal forms, and which must have existed potentially through the melted state—what of that, what is this "tendency" or force. The definition answers: "*the inherent powers of cohesive attraction.*"

So, here is "Cohesive Attraction," that we shall consider fully in forthcoming chapters of this book. "Inherent," too, the definition says. What is "Inherent"? Let us see, Webster defines "Inherent" as "permanently existing." So this power of Cohesive Attraction "permanently existed" in the Substance or else in connection with it. Let us take another look at Cohesive Attraction.

Cohesive Attraction is that form of Universal Attraction that causes the Molecules of a body to draw together—that "invisible power of" the Molecule, by which it draws another Molecule toward itself, and itself toward the other, the manifestation of which power by several Molecules tends to draw each of them together. (We shall learn of these particles of Substance called Molecules before long.) It is a primal cause of Motion, this mutual Attraction, and drawing-power. Now is it reasonable to suppose that this wonderful "power" is a mere blind-force? Is it not more reasonable to think of it as a form of vital-action—life-action? "Dead" things could not manifest this force and action.

And if this Cohesive Attraction is an evidence of Life, then all substance must have Life manifesting through it. Not only the rocks, but the soil and earth and dirt, for they are but crumbled rock.

And, when we thus consider Substance, as being the "body" through which Life is Manifesting, we must not lose sight of the Molecules and Atoms, in our consideration of the Mass. A bit of rock; crystal; or dirt; is but an aggregation of countless Molecules, grouped together in certain crystallized shapes and forms, each having characteristics of its own. These Molecules cling together, in accordance with their mutual Attractive powers.

And each of these Molecules is composed of a number of Atoms, which cling together in accordance with Chemical Affinity, or Chemism—but which is but another name for Attraction, or Cohesion—and which form a little family, called a Molecule. And these Atoms are composed of Corpuscles. We will waive the consideration of the Corpuscle, for the moment, but even if we consider it, we only carry the subject back a step farther. What we wish to say, could be said even if there were ten further divisions of Substance—or a million, for that matter.

The point we wish you to consider now, is that we must separate the Mass into its constituents—its Molecules, Atoms, and even Corpuscles—in our search for the Life in the Mineral and Chemical World. If there is Life in the Mass, there must be life in the Molecule, Atom, or Corpuscle. Now, do we find it there! Certainly, for the tiniest Atom manifests its Attractive Power, and not only does it draw other atoms to itself by virtue thereof, but it even goes a step further, and shows a "preference"—a degree of "liking" in its mutual relations with other atoms.

We shall see, in future chapters, that there is "desire," "love," "marriage," and "divorce" among the chemical Atoms. We shall consider the flirtations, and love-affairs of certain Atoms. We shall see how an Atom will leave another, and fly to a new charmer. We shall have many evidences of *the Atom's power to receive sensations, and to respond to the same.* Nothing "dead" about this, is there! The Atom is "very much alive." The Attraction; Affinity; and Motions, of the Atom, give a certain evidence of something "very much like Life," as we see it in higher forms. In the Atom exists all the Life that causes crystallization. And in the Atom lies that which causes Force and Motion to manifest. Verily, the Atom lives and moves and has its being.

And, so our journey is ended—we have traced Life to its last stages of manifestations—and we have found it there, and at each step of the journey. But, stop, we have not completed our journey—we have but begun it. "Why," some of us may cry, "how can we go back of the Atom, or Electron!" The answer is "into the ether"!

Yes, back of the Atom and the Corpuscle, is said by Science to lie that wonderful, paradoxical Something they call The Universal Ether—that Something that Science has considered the Womb of Matter and Force—Something that is different from Anything ever known or dreamed of by Man—that Something which Science has labored so diligently to build up, and which it has used as an "explanation" for so much phenomena, but regarding which, of very recent date, there has begun to grow a distrust and a suspicion, owing to the discovery of Radiant Matter, and things that followed in its train. But, notwithstanding these shadowy suspicions, Science still asserts in belief in the constancy and integrity of The Ether, and it behooves us to investigate that wonderful region in which it dwells, in order to see whether Life and Mind are also to be found there. We think that, in the words of the street, we shall find that they are "very much there."

And, so in later chapters of this book, we shall consider the Etherial Region very fully. But before doing so, we had better give Substance and Motion, in all their forms, a careful consideration, for a correct understanding of them is vitally necessary for an intelligent conception of the ideas underlying the philosophy to be herein set forth.

Now, pray do not leave this chapter with the belief that the writer has said that the Particles of Inorganic Substance are endowed with Conscious reasoning powers. Nothing of the kind has been said—nothing of the kind is meant. The Life and Mind evidenced in the Particles are but the faintest glimmerings.

There is no sign of "consciousness" or "reasoning"—the Mind exhibited is less than that of the plant, yes, less than even that of the cell of the plant. The Life is evidenced by power to move, and the Mind is evidenced by the ability to receive impressions and to respond to the same by evidencing Force and movement.

There is no evidence of "consciousness" or "understanding" in these mental processes. Consciousness is not an essential attribute of Life or Mind-action. In fact, but a small part of even the Mentation of Man is performed in the field of consciousness. Nearly all of his bodily functions are beneath the field of consciousness—one does not consciously regulate the beating of his heart; the circulation of his blood; the digestion and assimilation of his food; the tearing-down and building-up work of the cells; the work of the organs, etc., etc.

Yes, these processes are all mental processes, and far from mere "mechanical movements," or chemical processes, as some imagine. Let the spark of Life leave the body, and the processes stop, although all the chemicals are still there, and the "mechanical movements" might go on unhindered.

The Particles of Substance have enough Life and Mind to enable them to move, receive and respond to impressions, and to exert force in accordance with the Law of Attraction—but there it stops. The Crystals show signs of something like taking nourishment, but the real taking of food may be said to commence with the Monera. Not until very high degrees of Life and Mind are attained, do "creatures" begin to exhibit Consciousness, and that which is called "Understanding" is still higher in the scale, and not until Man is reached does the faculty of turning the mental searchlight *inward* manifest itself. These matters are mentioned here merely to prevent misunderstanding and misapprehension.

But still, do not forget—the Particles of Substance receive impressions and respond thereto—they *act* and exert Force and Energy—they manifest Life and Mentation.

5

The Story of Substance

As we stated in a former chapter, there are two Aspects of All-Things, viz., (1) Substance; (2) Mind. In this and the following two chapters we shall consider the first one, Substance, which Science calls "Matter." Perhaps it would be as well to begin by asking ourselves the question: "What is Substance?"

The answer seems to be: "Anything that takes up room; the Body aspect of Things; matter occupying space, etc." Some writers have spoken of Substance as "something tangible—that can be felt," but this definition will not do, for there are forms of Substance too fine to be felt. And so, perhaps the definition "The Body of Things," is as good a definition as any, taken in connection with the thought that it "takes up room."

Science divides Substance (which it calls "Matter") into four general classes, viz.:

(1) *Solid Matter*, which is Substance, the parts of which closely adhere and resist impression, such as stone, wood, flesh, etc., the degrees of solidity varying greatly, and sometimes shading into the next class, which is called:

(2) *Liquid Matter*, which may be described as Substance, the parts of which have a free motion among themselves, and easily yield to impression, such as water, molasses, etc., the degree of fluidity ranging from some liquids that flow very slowly, such as hot pitch, up to others that flow very freely, such as water, wine, etc., the property of fluidity being also shared by the next higher class, which is called

(3) *Aeriform Matter*, which is Substance in the form of "elastic fluid," such as air, gas, vapor, etc.; and

(4) *Radiant Matter*, which is of recent recognition, and which is an ultra-gaseous form of Substance, utterly unlike anything ever before known,

consisting of the tiniest particles of "corpuscles" of Substance finer and more subtle than the rarest form of atomic substance known to Science.

The three classes are well represented by (1) Earth (solid); (2) Water (liquid); (3) Air (aeriform); (4) The Corpuscles or Electrons, or particles of electrified substance, first noticed in connection with the X Rays, Radium, etc.

But it must be remembered that these four classes of Substance are not fixed or permanent—on the contrary they are changeable either under pressure, when subjected to heat, or under the influence of electricity, etc. In fact the word "condition" is more applicable than the term "class." The condition or class of a particle of Substance may be changed into another class or condition by the application of the agencies above named. The same substance may exist in two or three classes, under different circumstances. Solids may be changed into liquids, and liquids into gases, and *vice versa*. Metals may be melted, then changed into gas, according to the degree, of heat applied. Liquids may be changed into vapor by the application of heat, or into solids by the withdrawal of heat.

For an example we may turn to Water, which is a solid in the condition of ice; a liquid in the condition of water; and steam in the condition of vapor. Quicksilver is a metal which is in a liquid condition in our ordinary temperature, but which becomes a solid when subjected to a very low degree of temperature, and may be transformed into a gas, under a high degree of heat. Air is a vapor in our ordinary temperature, but has been transformed into "liquid air" under tremendous pressure, which produced a very low degree of temperature, and, theoretically, it may be transformed into a solid under a sufficiently low degree of temperature, although so far, Science has not been able to produce a degree of cold sufficient to "freeze" the liquid air. It is all a matter of "freeze," "melt," and "evaporate," in all forms of Substance—and any substance, at least theoretically, is capable of being subjected to any of the three conditions just named, and being manifested in the respective conditions, of Solid, Liquid, and Aeriform.

This may actually be accomplished with the majority of substances at this time, although in some instances we are not able to produce a sufficiently high temperature to "melt and evaporate" certain solid substances, on the one hand, or a sufficiently low degree of temperature to "liquify" or "freeze solid" certain vapors. But the intense heat of the center of the earth is able to melt rocks, and show them as liquid lava flowing from volcanoes, and Science teaches that the solid Substance of the Earth, and other planets, suns, etc., existed in the shape of a vapor at one time, and would again take on that condition in case of a collision with another great body, which convert motion into intense heat that would first melt, and then vaporize every solid particle of which the earth is composed.

If the sun's heat were completely to die out, the cold would be so intense that the air around the earth, and all the gases and vapors, would be frozen to solids. In physics the term "gas" is generally applied to a substance that is aeriform in our ordinary temperature, but which may be liquefied in a low temperature; the term "vapor" being generally applied to the aeriform condition of substances that are solid or liquid in our ordinary temperatures, but which may be "evaporated" by heat, and thus transformed into an aeriform condition, resuming their original form upon cooling. These terms, however, are technical, and practically there is no difference between a gas and a vapor.

In the above statements regarding the possibility of the transformation of each of the several forms of Substance, into other forms, the reference has been applied only to the three better known forms, *i.e.*, Solid, Liquid and Aeriform. The fourth form or state of Substance, known as Radiant Matter, is of too recent discovery to admit of its properties being accurately observed. The best and latest opinion of Science, however, is that it constitutes what may be called "Primal Matter"—that is substance from which all other forms, states, kinds and varieties of Substance arise—the "stuff" from which they are manufactured. Science seems to be discarding the Ether theory of the Origin of Matter, in favor of this "Primal Matter."

Physical Science divides Substance into Masses, Molecules, and Atoms— that is, the old Physical Science did, but the later investigators now see that even the Atom may be sub-divided. But the old terms may as well be used, at least for the time being. Let us consider these divisions.

A *"Mass"* is a quantity of Substance considered as a whole—but which is composed of a collection or combination of parts (molecules.) A lump of coal; a piece of iron; a portion of meat, even a drop of water, is a Mass. The only requisite for a Mass, is that it contains two or more parts or molecules. Therefore, a Mass is a collection or combination of two or more molecules, considered as a whole.

A *"Molecule"* is the *physical* unit of Substance, or, in other words, the smallest part of any kind of Substance that can exist by itself and still remain that particular "kind" of substance. (But not the smallest chemical part—the latter is called an Atom, and Atoms combine to form a Molecule.) The Molecule exists as a unit, and cannot be split or separated by physical means, although it may be separated into Atoms by chemical means. In order that we may form a clear idea of the Molecule, let us take a very small Mass of Matter—a drop of water, for instance.

This drop of water is a Mass composed of a great number of molecules. It may be divided, and sub-divided, into smaller and still smaller parts. This division may be carried on until it reaches a point where our sight and instruments are unable to make a further sub-division.

But, theoretically, the work may be carried on still further, until at last a limit is reached where we are unable to divide the water into any smaller parts, without separating its chemical constituents from each other, in which latter case there would be no water at all, its chemical constituents (or Atoms) having separated and now appearing as two atoms of Hydrogen and one atom of Oxygen, separated and apart and no longer forming a molecule of water.

Well, this smallest possible part of water (or any other form of Substance) is a Molecule. Remember the Molecule is the smallest part of that kind of Substance that can be produced by division and sub-division, without destroying the "kind" of the Substance. It is the smallest part of any kind of Substance that can exist by itself, and maintain its "kind."

In order that you may grasp the minuteness of the Molecule, we may mention that Science claims that no molecule, even the largest, is of sufficient magnitude to be seen under even the strongest microscope. It has been calculated that if a drop of water as large as a pea were magnified to the size of the Earth, the molecules would then appear no larger than the original drop. The space between the molecules is believed to be considerably larger than the molecules themselves.

The figures that are necessary to use in connection with molecular Substance are likely to stagger the imagination. Besides speaking of the molecules of inorganic Substance, it may be interesting to note that a spider's thread is so fine that a piece of it large enough to circle the earth would weigh only half a pound. And yet each thread is composed of six thousand filaments. And each of these minute filaments may be divided into tiny bits, and each bit will still be a Mass of Substance containing thousands of molecules and their constituent chemical atoms. There are living, microscopic creatures, so small that five millions of them might be crowded into a space the size of a pin head. And yet each of them have organs. And in these organs fluids circulate. Try to figure out the size of the molecules of the fluids circulating in these tiny organs, not to speak of the chemical atoms.

When you handle a coin, an infinitesimal portion of it is worn off—can you figure the size of the molecules composing that part? When a rose throws off its perfume, it emanates tiny particles of itself—can you measure or weigh the molecules composing that odor? The human mind is compelled to realize its finiteness when it considers these things—but we have only just begun to consider the smallness of Things.

An "*Atom*" is the *chemical* unit of Substance—that is, the smallest chemical part that can enter into combination. It has been considered indivisible—that is, incapable of further subdivision. That is, it has been so considered, until very recently, but the latest discoveries have exploded this idea, and have shown the Atom is composed of certain other Things, as we shall see a little later on. Still we may use the Atom as a very good unit of measurement, for it still represents the unit of *chemical* Substance, just as the molecule is the unit of *physical* Substance. In order that you may understand the difference between Molecules and Atoms—physical units, and chemical units, let us give you a few examples.

Take a molecule of water—the *physical* unit, you remember. When it is chemically separated or analyzed, it is found to contain two atoms of hydrogen, and one atom of oxygen—both chemical units, remember—which when united and combined, form water, but which when separated are simple atoms of certain chemical gases. The proportion in water is always the same, two of hydrogen and one of oxygen—this is the only partnership that will form water. The molecule of table salt contains one atom of sodium and one of chlorine. The molecule of air contains five chemical gases, of which nitrogen and oxygen are the principal ones, the proportion being about three parts of nitrogen to one of oxygen. Some molecules are far more complex, for instance the molecule of sugar is composed of *forty-five* chemical atoms, and sulphuric acid of seven. An atom is estimated at one-250,000,000th of an inch in diameter.

But this is not all. The old theory of the finality, and ultimateness of the Atom has been shattered by the recent discoveries of Science. The atom of Hydrogen was formerly considered to be the refinement of Substance—the Ultimate Atom—the smallest and finest Atom possible or known—the last thing that could be imagined about Substance. Some even went so far as to declare that the Atom of Hydrogen was the Ultimate Element, that is the Element out of which all other atoms were made—the mother of Atoms—the Origin of Substance. It was supposed that all other Atoms of Matter were composed of a varying number of hydrogen Atoms, which themselves were "vortex-rings in the Ether"—and that analysis could go no further. Science rested on its oars, and pronounced the work of a century completed.

But alas! no sooner was this position reached, than the discovery of Radiant Matter and the formulation of the "Corpuscle Theory" brought down the whole theoretical structure, and Science was compelled to take up the hunt again, and to probe further into the inner recesses of Things for the Ultimate

Thing. But, nevertheless, Atoms still exist, although their finality is no longer urged. The facts remain, although the theory has fallen.

Let us see about this latest theory—the Corpuscle or Electron Theory. The discovery of Radiant Matter, and the investigation of the late discovery of Radium, has led to the further discovery that each Atom, instead of being a "thing-in-itself" is a little mass containing numerous other "Things" called "Corpuscles" (or "Electrons," because electrified). The theory is this, briefly: That each Atom is a minute mass of Substance containing a number of "electrified particles," which are known as Electrons, in constant motion and vibration, revolving around each other, as do the planets, suns, and moons of the Universe—in fact each chemical Atom is like unto a Universe in itself. The simplest Atom—that which was supposed to be the "Ultimate Atom"—the Atom of Hydrogen—is supposed to contain within its tiny self no less than 1,000 minute Corpuscles, which because electrified are called "Electron," revolving in fixed and regular orbits within the containing globe of the Atom. The more complex forms of Atoms are supposed to contain a far greater number of Electrons, the authorities estimating those in an Atom of Oxygen at 10,000; those in an Atom of Gold, 100,000; and those in an Atom of Radium, 150,000. These figures are of course mere "scientific guesses" but when compared with the similar "guess" regarding the size of the Atom, they give a startling illustration of the size of the newly discovered Corpuscle or Electron.

Another authority, for an illustration, asks us to consider a great globe about 100 feet in diameter—that is, of course, 100 feet through its centre. Let the globe represent the Atom. Then imagine 1,000 minute "specks," each the size of a pin-point, composed of Substance, and each containing, as in a capsule, an atom of electricity. Each "speck" is revolving around each other in a regular orbit, in that great "100 feet through" globe, and keeping well away from one another. That will give you an idea of the relative size of the Electrons and Atoms, and the room that the former have to move about in—good many feet between each, you will notice. Lots of room, and plenty to spare. Try to figure out the size of an Electron.

Many readers of the magazines have been confused as to the relation between the Corpuscles and the Electrons (or Ions, as some have called the latter.) The matter is very simple. They are both the same. The Corpuscle is the tiny particle of Matter, which because it is electrified and has thus become the "unit of electricity," is called an "Electron." From the viewpoint of Substance we call the tiny particle a "Corpuscle"—from the viewpoint of Electricity, we call it an "Electron."

These Electrons are the tiny particles that pour forth from the pole in the

Crookes' Tube, and constitute what are known as "X Rays," "Cathode Rays," "Becquerel Rays," etc. They also are the particles that are thrown off and emitted by Radium, and similar substances. They exist in the Atom, as explained, but also are found "free" and independent, and in the last condition or state are thrown off in the aforesaid "Rays," and by Radium, etc. So far the Corpuscles are known only as charged with Electricity, and the Electron only as a tiny charge of Electricity with which the Corpuscle is charged. But Science dreams of Corpuscles of Substance other than Electrons, in which case the old Occult teachings of "light dust" and "heat dust," etc., will be verified.

The Electron contains a powerful charge of Electricity, as much in fact as an Atom, 1,000 to 150,000 times its size will carry. But Science is wondering how these highly charged particles manage to hold together in the Atom, so rigidly coherent as to appear indestructible. We think that we may get a hint at the matter a little later on in this book.

Science, or at least *some* scientists, are wondering whether the "whirl" or vibration of the Corpuscle might not produce that which we call "Electricity," and whether, when this motion is intensified, waves of Electricity will not be emitted. The writer fully agrees with this idea, and finds that it fits closely his own theories regarding Substance and Motion. But the reader is cautioned against falling into the error of many recent popular writers on the subject, some of whom have used terms calculated to convey the idea that the Corpuscle (Electron) is Electricity *itself*, rather than tiny particles of Substance called Corpuscles, charged with the unitary charge of Electricity, and therefore called "Electrons." But for that matter, Electricity is only known to us as associated with some form of Substance, and not as "a thing-in-itself." We shall see the reason for this as we proceed with this book. These Corpuscles are destined to play a most important part in the theories of Science from now on. They already have overturned several very carefully and laboriously erected theoretical structures—and many more will follow, among the many important ones evidently doomed to the dust-heap being the "vortex-ring" atomic theory, and other theories built upon the Etheric origin of Matter, and other theories concerning the Ether, even to the extent of breaking down the theory of The Ether itself, which theory had almost come to be considered a Law.

We shall further consider the Corpuscles, and their qualities, characteristics, etc., in the next chapter, for they have an important bearing upon the theories advanced in the course of the study of this book.

6

Substance and Beyond

Science has ascribed to Substance certain characteristic qualities which it calls "Properties." It divides these properties into two classes, viz.: (1) Molecular Properties (sometimes called Physical Properties); and (2) Atomic Properties (sometimes called Chemical Properties).

Molecular Properties are those which may be manifested by Substance without disturbing the Molecules, and consequently without affecting the "kind" of Substance.

Atomic Properties are those which concern the Atoms when free from Molecular combination, and which consequently cannot be manifested without changing the "kind" of Substance.

Science, before long, is likely to add a third class of Properties, namely, *"Corpuscular Properties,"* relating to the Corpuscles or particles of Radiant Matter, but, so far, it has not had the opportunity to sufficiently observe these qualities, except in a general way.

There are certain General Properties that seem possessed by both Mass, Molecules, and Atoms—and probably by Corpuscles.

These *General Properties* are as follows:

Shape: That property whereby Substance "takes up room."

This property manifests in three directions, called Dimensions of Space, namely, Length, Breadth, and Thickness.

Weight: That property whereby Substance responds to Gravity. Weight is simply the measure of the attraction.

Impenetrability: That property whereby two bodies of Substance are prevented from occupying the same space at the same time. A nail driven into a piece of wood, simply pushes aside the molecules, and occupies the Space between them. Substance is never actually "invaded" or its actual territory occupied by other Substance.

Indestructibility: That property whereby Substance is prevented from being destroyed or annihilated. Although the forms of Substance may be changed, or transformed into other forms, still, Substance *in itself* is not destroyed, and cannot be under the existing Laws of the Universe.

Mobility: That property whereby Substance responds to imparted Motion. We shall notice this property in our consideration of Motion. In addition to the Motion of the Mass, and the movements of Molecules and Atoms in response to its Attraction, there is another form of Motion constantly going on, without reference to the Attraction or impressed Motion of the Mass. The Molecules of all bodies are always in a state of rapid Motion, called Vibration. In solids this vibration is short; being restrained by the close cohesive position of the Molecules. But in Liquids, the Molecules being further separated, the vibration is far more rapid, and they move around and slide over each other with comparatively little resistance.

In gases and vapors the Molecules have a splendid field for Motion, and consequently vibrate in wide fields and orbits, and dash around with the greatest velocity. The Atoms also are believed to vibrate rapidly, in accordance with their own laws of vibration. And the Corpuscles are believed to far excel the last two mentioned particles in intensity, rapidity and complexity of their vibrations, as we shall see a little later on in the book. All Substance is in constant Motion and Vibration.

There is no Rest in Substance.

Inertia: That property whereby Substance may not move unless in response to imparted Motion; nor terminate its Motion, when it is once imparted, except in response to some other manifestation of impressed Force. Science holds that this "impressed Force" or "imparted Motion" must come from without, but the writer holds that Force may also be "expressed" from "within," as may be seen by reference to subsequent chapters of this book.

Attraction: That property whereby particles or bodies of Substance (1) draw other particles or bodies toward themselves; or (2) move toward other particles or bodies; or (3) are mutually drawn together. This property manifests in four forms, generally referred to as separate and distinct from each other, but which the writer believes to be but forms of the same Attractive Power, and which he believes to be a Mental Process, at the last analysis (a revolutionary claim, which will be supported by argument in later chapters of the book). These three forms of Attraction are known as (1) Gravitation; (2) Cohesion; (3) Adhesion; and (4) Chemical Affinity, or Chemism. We are invited to consider them briefly, at this point, further investigation being reserved for our chapters on Motion, and Dynamic Thought.

Gravitation: This term is usually applied to the attraction between Masses of Substance, such as the Sun, the Earth, and Masses of Substance on or about the Earth's surface. However, Newton, who discovered the facts of Gravitation, states the Law, as: "*Every particle of matter in the Universe, attracts every other particle,*" etc.

Cohesion: This term is used to indicate the attraction between Molecules, by which they are combined into Masses or Bodies. Cohesion causes the Molecules to unite and cling together, thus forming the Mass.

Adhesion: This term is used to indicate the attraction between Masses which causes them to "stick together" without a cohesion of their Molecules. Adhesion operates through the adjacent surfaces of the two Masses. It may be considered as a "lesser" form of cohesion.

Chemical Affinity (sometimes called Chemism or Atomic Attraction): This term is used to indicate the attraction between the Atoms, by which they combine, unite and cling together, forming the Molecule.

Science has before it the task of naming, and classifying, the attraction between the Corpuscles, by which they combine and form the Atom. But whatever the name, it will be seen that it represents but another manifestation of "Attraction."

Arising from Molecular Attraction, or Cohesion, are several "Properties" peculiar to Masses having Molecules, and resulting from the tendency of the latter to resist separation. We had better consider them briefly, in order to understand the power of Molecular Attraction, and its incidents.

Porosity: That property indicating the distances observed by the Molecules in their relation to each other, which varies in different "kinds" of Substance. All Substance is more or less Porous, that is, has more or less space existing between the Molecules—the degree depends upon the "closeness." Compressibility and Expansibility, sometimes mentioned as "properties," are but results of Porosity.

Elasticity: That property whereby bodies resume their original size and form, after having been compressed, expanded or "bent." The result is caused by the inclination of the Molecules to resume their original positions. What is sometimes called "Plasticity" is merely the reverse of Elasticity, and denotes a limited degree of the latter.

Hardness: That condition resulting from Molecular Attraction resisting the forcible entrance and passage of other Substance between the Molecules.

Tenacity: That condition resulting from Molecular Attraction resisting the forcible pulling asunder, or tearing apart of the Mass. This condition sometimes is called "Toughness."

Malleability: That condition resulting from Molecular Attraction resisting the forcible separation of the Mass by pounding, hammering or pressure. The resistance is "passive," and consists of the Molecules allowing themselves to assume a spread-out formation, rather than to be forced apart.

Ductility: That condition resulting from Molecular Attraction resisting the forcible separation of the Mass by a "drawing out" process. The resistance is "passive," and consists of the Molecules allowing themselves to be drawn out into a formation of the shape of wire or thread, rather than to be pulled apart.

In any of the above cases, we may intelligently, and with propriety, substitute the words, "Molecules, by means of cohesion, resisting, etc.," for the terms above used, "Molecular Attraction, resisting, etc."

All Masses of Substance (probably Molecules as well) are capable of *Expansion and Contraction*, both phenomena, in fact, and in degree, resulting from the relation of the Molecules. Contraction is a "crowding together" of the Molecules; Expansion a "getting apart" of them.

Density: The amount of Substance in relation to a given bulk. *Volume*—the "size" or "bulk" of a body of Substance. *Mass*—Besides being used to designate a "body" of Substance, composed of two or more Molecules, the term "Mass" is used to designate the "total quantity of Substance in a Body." An application of the above terms may be seen in the following illustration:

A quart of water occupies a certain space—and has a certain "volume," "mass" and "density." Convert the same "mass" of Water into Steam, and it expands to a "volume" of 1700 times that of Water—but, as no Molecules have been added, the "mass" remains the same—but as a quart of Steam weighs 1700 times less than the same "volume" of Water, the "density" of Steam is 1700 times less than that of Water. As the "volume" of a given "mass" increases, the "density" decreases in the same proportion—but the "mass" remains the same. "Mass" therefore has two factors, i.e., "Volume" and "Density." The "Density" of a "Mass" is determined by the *weight* of a certain "Volume" of it.

The above consideration of the "Properties" of Substance dealt only with the Molecular Properties, or Physical Properties, as they are sometimes called— that is, with properties depending upon the existence of the Molecules. When we consider the Molecules as being composed of Atoms, and when we consider the processes whereby these Molecules are built up of, or broken down through the separation of Atoms, we come to the subject of Atomic Properties, or Chemical Properties, as they are often called.

The Atomic Properties of Substance consist principally in the power and manifestation of Motion, in the direction of combination, separation, and the complex motions resulting from the same. This Motion is manifested by reason of Atomic Attraction, sometimes called "Chemical Affinity," which we shall consider a little later on in the chapter.

Atomic Principles, as above mentioned, are best illustrated by a reference to Chemical changes, and we shall now examine the same. And, the better way to consider Chemical Changes is by comparing them with Physical Changes, or Changes of the Molecules.

Some Physical Changes in Substance are brought about by Heat, which tends to separate the Molecules, or rather to allow them to spread out away from each other, so long as the high temperature is maintained, the degree of their nearness being influenced by temperature. Other Physical Changes are produced by outside Forces separating the Molecules to such an extent—to such a distance—that their cohesive force is lost, and the Solid matter is said to be "broken," or even reduced to dust. Other physical changes are brought about by Electricity, causing the Molecules to separate and disintegrate.

Chemical Changes, as distinguished from Physical Changes, do not involve or deal with Molecules, the action being solely upon the Atoms of which the Molecules are composed. Physical Changes *separate* Molecules from each other, while Chemical Changes destroy and break up the Molecule, so that its identity is forever lost, its Atoms thereafter either existing free from combinations, or else recombining with other Atoms, and forming new combinations. Chemical changes are occasioned by either physical or chemical agencies.

The physical agencies generally employed are heat, electricity, light, pressure, percussion, etc. The principle of Chemical Changes is that the Atoms are possessed of, and subject to, what is called "Atomic Attraction" or "Chemical Affinity," which may be defined as an attraction or "love" existing in varying degrees between Atoms. This Affinity causes Atoms of one element to seek out and ally themselves to Atoms of another element, the element of "choice" or "preference" being strikingly in evidence.

Atoms of different elements form marriages, and cling together in harmony, until, perchance, by some physical or chemical agency, the Molecule is brought in sufficiently close connection with another Molecule composed of different elemental atoms, when, alas! one of Atoms of our Molecule finds that it has a greater Affinity for some other elemental Atom in the second Molecule, and lo! it flies away, leaving its first partner, and seeking the new charmer. Divorce and re-marriage is a common thing in the world of Atoms—in fact, Chemistry is based upon these qualities.

Physical and Chemical Changes gradually transform solid rock to "earth" or "soil." Disintegration, by the action of changes in temperature, rains and atmospheric influences, and other Physical Changes, have slowly worn down the rocks into "dirt," gravel, clay, loam, etc. And Decomposition by Chemical Change that set the atoms free from their combinations has aided in the work.

There is no rest in the world of Substance. Everything is changing—constantly changing. Old forms give way to new, and these, grown old while being born, are, in turn replaced by still newer. And on, endlessly. Nothing persists but change. And yet nothing is destroyed, although countless forms and shapes have succeeded each other. Substance is always there, undisturbed and unaffected by the varieties of forms it is compelled to undergo. Masses may change—and do change. Molecules may change—and do change. Disintegration and decomposition affect both, and bring to them the death of form. But their substance endures in the Atom. Atoms may change, and decompose, or undergo whatever change that is their fate, and still the Corpuscles, or what lies beyond the Corpuscles will remain. The Atom was once regarded as Eternal, but now even it seems to be capable of dissolving into some finer division of Substance—and perhaps still finer subdivisions await it.

That familiar form of Substance that we call "earth," "dirt," "soil," etc., is but the result of disintegrated rock, which has crumbled and lost its former form through the action of air, water and atmospheric influences. And the rocks themselves, from which the "soil" came, were at one time a sea of melted, flowing liquid Substance, somewhat resembling volcanic lava. And this "melted rock" is thought to have been condensed from the same principles in the shape of vapor, that existed in the early days of our planetary system. Vapor, gas, liquid, semi-liquid, solid rock, "soil"—the Substance unchanged, the forms totally unlike.

Helmholtz estimates the density of the nebulous vapors of Substance as being so rare that it would take several millions of cubic miles of it to weigh a single grain. Oh, Nature, what a wizard thou art!

We have spoken of Air and Water, in a former chapter, and their constituent atoms have been named. And from these three great reservoirs of Substance—the Earth, the Air, and the Water—are obtained all the material that goes to form the bodies of the animal and vegetable kingdoms. The plant draws its nourishment from the soil, the air, and water, and in its wonderful chemical laboratory is able to transform the elements so drawn from these sources into a substance called "Plasm," which consists principally of carbon, oxygen, nitrogen and hydrogen, being nearly identical in composition to the white of an egg, and which constitutes the basis of animal and plant bodily structures. All the material of the physical bodies, of men, animals and plants, are but forms of Plasm. The animals, and man, obtain their nourishment, directly or indirectly, from the plant body, and so at the last we are seen to draw from the soil, air and water all our bodily nourishment, which we convert into bodily structure, bone, muscle, flesh, blood, veins, tissue, cells, etc. And the chemical atoms of our bodies are identical with those in the rock, the air, the water. And so you see the universality of Substance and its countless forms and appearances.

Chemistry resolves Substance back into about seventy-five simple substances, of which Atoms are the Units, which simple substances are called "Elements." From these Elements (by their Atoms) all other substances are formed by combinations, the number of such possible combinations being infinite. An Element (in order to be an element) must be a "simple" substance, that is, must be incapable of further analysis into some other elements. The seventy-five elements, now recognized by science, have never been resolved into other elements, by chemical analysis, and therefore are accepted as "simple." But, it is true that other substances that were formerly considered as simple elements were afterward decomposed by electricity, and found to consist of two or more simpler substances or elements. Thus new elements were discovered, and old ones discarded as "not-elemental." And this fate may be in store for a number of the elements now on the list—and many new ones may be discovered.

For a long time Science was endeavoring to trace all elements back to Hydrogen, the latter being considered the "Ultimate Element," and its atoms composing all the other atoms, under varying conditions, etc. But this theory is now almost abandoned, and Science rests on its list of seventy-five elements, the atoms of which are composed of "Electrons." Some have hazarded the theory that the Elements were all forms of Ether (see next chapter), their apparent differences resulting merely from the varying rate of vibration, etc. And, in fact, such theory was about finally adopted as a working hypothesis until the discovery of the Corpuscle. Everything in Substance now seems to be moving back to the Corpuscle, as we shall see a little further on.

The following is a list of the principal Elements, known to Science, today:

Aluminum. Bismuth. Calcium. Cobalt. Hydrogen. Magnesium. Nitrogen. Potassium. Sodium. Zinc. Antimony. Arsenic. Boron. Bromine. Carbon. Chlorine. Copper. Fluorine. Iodine. Iron. Manganese. Mercury. Oxygen. Phosphorus. Radium. Silicon. Strontium. Sulphur. Barium. Cadmium. Chromium. Gold. Lead. Nickel. Platinum. Silver. Tin.

Of the above, Hydrogen is by far the lightest in weight; in fact it is used as a unit of Atomic Weight, its weight being marked "1" on the scale; Gold, 197; Lead, 207; Silver, 108; Oxygen, 16; Nitrogen, 14; Iron, 56.

The discovery of the Corpuscle, or Electron, rudely shattered the vortex-ring theory of the origin of the Atom, and now, instead of the Atom being regarded as a "vortex-ring" in that hypothetical, paradoxical absurdity, the Ether, it is believed to be composed of a vast number of tiny particles called Corpuscles, as we saw stated in our last chapter. These Corpuscles seem to be the "last thing in Substance"—its last known state of refinement, and already it is being proclaimed as the long-sought for "Primal Matter," or "Ultimate Substance." Whether or not a still finer state of Substance will be discovered Science is unable to say, but thinks it unlikely. But we must not overlook the old Occult Teaching indicating a state of Substance so fine that it is imperceptible, and only recognizable as apparently "free force"; its covering, or vehicle of Substance not being evident. This would seem to indicate a still further refinement of Substance, although perhaps the "Corpuscle" or "Electron" will answer to "fill the bill" in the case.

As to the Corpuscle being "Primal Substance," it must be admitted that its advocates have presented a very strong case. One of their most important points is that although Molecules differ very materially from each other, according to their kinds; and while Atoms likewise manifest very plainly their "kind," the Corpuscle seems to possess *only one "kind"* no matter from what form or "kind" of Substance it is thrown off. Just think what this means. It means that the finest particles of Gold, Silver, Iron, Hydrogen, Oxygen, and all the rest of the Elements, *are composed of identically the same material, and exhibit no differences in "kind."* The Elements are no longer "Simple." *All Substance is One, at the last analysis!*

The Corpuscles seem to possess the same Mass—to carry the same charge of Electricity—to act precisely the same—irrespective of their source. No difference in size, mass or character, as in the case of the Atom—all are identical, save in the rate of their vibration at the time of observation, which is simply a matter of more or less Motion. Space seems to be flooded with these tiny particles—these Units of Substance.

They stream from the Sun; the Stars; and every body highly heated. Likewise they stream from the bodies of highly electrified Substance. Groups of these Corpuscles, absolutely identical in nature, size, mass, etc., constitute the Atoms of the Seventy-five Elements, the "kind" of Element seemingly being dependent upon the number and arrangement of the Corpuscles, and possibly by their rate of vibration. Every Atom is like a great bee-hive with a swarm of Corpuscles vibrating, moving around each other, and upon their own centres. And, if by the action of intense heat, transmitted, or caused by interrupted Motion—or if by a strong Electric charge—some of these Corpuscles are detached from the Atoms (or possibly an Atom broken up), they fly off through Space at a marvellous speed of many thousand miles an hour.

So we see that these wonderful Corpuscles look very much like Primal Matter or Ultimate Substance—the "Stuff" out of which Substance is made. And, taking you back to the chapter on "The Universality of Life and Mind," the writer would remind you that in their Motions and evident Attraction, etc., these Corpuscles evidence the same "Life and Mind" that we observed in the Molecules and Atoms. It must be so, for what is in the manufactured article must be in the material of which the article is made. And so, even here, Life and Mind have not escaped us. Nor will it in The Ether!

And speaking of the Corpuscles, as "manufactured articles," we are reminded of Herschel's thought about the Atoms, when they were regarded as Primal Matter and likely to be uniform, and, at the end, of one primal substance. Although Herschel's conception does not now apply to the Atoms, it may be transferred to the Corpuscles.

Herschel thought that the fact that the Particles of Substance were likely to be found to be uniform in size, and identical in nature and characteristics, indicated that they might be akin to "manufactured articles," turned out from the same great machinery of Creation. This idea would indicate that the Creator applied the rules of careful manufacture to the manufacture of the Particles, the uniformity operating in the direction of (1) Economy of Material; (2) Utility through interchangeability, replacing broken or discarded parts, etc.; and also (3) Conformity to a Standard of Size, Quality, etc.

The thought is interesting, and is mentioned here for that reason. It is not affected by the supposition that there may be a still finer and rarer form of Substance, from which the Particles are "manufactured"—in fact, the idea of Herschel, if closely analyzed, would seem to indicate some such "raw material" from which the articles were manufactured.

7

The Paradox of Science

In the days of the ancients, when the philosophers found themselves unable to account for any particular class of phenomena, they bundled it together and referred it to a suppositious Something that they called "The Ether." Finding this an easy way to get rid of vexatious questions, they fell into the custom— and the habit grew upon them. Soon there were a dozen or more different kind of Ethers in vogue, each explaining something else—the "something else," by the way, being things that Science *now* feels that it understands pretty well. These Ethers grew to be like the various "Vapors" of the ancients—a dignified term for "We don't know"—a respectable road for retreat under the semblance of an advance.

These Ethers became a scientific scandal, and caused a lax mode of thinking among students of those times. And so they were finally abolished and relegated to the scrap pile of Science, where they lay for many centuries until a comparatively recent period, when at least one of them was hauled forth, dusted, freshened up a little, and placed upon its old pedestal. This revamped Ether, referred to, was the "Ether of Aristotle." Aristotle, as we know, was a famous Greek philosopher who lived about 350 b. c.—about 2250 years ago. He was a good man and a celebrated philosopher, but was somewhat deficient in scientific knowledge. Although he knew many things, and uttered many wise thoughts, he was under the impression that the breath of Man entered the heart instead of the lungs—that the back part of the skull was empty, and so on. He was without the advantages of a modern training—which was not his fault, however.

Well, Aristotle conceived the idea of an Universal Ether, which he thought pervaded all space, and with which he accounted for the passage of light from the sun and stars; the movements of the planets, and various other physical phenomena. It is not known whether Aristotle really *believed* in this Ether, or whether he merely used it as a speculative hypothesis, following the Ether Habit of his contemporaries. At any rate, his theory served its purpose—lived, flourished, declined and died—at least seemed to be dead. But its corpse was resurrected in modern times, and used to account for diverse things.

This does not mean that modern thinkers really "believe" in the Universal Ether—they merely assume it as a working hypothesis until something better is offered.

Its principal modern use is to account for the transmission of Light from the Sun and Stars to the Earth. It was held that a thing could not act "where it was not," and so it became necessary to account for the transmission either by the theory that small particles of substance were thrown off from the Sun, and travelled to the Earth, or else that there was some medium of communication by means of vibrations, etc. Newton held to the first theory, but his hypothesis went down before the Ether advocates, who advanced the "wave-theory," although it seems that, like Banquo's ghost, Newton's theory will not stay down, and is now taking on a new lease of life, owing to the discovery of the Corpuscle and Radiant Matter.

The Wave-theory philosophers asserted that the Light and Heat of the Sun were thrown off in the shape of Force or Energy, and transformed into "waves" in and of a hypothetical Ether (Aristotle's own), which waves were carried to the Earth, where, meeting Substance, they were again transformed into Heat and Light.

It was known that Light and Heat travelled at the rate of 184,000 miles per second, and therefore the "waves" of the Ether were considered to have that speed. The Wave-theory seemed to fit the facts of the case better than the Newtonian Theory of Corpuscles, although the latter has always been considered as better explaining certain phenomena than the new theory. And so the Ether Wave became generally accepted, and remains so today, although recent discoveries are causing a disturbance in the scientific camp regarding the question.

Later it was discovered that the Electricity travelled at the same rate as Light and Heat, and the Wave-of-the-Ether theory was thus thought to have additional verification, and Electricity came under the Law and remained there until the Electron discovery, which is causing much disturbance, among those interested in the study of Electricity.

Briefly stated, the theory of the Universal Ether is this:

That pervading all Space in the Universe—not only between planets, stars and suns, but also "filling in the cracks" between molecules, and atoms as well—there is a subtle Substance in and through which the waves of Light, Heat, Electricity and Magnetism travel at the rate of 184,000 miles per second. This Substance is said to be "Matter that is not Matter"—in fact, Science does not venture to say just *what* it is, although it freely states just what some of its properties must be, and, alas! these properties are most contradictory and opposite to each other, as we shall see as we proceed.

This Universal Ether is purely hypothetical. It has been called a "necessity of Science"—something assumed for the purpose of explaining or accounting for certain phenomena. It is undemonstrated and unproved—in fact, may truthfully be said to be undemonstrable and unprovable. Some have gone so far as to say that its claimed properties and qualities render it "unthinkable" as well. And yet, Science finds itself compelled to assume that the Ether, or "something like it" exists, or else cease speculating about it. It belongs to the realm of pure theory, and yet, many writers treat it as if it were a positively demonstrated and proven fact. Let us examine into the nature of Science's problem, and her attempted solution, and the trouble arising therefrom.

Light travels at the rate of 184,000 miles a second. Remember, that Light and Heat are that which we call by those names only when considered in connection with Substance. According to the theory, Light in the Sun's atmosphere is transformed into a Light-wave of the Ether on its travels to the earth, and only when the "wave" comes in contact with the Substance on the earth's body or atmosphere does it become again transformed into Light as we know it. In its travels through space it meets with no Substance, and has nothing to "turn into light"—consequently Space (between worlds) is in a state of absolute darkness.

The same is true of Heat, and inter-world Space is absolutely cold, although passing through it are countless heat-waves of great intensity, which, later on, will be transformed into Heat when they reach the Substance, the earth. The same is true of Electricity and Magnetism.

Although the Ether, as we have seen, is a purely theoretical substance, yet Science has found it reasonable to conclude that it must be possessed of certain attributes in order to account for certain known facts. Thus, it is said to be frictionless, else the worlds, suns and planets could not pass freely through it, nor could the light and heat waves travel at such a tremendous rate. It also is thought to have something like Inertia, because Motion once started in it persists until stopped; because it is at a state of rest until Motion is imparted to it; and because it takes a fraction of time to impart motion to it. It is thought to be different from Substance in any of its known forms, for many reasons, among such being the fact that no known form of Substance could carry vibrations through space at the rate of 184,000 miles a second. And Light and Heat waves travel at that rate, and have forms and shapes, and lengths of their own. Light for instance, vibrates on two planes, and a light-wave is something like a Greek cross, thus (-|-), having a horizontal and a vertical line, or plane of vibration. And the Ether cannot be a fluid of any degree, because a fluid cannot transmit cross vibrations at all. And it cannot be a Solid, because a Solid could not stand vibrations at such a terrific speed, and still remain a Solid. And yet, to transmit the two-plane light waves, the Ether must have a certain degree of Rigidity, else the waves could not travel. Lord Kelvin estimated this degree of Rigidity as about 19,000,000,000th of the rigidity of the hardest steel. So, you see, Science is compelled to assume that the Ether is "a continuous, Frictionless medium, possessing both Inertia and Rigidity." Some scientists have thought it to be a kind of "elastic jelly."

Of the Ether, Prof. Oliver Lodge has said, "We have to try and realize the idea of a perfectly continuous, subtle, incompressible substance, pervading all Space, and penetrating between the molecules of ordinary Matter, which are imbedded in it, and connected to one another by its means. And we must regard it as the one universal medium by which all actions between bodies are carried on. This, then, is its function—to act as the transmitter of motion and energy."

To give you an idea of the wonderful thing that Science is compelled to think of the Ether as being, by reason of the qualities it is compelled to ascribe to it—although it confesses itself unable to "imagine" the nature of the "Thing" which it has created in bits by the adding and bestowing of qualities which were made necessary by the logical requirements of the case—let us take a hurried view of the Thing as the several departments of Science say it must be thought of.

To meet the requirements of the case, Science says that The Universal Ether must be Substance infinitely more rare and evanescent than the finest gas or vapor known to Science, even in its rarest condition. It must convey Heat in the manner of an infinitely Solid body—and yet it must not be a Solid. It must be transparent and invisible. It must be Frictionless, and yet Incompressible. It cannot be a Fluid. It cannot have Attraction for Substance, such as all Substance has. Nor can it have Weight—that is, it is not subject to Gravitation. It is beyond the reach of any known scientific instrument, even of the greatest power, and it refuses to register itself in any way, either to senses or instruments.

It cannot be known "of itself," but may only be recognized as existent by the "things" for which it acts as a medium or transmitting agent. It must convey Energy and Motion, yet it must not take up any part of either from the Matter in its midst. It must not absorb any of the Heat, Light or Electricity. It must fill up the spaces between the worlds, as well as the most minute space between the

Molecules, Atoms and Corpuscles, or any other minute particle of Substance, either known by name to Science now or which may be discovered or imagined later as a necessity of some conception regarding the nature of Substance. In short, The Universal Ether, in order to do the things attributed to it, must be more solid than Solids; more Vapor-like and Gas-like than Vapor or Gas; more fluid than Fluids; infinitely less rigid than steel, and yet infinitely stronger than the strongest steel. It must be a substance having the qualities of a vacuum. It must be continuous and not composed of Particles, Atoms or Molecules. It must be an "everything" in some respects, and yet a "nothing" in others. It must not be Substance, and yet it must carry Substance within its ocean of dimensions, and, besides, interpenetrate the most minute space between the particles of Substance. It must not be Energy or Force, and yet Science has been considering Energy and Force as but "interruptions of rest" or "agitations" within, and of, itself.

So you see that this mysterious, wonderful Universal Ether—in order to "be" at all—must be a "Something" possessing certain qualities or properties of Substance—many of the properties of qualities being exactly contradictory and opposed to each other—and yet it cannot be Substance as we know it. It is a Paradoxical thing. It could only belong to another and an entirely different order of existence from that of Substance as we know it. It must possess characteristics and properties of an order as yet unknown to us by name—for which the material world contains no analogy—for which Substance has no analogues. It must be a far more complex thing than is even the most complex thing we call Matter, or that which we call Force or Energy. And yet, it has been claimed that it would explain both—yes, contain within itself the possibility of both. And yet, in face of what has just been said, the writer must confess, humbly and with a full realization of the enormity of the offence, that he supposes advancing a theory, a little further on in this book that will attempt to identify this Something—this Universal Ether—with a Something else that we know, although not through the senses or by means of instruments. Bear with him kindly, he begs of you, while he proceeds gradually along the path that leads to the theory.

Scientists have compared Substance moving through the Ether as a coarse sieve moving through water, the latter making room for the passage of the sieve, and then closing up behind it. If this be amended by the idea that the moving sieve, while allowing the water to pass through it freely, still carries along with it a thin film of water which clings to the wires of the sieve by adhesion—if there be admitted this "clinging film" as well as the body of the water through which the sieve moves—then the illustration answers quite well as a crude illustration of Substance and "The Ether." This fact is important in view of the theory that will be advanced, further on in this book. Prof. Lodge, in his interesting work, "Modern Views of Electricity," mentions a number of experiments tending to prove the above mentioned fact, which is not so generally known as other facts relating to the Ether.

Until the discovery of Radiant Matter (bringing with it the new theories of the Corpuscle or Electron, etc.), brushed aside into the dust heap many generally accepted scientific theories regarding the nature of Substance, the favorite and most popular theory was what was known as the "Vortex-ring" theory of the Atom. This theory held that the atoms of Substance were but vortex-rings of the Ether, having had motion communicated to them in some way, and which afterwards acquired other motions, and which finally become apparent to our senses as Substance. In other words, the Atom was supposed to a vortex-ring of Ether, acted upon by Force, in some unknown way, the character, nature and properties of the Atom being determined by the shape and size of the vortex-ring; the rate of motion; etc., etc.

The new discoveries of Science, however, have set aside (at least temporarily) this "vortex-ring" theory, and at present Science seems to find its "latest thing in Substance," in the theory that Substance—at the last—seems to be the Corpuscle or Electron. In other words, after many years of fancied security in a settled theory regarding the nature of Substance, Science once more finds itself compelled to take up the search for the origin of things. But the theory of the Ether remains—and is likely to—although the names applied to it will change. By some it is still believed that in the Ether, a little further removed, rests the origin of Substance and that the Corpuscle may be the "vortex-ring" product, instead of the Atom.

It will be noticed that Science has made no serious attempt to connect the phenomenon of Gravitation or Attraction with the Ether. Gravitation stands alone—an "outsider" among the Forces, responding to none of their laws— needing no time in which to travel—needing no medium like the Ether in which to transmit "waves"—fearing no obstacle or interfering body, but passing right through the same—different, different, different. And we shall see *why* this difference, when we reach the point where our theory brings us to the point where we must substitute "something else" for that Great Paradoxical General Solvent of Modern Science—the Ether of Aristotle. We shall reach the point after a brief consideration of Motion, Force and Energy.

8

The Forces of Nature

The Substance filling the Universe is in constant and unceasing Motion. Motion is evidenced in every physical and chemical process and change, and manifested in the constant interchange of position of the Particles of Substance. There is absolutely no rest in Nature—everything is constantly changing—moving—and vibrating. Building-up processes are ever at work forming larger masses or bodies of the Particles—and tearing-down processes, disintegration and decomposition of Molecules and Atoms, and Corpuscles, are constantly at work also. Nature maintains a constant balance among her Forces. If the building-up energies and forces were allowed full sway, then all the Particles in the Universe ultimately would gravitate to a common centre, thus forming a compact and solid Mass, which would thus dwell for Eternity, unless the Creative Power should move upon it and again scatter its Particles in all directions. And, if the tearing-down, and dispersive forces and energies were allowed full sway, the Particles would fly apart and would remain asunder for Eternity, unless called together by some new Creative fiat.

But Nature pits one force against another, maintaining an equilibrium. The result is constant play and inter-play of forces, causing distribution, and redistribution of Particles, following the gathering-together and building-up processes.

There is no lost motion, or waste force. One form of force and motion is converted into another, and so on, and on. Nothing is lost—all force is conserved, as we shall see as we proceed.

In the public mind—or rather, in the mind of that part of the public which think of the matter at all—there seems to be an idea that "Force" is something of the nature of an entity, separate from Substance or Mind—something that pounces down upon Substance and drives it along by presence from without. The ancient philosophers regarded Substance as acted upon from *without* by an entity called Force, Substance being regarded as absolutely inert and "dead." This idea, which is still held by the average person, owing, doubtless, to the survival of old forms of expression, was generally held by philosophers until the time of Descartes and Newton. This old idea was due to the teachings of Aristotle—he of the Ether Theory—and Science and Philosophy were timid about shaking off the Aristotelian dogmas. Others held that Light, Heat and Electricity were "fluids" conveyed from body to body—in fact the general public still entertains this idea regarding Electricity, owing to the use of the term "the Electric *fluid*."

The present teaching of Science is that Force is the result of the motion of the Particles of Substance, and, of course, originates from *within*, rather than from without. It is true that Motion may be communicated to a body by means of another body in Motion imparting the same to it, but that does not alter the case, for the Original Motion came from the movement and vibration of the Particles of Substance, although it may have passed through many stages of transformation, change and transmission in its progress. The only exception to the rule is Gravitation, which is a form of Force, the nature of which is unknown to Science, although its laws of operation, etc., are understood. We shall learn some new facts about Gravitation in the forthcoming chapters of this book.

It will be well for us to remember *this* fact, in our consideration of Force and Motion—that Force and Motion *originate* from the inherent property of Motion passed by the Particles of Substance, and come from *within*, not from without. This is the best teaching of Modern Science, and also, forms an important part of the Theory of Dynamic Thought which is advanced in this book. Buchner, the author of "*Force and Matter*," vigorously insists upon this conception, saying, among many other similar expressions: "Force may be defined as a condition of activity or a motion of matter, or of the minutest particles of matter or a capacity thereof."

The term "Force" is generally defined in works on Physics as "That which causes, changes or terminates Motion." The word "Force" is generally used in the sense of "in action," while "Energy" is usually used in the sense of "Potential Force—capacity for performing work," the idea being that it is "stored-up" force, or "force awaiting use." The term "Power" is used in two senses, the first meaning "a measure of Mechanical Energy," such as a "forty horse-power engine," etc.; the second sense being "Capacity or Ability to Act, or exercise Force," this use being almost identical to the idea of "Energy," as above described, although, possibly, a little stronger expression.

The Materialistic school holds that Force is a property of Matter, the latter being regarded as the "real thing" of the Universe. Others hold that Force is the "real thing," and that what is called Matter, or Substance, is but a centre of Force, etc. Others hold that the two are but aspects of the same thing, calling the "thing" by the name "Matter-Force," or "Force-Matter." Haeckel calls this combined "thing" by the name of "Substance," claiming that what are called Matter and Force are but "attributes" of it, the third "attribute" being "Sensation," which he holds is akin to Mind—"Haeckel's Substance" is held to be Eternal, and Self-existent—its own Cause, in fact. (In this book the term" Substance" is not used in this sense, but merely as synonymous with what Science usually calls "Matter.")

The views advanced in this book differ materially from any of those above mentioned, it being held by the writer that "All Force is Vital-Mental Force," and, consequently, "Force" as a separate thing is considered an unreasonable proposition—what is called "Force" being considered merely an action of Mind upon Substance, causing Motion. The writer does not intend to advance this idea at this point beyond the mere mentioning of the fact—the theory being brought out and developed as we proceed—and he will proceed to a consideration of the phenomena of Force, along the lines of Modern Science, believing that in this way the subject may be better understood.

The term "Motion," as used in Physics, is defined as: "The act, process or state of changing place or position; "movement"—(Webster). So you see, Motion is the movement of Substance changing place or position; Force is that which causes, changes or terminates Motion; and Energy is the "capacity" for manifesting Force; and Power the Ability to Act. In works on Physics you will notice the expression, "Potential Energy," meaning Energy awaiting action; also "Kinetic Energy," meaning Energy in Action; that is, in Motion. We shall not need these terms in this book, but it is well to understand them.

Another term frequently met with, is "Conservation of Energy," which is used to indicate that Law of Physics the operation of which renders Energy indestructible. That is, Science holds that Energy can not be destroyed—that it is not lost, or created, but is merely transformed into other forms of Energy, Potential or Kinetic. Therefore, after Energy is used, it either passes into a state of Potential Energy or Rest, awaiting a future call to Activity, or else is immediately transformed into another form of Kinetic Energy; or Energy in Action. The theory holds that the quantity or amount of Energy in the Universe is fixed in its totality—none may be created or destroyed—there can be no addition to, or subtraction from the Totality of Energy—that all Energy used has been previously stored up, or else has been immediately transmitted or transformed. It is also held that when Energy manifests as the result of work performed, it is always found that it is at the expense of some previously manifested form of Energy—that the agency by which the work is performed always parts with its stock of Energy, and that the thing worked upon always acquires or gains the amount of Energy lost by the aforesaid agent, or worker—and yet there is no actual loss or gain, but merely transformation.

The above theory is mentioned as of interest in the general subject, although it does not play a prominent part in the subject of this book, for the writer holds that all Energy resides in Mind, and emerges therefrom, and, in the end, returns thereto. This being believed, it is seen that Energy is not to be thought of as a separate thing having a "totality," but merely as a quality of Mind— the question of its totality or fixed quantity not being inquired into, although both, probably, run along the lines of the nature of Mind, and depend upon the limitations, or lack of limitations, of the latter. However, the question does not assume a vital importance in our consideration of the subject. So far as the question of transmission, or transformation of Energy, is concerned, however, the principles of the Law of Conservation of Energy may be accepted as correct, although it more properly belongs to the principle of what has been called "The Correlation of Force," the idea of which is that one form of Energy may be, and is always, transformed into another form, and so on, and on, unto infinity. This idea is followed in this book, except that the idea of "From Mind originally, to Mind finally," is incorporated within it. This law of the "Correlation of Force" may be illustrated by the following quotation from Tyndall, the great scientist of the last century, who says:

A river, in descending from an elevation of 7720 feet, generates an amount of heat competent to augment its own temperature 10 degrees F., and this amount of heat was abstracted from the sun, in order to lift the matter of the river to the elevation from which it falls. As long as the river continues on the heights, whether in the solid form as a glacier, or in the liquid form as a lake, the heat expended by the sun in lifting it has disappeared from the universe. It has been consumed in the act of lifting. But, at the moment that the river starts upon its downward course, and encounters the resistance of its bed, the heat expanded in its elevation begins to be restored. The mental eye, indeed, can follow the emission from its source through the ether, as vibratory motion, to the ocean, where it ceases to be vibration, and takes the potential form among the molecules of aqueous vapor; to the mountain-top, where the heat absorbed in vaporization is given out in condensation, while that expended by the sun in *lifting* the water to its present elevation is still unrestored. This we find paid back to the last unit by the friction along the river's bed; at the bottom of the cascade, where the plunge of the torrent is suddenly arrested; in the warmth of the machinery turned by the river; in the spark from the millstone; beneath the crusher of the miner; in the Alpine sawmill; in the milk-churn of the chalet; in the supports of the cradle in which the mountaineer, by water-power, rocks his baby to sleep. All the forms of mechanical motion here indicated are simply the parcelling out of an amount of calorific motion derived originally from the sun; and, at each point at which the mechanical motion is destroyed or diminished, it is the sun's heat which is restored.

The following quotation, also, is interesting as illustrating another phase of this law:

"The work performed by men and other animals is due to the transformed energy of food. This food is of vegetable origin and owes its energy to the solar rays. The energy of men and animals is, therefore, the transformed energy of the sun. Excepting the energy of the tides, the sun's rays are the source of all the forms of energy practically available. It has been estimated that the heat received by the earth from the sun each year would melt a layer of ice over the entire globe a hundred feet in thickness. This represents energy equal to one horse-power for each fifty square feet of surface."—Anthony and Brackett.

From the above quotations, it will be seen that the principal and most familiar sources (or great storage batteries) of Energy, apparent to dwellers upon this planet, are (1) the Earth manifesting the Power of Gravitation; and (2) the Sun, manifesting solar heat. In Tyndall's illustration we see the force of the sun's Energy—heat—raising the water from the ocean, by evaporation (although aided by the earth's gravitation "pulling down" the heavier air, allowing the vapor to rise). Then we see the Force of Gravitation causes the condensed vapor to fall as rain or snow on the mountain-top—then causing the rain to run into little streams, and so on until the river is reached—then causing the river to start on its downward journey of over seven thousand feet—then causing it to plunge over the cascade; to turn the wheels that operated the machinery, and turned the millstone, and the crusher of the miner, and the saw-mill, and the milk-churn, and the cradle. And, as Tyndall might have added, had he lived a little later—in the running of the dynamo, which running, produced electricity, that in turn caused lights to burn; other machinery to run and manufacture things; stoves to cook; flat-irons to iron; automobiles and engines to run; and many other things along the lines of transmitting Energy, Force and Motion.

And in this consideration, let us not forget the important part that

Gravitation—that most wonderful of all Forces—plays in the grand scheme of Nature. Not only does this Force cause the planets to circle around the sun, and, perhaps that sun around another sun, and so on, and on until the matter becomes unthinkable—not only this, but it performs a million parts in the affair of earthly Matter, as we shall see in a later chapter. The Force of Gravitation is one of the greatest mysteries confronting Science today, although many believe it a simple question. Gravitation and the Universal Ether contain the great secrets of Nature that Man is striving to unveil. And yet, so "common" is Gravitation that the race, including almost all the scientists, take it as a "matter of course." We shall devote much attention to the question of Gravitation in the forthcoming chapters of this book, for it plays a very important part in the general theory of Dynamic Thought, upon which this book is based. We shall have a special chapter devoted to it, a little later on, and the matter will also come up for explanation further on in the book.

But, in the meantime, let us consider the other forms of Energy, *viz.*, Heat, Light, Magnetism and Electricity, which with Gravitation and Attraction of other kinds, form the Forces of Nature.

9

Radiant Energy

The "kinds" of Energy are very few, although the methods of using, applying and manifesting same are innumerable. Let us begin with one of the best known forms of Energy, namely, Heat.

Heat was formerly regarded as a very fine fluid or substance, called "caloric," which was supposed to enter into Substance and then manifest the phenomenon of "heat." This idea has long since been relegated to the scrap pile of Science. The present theory, which is supported by a mass of evidence obtained through investigation and experimentation, is that Heat is a form of Energy, arising from the vibratory motions of the Particles of Substance—a "Mode of Motion." The degrees of Heat are termed "Temperature." Temperature depends upon the rate of the heat-vibrations of the Particles of Substance, either arising from the Original Motion of the Particles, or else from vibrations or Motion aroused in them by transmission from Particles of other bodies of Substance—these vibrations being "contagious." Temperature then means "the measure of the vibrations of the Particles."

All bodies of Substance have *some* degree of Temperature—some degree of heat-vibration of its Particles. Science has a pleasant "scientific friction" of an Absolute Zero at the degree of 491 below Zero, Fahrenheit, but this is merely an imaginary something with which the grown up children of Science amuse themselves.

When two bodies are brought near each other—the "nearness" being comparative, and, in some cases, meaning a distance of millions of miles—Heat is transmitted from the warmer to the cooler body, until the temperatures are equalized—that is until the two bodies vibrate in unison.

In Physics we are taught that the "Transmission" of Heat may be accomplished in three ways, although the writer is of the opinion that the three ways are but three forms of *one* way.

The first form is called "Conduction," whereby the vibration, or Heat, is conveyed along a body of Substance, from its warmer to its cooler parts—for instance, an iron poker with one end in the fire. The second form is called "Convection," whereby the visible motion of heated Substance, moving along the air—for instance, hot-air, hot-water, steam, etc., either by means of pipes, or by allowing them to pass freely through the air. The third form is called "Radiation," whereby the vibrations are believed to be transformed into "waves of the Ether," which will be spoken of later, in addition to what has been said on the subject in our chapter entitled "The Paradox of Science."

The writer thinks that a little consideration will show us that the same rule operates in all of the above cases, and that "Conduction" and "Convection" are but forms of Radiation. For instance, in Conduction there must be a few Particles first set into vibration, the same gradually passing on to the others farther and farther away. Passing *how?* "By contact," replies Physics. But, the Particles are never in absolute contact—there always is "plenty of space" between them. And so there must be some kind of "waves" passing through the space between them, which space is not filled with "air," or other form of Substance, but only with "the Ether," or *something that takes its place.* So that, after all, Conduction is but a form of Radiation. And the same rule will apply in the case of Convection.

Heat arises from several causes, all of which, however, manifest through the vibration of the Particles of the body evidencing the Heat. These causes may be stated as (1) Original Motion of the Particles of a body of Substance, arising from some workings of the Law of Attraction, and including Motion arising from Chemical Action, Combustion, etc. (2) From transmission or "contagion" from some other body of Substance, the Particles of which are vibrating at the rate of Heat. (3) From interrupted Motion, including friction both of the moving body with the air or other Substance, and the friction of a current of Electricity passing through the body. In each of the above cases, the *actual* and immediate cause of the Heat is the vibration of the Particles of the Substance manifesting the Heat, although the transmitted vibratory waves, or the interrupted motion, friction, current, etc. may have been the instigator or provoker of such vibration. The interrupted motion, friction, or "wave" does not produce the Heat, but merely arouses or provokes the increased vibration of the Particles, that really manifest the Heat. At the last, remember, the Heat is in the Particles of the body that "feels" or experiences it.

The vibrations of Heat seem to have the properties of causing the Molecules to draw further apart, and to manifest less Attraction, or more Repulsion, whichever way one cares to express it. This "moving away" of the Molecules tend to cause the body to increase in volume or size, and occasions what is known as "Expansion" in Substance. In this way Heat transforms Solids into Liquids; Liquids into Gases or Vapors, the change being wholly a matter of the relative distances of the Molecules.

Magnetism is another form of Energy, and is generally believed to be a part of the phenomena of Electricity, if indeed, not a form of Electricity itself. Science knows very little about the nature of Magnetism, but in a general way holds to the theory that it results from the vibration or motion of the Particles of Substance, as do all other forms of Energy. The magnetic qualities of a body may be increased or decreased by motion affecting the relation of the Molecules, which fact has been regarded as having some bearing on the theory. *Electricity* is a form of Energy, that Science regards as also arising from the vibration or motion of the Particles of Substance. It is transmitted, like Heat, by Conduction and Radiation, the "waves" tending to provoke similar vibrations in the Particles of Substances receiving them. By many careful investigators, Electricity is believed to be very closely related to the phenomenon called light, both having much in common. Science seems to be discovering new points of resemblance between them, and it is probable that in the near future they will be seen to be but varying forms of the same thing. The purposes of this book do not call for an extended consideration of the properties of Electricity, the same being served by a consideration of its nature being akin to that of the other forms of Energy, namely, "vibration or motion in or among the Particles of Matter."

Light is a form of Energy, the study of which is of the greatest interest to Science, for the reason that the field seems to be widening out continuously, and reaching out into the territory formerly thought to be the special region of Electricity. And, in another direction, it seems to be reaching out into the territory of Heat, the latter being considered by many to be but a form of Light, in its lower vibrations. In fact, the writer of this book so considers the subject, and for the purposes of this book, in later chapters, he will combine Electricity, Heat, and Light, including, also, the phenomena known as the X-Rays, Becquerel Rays, Radium waves, etc., as forms of Light—the combined forms of Energy to be called "*Radiant Energy.*" In this combination, he believes that he is in line with the latest and best thought of Modern Science. However, he does not insist upon his readers following this idea, and so, if they prefer, they may think of each of these forms as separate and distinct, and yet not run contrary to the line of thought of the book.

Light is not the simple thing that it is considered to be by the general public. It is composed of many parts, qualities and manifestations. Its rays, when separated by the Spectrum, are seen to consist of "waves" or vibrations of differing degrees of rate and intensity. The lower range contains the heat rays, and it is interesting to know that there are rays of heat too far down in the scale to be evidenced by human senses that may be distinguished by delicate instruments. But there are rays still further down in the scale that are known to exist, theoretically, that cannot be registered even by the finest instruments. To gain an idea of the delicacy of these instruments, let us remember that Prof. Langley has an instrument called the "Bolometer," that is so delicate that it registers a change of temperature of one millionth of a degree, and will register the heat of a candle one and one-half miles distant from it. Light vibrations arise from combustion, friction electricity etc., causing the Particles to assume increased Motion.

Let us consider the report of the Spectrum. Beginning with waves or vibrations far below the sensibility of Man, the scale shows an advance until the first "warm" vibration of iron was reached. This first indication of warmth comes when the vibrations reach the rate of 35,000,000,000,000 *per second*. Then gradually they increase until a dull red glow is noticed—the *lowest* visible light ray—when the vibrations are 450,000,000,000,000 per second. Then come the orange rays, then the golden yellow, then the pure yellow, then the greenish yellow, then the pure green, then the greenish blue, then the ocean blue, then the cyanic blue, then the indigo, then the violet—the latter evidencing when the vibrations reach the rate of 750,000,000,000,000 per second. Then come the Ultra-violet rays—invisible to human sight—but evidenced by chemical media. In this Ultra-violet region lies the X-Rays, etc., and also the "Actinic Rays," that produce photographs, sunburn one's face and blister the nose—that cause violent explosions in chemicals—that transform forms of Substance—that are employed to cure skin diseases, etc. These Actinic or Chemical Rays have an important role to play in plant-life, for they act upon the green leaves of the plant, causing a chemical change by which carbonic acid and water are transformed into sugar and starches.

Some of the rays of the Ultra-violet region of Light penetrate substances formerly considered solid and impenetrable. And some of them emitted from Radium, etc., would destroy organic life if applied in sufficient quantities. Some of them are practically waves of Electricity so that Light and Electricity are seen to be closely related.

To give one an idea of the differences produced by different rates of vibration, let us imagine a Mass of Iron, shaped like a great "Top," capable of being impelled to "spin" at a constantly increasing rate of speed, by some Mighty

Will. At first it is seen as a slowly spinning Top, manifesting nothing but slow motion, to our senses.

Now, imagine our Top spinning at a rate doubling each second. The first second the Top spins at the rate of two revolutions per second. We notice no change, except that we can see the movement. The next second the revolutions are doubled to four per second. Then, doubling each second, we have, respectively, revolutions of eight per second, then sixteen, and then in the fifth second thirty-two per second. Then we begin to notice a change.

When the revolutions reach thirty-two per second the friction of the moving Top on the air causes it to give forth a very low, deep, bass note of sound. This note is like a low, deep "hum," and is the lowest possible of perception by the human hearing, although it is possible that some of the lower forms of life may be conscious of still lower vibrations.

The sixth second the revolutions reach sixty-four, and the low note has grown much higher in the scale. The seventh second records a rate of 128, and the note has correspondingly increased. Then, as the seconds pass, we have, successively, 256, 512, 1,024, 2,048, 4,096, 8,192, 16,384, 32,768, the latter in the fifteenth second, and representing the highest note recognizable by the human ear, although it is believed that some of the lower animals may recognize sounds too acute for our sense of hearing. During this increase in revolutions from the fifth second to the fifteenth, the sound-note has risen rapidly in the scale from the low sullen "hum," on through the notes of the musical scale, and beyond the range of instruments, until the shrillness becomes so intense as to be almost unhearable, and finally terminating in a shrill, piercing shriek like the "squeak" of the bat, only long-drawn out.

Then from the termination of the sound (by reason of the rate of vibration having become too high) silence reigns for thirty seconds—absolute silence, in spite of the rapidly increasing rate of vibrations, in fact, because of it.

When the forty-fifth second is reached, and the revolutions have reached the rate of 35,184,372,088,832 per second, our Top begins to emit heat-rays, increasing each second. Then a little later a dull, dim glow may be noticed. Then, as the seconds fly, the dull glow manifests a deep dark red color, such as one notices in the iron of the blacksmith's shop, soon after it begins to "glow." Then, on and on, as the seconds fly, the deep red grows lighter and brighter, gradually changing into orange, then into yellow, then into green, then into blue, then into indigo, then into violet, and then into the color of "white-heat." Then this "white-heat" changes into a still more dazzling white, and then a white impossible to describe appears, so bright, clear and brilliant that the eye cannot bear the sight. Then, suddenly, the intense brightness is succeeded by absolute darkness, and the moving Top cannot be seen by the eye—and yet it moves on. The highest recorded chemical rays of light are estimated to equal a rate of vibration of 1,875,000,000,000,000 per second. The vibration of the lowest shade of red light is estimated at 450,000,000,000,000, and the highest of violet at 750,000,000,000,000 per second, so we may imagine what the highest line on the spectrum is like.

Still vibrating, our Top, which has become now a Mass of Vaporized Iron, rapidly tending toward still more ethereal forms.

It has passed out from the region of light-waves, into another "Unknown Region" of Vibrations, in which region, however, exist the vibrations known to us as the "X-Rays," etc. It is throwing off great quantities of Electrons. If we were to use a fluorescent screen we would be able to observe the phenomena of the Roentgen Rays, and similar manifestations of Radiant Energy. On and on vibrates the Top of what we once called Iron—cold iron, warm iron, hot iron, melted iron, gaseous iron, etherealized iron, if you like. What it is like now, the imagination of Man cannot conceive. Still the revolutions continue, doubling each second. *What is being produced?* The imagination cannot conceive of what this state of Substance, now being reached, is like. By a scientific form of poetry we might think of it as melting into Energy—pure Energy, if there were such a thing. Long since it has been resolved into its original Particles—its Corpuscles, and perhaps into the "stuff" from which particles are made. But we must let the curtain drop—the wildest fancy cannot follow the Dance of Substance any further.

The theory of the transmission of vibrations of Radiant Energy by means of "waves" in the Ether, or "something that takes the place of the Ether," has been mentioned in other parts of the book. Referring again to it, the writer would say that he thinks it probable that the "waves" coming in contact with the countless Corpuscles in the Earth's atmosphere, communicate a high rate of motion to them, the result being that they take on the vibrations immediately, and pass along with the "wave" current—the result being that much that we consider as waves of Light, Heat and Electricity are but streams of these Corpuscles in which vibrations have been awakened by the "waves." This idea will help to explain some of the phenomena of Light, which seemed more understandable under the old Light-Corpuscle theory of Newton than under the "wave" theory of recent years. The idea is advanced merely for the purpose of setting down the thought, for it plays no important part in the theory of the book.

Another matter that should not be overlooked in connection with Light and Heat and Electricity is that Particles absorb or "catch" the vibrations in different degrees, their receptivity depending upon their particular vibratory mode, or "custom of their kind." If unable to "absorb" the vibrations, they "reflect" them. Substance, of any particular kind, absorb Heat in the degree of its atomic weight.

In the next chapter we shall learn something of The Law of Attraction, that wonderful Law that makes possible any Motion or Radiant Energy.

10

The Law of Attraction

In the previous chapters we have seen that all forms of Radiant Energy, *viz.*, Light, Heat, Electricity and Magnetism, arose from the Motion of the Particles of Substance. It now becomes important to learn just what causes this "Motion of the Particles." Science is somewhat hazy and foggy on this subject, but in a general way decides that it is caused by "the mutual relations and positions of the particles, arising from their respective attractive qualities," as a recent writer has expressed it. Well, this is better than the old way of seeking refuge and retreat in a mere volume of dense words. It is indeed the only logical conclusion, this one that the operations of the Law of Attraction are manifested in the Motion of the Particles.

This great Law of Attraction is the greatest Law in Nature. It operates on all planes of life. It is always in evidence. Let us consider it.

Let us begin by considering the most magnificent and constant exhibition of that Law—Gravitation. Gravitation is the Riddle of the Universe, and the one form of Energy that balks Science—so much a mystery that Science does not even hazard a "guess" at its nature—no theory of the origin and nature of Gravitation is to be found in "the books." Let us see what Gravitation is.

It is more than the power that "pulls things to the earth," as the average man would define it. It does more than cause water to run down hill, and turn mill-wheels to drive machinery. Water-power results from Gravitation, but even the Energy of Niagara Falls is insignificant when compared to the other manifestations of the Mother of Energy—Gravitation.

Webster defines Gravitation as: "That attraction or force by which all bodies or particles in the universe tend toward each other."

Following that definition, let us add that: *Every particle of Substance has an attraction for every other particle.*

In view of our belief that this "attraction" is a form of mental effort, let us regard the term "Attraction" as being a form of what we call "Desire," or even "Love," in the mental world. If you will think of it in this way, you will be better able to fall in with our lines of thought.

And, in addition to every particle of Substance having an attraction (love or desire) for every other particle, *it has the means and power to draw that other particle toward itself, and to move toward that other particle at the same time.* Webster gives a very clear idea of this when he defines Attraction as: *"An invisible power in a body by which it draws anything to itself; the power in nature acting mutually between bodies, or ultimate particles, tending to draw them together, or to produce their cohesion or combination, and conversely resisting separation."*

The majority of persons, when thinking of "Gravitation," are satisfied with the idea that it is a power that "pulls things down to the ground," and do not think of it as a force that "pulls things" other ways besides "down," and which is possessed and exercised by the speck of dust as well as by the whole earth—by the molecule as well as by the mass. The reason of this is that this power is so slight in small bodies of Substance that it is unnoticed; and that only when the mass is sufficiently large to make the "pull" strong does one perceive and appreciate that the force exists. The lack of information on the part of the average person regarding this subject is amazing, particularly when the importance of the knowledge is understood.

The attraction that holds the molecules of Substance together is Gravitation. The attraction that "pulls" a piece of Substance to the earth is Gravitation. The attraction that keeps the suns and planets in their orbits is Gravitation. Let us see the operations of the Law.

In Astronomy you may learn that the movements of the planets around the sun and the moons around their planets—their regular and constant relative positions—are caused by the force of Gravitation. If it were not for this attraction by the Sun, the planets would fly out into space, like a stone from a sling. The Attraction of Gravitation acts on the planets just as does the string of the whirling sling that keeps the stone from flying away during the whirling until the string is released. Some astronomers think that our sun revolves around some greater sun, and this again around a greater, and so on to infinity. If this be so, then the Attraction of Gravitation is that which holds them all in their orbits and places in spite of their motion.

And in Physics, you may learn that this same Attraction of Gravitation prevents the people and objects on the surface of the earth from flying off into space. And that it holds the portions of the earth together, preventing them from flying apart.

And, remember this, for it is important—the Attraction of the Earth, great and powerful as it is, is nothing more than the *combined* attractive power of its constituent molecules, or atoms, or parts. The centre of the Earth is the Centre of the Attraction, because it is the centre of the aggregation of its Particles.

It must not be supposed that the Earth simply attracts "downward," that is, toward its centre. On the contrary, large masses of earth—large mountains, for instance—exert a certain degree of Attraction of Gravitation, and experiments have shown that a "plumb" is slightly deflected by reason of the proximity of a large mountain. And the reason that bodies "lose weight" as they descend from the surface of the earth is because they leave "above" them a certain large portion of the molecules composing the earth, which mass of molecules exert an attraction proportionate to their mass, which attraction balances the attraction of the mass of earth "beneath them."

Science teaches that if the earth were hollow in the centre, the weight there would be Zero, or nothing at all, and that a body would float in the space at the centre of the earth just as does a balloon in the air, the reason thereof being that the attraction would be equalized—equal attraction from every direction, counterbalancing each other. Considering the earth's radius to be 4000 miles, a body that weighed 100 pounds on the surface would weigh but 75 pounds at the depth of 1000 miles; but 50 pounds at a depth of 2000 miles; but 25 pounds at a depth of 3000 miles; and Nothing, or Zero, at a depth of 4000 miles, which would be the Centre of the Earth. This, of course, supposes that the Substance of which the earth is composed is of uniform density from surface to centre.

From an equal distance above the surface of the earth, bodies released, or dropped, will reach the surface at exactly the same degree of speed, and in exactly the same time—this irrespective of weight or size. In other words, a cork or piece of lead, no matter what their sizes may be, will travel with equal rapidity. In case where the "lighter" substance travels more slowly (compare a feather and bullet, for instance) the difference is caused by the light object meeting with more resistance from the air. This apparent exception has been explained away by the experiment of dropping the bullet and the feather in a vacuum tube, in which there was no resistance from air, the consequence being that both descended precisely at the same instant. Another similar experiment is to place the feather upon a piece of iron whereby the resistance of the air is prevented, and the feather will maintain its position during the drop, and will reach the ground resting on top of the iron, just as it started.

And, remember this please, that the small object attracted by the earth exerts an attraction on its own account. If the two were of the same size they would exert an equal attracting power, but as one is smaller its attracting power is very slight compared with that of the large mass. But it is true that the particle of dust attracts the earth precisely as the earth attracts the particle of dust— the difference being solely a matter of degree depending upon the "mass" of the body. The amount or degree of the *combined* attracting power is determined by the combined total of the two masses. Distance lessens the degree of attraction—thus as bodies are lifted above the earth the weight decreases very gradually, and by very slight degrees, but constantly and invariably. The poles of the earth are flattened, and, consequently, the weight of an object slightly increases as it is carried from equator to pole.

Concluding our consideration of Gravitation, it will be well to call your attention to the fact that Gravitation differs from the forms of Radiant Energy known as Heat, Light, Electricity and Magnetism in several very important particulars, which seems to go far in the direction of proof that the latter are by incidents or consequences of the former.

In the first place, Gravitation, so far as is known, is not dependent upon, caused by, or maintained by, any other Force or form of Energy. Nor does it seem to be derived from some great reservoir, from which it obtains its supply of Energy. On the contrary, it seems to be a "thing-in-itself," self-supporting, self-existing—an intrinsic thing, in fact. It does not seem to be lost to bodies by radiation. And consequently there seems to be no need of a body replenishing its supply, as there is no loss. Gravitation seems to be a constant *something*, remaining always with bodies and neither being lost or acquired. It exists between the Atoms, Molecules, Masses—all in the same way. In fact, one is tempted to think of the planets and worlds in space, as Molecules of some greater Mass held together by Gravitation just as are the Molecules held together. Remember, that the Molecules and Atoms are not in absolute contact, *but there is always a "space" between them*, although the space or distance may be "insensible" to us. "As above, so below," says the old occult aphorism, and it seems to be so.

Then again, Gravitation is believed to act *instantaneously*, and does not require Time to pass between bodies, as does Light, Heat, Electricity, Magnetism—Radiant Energy. Light travels through the Ether (as light-waves) at the rate of 184,000 miles a second. The same is true of Heat and of Electricity. But Gravitation travels instantaneously. For instance, if a new star were to spring into existence at some inconceivable distance from the earth it would require thousands of years for its light to reach us. But its Attraction of Gravitation would be felt *instantly*. Do you realize what this means! It means that Gravitation is in some way connected with the Ether, or "conveying medium," that an impulse communicated at some point of space trillions of miles away is felt *at once* at our point in space, and vice versa. There is some awful mystery here, and the laws of Substance, and Force, as generally understood, do not account for it. And the theories regarding the Ether do not throw light upon it. *But wait a bit!*

But more than this. Science holds that Gravitation *does not require a medium*—that it seems to be its own medium—needing no "Ether" or other medium to transmit its influence. In this respect also, Gravitation differs from the form of Radiant Energy. And more, it is not "cut-off" or interfered with by any intervening body, for its force operates through such intervening bodies. For instance, in an eclipse of the Sun, the Moon passes between the Earth and the Sun, but the Gravitation is not affected in the slightest, for the bodies would evidence such change immediately were it to occur. So Gravitation acts instantaneously; is its own medium, and may not be interfered with by an intervening body. It, indeed, is in a different "class" from Light, Heat and Electricity.

And now let us consider the other forms of Attraction.

In the previous chapters we saw that the form of Attraction called "Cohesion" caused the molecules to tend to each other, and to remain in more or less close contact, the differing degrees of Cohesion determining the Density, etc., of the body. Were the Attractive force of Cohesion suddenly removed, the most solid bodies, as well as the lightest ones, would instantly fly into very fine powder, thus being resolved into their constituent molecules. The separation of the Molecules, that is, the "setting further apart," occasioned by Heat, is spoken of by Physicists as "Repulsion." But the writer holds that repulsion is an entirely different thing, and that the heat merely causes the Molecules to lose a portion of their Attractive power for each other. Until the heat being withdrawn, the Molecules respond to the uninterrupted Attraction. The Molecules are like lovers who are attracted toward each other, and remain attached unless separated violently, or by some fading of Attraction. Consider Heat as a disturbing element—a "misunderstanding" between the molecular lovers, who under its influence draw somewhat apart, and are only reunited when the obstacle is removed, and harmony again manifested.

As we have shown you in a previous chapter, the so-called "properties" of Matter, i.e., Hardness, Tenacity, Malleability, Ductility, etc., are simply evidence of a persistent Cohesiveness of the Molecules—a strong "love" or "desire" for each other that caused them to adopt every possible means in their power to resist, and prevent, the separation of the Molecules forming the mass. It was like a desperate attempt to prevent the "breaking up of the family."

Each so-called Special Physical Property of Matter is seen to be but the

action of the Molecule resisting separation, in obedience to that law of its being called "Attraction," or "Gravitation," or "Cohesion," or "Adhesion"—but
which might as fitly be called "Desire," or "Love." And, remember, that this
law does not seem to be merely one of self-preservation of the Molecule—for
it remains intact even after the separation from its companions or family. It is
more, for it is a law that causes it to bend all its energies in remaining within
"molecular distance" or close companionship with its family, and resisting disintegration. It is like the "social instinct" in Man, if one may be pardoned from
using the figure.

Now for the Attraction of the Atoms—"Chemical Affinity," or "Chemism,"
as it is called. An Atom, you know, is the chemical unit of Matter, and the
smallest particle of Matter that can enter into combination (leaving the Corpuscle out of the consideration, for the moment). These Atoms exhibit and
manifest an Attraction for each other that causes them to form combinations
or "marriages," and thus to combine, forming a molecule. But remember, always, that when Atoms "combine" they do not merge their identities—they
simply "marry," and nothing more. Each atom maintains its own identity,
and is found intact if the "marriage" is destroyed by chemical process, which
might be called the termination of the molecular marriage, by "divorce," that
is, by one Atom forsaking its mate and seeking a new "affinity" in the shape
of some more attractive (or attracting) Atom. For, alas, the Atoms are more or
less fickle, and often leave their life-partners for some other fascinating Particle.
At times there is manifested a condition of "how happy could I be with either,
were t'other fair charmer away"—there is a conflict of attractions.

There is more "flirting" and "affairs of the heart" in the world of Atoms
than in the region of the Molecules, for while the latter are apt to seek only
the companionship of their own "family," or some nearly related family, the
Atoms have quite a number of possible "affinities," and will invariably desert a
lesser attraction for a greater one (thus forming a new molecule) and leave the
deserted one to get along alone as best it may, or else form a new alliance with
some other affinity who is either impervious to the attraction of the more brilliant charmer, or else is out of the danger of temptation.

But, if we analyze and carefully consider this "Chemical Affinity,"
"Chemism," we will see that it comes well under the definition of "Attraction"
as given by Webster, and quoted in the first part of this chapter. It certainly
comes under the rule of "*the power in nature acting mutually between bodies, or
ultimate particles, tending to draw them together,*" etc.

The writer thinks that he is justified in asking you to consider Gravitation,
Cohesion, Adhesion and Chemical Affinity as related forms of the same thing.

If you do not like to call this "same thing" by the name of "Gravitation," suppose we call it "The Law of Attraction," of which Gravitation, Cohesion, Adhesion, Chemical Affinity or Chemism are but different aspects. (This "relation" is described in Chapter xiii.)

And the writer believes that this "Law of Attraction" is the underlying cause of all that we call Energy, Force, Power, Motion, etc., in the Physical world. For if "Gravitation" accounts for all "Mass Motion," or "Mechanical Motion"—if Molecular Cohesion, and the vibrations accompanying it, manifest in forms of "Molecular Motion"—and if Atomic "Chemical Affinity" or "Chemism," manifest in "Atomic Motion"—and if even the Corpuscles in their movements obey this same "Law of Attraction" in some form—and if all Force and Energy is but a "Mode of Motion"—then, if all this be true, are we not justified in claiming that this "Law of Attraction" is the Basis of All Energy, Force and Motion? And are we not justified in thinking of this "Law of Attraction" as always manifesting in the direction of drawing together particles of Substance—be those particles suns, planets, masses, molecules, atoms or corpuscles—in pursuance of some basic law imposed upon All-things, by That-which-is-above-Things?

The following quotation is interesting, in our consideration of this subject: "There are other forces besides gravity, and one of the most active of these is chemical affinity. Thus, for instance, an atom of oxygen has a very strong attraction for one of carbon, and we may compare these two atoms to the earth and a stone lodged upon the top of a house. Within certain limits, this attraction is intensely powerful, so that when an atom of carbon and one of oxygen have been separated from each other, we have a species of energy of position just as truly as when a stone has been separated from the earth. Thus by having a large quantity of oxygen and a large quantity of carbon in separate states, we are in possession of a large store of *energy* of position. When we allowed the stone and the earth to rush together, the *energy* of position was transformed into that of actual motion, and we should therefore expect something similar to happen when the separated carbon and oxygen are allowed to rush together. This takes place when we burn coal in our fires, and the primary result, as far as *energy* is concerned, is the production of a large amount of heat. We are, therefore, led to conjecture that heat may denote a motion of particles on the small scale just as the rushing together of the stone and the earth denotes a motion on the large. It thus appears that we may have invisible molecular energy as well as visible mechanical *energy*."—*Balfour Stewart*.

To the writer it seems that the Particle of Substance finds within its Mind-principle (for you know we have seen that all Substance had something akin to

Life and Mind) a constant craving, imbedded in its very nature, which causes it to seek Satisfaction. This craving for Satisfaction results in Unrest, and seeks a solution along two lines. These two lines are indicated by two entirely different Desires that it finds within itself—the first being a Desire or Inclination to seek the companionship of some other Particle—the second being a Desire or Inclination to be Free of Attachment or Entanglement.

The Desire for Attachment arises from the force of the Law of Attraction that exists between each Particle of Substance. The Desire for Non-attachment arises from some inward inclination for Freedom. These two Desires or Inclinations may be called the Desire for Impression and the Desire for Expression.

The Desire for Impression (or pressing in) manifests along lines of action tending toward Attachment, Moreness, Companionship, Combination. The Desire for Expression (or pressing out) manifests along the lines of action tending toward Individuality, Freedom, Independence, Unattachment, etc. And both are strong cravings—and both tend to produce Unrest, which results in Motion. The "pull" of the Desire of Impression exists always, and is always modified and counteracted by the "push" of the Desire for Expression. And, resulting from the play of these two Desires, or Forces, result Activity, Motion and Change. Like the two conflicting angels in the Persian mythology—Ahriman and Ormuzd—these two Desires wrestle with each other in the theatre of the Universe—constant Motion and Change being the results.

And, if the writer may be pardoned for dropping into Mysticism for the moment, may it not be that these conflicting Desires for Separateness and Unity, respectively, are but different forms of the Desire for Satisfaction through Oneness. Impression seeks Oneness by combination with other separated Particles, *but finds it not.* Expression seeks Oneness by drawing apart and endeavoring to realize it in that way, *but finds it not.* But both are but different aspects of the same Desire for Satisfaction, and only when the Mind recognizes Oneness in Diversity does Satisfaction come. And thus the lesson of the Particle becomes the Lesson of the Man.

These conflicting Desires of Inclinations of the Particles—the one urging it along the lines of Attraction—the other along the lines of Separation—produce the Dance of the Atoms—the Motion of the Particles.

When the Particle manifests along the lines of Expression it pushes itself away from the other Particle, and, consequently, also pushes the other Particle away. When it manifests along the lines of Impression, it pulls itself toward the other Particle, and at the same time pulls the other Particle toward itself. In both cases the "medium" of the pulling extends over the space separating them, as will be described in future chapters. This pulling and pushing is called by Chemistry "Attraction and Repulsion" of the Particles.

It is perhaps unnecessary to state that the Force of the Attraction of Cohesion or of Chemical Affinity is much stronger than that of Gravitation, in the case of the same Particles. Otherwise, if one picked up a piece of iron, the Attraction of Gravitation would cause its particles to separate and fall to the ground, whereas, the Attraction of Cohesion and that of Chemical Affinity enable the Particles to counteract the pull of Gravitation, and thus remain intact. Compared with Cohesion or Chemical Affinity, the pull of Gravitation is incomparably weak. The force which holds together two atoms of water represents a high degree of dynamic power, and the shock of forcible separation of chemical atoms produces something akin to an explosion. So we see that the Attraction of the Particles, while of the same nature as Gravitation, is much higher in intensity.

But notwithstanding the power of the Attraction, it seems to be a matter inherent in the nature of the Particle, and to represent a something like Will, in response to Desire.

The varying "push and pull" or the two Desires, would necessarily cause a revolution of each Particle on its own axis, and a revolution around each other—besides many instances of rushing together and away from each other. In these forms of Motion is to lie found the cause of the vibrations producing Radiant Energy, known as Light, Heat, Electricity and Magnetism.

11

The Theory of Dynamic Thought

From the preceding chapters we have learned that:

(1) The forms of Force or Radiant Energy, known as Light, Heat, Magnetism and Electricity, are "Modes of Motion," arising from the Original Motion of the Particles of Substance (Molecules, Atoms, Corpuscles or Electrons). And that such Original Motion of the Particles arises from the Operation of The Law of Attraction;

(2) That the forms of Attractive Force or Energy, known as Gravitation, Cohesion, Adhesion, Atomic Attraction, Chemical Affinity or Chemism, and Corpuscular Attraction, also arise from the operation of the Law of Attraction;

(3) That, from the above, it follows that: All Manifestations of Force and Energy in Inorganic Substance (*viz.*, both Radiant Energy in its forms of Light, Heat, Magnetism, Electricity, etc.; and also Attractive Energy in its forms of Gravitation, Cohesion, Adhesion, Chemical Affinity or Atomic Attraction and Corpuscular Attraction) arise from the operation of the Law of Attraction.

It will be well to remember that the fact that some of the above forms of Radiant Force or Energy, such as Heat, Light, Magnetism and Electricity, may arise from Motion transmitted from other Substance, does not alter the matter. For if they arise from "waves" from some other Substance, it merely follows that the Original Motion that gave rise to the "waves" arose from the operation of the Law of Attraction. Or, if they arise from "interrupted Motion," it merely follows that the Motion that is interrupted may be traced back to Original Motion that arose from the operation of the Law of Attraction. So that all Mechanical Power, and all the forms of Energy or Force producing the same (omitting for the moment the forms of Energy or Force of "Living Organisms," which will be described later on) arise from the operation of the Law of Attraction.

Now, for the next step. We have seen that the operation of the Law of Attraction results from Vital-Mental Action on the part of the Life and Mind Principle inherent in the nature of the Particles of Substance. Consequently, all forms of Energy and Force arising from the operation of The Law of Attraction—the latter being the result of Vital-Mental Action—then it follows that:

All forms of Energy and Force having its origin in the Law of Attraction are manifestations of Vital-Mental Action.

But this is not all—for we have not considered the Energy and Force abiding in, and manifested by, what are called "Living Organisms," such as human, animal and plant life, which are manifested by the physical organisms or "bodies" of man, animal and plant. In order to avoid a long digression into the realms of biology, we will omit all but a passing reference to the theories that seek to identify the action of the cells of organic life with those of the particles of inorganic life—for remember, that Organic Substance has its Molecules, Atoms and Corpuscles, as well as its higher combinations known as "Cells"— and we will seek the ultimate source of all forms of Force and Energy, exhibited by "Organic Life," in that which lies back of "Physical Action." We need no argument here—for all will readily recognize that behind the physical action of man, animal and plant, lies Life and Mind, and that therefore all Force and Energy arising from such action must be manifestations of Vital-Mental Action.

And so, summing up our conclusions regarding Force and Energy and Motion in Inorganic Substance—and then in Organic Substance—we arrive at an understanding of the Basic Proposition of the Theory of Dynamic Thought, which is as follows:

Basic Proposition—*That All forms and exhibition of Force, Energy, Motion and Power are manifestations of Vital-Mental Action. And that, consequently, at the last there is no Force but Vital-Mental Force; no Energy but Vital-Mental Energy; no Motion but Vital-Mental Motion; no Power but Vital-Mental Power.*

It is possible that the average reader will fail to recognize the tremendous importance of the above proposition. It is most revolutionary, and is not only directly opposed to the Materialistic theory which makes Matter the dominant factor—the only factor, in fact, in Life; but it is also far different from the opinion of the average person who has been taught to think of "blind force," "dead matter," "mechanical energy," "power of machinery, engines," etc. And yet, you are invited to go back over the path that leads up to the theory, and test and examine every bit of the road for weak spots—insecure bridges, etc.—the writer feels that the work will bear examination. He thinks that he has succeeded not only in proving that (1) The Universe is Alive and Thinking; and (2) That Mind is Dominant—but he believes, also, that he has made at least partially understandable the old occult and metaphysical aphorism that has been heard so much in these later days—the statement that "All is Mind—Mind is All."

The only fact needed now is the proof of the old occult theory that Matter or Substance blends gradually into Mind, and that in the end it is found to have its origin there. So far, Science has not given us this proof, but it begins to look that way, although Science does not dream of what lies at the end of the road she is traveling. She tells us that she sees Matter melting into Force or Energy, and that perhaps the Universe may be found to be Energy or Force, at the last. But she ignores the fact that her investigations have already proven (to those who know how to combine them) that Mind is back of Force—that all Force is Mental Force, at the last. And, so, you see it is not so far a cry from Matter to Mind in these days of the Twentieth Century. The bridge is being erected by the Materialists, but the Mentalist will be the first to cross over it.

But there are many important questions ahead of us for consideration in relation to the Theory of Dynamic Thought. And we must hasten on to them.

One of the first questions that must be considered is that of the transmission of Force, Energy or Motion. Science has told us that Light travels and is "contagious," that Heat travels and is "contagious," that Electricity travels and is "contagious," that Magnetism travels and is "contagious." But it has failed to find evidences of Cohesive Force, or Adhesive Force, or the Force of Gravitation, or the Force of Chemical Affinity, or the Force of Corpuscular Affinity, being "contagious," and although it recognizes that they must "travel" beyond the limits of the bodies manifesting them, yet it has hazarded no theory or hypothesis, worthy of the name, to account for the phenomenon. It informs us that Light, Heat, Magnetism and Electricity "travel" (via waves of the "Ether") at the rate of 184,000 miles per second—and that when they reach their destination the "Ether waves" set up similar vibrations in the Substance with which they come in contact. The only explanation of the method or medium of "travel" is the "Aristotle's Ether" Theory, which, while generally accepted as a working hypothesis, nevertheless, brings a broad smile to the face of any thoughtful scientist who considers it in detail. As for the medium of the transmission of Gravitation, Cohesion, Chemical Affinity and Molecular Affinity, Science is mute. All that she says is that Gravitation is believed to travel *instantaneously* over distances that it takes Light, traveling at the rate of 184,000 miles per second, *over two thousand years* to travel. Verily, Gravitation defies Scientific theories and estimates, and laughs at the "Ether." Let us see if the Dynamic Thought Theory throws any light on the subject! The first step in the solution of the problem of the transferring and communication of Energy is the remembrance of the fact that the Energy is *purely Mental*. Be it Gravitation, Affinity or Attraction, on the one hand—or Light, Heat, Magnetism or Electricity on the other—it is all Mental Force. Attraction in all of its forms has been recognized as Mental Action. And the vibrations that cause Light, Heat, Magnetism and Electricity have been seen to result from the Law of Attraction, and, therefore, are Mental. This being the case, would it not be wise for us to look for a solution of the transmission of Force and Energy in the region from which it originated—*the Mental Region?* Does not this seem reasonable? Should not the explanation for Mental Effects be sought in a Mental Cause? And should not the medium between Mind and Mind be looked for in the Mental Region?

Taking the liberty of peeping into some of the succeeding chapters of this book—getting a little ahead of the story, as it were—let us consider the operation of Mind in the higher forms of Life. Without argument, or proof at this point, let us remember the well-founded statements of fact—and the old occult teachings as well—that the Mind is not confined to the limits of the body, but extends as an "Aura" for some distance beyond the physical form. Let us also remember the phenomena grouped together under the general subject of "Thought-transference," "Thought-transmission," "Telepathy," or (the best term of all) "Telesthesia" (meaning, literally "far-off sensation"). The writer imagines that he hears the yell of derision go up at this point from the materialistic personage, or "man on the street," who has been induced to read this book by some well meaning friend. "Thought-transference, Fiddlesticks," we may hear him cry, in imagination. But let this reader remember—Fiddlesticks, or no Fiddlesticks—that Thought-transmission is a proven fact—and that thousands of people know it to be so, absolutely, from their own experience. It is too late in the day for sneers at the mention of the term.

Well, then, since Force is Mental, and we are looking for a Mental explanation for the phenomenon of Transmission of Force, does it not seem natural to consider Thought-transmission in that connection? Answering a possible objection of some critical reader, to the effect that before a "sensation" may be received, the receiver must have "sense-organs"—a very good objection, but one that is answered by Science itself—let us read on.

Haeckel, the distinguished scientist, in his endeavor to prove that Man's senses are but a development of something in inorganic life, has called our attention to the fact that Molecules, and Atoms, are capable of "receiving" sensations and "responding" thereto. He makes quite a point of this in his latest works, and remarks, among many other things showing his positive views on the subject of "sensation in the inorganic world": *"I cannot imagine the simplest chemical and physical process without attributing the movements of the material particles to unconscious sensation"*; and again: *"The idea of chemical affinity consists in the fact that the various chemical elements perceive the qualitative differences in other elements—experience 'pleasure' or 'revulsion' at contact with them, and execute specific movements on this ground."* He also quotes, approvingly, the remarks of Nageli, who said: *"If the molecules possess something that is related, however distantly, to sensation, it must be comfortable to be able to follow their attractions and repulsions; uncomfortable when they are forced to do otherwise."* Haeckel also says that in his opinion *the sensations in animal and plant life are "connected by a long series of evolutionary stages with the simpler forms of sensation that we find in the inorganic elements, and that reveal themselves in chemical affinity."* Is not this strong enough! Perhaps we may now be permitted at least to "assume" that even the Atoms, Molecules and Corpuscles have "something like sensation."

Someone may now object that Haeckel speaks of "contact" between the particles, and that sensation by contact (even in an atom) is far different from sensation without contact, at a short distance. Quite right, but if the objector will take the trouble to review the teachings of Science regarding the relation of the Particles, he will see that the Particles are *never "exactly" in contact*, except in moments of collision, which, by the way, they carefully avoid. The Corpuscles, as we have shown, have *"plenty of room" in which to move about*, and they move in orbits around each other. The Atoms combine, *but there is always room between them*, as may be seen by reference to the teachings regarding the "Ether," which "fills up the cracks" according to the theory. And the Molecules *also have "plenty of room,"* as may be seen by reference to that part of the subject, particularly to the comparison of the drop of water magnified to the size of the Earth, in which the Molecules would appear about the size of the original drop *with more room between each than their own size.*

In fact, as we have been shown in a previous chapter, the particles are attracted only to a certain distance, at which they resist the impulse or attraction and "stand off" a bit. They will not be forced too near without creating disturbances, and manifestations of force, and if they are separate beyond a certain distance the attractive power ceases to operate. But *there is always some room between them*, and they bridge over that room and exert and receive the attractive power *in some way.*

This is true not only of the particles but of the great bodies, like the Earth and planets, that are attracted, and attract over great distances. Now for the question: "How do they exert sense and attractive power over the great comparative distance—great, comparatively, as well in atom, as in planet and sun? Someone may answer the question closing the last paragraph with the word "*Electricity.*" Very good—Electricity, like the "Ether," comes in quite handy when one is forced to explain something not known. "Electricity," like the "Glacial Period," "Aristotle's Ether," "Natural Laws," and "Suggestion," is a most handy weapon of argument, and often acts as a preventative to further inquiry and investigation until some sufficiently irreverent of precedent arises to ask, "But Why and How!" and starts the ball rolling again.

But "Electricity" will not answer in this case, for the rate of the "travel" of Electricity is well known—184,000 miles per second, which, fast as it is, assumes the crawl of a "slow-freight" when compared with the "instantaneous" rate of travel of Gravitation. And then Electricity requires a "medium" and Gravitation does not, and in many other ways the two are seen to be totally different. And in the case of the Space between the Atom and Molecule and Corpuscle, it is no more reasonable to say "Electricity" than it would be to say "Heat" or "Light"; and "Magnetism" is not available for obvious reasons. Remember that Electricity, Light and Heat are *caused* by Motion resulting from Attraction, and *the child cannot procreate the parent.* Heat, Light and Electricity may beget each other (and they do). And Gravitation may procreate Heat, Light and Electricity. But Heat, Light and Electricity *cannot procreate Gravitation*—Never! And Light, Heat and Electricity require replenishing from the common source of Energy, but Gravitation is self-sufficient and asks no replenishing or storage-battery or power-house. Electricity, Heat and Light come and go, appearing, manifesting and disappearing, swallowed up by each other, or by Substance. But Gravitation is always there—unchangeable—unwavering—immutable—invariable—Something above Matter and Force—something majestic, awe-inspiring, sublime! Does it take a wild flight of the imagination to see that this Something, that is not Matter, and nor Force, *must be a manifestation of Mind?*

Let us first apply this idea of Thought-transference to the operation of the Law of Attraction between the Corpuscles, Atoms and Molecules of Substance—the Particles of Substance. The particles are believed to move to or away from each other in accordance with the workings of Attraction and Affinity, in its various degrees. First they must *desire* to move—not Desire in the developed sense that we feel it, but still elementary "feeling," or "inclination," or "tendency"—call it what you will, but it remains rudimentary Mental

Emotion—an E-motion leading to Motion. (This is not a pun—look up the meaning of the word Emotion and you will see its application.)

Then, following the Desire, comes the action in the direction of gratifying it. The Particles act to gratify Desire in two ways—acting at a "distance," remember—they exert the Attractive Force, which the writer believes to be Mental Force, *transmitted by Mind, projection*, a mental or psychic bond or connection being thus established. By means of this bond of Mind, the Particle endeavors to (1) draw itself to the object; and (2) to draw the object toward itself. In the case of the Molecule, this Desire and Movement seems to be mutual, and evidenced by and to all Molecules alike, *providing they be within Molecular Distance*, as Science calls it. But in the case of the Atoms, it seems to be different—for there is found a greater degree of "choice," or "elective affinity." This "election" or "choice" is not altogether free, but depends upon the relative likes and dislikes of certain "kinds" of elements, as we have seen in previous chapters, although, to be sure, these Elements are all made out of the same "stuff" in different combinations.

The details of Corpuscular Attraction are not known, so it cannot be told whether "preferences" exist, or whether (in the words of the street) all Corpuscles "look alike" to each other. It would appear, however, that there must be some reasons for preference, among the Corpuscles, else they would always form in the same combinations—always act alike to each other, as they are alike in other actions—and thus there would be but *one* Element or kind of Atom, formed, instead of the *seventy-five*, already known. To be sure, in this case, it *might* be that the *one* kind of Atom formed would be the Atom of Hydrogen, and that all other Elements, or Atoms, were modifications of that one—just proving the dream of the Scientists of the Nineteenth Century. But, as Kipling would say, "that is another story."

To return to the Particle which we left trying to draw the other Particle to itself, and itself toward the other. There is no *material* connection between them (and Electricity and Magnetism will not answer), so what is to be done! Evidently the Particle knows, for it exerts a "*drawing" power or force by means of the Mental-connection*, and two come together. The Particle evidently is able to exert a repelling or "moving away" power by reversing the process, the Mental-bond acting as the medium. This may cause a smile, because we have never seen an instance of bodies pulling themselves together by intangible "bonds." *Haven't we?* Then how about two pieces of magnetised steel, or two electrified substances? Oh, that's different, you say. *Why, different?* Isn't *the bond intangible?* And, haven't we seen that both Electricity and Magnetism were Mental

Actions also! Oh—er—but well—oh yes, *that's* it—perhaps the Attracting Force is Magnetism or Electricity. No, that will not do, for we have seen that Electricity and Magnetism were *products* of this Attraction, not *producers* of it—the Attraction must come *before* Electricity and Magnetism, not *after* them—you are mixing Cause and Effect. And, even if you were right—and you cannot be—wouldn't the Electrical or Magnetic Force be *called into operation, and directed by the Mental Action*, arising from the Desire? You cannot get away from Mental Action when you study the Law of Attraction.

"But, how about the fact that Heat causes the Particles to change their vibrations, and draw apart, and all that sort of thing—and Electricity, likewise!" you may ask. "Surely this takes the matter away from Mental Action, doesn't it!" Well, the writer thinks that the phenomenon referred to only helps to prove his theory. And he will endeavor to so prove to you.

The consideration of the facts related in this chapter, leads us to a supplemental proposition to our Basic Proposition, which may be stated as follows:

Supplemental Proposition i.—*Not only is the Law of Attraction the manifestation of a Mental Process, or Vital-Mental Action; but also the actual Force or Energy used in bringing the Particles of Substance in closer relation, in accordance with that Law, is in its nature a Vital Mental Force or Energy, operating between bodies or particles of Substance, without a material medium.*

12

The Law of Vibrant Energy

In previous chapters we have seen that the phenomena of Radiant Energy, known as Light, Heat, Magnetism and Electricity, had their origin in the Motion of the Particles, the different classes of phenomena depending upon the particular degree and nature of the aforesaid Motion of Particles.

We have seen also that Radiant Energy could be communicated or transmitted from one body of Substance to another. And that the communication of transmission might be accomplished not only by close contact of the bodies, but by "waves" of some sort which were caused in some "medium" (the Ether) by the vibrations of the Particles of the body, and which "waves," when they reached the other body, were transformed into vibrations of the Particles corresponding to those manifested in the first body. The idea has been illustrated by the sending telephone, the sound waves in the diaphragm of which were transformed into waves of the Electric current, and thus passing along the wires were transformed again into sound-waves by the diaphragm of the receiving instrument.

We have seen, also in the preceding chapter, that the medium by which these vibrations were transferred, transmitted, or communicated, might be supposed to be Mind, the operation being akin to Thought-transference. Now let us examine into the workings of the matter.

In the first place, we assume a certain state of vibration, existing in a certain body of Substance—Heat, or Electricity for instance (either illustration will answer.) Another body of Substance is brought in close contact with the first body, and the vibrations of Energy pass on to the second, not by "waves" but by a seeming actual passing of vibrations without the need of intervening "waves." This, Science calls transmission by Conduction, the theory being that the particles rapidly "pass on" the vibrations from one to another. Convection or conduction along other forms of Substance, such as hot-air, hot-water-steam, etc., is but a variation of the above, as Substance is the medium in both cases. The third form of transmission is by Radiation, whereby the vibrations are transmitted by "waves" in some medium other than Substance (according to the theory), as we have described in a preceding paragraph, as well as in previous chapters. As a matter of fact, a careful analysis of the matter will show that even in the "Conduction" of the most solid Substance, there must be a *"medium not Substance"* between the Particles of the Substance, *for the Particles always have Space between them*—this being true of the Particles of Air, as well as those of Iron. *So there is always Space to be traversed by a "medium not Substance."* But we need not stop to split-hairs regarding this question, for the general explanation will explain this also.

Now, to get back to our body of Substance vibrating with Radiant Energy, separated from a second body of Substance by a great distance—thousands of miles in fact—millions would be better—let us take two worlds, for instance—the Sun and the Earth. Ignoring for the moment the explanation of Gravitations (which will be given later) and realizing that there *is no medium of Substance* existing between the two bodies, we must grant that there is a *"medium not Substance"* existing between them, either permanently or thrown out for the purpose of this special transmission. We shall assume a medium existing before the need of the transmission (for reasons to be seen later.) Our Theory of Dynamic Thought, and Thought-Transference between bodies of Substance, compels us to suppose that this medium *is a Mental Connection, or Mental Relation, existing between the two bodies of Substance.* So, we must consider the question of this medium of Mind transmitting the vibrations of Radiant Energy from the Sun to the Earth. How can Mind conduct Radiant Energy? *It does not conduct Radiant Energy,* but it does *transmit*—not Radiant Energy—but the *Mental State that causes Radiant Energy Vibrations.*

This statement of a "Mental State causing Radiant Energy Vibrations" seems rather startling at first sight—but let us examine it. We have seen that the Radiant Energy was caused by the Motion or Vibrations of the Particles, which Motion or Vibration was the result of the workings of the Law of Attraction, and which Law was but the manifestation of Vital-Mental Action. And, at the last, the Vibrations of Radiant Energy are the result of peculiar or particular "states" of the Life and Mind of the Particle. The word "State" is derived from the Latin word *Status*, meaning "position; standing," and is used generally in the sense of "condition."

This Mental State of the Particle may be described as a state of *"Emotional Excitement."* Let us pause a moment to consider the meaning of these words—

it often helps us to understand a subject, if we examine the real meaning of the words defining it.

"Emotion" is derived from the Latin word *Emotum*, meaning "to shake; to stir up"—the Latin word being made up of two other words, *i.e.*, *E*, meaning "out"; and *Motum*, "to move." "Emotion" is defined as "a moving or excitement of the mind." "Excitement" is derived from the Latin word *Excitare*, meaning "to move out"—the English word being defined as "a calling to Activity; state of Active feeling; aroused Activity." So you see that the idea of *Active Motion*, and *Aroused Activity*, of Mind, permeates the term "Emotional Excitement," that is used by the writer in connection with the Mental State causing vibration of the Particles of Substance. The single word, "Excitement," will be used by the writer, hereafter, in the above connection, in order to avoid complex terms. To those who still object to the use of a mental term in reference to motion of Substance, he might remark that Science makes use of the term—"Excite," and "Excitement"—in reference to Electrical phenomena, so that he is not altogether without support in the use of the word.

Now to return again to our body of Substance—the Sun—the Particles of which are manifesting a great degree of "Excitement," evidencing in Vibrations producing the phenomenon of Radiant Energy. The excitement is shared equally by its Particles, the "contagion" having spread among them. Even the Particles of its atmosphere are vibrating with Excitement, and evidencing Radiant Energy. The Sun is in direct Mental Connection with the Earth (as we shall see presently) and the Excitement is transmitted by Thought-Transference (along this Mental Connection) in the shape of Dynamic Thought-waves of Excitement. These waves have a rate of speed of 184,000 miles per second—why this particular rate, or any rate at all, is not apparent; it being very evident, however, that this particular kind of Mental Action—Excitement, or Thought—is not transmitted *instantaneously* as is the Mental Quality known as Desire, resulting in Attraction, or Gravitation, which seems to be rather a Basic quality, rather than a temporary disturbance or emotional excitement. But the writer must not get ahead of his story.

The Excitement of the Particles of Substance composing the Sun is "contagious," and the Thought-waves travel along the Mental Connection, or medium, at a wonderful rate of speed. Soon they come in contact with the Mental Atmosphere of the Earth and the Excitement becomes manifest in Action, the Emotional Excitement being reproduced by the Particles of the Earth's Substance nearest the surface which vibrate and manifest the Radiant Energy in spite of themselves, for the tendency among Particles is to "settle down," and remain "calm," rather than to participate in Emotional Excitement. They have acquired a normal and fixed rate of Vibration, or Mental State, after many years, gradually changing from a high state of Excitement, to a comparative calm state. And, their tendency and inclination is Conservative, and they are disposed to resent and repel Radical states of Excitement or Disturbance, coming from other less Conservative Bodies.

The above fact partially explains why the communicated Excitement manifests itself more strongly on the surface of the body "exposed" to the contagion of Excitement. The Conservative influence is always at work, and manages to absorb and equally distribute the Energy that is beating down upon it, without allowing it to penetrate very far. The Energy is used-up or absorbed, and neutralized by the lower vibrations of the Mass. The effort of the Energy coming from the sending Body is to "bring-up" the vibrations of the receiving body to the rate of the sender; while the effort of the receiving body is to resist this effort, and to reduce and "bring-down" the transmitted increased rate of vibration of the Particles immediately exposed to the contagion. In both cases the effort is toward "equalization" of the rate of Vibrations. This working of the law may be observed plainly in the case of Heat vibrations—the Energy seeming to wish to "bring-up" the vibrations or temperature of the second body, while the latter resists this effort, and strives to "bring-down" the vibrations or temperature of those Particles of itself that have "caught the Motion." The Energy is like a Radical Agitator who wishes to stir up an Excitement, leading to "a change," while the Body is like the Conservative element that prefers to "let well enough alone," and resists the stirring-up process, and exerts itself to restore quiet, and to maintain accustomed conditions.

The explanation of the phenomenon given in any work on Physics or Natural Philosophy will answer fairly well in the consideration of this Theory of Dynamic Thought, the only important change being required, being the substitution of "Thought-waves" for "Waves of the Ether" of Science. Science has described the "working operations," as might be expected from her years of careful study and examination. She has erred only in the Theory or Hypothesis advanced to account for the facts. Her "Ether" handed down by Aristotle, is admitted by her to be paradoxical and "unthinkable"—but she has had none other to substitute for it. She will probably sneer at the Dynamic Thought, and Thought-Transference theory advanced in this book—if indeed she takes the trouble to examine it. But sometime, from her own ranks—among her most advanced members—will arise a man who will claim that "All Force is Mental Force," and that "Transference of Energy is Thought Transference." And the Scientific World will accept the doctrine after it finds itself unable to fight it down and it will give new names and terms to its workings. And it will proclaim loudly the "new" Truth. And this little book, and its writer will be ignored— but its work will go on. The writer although probably doomed to have himself and his theory laughed at by the masses of people (whose children will accept the teachings of this book) does not feel discouraged by the prospect. He cares nothing for personal credit—the truth being the important thing. Like Galvini, (whose words appear on the title page of this book) he may cry: *"I am attacked by two very opposite sects—the scientists and the know-nothings. Both laugh at me, calling me the 'Frog's Dancing Master,' but I know that I have discovered one of the greatest Forces in Nature."*

The illustration given above of the transmission of the Excitement of the Particles of the Sun to the Particles of the Earth, will answer equally well in the case of Light, Heat, Magnetism and Electricity. And it will answer in the case of the transmission of these Forces between Atoms, Molecules, and Masses as well as between Worlds and Solar Systems. Any bodies subject to the Law of Attraction may and do, so transmit Vibrations. In our consideration of "The Riddle of the Sphinx," which forms the subject of the next chapter, we shall obtain further particulars of the workings of the Law.

The consideration of the facts and principles stated in this chapter brings us to a second Supplemental Proposition, which may be stated as follows:

Supplemental Proposition ii.—*The rates of vibration of the Particles of Substance may be likened to "Mental States"; and a high degree of the same may be called an "Excitement." This "Excitement" may be, and is, communicated from the Particles of the body manifesting it, to the Particles of other bodies—the medium of such communication being a Mental Connection or Mental Relation existing between the two bodies of Substance, without the employment of any material medium—and which Excitement, so communicated, reproduces in the second body the vibrations manifested in the first body, subject, always, to the counteracting efforts of the second body to maintain its accustomed, and former, rate of vibration, and Mental State.*

13

The Riddle of the Sphinx

It is with no light emotion, or jaunty air, that the writer approaches this part of his subject. On the contrary, he feels something like awe when he contemplates the nature of that great Something which he is called upon to attempt to "explain" in a few pages. He feels, in only a lighter degree, the emotion that one experiences when, in occasional moments, his mind leads to a contemplation of The Infinite. He feels that that which men mean when they say "Gravitation" and "The Ether," are but symbols and feeble concepts of Something so far above human experience that the Mind of Man may grasp only its lowest shadings, the greater and higher part of it, like the higher rays of the Spectrum, being hidden from the experience of Man.

In his endeavor to pass on to you his ideas regarding the Something that explains both Gravitation and the Ether, he must ask you to endeavor to form a Mental Picture of a "Something." This Something must fill all Space within the Limits of the Universe, or Cosmos—if limits it has. It must be an expression of the first of the attributes of The Infinite—the one called Omnipresence, or Presence-everywhere—and *yet it must not be The Infinite Presence*. It also must be an expression of the second of the attributes of the Infinite—the one called Omnipotence, or All-Power—*and yet it must not be The Infinite Power*. It also must be an expression of the third attribute of The Infinite—the one called Omniscience, or All-Knowing—and *yet it must not be The Infinite Wisdom*. It must be an expression of All the Attributes that *we think of* as belonging to The Infinite—*and yet through them All we may see The Infinite, Itself, in the background, viewing its expressions*.

This Something that you are asked to think of is that Something regarding which the mystics have dreamed; the philosophers have speculated; the scientists have sneered and smiled—that Something that Men have thought of as The Universal Mind or the Cosmic Mind.

You are asked to think of this Something as a great Ocean of Pure Mind, permeating all Space—between Solar Systems—between Worlds—between Masses of Substance—between the Molecules, Atoms, and Corpuscles. In and about and around everything—yes, even in Everything—in the very essence of the Corpuscle it is—in truth *it is that Essence itself.*

Bound up in the bosom of that Mighty Ocean of Mind must reside all Knowledge of the Universe—of all "this side of God." For that All-Knowledge is but a knowing of its own region. Latent within itself must be locked up all Energy, or capacity for Force or Motion, for all Force or Energy is Mental. In its very presence it exemplifies the capacity of filling All Space. Omnipresent; Omnipotent; Omniscient—all the attributes of The Infinite are manifested in it—*and yet it is but the outward expression of That-Behind-the-Veil, which is the Causeless Cause of All.*

In that Great Ocean of Universal or Cosmic Mind, bodies of Substance are but as floating specks of dust—*or even bubbles formed of the substance of that Ocean itself*—on the surface of that Ocean, there may arise waves, currents, ripples, eddies, whirlpools, storms, hurricanes, tempests—from its bosom may rise vapor, that after stages of clouds, rain-drops, flowing in streams, rivers, bays, at last again reach the source of its origin. These disturbances and changes we call Energy, Force, Motion—but they are but surface manifestations, and the Great Ocean is serene in its depths, and, in reality, is unchanged and undisturbed.

This, friends, is that which the writer asks you to accept in the place of Aristotle's Ether. Is it a worthy exchange?

We have seen that the Attraction of Gravitation was different from any other so-called form of Force and Energy—both in its operations and laws, as well as in its constancy and self-support. And that it was different from the other forms of Attraction such as Cohesion, Chemical Affinity, etc. And, so we must consider it as more than a mere "Emotional Excitement" in the Mind of the Particle—that bubble on the surface of the Ocean. And it must be different from the special forms of Attraction manifested by the Atom and Molecule. It must be a simpler, more basic, and yet a more constant and permanent thing. It must exist before and after "Excitement; Vibration; Cohesion; and Chemical Affinity." *It must be the Mother of the Forces.*

Let us imagine the Cosmic Mind as a great body of Something filling Space, instead of as the surface of the Ocean, which figure we used just now—either figure is equally correct. This great Cosmic Mind is to be thought of as filling

Space, and containing within its volume (Oh, for a better word!) countless worlds, and suns, as well as smaller bodies of Substance. These suns and worlds and bodies are apparently free and unconnected, floating in this great volume of Mind. But they are not free and unconnected—they are linked together by a web of lines of Gravitation. Each body of Substance has a line reaching out in a continuous direction, and connecting it with another body. Each body has one of such lines connecting it with each particular "other body." Consequently, each body has countless lines reaching out from it; some slender, and some thick—the thickness depending upon the ratio of distances maintained by, and relative sizes of, the particular bodies that it connects. This system of "lines" form a great net-work of connections in the volume of Mind, crossing each other at countless points (but not interfering with each other.) And although the number may be said to be "countless," still these lines do not begin to cover the entire dimensions of Space, or of the Mind that fills it. There are great areas of Space entirely untouched by these lines. If one could see the system of lines, it probably would appear as a sheared off section of a great spider's web, with lines in all directions, but with "plenty of room" between the lines. *Perhaps these lines converge to a common centre, and that centre may be——! * But this is transcendental dreaming—let us proceed with our consideration of the use of these lines.

It is to be understood, of course, that these "lines" *are not material lines*— not made of Substance—but rather, "conditions" in the Cosmic Mind. Not Thought-waves arising from the Excitement of Particles, but Something more basic, simpler, and more permanent. Let us look closer and we will see that the great lines of Gravitation radiating from, and connecting world with world— sun with planet—are really cables composed of much smaller lines, the finest strands of which are seen to emanate from each Corpuscle or Particle of Substance—the "line" of Gravitation reaching from the Earth to the Sun being composed of a mass of tiny strands which connect each Particle of one body with each Particle of the other. The last analysis shows us that *each Particle is connected with every other Particle in the Universe by a line of Attraction.*

These "Lines of Attraction" are what we call Gravitation—purely Mental in nature—Lines of Mind-Principle in the great volume of mind.

These lines of Gravitation must have existed from the creation of the Particle, and the connection between Particle and Particles must have existed from the beginning, if beginning there was. The Particles may have changed their positions and relations in the Universe, but the lines have never been broken. Whether the Particle existed as a free Corpuscle—whether combined as Atom or Molecule—whether part of this world or sun or planet, or that one countless millions of miles removed—it mattered not. The Line of Gravitation always was there, between that Particle and every other Particle. Distance extended and thinned the line, or the reverse, as the case might be—but it was there, always. Obstacles proved no hindrance to passage, for the lines passed through the obstacle. Can it not be seen that here is the secret of the fact that no "time" is required for the passage of Gravitation—it apparently traveling instantaneously, whereas, in fact, it does not "travel" at all. And does not seem that this theory also explains why no medium is required for the "travel" of Gravitation! And does it not explain why Gravitation is not affected in its "passage" by intervening bodies! Gravitation does not "travel" or "pass"—it remains constant, and ever present between the articles, varying in degree as the distance between the Particles is increased, and *vice-versa*; and increasing and decreasing in effect, according to the number of Particles combining their lines of Attraction, as in the case of Atom, Molecule, Mass, World. Gravitation is a Mental Connection or Bond uniting the Mind in the several Particles, rather than their Substance or Material.

Along these lines of Gravitation pass the "Thought-waves," resulting from the Excitement of the Particles—these fleeting, changing, inconstant waves of Emotion—how different they are from the changeless, constant exhibition of Gravitation. And along these same lines—when shortened by close contact, travel the impulses of Cohesion and Chemical Affinity. Gravitation not only performs its own work, but also acts as a "common-carrier" for the waves of Desire-Force, and the Thought-waves of Excitement of the Particles, manifesting as Attractive Energy, and Radiant Energy, respectively.

The writer asks you to remember, particularly, that while the Desire-waves of the Particles—and their Thought-waves of Excitement—are changeable, disconnected, and inconstant; the Line of Gravitation is never broken, and could not be unless the Particle of Substance was swept out of existence, in which case the balance of the Universe would be overturned, and chaos would result. The Divine Plan is perfect to the finest detail—every Particle is needed—is known—is counted—and used in the Plan. And Gravitation is the plainest evidence of the reality of The Infinite that is afforded us. *In it we see the actual machinery of The Infinite.* No wonder that great thinkers have bowed their heads reverently before its Power and Awfulness, when their minds have finally grasped its import. Verily the sparrow's fall is noted, and known, as the Biblical writer has recorded, for the fall is in obedience to that great Law that holds the Particles in their places—that makes possible the whirl of worlds, and the existence of Solar Systems—that, indeed, makes possible the Forms of Life as we know them—that Something that forever and ever has, and will, silently,

ceaselessly, untiringly, and without emotion, fulfilled its work and destiny—
gravitation.

The Theory of Dynamic Thought also holds that in addition to the existence
of the Cosmic Mind, or Ocean of Mind-principle—and the Lines of Attraction that run through it, each particle has its Mental Atmosphere, or Aura.
The Aura is an Atmosphere of Mind that surrounds the Particle—and also the
larger bodies—and also living forms higher in the scale. This Aura is merely an
extension of the bit of Mind that is segregated or apparent separated from the
Cosmic Mind, for use by the individual Particle, Mass, or Creature. Through,
and by means of this Aura the Particle takes cognizance of the approach and
nature of the other Particles in its vicinity. The same rule holds good in the case
of the Creatures, including Man, as we shall see in a later chapter. The fact is
mentioned here, merely in order to connect the several manifestation of Mental
Phenomena mentioned in the several parts of this book.

Some may object to the Theory of the Lines of Gravitation being the only "car-
riers" of the Energy of the Sun, as being contrary to the conception of Science
that the Sun radiates Energy *in all directions equally*, just as does a piece of hot
iron, or a lamp. Answering this objection, the writer would say that there is a
decided difference in the two cases. The iron or lamp radiates its heat and light
to the particles of the surrounding air and other Substance in close distance,
the "lines" being very close together,—so close in fact that they seem to be
continuous and having no space between them, at least no Space sufficiently
large to be detected by the eye of Man, or his instruments. But with the Sun
the case is different, for the distances are greater and the lines spread apart
as the distance is increased. Draw a diagram of many fine rays emanating
from a central point, and you will have the idea at once. If Space were filled
with Substance, just as is the Atmosphere of the Earth—the Air, is meant of
course—then indeed would the lines practically be joined together, but as
Space between the worlds is almost devoid of Substance, the lines between the
Sun and the other worlds, and planets, spread out rapidly as the distance from
the Sun increases.

To show how this objection is really an additional proof of the Theory the
writer begs to call your attention to the fact that according to the calculations
of the physicists in Science, the Sun's energy would have been exhausted in
20,000,000 years, granting that it was dispersed equally in all directions during

that time. But, *note this*, Science in its other branches, namely in Geology, etc., holds that the Sun already has been throwing out energy for 500,000,000 or more years, and seems able to stand the strain for many millions of years more.

Thus Science is arrayed against Science. Does not this Theory harmonize the two, by showing that the Sun does *not* emanate Energy in *all* directions, equally, and at all times—but, on the contrary radiates Energy *only along the lines of Gravitation, and in proportion to the relative distances and sizes of the bodies to whom such Energy is radiated*?

The writer need scarcely state that in the short space at his disposal, in the pages of this book, he has been able merely to outline his Theory of Dynamic Force, as applied to the Inorganic World. The patience of the average reader has limits—and he must pass on to other features of the workings of the theory, namely the Mental Life of Man, in which the same laws are manifested. But, he feels that those interested in the phases of the subject touched upon, may explain for themselves the missing details by reference to the teachings of Modern Science on the subjects of Physics, remembering, *always*, to substitute the Theory of Dynamic Thought for the "Ether" theory that Modern Science borrows from Aristotle as a temporary "makeshift." The writer believes that this Theory will account for many of the missing links in Physics—a broad statement, he knows, and one either extremely impudent or superbly confident, according to the view-point of the critic.

The writer may be able to throw a little additional light, probably, upon the question of the relation between Gravitation, and the Excitement-waves of Radiant Energy. Without attempting to go into details, he wishes to suggest that in view of the fact that the Particles are connected by the "Lines of Gravitation," any great, extended, and rapid disturbance of a number of Particles would cause a series of undulating or wave-like movements in the "lines," which might be spoken of as waves of "Agitation or Unrest" in the Lines of Gravitation. This Agitation, or Unrest, of course, would be thus communicated to all other Particles toward whom lines extended, the intensity or effect of such Agitation or Unrest depending upon the relative distances, and the number of Particles involved. We may easily imagine how the intense and high rate of vibration among the Particles of the Sun, manifesting as intense Heat, would cause a like high degree of Agitation or Unrest among the Lines of Gravitation—the "lines" dancing backward and forward; around and about; following the movements of the Particles, and thus producing "waves" of Gravitational Agitation and Unrest, which when communicated to the Particles of the Earth, would produce a similar Excitement among the Particles of the latter. In the same way the "Sun-spots," and consequent terrestrial electrical disturbance may be explained.

While not absolutely tying himself to this particular conception of the details of the workings of the law, the writer feels free to say that he considers it a very reasonable idea, and one that in all probability will be found to come nearer to explaining the phenomena, than any other hypothesis. It certainly coincides with the "undulatory wave" theory of Science. The idea is but crudely expressed here, for lack of space, it being impossible to attempt to go into details—the mere mention of general principles being all that is possible at this time and place.

And now, for a few additional words on the subject of our theory that in place of the hypothetical Ether of Science—a Substance that is not Substance— there exists a great Ocean of Cosmic Mind. The idea is not without corroborative proof in the direction of the thought of advanced thinkers even among the ranks of Science.

While Science has accustomed the public to the idea that in the Universal Ether might be found the origin of Matter—the essence of Energy—the secret of Motion—it has not spoken of "Mind," in connection with this Universal Something. But the idea is not altogether new, and some daring Scientific thinkers have placed themselves on record regarding same. Let us quote from a few of them—it will make smoother our path.

Edward Drinker Cope, in several of his writings, hinted at the idea that *the basis of Life and Consciousness lay back of the Atoms, and might be found in the Universal Ether.*

Dolbear says: *"Possibly the Ether may be the medium through which Mind and Matter react."*

Hemstreet says: *"Mind in the Ether is no more unnatural than Mind in flesh and blood."*

Stockwell says: "The Ether is coming to be apprehended as an *immaterial,* superphysical substance, filling all space, carrying in its infinite throbbing bosom the specks of aggregated dynamic force called worlds. *It embodies the ultimate spiritual principle,* and represents the unity of those forces and energies from which spring, as their source, all phenomena, physical, *mental and spiritual,* as they are known to man."

Dolbear speaks of the Ether as a substance, which, besides the function of energy and motion, has other inherent properties *"out of which could emerge, under proper circumstances, other phenomena, such as life, or mind or whatever may be in the substratum."*

Newton spoke of it as a *"subtle spirit, or immaterial substance."*

Dolbear says: "The Ether—the properties of which *we vainly strive to interpret in the terms of Matter,* the undiscovered properties of which ought to warn every one against the danger of strongly asserting what is possible and what is impossible in the nature of things."

Stockwell says: "That the Ether *is not Matter in any of its forms,* practically all scientists are agreed. *Dolbear,* again, says: If the Ether that fills all space is not atomic in structure, presents no friction to bodies moving through it, and is not subject to the law of gravitation, it *does not seem proper to call it Matter.* One might speak of it as a substance if he wants another name for it.

As for myself, I make *a sharp distinction between the Ether and Matter,* and feel somewhat confused to hear one speak of the Ether as Matter." And yet, in spite of the above expressions, no Scientist has dared to say in plain words that the Ether, or whatever took the place of the Ether, *must be Mind,* although several seem to be on the verge of the declaration, but apparently afraid to voice their thought.

In view of what we have seen in our consideration of the facts and principles advanced in this chapter, we are invited to consider the following two Supplemental Propositions:

Supplemental Proposition iii—*Connecting each Particle of Substance with each and every other Particle of Substance, there exists "lines" of Mental Connection, the "thickness" of which depends upon the distance between the two particles, decreasing in proportion as the distance is increased. These "lines" may be considered as "conditions" of the great Ocean of Cosmic Mind which pervades and fills all Space, including the essence or inner being of the Particles of Substance, as well as the space between the said Particles. These "lines" are the "Lines of Gravitation," by and over which the phenomenon of Gravitation is manifested.*

These Lines of Gravitation have always existed between each Particle and every other Particle, and have persisted continuously and constantly, throughout all the changes of condition, and position, and relation, that the Particles have undergone. There is no "passage" or "transmission" of Energy or Force of Gravitation over these lines, or any other channel, but, on the contrary the Energy or Force of Gravitation is a constant and continuous "Mental Connection or Bond existing between the Mind of the Particles, rather than between their Substance or Material.

Supplemental Proposition iv.—*The Lines of Gravitation, mentioned in the preceding proposition, are the medium over which travel, or are transmitted the "Thought-waves" resulting from the Excitement of the Particles, and by which waves the "Mental States" are communicated or transmitted. The same medium transmits or carries the Mental Force of Attraction—Cohesion, Chemical Affinity, etc., evidencing in the relation of the Particles to each other. Thus Gravitation not only performs its own work, but also acts as a "common carrier" for the "waves of Excitement," manifesting as Radiant Energy; and the waves of Desire-Force, manifesting as Attractive Energy.*

And here, the writer rests his case in the action in the Forum of Advanced Thought, entitled "*The Theory of Dynamic Thought vs. The Theory of Aristotle's Ether,*" in which he appears for the Plaintiff. He begs that you, the members of the jury, will give to the evidence, and argument, due consideration, to the end that you may render a just verdict.

14

The Mystery of Mind

The writer, in this book, has treated the two manifestations of Life, *viz:*, Mind and Substance, as if they were separate things, although he has hinted at his belief that Substance, at the last, might be found to emanate from Mind, and be but a cruder form of its expression. The better way to express the thought would be to say that he believes that both Substance, and Mind *as we know it*, are but expressions of a form of Mind as much higher than *that which we know as Mind*, as the latter is higher than Substance. But he does not intend to follow up this belief, in this book, as the field of the work lies along other lines. The idea is mentioned here, merely for the purpose of giving a clue to those who might be interested in the conclusions of the writer, regarding this more remote regions of the general subject.

The writer agrees with the Ancient Occult Teachings regarding the existence of The Cosmic Mind, as he has stated in the last chapter. This Cosmic Mind, he believes, is independent of Substance, in fact it is the Mother of Substance, and its twin-brother, *Mind as we know it.*

Mind, as we know it, and Substance are always found in connection with other. It is true that the form of Substance, used by Mind as its body, may be far finer than the rarest vapor that we know, but it is Substance nevertheless. The working of the Great Plan of the Universe seems to require that Mind shall always have a body with which to work, and this rule applies not only in the case of the densest form of Substance and the Mind-principle manifesting through it, but also in the case of the highest manifestation of Mind, as we know it, which requires a body through which to manifest.

This constant combination of Mind and Substance—the fact that no Substance has been found without at least a trace of Mind, and no Mind except in relation to and combination with Substance, has led many scientific thinkers to accept the Materialistic idea that Mind was but a property of Substance, or a quality thereof. Of course, these philosophers and thinkers have had to admit that they could form no idea of the real nature of Mind, and could not conceive how Substance really *could* "think," but they found the Materialistic idea a simpler one than its opposite, and so they fell into it. Notwithstanding the fact that there was always a Something Within that would cry "Pshaw!" at the conclusion of the argument or illustration, these men have thought it reasonable to believe that there was no such thing as Mind, except as a result of "irritation of tissue," etc. But, nevertheless, there is always a Something in us that, in spite of argument, keeps crying like a child, *"'taint so!"* And, wonderful to relate, we heed the little voice.

This Materialistic theory is a curious reversal of the facts of the case. Even the very conclusions and reasoning of these thinkers is made possible only by the existence of that Mind which they would deny. The human reason is incapable of "explaining" the inner operation of the Mind, upon a strictly and purely physical basis. Tyndall, the great English scientist, truthfully said, *"the passage from the physics of the brain, to the corresponding facts of consciousness, is unthinkable. Granted that a definite thought and a definite molecular action of the brain occur simultaneously, we do not possess the intellectual organ, nor apparently any rudiment of the organ, which would enable us to pass by a process of reasoning from the one phenomenon to the other."*

The Materialist is prone to an attempt to rout the advocates of "Mind" with a demand for an answer to the question, "What *is* Mind?" The best answer to that question lies along the proverbial Irishman's lines of answering a question by asking another one, resulting in the "answering question," "What is *Matter?*" As a fact, the human reason is unable to give an intelligent answer to either question, and the best opinion seems to be to consider them as but two aspects of Something, the real origin of which lies in Something Higher, of which both are aspects or forms of expression.

The Occult Teaching, with which the writer agrees, is that the "Mind" inherent in any portion of substance, from the Corpuscle up to the Brain of Man, is but a segregated (or apparently separated) portion of the Universal Mind-principle, or Cosmic Mind. This fragment of Mind is always connected with Substance, and, in fact, it is believed that it is separated from the Universal Mind, and the other Separate Minds by a "film" of the rarest Substance, so fine as to be scarcely distinguishable from Mind. This separation is not a total separation, however, for the fragment of Mind is in connection with all other fragments of Mind, by "mental filaments," and besides is never out of touch with the Cosmic Mind.

But, comparatively, the fragment of Mind is *apart* from the rest, and we must consider it in this way, at least for the purpose of study, consideration, and illustration. It is like a drop in the Ocean of Mind, although connected, in a way, with every other drop, and the Ocean itself.

The individual Mind is not closely confined within the Substance in which it abides, but extends beyond the physical limits of the Substance, sometimes to a quite considerable distance. The Aura, or egg-shaped projection or emanation of Mind, surrounding each Particle and each Individual, is an instance of this. In addition to the Aura, there is possibly an extension of Mind to a considerable distance beyond the immediate vicinity of the physical limits, the connection, however, never being broken during the "life" term.

Mental influence at a distance, however, does not always require the above mentioned projection of the Mind. Thought-waves often answer the purpose, and, besides, there is such a thing as the imparting of Mental vibrations to the small particles of Substances with which the atmosphere is filled, which vibrations continue for quite a time, often for a long period after the presence of the individual producing them.

These matters shall be discussed in later chapters of this book. The Mind of Man is a far more complex thing that is generally imagined by the average man. Not only in its varied manifestation of consciousness, but its great region of "below-consciousness" or Infra-Consciousness, as it is called. It shall be the purpose of the sequel to this book (now in preparation) which will be titled "The Wonder of the Mind," to describe these inner workings, and to point out methods of utilizing the same.

Our next chapter, entitled "The Finer Forces of the Mind," will lead us into this field.

15

The Finer Forces of the Mind

It was the writer's original intention to close the book with the chapter in which he brought to a close his argument, and presentation of the case of "Dynamic Thought." The book was written for the purpose of demonstrating that Theory, and it naturally should have closed there. The writer has in simultaneous course of preparation a companion book, entitled "*The Wonders of The Mind*," in which, in addition to information and instruction regarding the latent powers and hidden regions of the mind—including an investigation of the Infra-conscious and Ultra-conscious Regions; Automatic Thinking; Occult Systems of Mentation; Mental Development, and Unfoldment, etc.—he purposes taking up the subject of "Dynamic Thought," from the Mental Plane of Man. And he thought it better to keep the two branches of the subject separate and apart.

But, notwithstanding the above facts, he feels that he cannot close the present book—the consideration of the present phase of the subject, without at least a passing reference to the fact that "Dynamic Thought" is fully operative on the Plane of Human Mentation, as on the Plane of Atomic Mentation. In fact, Man has the same power, potentially, that is possessed by the Atom, only refined to a degree corresponding to the development of Man as compared to that of the Atom. The Power is raised to a higher Plane of Mentation, but is fully operative.

Just as the body of Man contains physical life corresponding with the different stages of lower physical life, mineral, vegetable, and animal—for instance, the mineral-like bones, and the mineral salts in the system; the plant-like life and work of the cells; and the animal-like flesh, and physical life; in addition to the wonderful brain-structure and fine brain development, peculiar to Man—so has Man the lower Mental Qualities of the lower life, in addition to his glorious Human Consciousness that is reserved for the Highest Form of Life on the globe.

In his Mental regions, man has the power of the Atom of attracting particles of Substance to him, that he may combine it with other Substances in building up his body—then he has the plant-like cell mentation, that does the building-up work, and repairs wounds, and damaged parts, etc.—then he has the animal mentation evidencing in the passions, desires, and emotions of the purely animal nature, and which mentation, by the way, keeps Man busy in controlling by means of his higher mental faculties, that are God's gift to Man, and are not possessed by the animals. But all this will form part of the sequel, "*The Wonders of The Mind*," and are merely mentioned here in passing.

And, just as Man is enabled to use elementary the physical qualities that he finds in his body, and to turn same to good account in living his "human life, so does man, consciously, or unconsciously, make use of these elementary Mental powers in his everyday mental life. And if he but realizes what a *conscious* use of these faculties, guided by the Human Will, will do, Man may become a different order of being. This is the basis of the Occult Teachings, and the Mysteries of the Ancients, as well as the teachings of the modern secret esoteric bodies and societies, such as the "Rosicrucians" and "Hermetic Brotherhood," and several other societies whose names are not known—the *real* societies are referred to, not the brazen imitations that unscrupulous men are holding out to the public as the original orders, membership being offered and urged for the consideration of a few dollars. It is needless to say that membership in the *real* Occult orders is *never urged*, and *cannot be bought*.

But to return to the subject—the Individual Mind of Man is in direct touch, not only with the great Cosmic Mind, but also with the Individual Mind of every other Man. Just as the Particles are bound by lines of Attraction, so are the Minds of Men bound together by lines of Mind, or Mental filaments. And just as special forms of Attraction exist between the Particles, so do special forms of Attraction exist between Men. And just as Particles are influenced at a difference by other Particles, so are Men influenced at a distance by other Men. And just as the Particle draws toward itself that which it Desires, so do Men draw toward themselves that which they Desire. And just as Mental-States and "Excitement" are transmitted, or communicated from Particle to Particle, so are Mental States or "Excitement" transmitted or communicated from Men to Men.

"*As Above so Below—as Below so Above*," says the old Occult Maxim, and it may be found to operate on every plane.

The phenomena of Thought Transference; Telepathy; Telesthesia; Mental Projection; Suggestion; Hypnotism, Mesmerism, etc., etc., may be explained and understood, by reason of an acquaintance with the "Theory of Dynamic

Thought," as explained in this book. An understanding of one gives you the key to the other—for the Law operates precisely the same on each particular plane. If the reader will think over this statement, and then apply it to his investigations and experiments, he will find that he has the key to many mysteries—the loose end of a mighty ball of thread, which he may unwind at his leisure.

Let us begin by a consideration of the process of Thought-production in the Human Mind. In this way we may arrive at a clearer idea of the Mental Phenomena known as Thought-Force; Mental Power; Thought-waves; Thought-vibrations; Mind-transference; Mental Influence, etc. To understand these things we must begin by understanding the Process of Thought-production. Here is found the Secret of the phenomena named, and much more.

In the first place, while the Brain is the Organ of the Mind—the Instrument that the Mind uses in producing Thought, still the Brain does not do the thinking, nor is the brain-matter visible to the eye, the material instrument of thinking. The Brain (and other portions of the nervous systems, including the "little brains" or ganglia, found in various parts of the body) is composed of a certain substance—a fine form of Plasm, which however is but the groundwork of foundation for finer forms of Substance used in the production of Thought. Science has not discovered this finer Substance, for it is not visible to the eye, or to the finest instruments, but trained Occultists know that it exists. This fine Substance escapes the scalpel and microscope of the biologists and anatomists, and, consequently, their search for "Mind" in the Brain is futile. There is something more than "tissue to be irritated" in the Brain. But, remember, that this "something more" is still Substance, and not Mind itself.

Thought is a form of "Excitement" in this fine brain-substance, which we may as well call Psycho-plasm, from the two Greek words meaning "the mind," and "a mold, or matrix," respectively—the combined word meaning the "mold or matrix of Mind," in other words the material Substance used by the Mind in which to "cast" or "mold" Thoughts.

This Excitement in the Psychoplasm manifests in vibrations of its particles—for, like all Substance, it has "particles." All scientists agree that in the process of thinking there is an expenditure of Energy, and a "using-up" of material Substance. Just how this is effected, they do not know, but their experiments have shown that there is Energy manifested and used, and also Substance consumed.

The secret of the production of Thought does not lie in the Brain or nervous system, which are but the material substratum upon which the Mind works, and which it uses as a mold or matrix for the production of Thought. Thought is the product of Mind directing Force upon Substance in the shape of Psychoplasm. And Energy is manifested in the production of Thought just as much as in the operation of the Law of Attraction, or Chemical Action. "*What* Force and Energy?" may be asked. The answer is "*Mental* Force!" But although the answer stares them right in the face, scientists deny that Mind contains Force or Energy within itself, and persist in thinking of Force as a "mechanical thing," or as necessarily derived from the common forms of Energy, such as Heat, Light or Electricity.

They ignore the fact that Mind has a Finer Force which it uses to perform its work.

How do the Atoms attract each other and move together? There is an evidence of Force and Energy here that is not Heat, Light or Electricity—what is it? When a man wishes to close his hand, he Wills that it be closed, and sends a current of this Finer Force of the Mind along the nerve to the muscle, and the latter contracts and the hand is closed. A similar process is used in every muscular action. *What is the Force used?*

Science admits the existence of this Force, and calls it "Nervous Energy," or "Nerve Force." It holds that it must be "something like Electricity, and some even go so far as to say that it is Electricity. They base their ideas upon the fact that when Electricity is applied to the muscle of living or dead animals, they contract just as they do when this "Nerve Force" is applied, and every movement of the muscles may be so produced by Electricity, which becomes a counterfeit Nerve Force. But, here is the point, this Force cannot be identical with Electricity, *for none of the appliances for registering electric currents will register it.* It is not Electricity, *but is some Finer Force of the Mind*, generated in the material substratum that the Mind uses as a base of operation.

This Fine Force of the Mind is generated in some way in the Brain and Nervous System, by action upon the Psychoplasm. The Brain, or brains (for Man has several centres worthy of that term) are like great dynamos and storehouses of this Force, and the nerves are the wires that carry it to all parts of the system. More than this, the nerves have been found to be generators of Force, also, as well as the Brain. Experiments have shown that the supply of Force in a nerve vanishes when the nerve is used, in which case it draws upon the storehouses for an additional supply.

This Fine Force of the Mind is really the source of All Energy, for as we have shown in previous chapters, all Motion arises from Mental Action, and this form of Force or Energy is the primal Force or Energy produced by the Mind. And this Force is in operation in all forms of Life, from the Atom to the Man. And not only may it be used by the Particle, but Man, also, has it at his disposal.

As a proof that Substance is "used-up," and Energy manifested in the production of Thought, Science points to the fact that the temperature of a nerve rises when it is used, and the temperature of the Brain increases when it is used for extended Thought. Scientists have claimed, and advanced a mass of proof to back up the same, that Thought was as much a form of Energy as was the pulling of a train of cars, and was attended by the production of a definite amount of Heat, resulting from the activity of the fine substance of the physical extended resistant and composite substratum.

But, Science has taken all this to mean that Thought and Mind were purely material things, and properties of Matter. It has claimed that "Matter Thinks," instead of that Mind uses the Matter or Substance, in its finer forms, as a *substratum for the production of Thought*. Buchner, the leader of the purely Materialistic school, claims positively that Thought is but the product of Matter. He says: "Is it not a patent fact, obvious to all but the willfully blind that *matter does think?* De la Mettrie made merry over the narrowness of the mentalists, in saying: "When people ask whether matter can think, it is as though they asked whether matter can strike the hours! Matter, indeed, as such, thinks as little as it strikes the hours; but it does both, when brought into such conditions that thinking, or hour-striking results as a natural action or performance."

The above quoted opinion of Buchner shows how narrow and one-sided a talented man may become by reason of shutting out all other points of view, and seeing only one phase of a subject. The example of the "hour-striking" is a poor figure for the Materialists, for although matter *does* strike the hours, it does so only when wound up by Man under direction of his Mind. And in the manufacture, adjustment, and winding of the clock, Mind is the Cause of the Action. And, more than this, the very action of the coiled spring that is the immediate cause of the striking, results from the *mental* effort of the Particles of the spring endeavoring to resume their accustomed position, under the law of Elasticity, as explained in our chapters on Substance.

Science renders valuable service in showing us the details of the "mechanism" of Thought, but it will never really *explain* anything unless it assumes the existence of Mind, back of and in everything. It may dissect the brain-cells, and show us their composition, but it never will find Mind under the scalpel, or in the scale or test-tube. Not only is this true, but it cannot even discover the fine Psychoplasm which is used in the production of Mind. But we may make use of its investigations regarding the matter of Activity of Brain-substance in the process of Thought, and by combining them with our belief regarding the existence of Mind we may form a complete chain of reasoning, without any missing-links—these missing-links appearing both in the case of the "no-mind" philosophers, and the "no-matter" metaphysicians.

This theory of Mind and Substance considered as the two aspects of Something Higher, from which both have originated or emanated, will come to be regarded as the only "thinkable" proposition, in the end. And, with this idea in view, we may use the facts and experiments of the Materialists, while smiling at their theories. And, with but a slight change of words, we may turn against them their own verbal batteries. In this way, we may take Moleschott's famous statement: "*Thought is but a motion of Matter*," and render it intelligible by making it read as follows: "*Thought produces Motion in Matter*."

This Finer Force of the Mind is in full evidence to those who look for it, and although it may not be registered by the scales or instruments designed to register the coarser grades of Force, still it *is* registered in the minds of men and women, and in the actions resulting from their thoughts. These living registers of the Force respond readily to it—and every one of us is such a register. Just as is the Force a much higher grade of Energy than the forms usually considered as comprising the entire range of Energy, so are the instruments required for its registration much higher than those used to determine the degrees of Heat, Light, Electricity, and Magnetism. It may be that the future will give us instruments adapted for the purpose—in fact it begins to look even now as if the same were forthcoming. But whether we have such mechanical instruments, or not, the living instruments give us a sufficient proof of the existence of the Force, and its operation.

Well—the writer still finds himself unable to bring the book to a close. He added this chapter, to show that the property of Dynamic Thought extended to the highest development of Mind, as well as abiding in the lowest. And, now that he has ventured upon the subject, he finds himself impelled to give you a few instances of the workings and operations of that Law, in the case of Human Mental Life. And this means one more chapter—but only one, remember. The book must come to an end sometime remember. And, so we will pass over into another chapter, which will be entitled, "Thought in Action."

16

Thought in Action

Without attempting to go into details, or to enter into explanations, the writer purposes taking his readers on a flying trip through the region of "Thought in Action," or "Dynamic Thought in Operation in Human Life." The details of this fascinating region must be left for another and more extended visit, in our next book (before mentioned) which will be called "*The Wonders of The Mind*." But he thinks that even this flying trip will prove of interest and instruction.

Let us start with a hasty look at Man himself. Not to speak of his "Seven Planes of Mind," which belongs to the next visit, we find him a very interesting object. Not only has he a physical body, apparent to our senses, but he has also a finer or "astral body," which he may use (unconsciously, or consciously, when he learns how) for little excursions away from the body, during his lifetime. This Astral Body is composed of Substance just as his denser physical body. The field and range of Substance extends far beyond the powers of ordinary vision, as even the Materialists must admit when they talk of "Radiant Matter," "Etherial Substance," etc. Then he has currents of Fine Force coursing through his nervous system, which may be seen by those possessing "Astral Vision," if the teachings of the Occultists be true.

Then he, like the Particle, has an "Aura" or egg-shaped projection of Mind and fine particles of Psychoplasm, which has been thrown off in the process of Thought, and which clusters around him, producing a "Mental Atmosphere," which constantly surrounds him, and makes itself "felt" by those coming in his presence. Those who read these words may remember, readily, the "feeling" they have experienced when coming in contact with certain people—how some radiated an atmosphere of cheerfulness, brightness, etc., while others radiated the very opposite. Some radiate a feeling of energy, activity, etc., while others manifest just the reverse. Many likes and dislikes between people meeting for the first time, arise in this way, each finding in the mental atmosphere of the other, some inharmonious element. These radiations are perceived by others coming into their range.

Occultists tell us that the character of a man's thought vibrations may be determined by certain colors, which are visible to those having "Astral Sight." There is nothing so wonderful about this, when it is remembered that the various "colors" of light, comprising the visible colors of the spectrum, ranging from red, on through orange, yellow, green, blue, indigo, and terminating in violet, arise simply from different rates of vibration of the Particles of Substance. And as Thought is produced by Mind causing vibrations in the Psychoplasm, why is not the Astral Colors reasonable? We cannot stop to consider these colors in detail, but may run over the ones corresponding to each marked Emotion of Thought, as reported by the Occult teachings.

For instance the shade of the thought manifesting in physical or organic functions, is of a colorless white, or "color of clear water"; and the color of the thought manifesting in Fine Force or Vital Energy, is that of air—heated air arising from a furnace or heated ground—when it emerges from the body although of a faint pink when in the body itself. Black represents Hate, Malice, etc.; Gray (bright shade) represents Selfishness, while Gray of a dark dull shade represents Fear. Green represents Jealousy, Deceit, Treachery, and similar emotions, ranging from the dull shades which characterize the lower and cruder forms, to the bright shades which characterize the finer, or more delicate forms of "Tact," "Politeness," "Diplomacy," etc. Red (dull shade) represents Sensuality and Animal Passion, while Red (bright and vivid) represents Anger. Crimson, in varying shades; represents the phases of "Love." Brown represents Avarice or Greed. Orange represents Pride and Ambition; and Yellow, in varying shades, represents grades of Intellectual Power. Blue is the color of the Religious thoughts, ranging, however, through a great variety of stages, from the dull shade of superstitious religious belief, to the beautiful violet of the highest religious emotion or thought. What is generally known as "Spirituality" is characterized by a Light Blue of a peculiarly luminous shade. Just as there are ultra-red, and ultraviolet rays in the spectrum, which the eye cannot perceive, so Occultists inform us there are "colors" in the Aura or Mental Atmosphere of a person of unusual psychic or occult development, the ultra-violet rays indicating the thought of one who is pursuing the higher planes of occult thought and unfoldment, while the ultra-red is evidenced by those possessing occult development, but who are using the same for base and selfish purposes—"black-magic" in fact. There are other shades, known to Occultists, indicating several highly developed states of Mind, but it is needless to mention them here.

But the influence of these Particles of "Thought-stuff" thrown off from the

Mind Psychoplasm under the vibrations produced by the Mind during the process of Thought, does not cease with the phenomena surrounding the Aura. They are radiated to a considerable distance, and produce a number of effects. We will remember how the Corpuscles or Electrons are thrown off by Substance in a high state of vibration. Well, the same law manifests in the vibrations attendant upon the production of Thought. The particles are thrown off in great quantities each vibrating at the rate imparted to it during the process. No these particles of "Thought-stuff" do not compose the "Thought-waves"—the latter belong to a different set of phenomena.

These particles of vibrating "Thought-stuff" fly off from the brain of the thinker, in all directions, and affect other persons who may come in contact with them. There is an important rule here, however, and that is that they seem to be attracted by those minds which are vibrating in similar thought-rates with themselves, and are but feebly attracted—and in some cases, actually repelled—by minds vibrating on opposite lines of Thought. "Like attracts Like," in the Thought World, and "Birds of a feather flock together," here as elsewhere.

Some of these particles of "Thought-stuff" are still in existence, and vibrating, which proceeded from the minds of persons long since dead, the same being emitted or thrown off during the lifetime of the persons, however. Just as a distant star, which was destroyed hundreds of years ago, may have emitted rays which are only now reaching our vision, years after the destruction of the star which emitted them—and just as an odor will remain in a room after the object causing it has departed the particles still remaining and vibrating—and just as a stove removed from a room may leave heat vibrations behind it—so do these particles persist, vibrate, and influence other minds, long after the person who caused them may have passed out of the body. In this way, rooms, houses, neighborhoods, and localities may vibrate with the thoughts of people who lived there long ago, but who have since passed away, or removed. These vibrations affect people living in these places, to a greater or lesser extent, depending upon circumstances, but they may always be counteracted or changed (if they are of undesirable nature) by setting upon positive vibrations on a different plane of mind, or character of thought.

The mind of a thinker is constantly emitting or throwing off these particles of "Thought-stuff"; the distance and rate of speed, to and by which they travel, being determined by the "force" used in their production, there being a great difference between the thought of a vigorous thinker, and that emanating from a weak, listless mind. These projections of Thought-stuff have a tendency to mingle with others of a corresponding rate of vibration (depending upon the character of the thought.) Some remain around the places where they were emitted, while others float off like clouds, and obey the Law of Attraction which draws them to persons thinking along similar lines.

The characteristics of cities arise in this way, the general average of Thought of their inhabitants causing a corresponding Thought-atmosphere to hang over and around it, which atmosphere is distinctly felt by visitors, and often determines the mental character of the persons residing there, in spite of their previous characteristics—*that is, unless they understand the Laws of Thought.* Some neighborhoods, also, have their own peculiar Mental Atmosphere, as all may have noticed if they have visited certain "tough" neighborhoods, on the one hand, and neighborhoods of an opposite kind, on the other. Certain kinds of Thoughts and Actions seem to be contagious in certain places—*and they are* to those who do not understand the Law. Certain shops seem to have their own atmosphere—some reflecting confidence and honest dealing, and others radiating an atmosphere that causes patrons to hold tightly to their pocketbooks, and, in some extreme cases, to be certain that their buttons are tightly sewed on their garments. Yes, places like people, have their distinctive Mental Atmospheres, and both arise from the same cause.

And each person draws to himself these particles of vibrating "Thought-stuff" corresponding with the general mental attitude maintained by him. If one harbors feelings of Malice, he will find thoughts of malice, revenge, hate, etc., pouring in upon him. He has made himself a centre of Attraction, and has set the Law into operation. His only safe course is to resolutely change his thought vibrations.

A most remarkable form of these particles of Thought-stuff is evidenced in the case of what are known among occultists as "Thought-forms," which are aggregations of Particles of Thought-stuff energized by intense and positive thought, and which are sent out with such intensity and positiveness, that they are almost "vitalized," and manifest almost the same degree of mental influence that would be manifested by the sender if he were present where they are. This highly interesting phase of the subject would take many chapters to describe in detail, and we must content ourselves with a mere passing view. To those who are interested in the subject, the writer would say that he purposes considering them at considerable length, in the forthcoming book "*The Wonders of The Mind*," which has been alluded to elsewhere.

Besides the operation of these particles of Thought-stuff emitted during the production of Thought, there are many other phases of Thought Influence, or Thought in Action. The principal phase of this phenomena arises from the working of the Law of Attraction between the respective minds of different people. Just as are the Particles of Substance united and connected by "lines" of connection, so are the minds of Men connected. And the strong "pull" of Desire manifests along these lines, just as it does in the case of the Atoms. There has been much written of recent years regarding this "Drawing Power of the Mind," and although some of what has been written is the veriest rubbish and nonsense, yet under it all there remains a strong, form, substantial substratum of Fact and Truth. Men *do* attract Success and Failure to them—people *do* attract things to them—as strange as it may seem to the person who has not acquainted himself with the laws underlying the phenomenon.

There is no "miracle" about all of this—it is simply that the Law of Attraction is in full operation, and that people of similar thoughts are drawn together by reason thereof. The workings of this Law are somewhat intricate, but all of us are constantly using them, consciously or unconsciously. We draw to ourselves that which we Desire very much, or that which we Fear very much, for a Fear is a Belief, and acts in the direction of actualizing itself, *sometimes*. But, again, as Kipling would say: "But, that's another story." This phase of the subject is a mighty subject in itself, and "the half has not been told" even by the many who have written of it. The writer intends to try to remedy the deficiency in his next book, however.

Then, again, the "Excitement" of Thought, in the minds of people may be transmitted or communicated to the minds of others, and a similar vibration set up, under certain conditions, and subject to certain restraining influences— just as in the case of the Particles of Substances in a body or Mass of Substance. And, in many ways that will suggest themselves to the reader who has mastered the contents of the earlier chapters of this book, the phenomena of Dynamic Thought in the case of the Atoms, and Particles, may be, and are duplicated in the case of Individual Minds of Men.

The reader will see, readily, that this theory of Dynamic Thought, and the facts noted in the consideration thereof, give an intelligent explanation for the respective phenomena of Hypnotism, Mesmerism, Suggestion, Thought-transference, Telepathy, etc., as well as of Mental Healing, Magnetic Healing, etc., all of which are manifestations of "Dynamic Thought." Not only do we see, as Prentice Mulford said, that "Thoughts are Things," but we may see "*just why*" they are Things. And we may see and understand the laws of their production and operation. This theory of Dynamic Thought will throw light into many dark corners, and make plain many "hard sayings" that have perplexed you in the past. The writer believes that it gives us the key to many of the great Riddles of Life.

This theory has come to stay. It is no ephemeral thing, doomed to "die a-borning." It will be taken up by others and polished, and added to, and shaped, and "decorated"—but the fundamental principles will stand the stress of Time and Men. Of this the writer feels assured. It may be laughed at at first, not only by the "man on the street," but also by the scientists. But it will outlive this, and in time will come to its own—perhaps long after the writer and the book have been forgotten.

This must be so—for the idea of "Dynamic Thought" underlies the entire Universe, and is the cause of all phenomena. Not only is all that we see as Life and Mind, and Substance illustrations of the Law, but even that which lies back of these things must evidence the same Law. Is it too daring a conception to hazard the thought that perhaps the Universe itself is *the result of the Dynamic Thought of The Infinite?*

Oh, Dynamic Thought, we see in thee the instrument by which all Form and Shape are created, changed and destroyed—we see in thee the source of all Energy, Force and Motion—we see thee Always—present and Everywhere—present, and always in Action. Verily, thou art Life in Action. Thou art the embodiment of Action and Motion, of which Zittel hath said:

"Wherever our eyes dwell on the Universe: whithersoever we are carried in the flight of thought, everywhere we find Motion." Suns, planets, worlds, bodies, atoms, and particles, move, and act at thy bidding. Amidst all the change of Substance—among the play of Forces—and among and amidst all that results therefrom—there art thou, unchanged, and constant. As though fresh from the hand of The Infinite, thou hast maintained thy vigor and strength, and power, throughout the aeons of Time. And, likewise, Space has no terrors for thee, for thou hath mastered it. Thou art a symbol of the Power of The Infinite—thou art Its message to doubting Man!

Let us close this book with the thought of the Greatness of this Thing that we call Dynamic Thought—which, great as it is, is but as the shadow of the Absolute Power of The Infinite One, which is the Causeless Cause, and the Causer of Causes. And in thus parting company, reader, let us murmur the words of the German poet, who has sung:

> Dost thou ask for rest? See then how foolish is thy desire; the stern yoke of motion
>   holds in harness the whole Universe.
> Nowhere in this age canst thou ever find rest, and no power can deliver thee
>   from the doom of Activity.
> Rest is not to be found either in heaven or on earth, and from death and dying
>   break forth new growth,—new birth.

All the life of Nature is an ocean of Activity; following on her footsteps, without ceasing, thou must march forward with the whole.

Even the dark portal of death gives thee no rest, and out of thy coffin will spring blossoms of a new life.

LET A LITTLE
SUNSHINE IN

The young people's song—Good "New Thought" doctrine—Plenty of sunshine in life, if you look for it—Don't make a dark dungeon of your mind—Throw open the windows of your soul—How to let a little sunshine in.

The other night, just as I was dropping off to sleep, a crowd of young people passed along, returning from some social gathering. They were bubbling over with mirth and joy, and every girl seemed to be talking at the same time, the voices of the young men serving merely to punctuate the sentences of their fair companions. Just after they passed my window, someone started up a song, and the rest joined in. I do not know the song they sang, but the chorus went something like this:

Let a little sunshine in;
Let a little sunshine in;
Open wide the windows,
Open wide the doors,
And let a little sunshine in.

I listened with pleasure to the words and cheerful air of the song and said to myself: "Well, that's good enough 'New Thought' doctrine for me."

The young people went on their way singing. I, now wide awake, listened and thought. The song grew fainter and fainter as the distance between us grew greater, and at last I could not clearly distinguish the words they sang, but the faint vibrations of the tune still reached me, and I imagined that I could just hear the last words of the refrain: "Let a little Sunshine in."

Oh, if only those young people—and all young people—and all people young or old—would take to their hearts these words, and "let a little sunshine in." It is not sufficient that you merely agree that the advice is good—that you merely repeat the words mechanically—you must make thought take form in action, and not only say the words—not only think them—but you must ACT them. Make them a part of your life—incorporate the idea in your being— train yourself into the habit of opening yourself to the sunshine of Life—get into the way of letting it flow in.

"Let a little Sunshine in."

There is plenty of sunshine in life, if you only look for it. And there is plenty of shadow in life, if you only look for it. But in the things that seem all shadow to others, you will be able to find the sunshine if you but train yourself to always look for it. And in that which may seem bright sunshine to some, others will find nothing but shade—they are troubled with a mental cataract that shuts out all the rays of the sunshine of life.

"Let a little Sunshine in."

And when you learn to love the sunshine and look forward to seeing it always, you seem to draw it to you. The Law of Attraction brings to you your share of the sunshine with which the world is plentifully supplied. And, if you fall into the habit of looking for and expecting the shadow, the shadow will always be found.

"Let a little Sunshine in."

It is astonishing what a change the Mental Attitude of the person will make. Change your Mental Attitude, and the whole world seems to change. It is like taking off the smoked glasses that have caused the world to seem dark and gloomy, and seeing the brightness and colors of the world.

"Let a little Sunshine in."

Many of you have been making dark dungeons of your minds. You have steadily shut out the sun, and your minds have become musty, damp and mildewed. Across the floor crawl noxious creatures. The slimy form of Fear drags itself slowly along, leaving its track behind; the hideous shape of Jealousy eyes you from one corner—a creature of darkness; the venomous reptile Hate shows its fangs; the vampire Worry flits across the chamber. Fearful shapes are there glowering in the darkness—frightful forms crouch in corners and recesses. All is gloom, darkness, horror. A fit breeding place for the foul creatures who fear the light—a fit nursery for monsters. Look within the dark chambers of your mind—see what it really is—see what it generates. Look within—look within. Ah, you see at last. No wonder you shriek with terror—no wonder you turn away with horror. No, no, do not turn away—look and see yourself as you are. You need the lesson. Now that you see what you have been carrying around with you, and are sickened at the sight, start to work to remedy the evil. Throw wide open the doors; throw open the windows of the soul.

"Let a little Sunshine in."

Ah, yes, never fear, there is plenty of sunshine in the Universe. Plenty for all of you. There is an infinite supply. Draw it to you. Take it freely. It is there for *you*. It is your own—your very own. It is as free as air and the material sunshine. There is no tariff on it. It is not controlled by any trust or combine. It is not adulterated. It is everywhere, everywhere. Ho! ye who are dwelling in darkness! Here is Life and Happiness for you! Here is Peace for you! Here is Joy for you! Joy, comrades, Joy! Open wide your windows; open wide your doors.

"Let a little Sunshine in."

Yes, yes! I hear you say that you cannot dispel the gloom with which you are surrounded. Nonsense. Do you not know that darkness is not a positive thing—it is the essence of negation. It is not a real thing at all—it is merely the absence of light. And here you have been for all these years, believing that the darkness was a real thing that you could not get rid of. Just stop for a moment and think. If a room in your house is dark and gloomy, do you hire a man to shovel out the darkness—do you attempt to do it yourself in your desire for light? No, no, of course you do not. You just raise the shades, and throw open the shutters and the sunshine pours in and lo! the darkness has vanished. So it is with the gloom of the soul, the darkness of the mind. It is a waste of energy to attempt to dig away the darkness—to cast out the shadows. You'll never get light in that way. All that you need to do is to recognize the advantage of light—the fact that light is to be had—that there is plenty of it anxiously waiting to be let in. Then all that you need to do is to

"Let a little sunshine in;
Let a little sunshine in;
Open wide the windows,
Open wide the doors,
And let a little sunshine in."

PRACTICAL
MENTAL
INFLUENCE

Contents

1

The Law of Vibration

Students of history find a continuous chain of reference to the mysterious influence of one human mind over that of others. In the earliest records, traditions and legends may be found reference to the general belief that it was possible for an individual to exert some weird uncanny power over the minds of other persons, which would influence the latter for good or evil. And more than this, the student will find an accompanying belief that certain individuals are possessed of some mental power which bends even "things" and circumstances to its might.

Way back in the dim past of man's history on this planet, this belief existed, and it has steadily persisted in spite of the strenuous opposition of material science, even unto the present day. The years have not affected the belief, and in these dawning days of the Twentieth Century it has taken on a new strength and vitality, for its adherents have boldly stepped to the front, and confronting the doubting materialistic thinkers, have claimed the name of "Science" for this truth and have insisted that it be taken, once and for all, from the category of superstition, credulity and ignorant phantasm.

Were it not pitiable, it would be amusing to glance at the presumptuous, complacent, smug, self-satisfied position of the materialistic school of thinkers, who would brush aside as a foolish delusion that which man of the wisest men of a past ages have accepted and taught as the truth. The modern "know-it-alls" would sneer contemptuously at facts that are known to be of actual occurrence in the daily lives of thousands of intelligent people, and which the experience of human-kind has demonstrated for many centuries, in all lands and all races.

The trouble lies in the dogmatic assumption of the materialistic school that what is known as "mind" is merely some peculiar action of the material brain, some writers even holding that the brain secretes thought, just as the liver secretes bile. They refuse to see that the operation of Mind is a manifestation of energy known as electricity, magnetism, light, heat, gravitation, cohesion, etc. Because mental energy does not register the vibrations of these lower forms of energy, they conclude that the higher mental energy does not exist. Having formulated a theory to suit their materialistic conceptions, they try to ignore all facts not consistent with their theory. If they find a fact that will not squeeze into their narrow theory well, "so much the worse for the fact," as a writer has said and they promptly ignore or dispute it.

As a matter of truth, the investigator is not compelled to resort to metaphysical explanations to account for the phenomena of Mental Influence. The very facts of physical science itself, if rightly interpreted, will give the clue to the mystery, and will point the steps of the honest investigator toward the path where he may find the solution of the perplexing riddle. Although we know that the real solution lies in the metaphysical realm, still even physical science will corroborate the facts of its metaphysical sister science, and instead of contradicting the latter will actually go far toward furnishing analogous facts and principle basis for a theory of metaphysical facts.

The student will see at once that so far as physical science is concerned, it must begin at the phenomenon of "Thought Transference" for in that phase of the subject may be found an elementary principle in evidence in many other forms of phenomena. We have given many instances of "Thought Transference" in the two proceeding volumes of this series, entitled "Mind Reading" and "Psychomancy," respectively, and so we need not repeat the same in this place. The main fact is that "Thought Transference" does exist, and may be accounted for upon purely scientific grounds, without calling in the truths of metaphysical thought. We know that this is a strong statement, and a positive assertion, but we also know that the same may be demonstrated. Let us consider this phase of the subject.

In the first place, physical science teaches that underlying all forms, degrees and apparent differences in matter and energy, there is to be found a manifestation of some elementary energy, which manifests in what is known as "Vibrations." Everything in the material world is in vibration—ever manifesting a high degree of motion. Without vibration there would be no such thing as a material universe. From the electronic-corpuscles which science teaches compose the atom; up through the atom and molecule, until the most complex forms of matter are manifested, there is the ever-present Vibration. And through all forms of energy, light, heat, electricity, magnetism and the rest, Vibration is also ever present. In fact, physical science itself teaches that not only is Vibration the basic force underlying other forces and the various forms of matter, but also that the apparent differences between the various forms of matter, and also between the various forms of energy, are caused simply and solely by the varying degrees of Vibration manifested.

Just as the difference between the lowest tone that can be distinguished by the ear of man, and the highest note that can be distinguished by the same organ of sense, is merely a difference between the rate of Vibration—just as is the difference between the dull red color at one end of the spectrum, and the violet at the other end, with the intervening colors known as indigo, blue green, yellow and orange, with all the combinations of shades arising from them—just as the difference between the greatest degree of cold known to science, and the greatest degree of heat that can be conceived of—just as these great differences due solely and wholly to varying rates of Vibration—so is the difference between and all forms of matter or force simply a matter of the rate of Vibration. In short, all material and physical "Things" are simply manifestations of some "infinite and eternal energy from which all things proceed," their differences resulting merely from the different degree of Vibration being manifested in them. Remember, that this is not "vague philosophy" or "airy metaphysics" or "spiritualistic vagaries" (to quote from the materialistic writers), but facts claimed and admitted by the greatest physical scientists of the age, as a reference to their lectures and text-books will prove to anyone.

And, more than this, any intelligent physical scientist will tell you that Science has every reason to believe that there are great fields of energy and force, the Vibrations of which are far too high for even the delicate instruments of science to record, but which nevertheless exist and manifest effects. It was only the other day that Science was able to "catch" the "X-Rays" and other forms of high Radioactivity, and yet these rays and forces had always existed. And tomorrow Science will perfect instruments capable of registering still higher forms of energy. And by and by, some scientist will perfect an instrument capable of registering and recording the subtle vibrations of Thought, and perhaps in time someone will perfect that instrument so that it will not only record such Thought vibrations and waves, but, like the phonograph, it will be able to reproduce and send forth similar vibrations so that others may feel the thoughts, just as they now hear the sounds from the phonograph. Such a prediction is no more wonderful than would have been the prediction of the telephone, the phonograph, the wireless telegraph and sundry other discoveries and inventions a hundred years ago.

Did you ever think that there are colors that the eye cannot see, but which delicate instruments clearly register? In fact, the rays of light which sunburn the face, and which register on the photographic plate are not visible to the eye. The eye sees the lower rays, but only instruments adapted for the purpose detect the higher ones. Your eye cannot see the X-Ray as it passes through the room, but the plate will catch it, and its light may make a photograph. The rays of light visible to the eyes are only the lower ones—the higher ones are far beyond the power of the eye to record, and beyond even the range of the most delicate instrument there exist rays and waves of light of such high vibratory rate as to defy even its power to record.

Did you ever know that there are sounds unheard by human ears that the microphone will catch and magnify? Scientific imagination dreams of instruments that will catch the songs of the mitelike insects, and magnify them until they can be distinguished. There are waves of electricity that may pass through your body, unperceived by you, and yet powerful enough to run light electric lights. Listen to the words of certain eminent scientists.

Prof. Elisha Gary, a celebrated scientist and teacher, has said: "There is much food for speculation in the thought that there exists sound waves that no human ear can hear, and color waves of light that no eye can see. The long, dark, soundless space between 40,000 and 400,000,000,000,000 vibrations per second, and the infinity of range beyond 700,000,000,000,000 vibrations per second, where light ceases, in the universe of motion, makes it possible to indulge in speculation."

Prof. Williams, the well-known scientific writer, has said: "There is no gradation between the most rapid undulations or trembling that produces our sensations of sound, and the slowest of those which give rise to our sensations of gentlest warmth. There is a huge gap between them, wide enough to include another world of motion, all lying between our world of sound and our world of heat and light; and there is no good reason whatever for supposing that matter is incapable of such intermediate activity, or that such activity may not give rise to intermediate sensations, provided that there are organs for taking up and sensitizing their movements."

And, so you see that in the scientific theory of Vibrations, there may be found plenty of room for a scientific explanation of all that is claimed by adherents of the truth of Mental Influence, without getting out of the region of physical science, and without invading the plane of metaphysics. And there are many more proofs from the same source, which we may touch upon as we proceed.

There is but one Truth, and it manifests on all planes—the Spiritual; the Mental; and the Physical—and manifestations agree and coincide. So no Mentalist need fear the test of Physical Science, for each plane will bear out the facts and phenomena of the ones below or above it—the Three are but varying phases of One. In this little work we shall hug close to the plane of Physical Science, because by so doing we will be able to make the subject much clearer to many than if we had attempted to express the teaching in Metaphysical terms. There is no contradiction in the end. Each bit of Truth must dovetail into every other bit, for all are parts of the Whole.

2

Thought Waves

In our last chapter we have seen that Vibration was to be found underlying all manifestations of energy, and all forms of matter. We also quoted two distinguished scientists whose words showed that there were fields of vibratory energy not filled by any known forms of energy, the inference being that inasmuch as there are no gaps in nature's processes these unknown fields must be occupied by certain forms of energy no known as yet to physical science. The teachings of the occultists of all lands and ages, as also those of modern Mental Science, are to the effect that the Mind, in its manifestation of Thought in the brain, generates a form of energy of intensely high Vibration, which energy may be, and is, projected in vibratory waves from the brains of other persons within its field of influence.

All students of Mental Influence have noticed the close resemblance that is manifested between the phenomena of electrical and magnetic energy on the one hand and the phenomena of mental energy on the other. So close is the analogy that one may take the proven facts of science relating to electrical and magnetic phenomena and confidently proceed with the certainty of finding a strikingly close correspondence in the field of mental phenomena. And the recognition of this fact is helping the workers in the mental field group together the varied phenomena that come under their notice, and to work out the theory and practice of Mental Influence.

In the first place, it is now a fact well known and accepted by investigators that the generation of Thought and the manifestation of Mental States occasions a "burning up" of brain matter, and the consequent production of a form of energy of high vibratory power. Physiologists recognize this fact, and the textbooks make reference to it. Experiments have shown that the temperature of the brain is increased in accordance with the intensity of Feeling and Thought, and that there is undoubtedly a generation of energy and a consumption of brain matter which bears a very close resemblance to the process of the generation of electrical energy. And this being conceded, it follows that this energy once released must be emanated or sent forth from the brain in the manner akin to the emanation of other known forms of energy, i.e., in the form of "waves" of vibratory force. Light and Heat travel in this way—so do electricity and magnetism—so do the forces of Radioactivity. And the investigators of Mental Influence have demonstrated by their experiments that there is such a thing as Thought-Induction, and many other phases of manifestation similar to that exhibited by electricity and magnetism.

Flammarion, the well-known and eminent French scientist, has said on the subject: "We sum up, therefore, our preceding observations by the conclusion that one mind can act at a distance upon another, without the habitual medium of words, or any other visible means of communication. It appears to us altogether unreasonable to reject this conclusion if we accept the facts. The conclusion will be abundantly demonstrated. There is nothing unscientific, nothing romantic in admitting that an idea can influence a brain from a distance. The action of one human being upon another, from a distance, is a scientific fact; it is as certain as the existence of Paris, of Napoleon, of Oxygen, or of Sirius." The same authority also states: "There can be no doubt that our physical force creates a movement in the ether which transmits itself afar like all movements in the ether, becomes perceptible to brains in harmony with our own. The transformation of a psychic action into an ethereal movement, and the reverse, may be analogous to what takes place on a telephone, where the receptive plate, which is identical with the plate at the other end, reconstructs the sonorous movement transmitted, not by means of sound, but by electricity. But these are only comparisons."

When a Thought or Feeling is generated in the mind or brain of a person, the energy generated flows forth from the brain of the person in the form of waves of mental energy, spreading from the immediate neighborhood of the thinker to a distance proportioned to the strength of the thought or feeling.

These Thought-Waves have the property of awakening similar vibrations in the minds of other persons coming within their field of force, according to the laws of Mental Influence, which law shall be explained in the next chapter.

As we proceed with our consideration of the subject of Mental Influence, in the succeeding chapters, we shall see the many and varied forms of manifestation of Thought-Waves. At this point we shall merely view the phenomena in a general way.

Thought-Waves are manifested in a variety of forms and phases. Some are the waves emanated from the minds of all thinkers, unconsciously and without purpose, and usually without much force. Others are sent forth with great force, and travel far, manifesting a degree of influence commensurate with the force with which they are projected. Others are directed purposely toward certain individuals or places, and travel along rapidly in a straight line to the point, which they have been directed or aimed. Others are sent forth with great strength and power, but instead of being directed toward any particular person or place, are designed to sweep around in great whirlpools of energy affecting all who happen to fall within their field force.

You will readily understand that there is a great difference between Thought-Waves sent forth idly and unconsciously, and without knowledge of the underlying laws of Mental Influence, and those projected with a full knowledge of the laws governing the phenomena and urged on and directed by a powerful Will of the sender. The force is the same, but the degree of its power, and the measure of its effects are determined by the conditions of its sending force.

The vibratory force of these Thought-Waves does not cease with the sending forth of the wave, but persists for a long time afterward. Just as heat in a room persists long after the fire in the stove has been extinguished—just as the perfume of the flower exists in a room long after the flower has been removed—just as a ray of light travels through space for millions of miles, and for centuries after the star itself has been blotted out of existence—just as any and all forms of vibratory energy persist in manifesting after the initial impulse has been withdrawn—so do the vibrations of Thought continue long after the thought, yes, long after the brain which sent them forth has passed into dust.

There are many places today filled with the thought-vibrations of minds long since passed outside of the body. There are many places filled with the strong vibrations of tragedies long since enacted there. Every place has an atmosphere of its own, arising from the thought vibrations set in motion by the various persons who have inhabited or occupied them. Every city has its own mental atmosphere, which has an effect upon persons moving into them. Some are lively, some dull, some progressive, some old-fogeyish, some moral, some immoral—the result of the character of the early settlers and leading spirits of the places.

The atmosphere affects persons moving into these towns, and either sinks to the general level, or else, if strong enough, help to change the mental tone of the place. Sometimes a change in conditions brings a large influx of new people to the town, and the mental waves of the newcomers tend to bring about a marked change in the local mental atmosphere. These facts have been noticed by many observing people who were, perhaps, not familiar with the laws and principles underlying the phenomena.

Many have of course noticed the differing atmosphere of stores, offices and other places of business. Some of such places give one and air of confidence and trust; others create a feeling of suspicion and just trust; some convey an impression of active, wide awake management, while others impress one as being behind the times and suffering from alert active management. Did you ever stop to think that these different atmospheres were caused by the prevailing mental attitudes of those in charge of the places? The managers of business places send forth Thought-Waves of their own, and their employees naturally falling into the pace set for them, sending forth similar vibrations, and before long the whole place is vibrating on a certain scale. Let a change in the management occur and see what a change soon manifests itself.

Did you ever notice the mental atmospheres of the houses you happened to visit? You may experience and recognize all of the varying notes in the mental scale of their occupants. From some thresholds Harmony manifests itself, while others breathe in harmony as soon as you step over the threshold. Some radiate mental warmth, while others seem as cold as an iceberg. Think for a movement and recall the various houses or places you visit, and see how the mental vibrations of the inmates manifest themselves to a visitor.

The low quarters of our cities, the dens of vice and haunts of dissipation vibrate with the character of thought and feeling of those inhabiting them. And the weak-willed visitor is thus tempted.

And, in the same way, certain places are filled with strong, helpful, elevating vibrations, which tend to lift up and elevate those coming within their circle of influence. Thoughts and Feelings are contagious, by reason of the Law of Vibration and Mental Induction. When this law is understood the individual is enabled to protect and improve himself. Such Knowledge brings Strength.

3

Mental Induction

As we stated in the preceding chapter, the phenomena of Mental Influence bears a striking analogy to that of the electrical or magnetic energy. Not only is this so in the phase of wave motion and transmission, but also in the phase of induction, as we shall see presently.

In physical science the term Induction is used to indicate that quality in a manifestation of energy which tends to reproduce in a second object the vibrations manifesting in the first object, without direct contact between the two bodies. A magnet will induce magnetism in another object removed from its space. An electrified object will tend to produce similar vibrations in another object by induction, over great spaces. Heat waves travel along the ether, and tend to produce heat vibrations in objects far removed, notably in the case of the sun and the earth. Even sound waves will affect other objects in this way, as in the well-known instance of the glass or vase "singing" in response to the musical note sounded afar off. In fact, we see and hear by processes similar to those described.

And in this same manner that Thought-Waves carry the vibrations of the mind sending them forth to great distances, or lesser ones, tending to set up similar vibrations in the middle of other persons within their field force. Thus a person feeling a strong degree of anger will pour forth waves of that degree of mental vibration, which, coming in contact with the brains of other persons, tend to set up a similar feelings or emotions and thus cause the person to "feel cross" or "peevish" or even to manifest a similar angry state of mind. We all know how easily a fight is started by a very angry person in a room sending forth violent vibrations. One has but to remember the instances of mob violence to see how easily the "contagion of hate and anger" spread among people who allow themselves to be influenced. And not only is this true of undesirable emotions and feelings, but also of desirable ones. The influence of a good man who happens to be strong mentally spreads among those around him, influence in them for good.

Orators, actors, preachers and teachers send forth strong mental currents, which tend to produce mental conditions on the part of their hearers corresponding to the feeling held by the mind of the speaker. When you remember how this speaker swayed your feelings, or how that actor made you weep with pity, shiver with fear, or laugh with joy, you will see how Mental Induction acts.

But not only is this true when we are in the actual presence of the person sending out the Thought-Waves, but it is equally true that we are influenced by persons far removed from us in space, often without their knowledge or intent, although sometimes (in the case of one who understands the principal post) with full knowledge and intent.

The ether with which space is filled carries these Thought-Waves in all directions, and the surface of the earth, particularly in the densely occupied portions, is filled with these waves. These waves, carrying the mental vibrations, coming in contact with each other, tend to set up combinations on one hand, or else neutralize each other on the other hand. That is to say, if two sets of waves of a similar nature meet there is likely to be a combination formed between them just as between two chemicals having an affinity for each other. In this way the "mental atmosphere" of places, towns, houses, etc., is formed. On the other hand if currents of opposing vibrations come in contact with each other, there will be manifested a conflict between the two, in which each will lose in proportion to its weakness, and the result will be either a neutralization of both or else a combination having vibrations of an average rate. For instance, if two currents of mental energy meet, one being a thought of Love and the other Hate, they will neutralize each other if they are equal, or if one is stronger than the other, it will persist but robbed of much of its strength. If it were not for this neutralizing effect we would be largely at the mercy of stray currents of thought. Nature protects us in this way, and also by rendering us immune to a considerable extent.

But nevertheless we are affected by these waves to a considerable extent, unless we have learned to throw them off by knowledge of the laws and an enforcement of them by practice. We all know how great waves of feeling spread over the town, city or country, sweeping people off their balance.

Great waves of political enthusiasm, or war spirits, or prejudice for or against certain people, or groups of people, to sweep over places and cause men to act in a manner that they will afterward regret when they come to themselves and consider their acts in cold blood. Demagogues will sway them or magnetic leaders who wish to gain their votes or patronage; and they will be led into acts of mob violence, or similar atrocities, by yielding to these waves of "contagious" thought. On the other hand we all know how great waves of religious feeling sweep over a community upon the occasion of some great "revival" excitement or fervor. The effect of these Thought-Waves, so far as the power of induction is concerned, of course depends very materially upon the strength of the thought or feeling being manifested in the mind sending them forth. The majority of persons put but little force into the mental manifestations, but here and there is to be found a thinker whose Thought-Waves are practically "a stream of living will" and which of course have a very strong inductive effect upon the minds of others with whom the waves come in contact. But it likewise follows that a number of persons thinking along the same lines will produce a great volume of power by a combination of their thought currents into great streams of mental force.

Then again there is another feature of the case that we must not lose sight of, and that is the Attraction between minds, by virtue of which one draws to himself the Thought-Waves of others whose thoughts are in accord with his own. The contrary is true, for there is a Repulsion between the minds of persons and the Thought-Waves of others whose thoughts are in accord with his own. The contrary is true, for there is Repulsion between the minds of persons and the Thought-Waves of others antagonistic to their thoughts. To quote a well-worn and much-used expression to illustrate this truth, "Like attracts Like" and "Birds of a Feather flock together". There is ever in operation this marvelous Law of Attraction and Repulsion of Mental Energy. Persons allowing their thoughts to run along certain lines, and permitting the feelings to be expressed in certain ways, draw to themselves the Thought-Waves and mental influences of others keyed to the same mental keynote. And likewise they repel the waves and influences of an opposing nature.

This is an important fact to remember in one's everyday life. Good attracts Good and repels Evil. Evil attracts Evil and repels Good. The predominant Mental Attitude serves to attract similar influences and to repel the opposing ones. Therefore watch carefully the character and nature of your thoughts—cultivate the desirable ones and repress the undesirable ones. Verily "As a man thinketh in his heart, so is he."

Some Thought-Waves sent forth with but little strength travel slowly and do not proceed very far from their place of emanation, but creep along like some smoke or fog, lazily and yielding. Other thoughts charged with a greater intensity of desire or will, dart forth vigorously like an electric spark, and often travel great distances. The weak Thought-Waves do not last a very long time, but fade away or become neutralized or dissipated by stronger forces. But the strong thoughts persist for a long time, retaining much of their vitality and energy.

In the same manner the Thought-Waves of a person will continue to vibrate around him wherever he goes, and those coming in contact with him will be impressed by the character of his vibrations in this way.

Some men send forth gloomy vibrations, which you feel when you come in contact with them. Others radiate good cheer, courage and happiness, which conditions are induced in those with whom they come in contact. Many people will manifest these qualities so strongly that one can notice the effect the moment such persons enter a room. They carry their atmosphere with them, and the same is induced in the minds of others around them.

In the same way some people carry with them vibrations of Willpower and Masterfulness that beat upon the minds of others, making them feel the power of such persons and conquering their own willpower and changing their desires. Others manifest a strong power of Fascination or Attraction, in a similar manner, which tends to draw others to them and to their desires and wishes. Not only does this principle operate in the phase of general mental atmospheres, but also in the phase of direct personal influence.

All forms of Mental Influence operate along the lines of Mental Induction, as herein described. The principle is the same in all cases and instances, although the manner of operation varies according to the particular phase of the phenomena manifested. Remember this as we proceed, and you will be able to understand the subject much better.

4

Mental Concentration

The two principal factors in the manifestation of Mental Influence, in all of its forms, are what are known as (1) Concentration, and (2) Mental Imagining. The first of these factors shall be considered in this chapter, the succeeding chapter taking up the consideration of the second.

"Concentration" is a word derived from two Latin words, i.e., "con," a prefix meaning "to," and "centrum," meaning "center" or "fixed central point." The two words combined mean, literally, "to bring to a common point; to focus," etc. Thus the word "Concentration" is seen to mean, literally, "the act or state of bringing to a fixed point or focus."

Borrowing an analogous illustration from physical science, we readily see that the highest forms of energy, force or power are manifested by bringing the force to a focus, center, or common point thereby directing to that point the entire energy employed, instead of allowing it to become dissipated over a larger area. The electricity generated by a battery or dynamo, if allowed to diffuse itself over a large surface manifests but a small degree of the power that may be obtained from it by compelling it to discharge itself from a small point of focus. The same is true regarding the power of steam, which manifests great power by being forced to discharge itself through a small point or opening instead of being permitted to spread itself widely in the air. The same law applies to gunpowder, which manifests force by its gases being compelled to escape through the small gun-barrel instead of spreading in all directions, which it would do if unconfined.

Another familiar example is that of the sunglass, or "burning-glass," which brings the rays of the sun to a common point or focus, greatly intensifying the heat and light by reason thereof.

The occult masters have ever impressed upon their pupils the importance and necessity of acquiring the power of Mental Concentration and all trained and developed occultists have practiced and persevered toward this end, the result being that some of them attained almost miraculous mental powers and influence. All occult phenomena are caused in this way, and all occult power depends upon it.

Therefore, the student of Mental Influence should devote much thought, time and practice to this most important branch of the subject.

It is a fact known to all students of mental phenomena that very few persons possess more than a very small degree of concentration. They allow their mental forces to become scattered and dissipated in all directions, and obtain little or no results from the same. In the degree that a man is able to concentrate, so is he able to manifest mental power. A man's power of mental concentration is to a great extent his measure of greatness.

Mental Concentration, in practice, consists of focusing the mind upon a given subject, or object, firmly and fixedly, and then holding it there for a certain time, fully intent upon its object, and not allowing itself to be diverted or attracted from its object. It likewise consists in the correlative power of then detaching the mind from that subject, or object, and either allowing it to rest, or else focusing it upon another object. In other words, it either gives undivided attention or else inhibits (or "shuts off") attention from the given subject or object.

To the reader who has had no experience along the lines of Mental Concentration, it may seem like a very easy task to focus the mind upon a subject, and then hold it there firmly and fixedly. But a little practice will undeceive such a person and will bring him to a realizing sense of the difficulty of the task.

The mind is a very restless thing, and its tendency is to dance from one thing to another, darting here and there, soon tiring of continued attention, and like a spoiled child, seeking a new object upon which to exercise itself. On the other hand, many people allow their minds to concentrate (involuntarily) upon whatever may strike their fancy, and, forgetting everything else, they give themselves up to the object attracting their attention for the moment, often neglecting duties and important interests, and becoming daydreamers instead of firm thinkers. This involuntary concentration is a thing to be avoided, for it is the allowing of the attention to escape the control of the will. The Mental Concentration of the occultists is a very different thing, and is solely in control of the will, being applied when desirable and taken off or inhibited when desirable.

The trained occultist will concentrate upon a subject or object with a wonderful intensity, seemingly completely absorbed in the subject or object before him, and oblivious to all else in the world. And yet, the task accomplished or the given time expired, he will detach his mind from the object and will be perfectly fresh, watchful and wide-awake to the next matter before him. There is a difference in being controlled by involuntary attention, which is a species of self-hypnotizing, and the control of the attention, which is an evidence of mastery.

The secret of Mental Concentration lies in the control of the Attention. And the control of the Attention lies in the exercise of the Will. A celebrated French psychologist has well said: "The authority is subject to the superior authority of the Ego. I yield it or I withhold it as I please. I direct it in turn to several points. I concentrate it upon each point as long as my will can stand the effort." Sully says: "Attention may be roughly defined as the active self-direction of the mind to any object which presents itself at the moment."

All of the occult authorities begin teaching their pupils Attention as the first step toward Mental Concentration. They instruct the pupil to examine some familiar object, and endeavor to see as many details as possible in the object. Then after hearing the pupil's report, the master sends him back to the task, bidding him seek for new details, and so on until at last the pupil has discovered about all concerning the object that can be discovered. The next day a new object is given to him, and the process is repeated. First simple objects are given, and then more complex ones, until at last objects of great complexity are easily mastered. In this way not only is the power of close observation highly developed, but also the faculty of Attention becomes so highly strengthened that the pupil is able to exert the greatest amount of Mental Concentration with scarcely the consciousness of effort. And such a person then becomes a very giant in the manifestation of Mental Influence. For he is able to mold his mind "one-pointed," as the Orientals describe it, until he has focused and directed a mighty degree of Mental Influence toward the desired object.

Among the practices imposed upon their pupils by occult masters may be named Mathematics, Drawing, Analysis, etc. You will readily see why this is. To begin with, Mathematics requires the undivided attention of the student—unless he concentrates upon his examples, he will not be able to work out their solution. And, according to the principle in Nature that "practice makes perfect," and that "exercise develops power," the practice of the mind along lines requiring voluntary attention and mental concentration will inevitably result in the acquirement of the mental control and power, which renders possible the strongest manifestation of Mental Influence.

The person who uses Mental Influence must certainly possess the power of focusing the force to a common point, in order to manifest the greatest amount of power and influence. And that faculty of focusing results from the training of the mind along the lines of Concentration. And Concentration arises from the mastery of Voluntary Attention. So there you have the whole matter in a nutshell. So your first step toward acquiring Mental Influence should be to cultivate Voluntary Attention.

We might fill page after page with exercises designed to strengthen your faculty of Voluntary Attention, but what would be the use? The best plan is to set you to work to find something upon which to concentrate, for the very search will develop attention. Look around you for some object to study in detail. Then concentrate your attention upon it until you have seen all there is about it to be seen, then take up another object and pursue the practice further. Take a page—this page, if you will, and count the number of words on it.

Then see how many words are required to fill each line, on an average; then see how many letters there are in each word, in each line, on the whole page. Then go over the page and see if any words are misspelled, or if any of the letters are imperfect, etc. In short, get acquainted with this page, until you know all about it. Then take up another page, and after studying it in the same way, compare the two. And so on. Of course this will be very dry and tedious unless you take an interest in it. And, remembering just what the exercise is designed for may arouse this interest. After practicing this way for a short time each day, you will begin to find that you are able to bestow greater attention upon objects upon which you are trying to manifest Mental Influence. You are developing Concentration, and that is the great secret of the use of Mental Influence, and explains the difference in its manifestation among men. Think over this.

5

Mental Imaging

In our last chapter we called your attention to the first of the two principal factors in the manifestation of Mental Influence, namely, "Mental Concentration." In the present chapter we shall consider the second factor tending to render possible the said manifestation, namely, "Mental Imaging."

What is known as a "Mental Image" in occultism, is the mental creation, in the imagination of a "picture" of the things, events or conditions that one desires to be manifested or materialized in actual effect. A moment's thought will show you that unless you know "just what" you desire, you can take no steps toward attaining it on any plane of manifestation. And the more clearly your desires are perceived in your imagination, the clearer is the work of proceeding toward the realization of that desire. A Mental Image gives you a framework upon which to work. It is like the drawing of the architect, or the map of the explorer. Think over this for a few moments until you get the idea firmly fixed in your mind. And now the same rule holds well on the plane in which the manifestation of Mental Influence takes place. The occultist first builds up, in his imagination, a Mental Image or Picture of the conditions he wishes to bring about, and then by concentrating his influence strongly, instead of in a haphazard way as is the case with the majority of people who do not understand the laws and principles underlying the manifestations of the forces of mind. The Mental Image gives shape and direction to the forces, which is being concentrated upon the desired object or subject. It may be compared to the image on the glass of the Magic Lantern, through which the focused rays of the lamp pass, the result being that a corresponding image is reproduced upon the screen or curtain beyond. The analogy is a very close one indeed, if we remember that the minds of the majority of people are more or less blank screens or curtains upon which play the pictures produced there by outside influences, suggestions, environments, etc., for very few people realize their individuality, and are merely reflections of the thoughts and ideas of other people.

An eminent authority, Sir Francis Galton, who was one of the leading authorities upon psychology of preceding generations, has said on this subject: "The free action of a high visualizing faculty is of much importance in connection with the higher processes of generalized thought. A visual image is the most perfect form of mental representation whatever the shape, position and relations of objects to space are concerned. The best workmen are those who visualize the whole of what they propose to do before they take a tool in their hands. Strategists, artists of all denominations, physicists who contrive new experiments, and in short, all who do not follow routine, have a need for it. A faculty that is of importance in all technical and artistic occupations, that gives accuracy to our perceptions and justice to our generalizations is starved by lazy disuse instead of being cultivated judiciously in such a way as will, on the whole, bring the best return. I believe that a serious study of the best way of developing and utilizing this faculty, without prejudice to the practice of abstract thought in symbols, is one of the many pressing desires in the yet unformed science of education."

And what Galton has said of the value of the use of this faculty of the mind in the affairs of the material plane, so it is likewise true of the manifestations on the mental plane. You know that the clearer a Mental Picture you possess of anything that you want—the better you know just what you want—and the better you know the latter, the better able you are to take steps to get it. Many people go through life wanting "something," but not really knowing "just what" they do want. Is it any wonder that they do not realize or materialize their desires any better? And the same thing holds well on the plane of manifestation of Mental Influence. If one wishes to materialize anything by the use of the influence, is he not handicapped by a lack of Mental Image of just what he wants to materialize, and is he not helped very much by the creation of a mental "pattern" or plan, in the shape of a mental picture, through and around which he may direct his thought-currents?

The occultists manifesting the greatest degree of Mental Influence acquire by practice this art of creating Mental Images of that which they wish to materialize. They train their Imagination in this way until the very act of creating the Mental Image acts strongly toward the actual materialization or event, as "actually existing" in their minds before they attempt to concentrate their Thought-Waves upon the task of accomplishing it. Then the Mental Picture, being completed and standing in strong outline, they focus their mental force through it, just as in the case of the magic lantern before referred to, and the picture is reproduced on the screen of mentality of other people.

The imagination may be strengthened in many ways, the principle being constant and persistent practice. The practice of recalling to the memory of scenes previously witnessed, and then whether describing them to others or else drawing a rough picture of them will help in this matter. Describe to others scenes that you have witnessed, occurrences, details of appearances, etc., etc., until you are able to reproduce mentally the aspects and appearances of the things. Then you may begin to draw mental pictures of things desired as if they were being drawn on the screen of your mind. See, mentally, the things as actually occurring—create a little playhouse of your own, in your mind, and there enact the plays that you wish to witness in actual life. When you have acquired this, you will be able to project your mental pictures on the screen of objectivity in actual life with far greater effect.

In thinking of this subject, you would do well to remember the illustration of the magic lantern, for the figure is a good one, and will enable you to carry the idea better in your mind. You see, in giving you this suggestion, we are really telling you to form a mental picture of the mental magic lantern, using the illustration given—you see how much easier it is for you to think of it in this way and how much easier it is for you to manifest it in practice.

Build your Mental Images by degrees, commencing with the general outlines, and then filling in the details. Always commence by trying simple and easy things, and then working up to the more complex and difficult feats.

And now, I offer a word of warning at this point to all. Do not allow your imagination to "run away with you"—do not become a dreamer of dreams and a doer of nothing. You must master your imagination and make it your servant and not your master. You must make it do your bidding, instead of allowing it to dictate to you.

You will see in the succeeding chapters the important part that Mental Imaging plays in the different phases of Mental Influence. Even when we do not refer directly to it by name, you will see that the "idea" sought to be conveyed by one mind to another—the feeling, desire or mental state sought to be transferred from one mind to others—must and does depend very materially for strength upon the clearness and completeness of the Mental Image held in the mind of the person seeking to do the influencing, the "projector" of the Mental Image of his mental magic lantern, upon the screen of the minds of others. Carry this principle well in mind that you may see its operation in the different forms.

6

Fascination

In this and the next chapter we shall present to you information regarding the effect of Mental Influence manifested when there is personal contact between the persons using the power and the person affected. Then we shall pass on to a consideration of the effect produced when the persons are not in direct contact with each other.

There are two general forms of the direct use of Mental Influence, which, although somewhat resembling each other, may still be separated into two classes. The first we shall call "Fascination" and the second "Hypnotism".

By Fascination we mean the manifestation of Mental Influence when the two persons are together, without passes or the usual hypnotic methods. By Hypnotism we mean the use of the power, also, when the two parties are together, but accompanied by passes or hypnotic methods.

Under the head of Fascination are to be found the manifestations generally known as "Personal Magnetism," "Charming," etc., are quite commonly employed, in varying degrees by many persons, often without their conscious knowledge of the principles employed. Many persons are possessed of the power of Fascination "naturally" and without having studied or practiced the principles. Many others, not originally possessing the power, have acquired by study and practice the power to influence people in this way. For, it must be known, the power may be acquired by study and practice just as may any other power of mind and body. To some it is easy, to others difficult—but all may acquire a very great degree of the power by intelligent study and practice of the underlying principles.

Fascination is one of the oldest forms of the manifestations of Mental Influence. It was known to, and employed by, the earliest races of men. It is even found among the lower animals that pursue their prey or capture their mates by its use.

A recent writer on the subject has defined the word, used in this connection, as: "Acting upon by some powerful or irresistible influence; influencing by an irresistible charm; alluring, exciting, irresistibly or powerfully, charming, captivating or attracting powerfully, influencing the imagination, reason or will of another in an uncontrollable manner; enchanting, captivating or alluring, powerfully or irresistibly."

As we have just said, this power is observable even among the lower animals in some cases. Instances are related by naturalists, which scorpions have fascinated other insects, causing them to circle around and around until finally the insect would plunge down right within striking distance of the scorpion, which would then devour its prey. Birds of prey unquestionably fascinate their game, and men who have been brought in contact with wild tigers, lions, etc. have testified that they felt paralyzed in some manner, their legs refusing to obey their will, and their minds seeming to become numbed and stunned. Those who have seen a mouse in the presence of a cat will testify to the effect of some power exerted by the latter. Birds in the presence of a cat and serpents also manifest symptoms of a conquered will. And naturalists cite many instances of the employment of this force by birds seeking to captivate and charm their mates at the beginning of the season.

Among men it has been noticed that certain individuals possess this power to a great degree, some of the "great men" of ancient and modern times having been so filled with the power that they could manage their followers almost as one would move automatons. Julius Caesar had this power developed to a great degree, and used it from youth to his last days. He was worshipped—almost as a god by his soldiers—who would undertake almost any task at his bidding. Napoleon also possessed this charm to a wonderful degree. It enabled him to control men with whom he came in contact, and to bend them to his will. He rose from a poor student to the dignity and power of the Emperor of France. When banished to Elba he escaped, and landing in France, alone and unarmed, confronted the ranks of the French army drawn up to capture him, and walking towards the soldiers compelled the latter to throw down their guns and flock to his support. He entered Paris at the head of the great army, which had been sent forth to capture him. This is no wild legend, but a sober fact of history. And in our own times we see how certain leaders of men sweep people before them and move them around like pawns on the chessboard of life.

All of the above-mentioned phenomena come under the head of Fascination, and is the result of the emanation of streams of active Thought-Waves from the mind of a person, the same being strongly concentrated and directed toward those whom the person wishes to affect. The person forms a strong thought in his mind and sends it out to the others charged with the force of concentrated will, so that the other person feels it most strongly and forcibly. The fundamental idea is the forming of the thought, and then sending it out to the other person.

For instance, if you wish a person to like you, you should form in your mind this thought: "That person likes me," fixing it in your own mind as a fact. Then project to him the concentrated thought, "You like me—you like me very much," with an air of assurance and confidence, and the other person is bound to feel the effect unless he or she has acquired a knowledge of the subject and is using self-protection. The thought should be sent forth with the strength that usually accompanies a strong spoken statement, but you must not actually "speak" the words aloud—you should merely say them strongly "in your mind."

If you wish to produce an effect or impress Strength upon another person, the same process may be used, changing the Thought and vibrations to the idea that you have a stronger Will than the other person, and are able to overcome his Will—using the silent message of "I am Stronger than you—my Will overcomes yours," etc.

Some successful agents and salesmen use the following method in reaching their customers. They form a thought that the other person desires their goods very much, and then they send out the Thought-Waves that "You desire my goods—you want them very much—you have an irresistible longing for them," etc.

Others use the following when they wish another to comply with their wishes: "You will do as I say—will do as I say—you will yield to me fully and completely," etc.

You will readily see from the above examples that the whole principle employed in any and all of these cases consists of:

(1) The Thought of what the person wishes the other to do held firmly in the mind; and

(2) The projection of that Thought to the other, silently, in the shape of unspoken words.

In the above you have the whole secret of Fascination condensed to a small space. You will understand, of course, that the words are only a means of concentrating and vitalizing the thought. Animals merely feel Desires, but are able to fascinate by the strength of them, although they cannot use words. And one person may fascinate another without understanding a word of his language, the real strength coming from the strength of the desire behind the words. The formation of the desire-thought into words is merely for the purpose of concentrating and focusing the thought, for words are concentrated symbols of ideas, thoughts or feelings.

The exact process of "sending forth" the Thought-Wave to the other is difficult to describe. You know how you feel when you say something very forcible and emphatic to another person. You can fairly "feel" the force of the words being hurled at the other person. Well, cultivate that same power in sending forth the "unspoken word" in the above manner, and you will soon be able to notice the effect of the thought on the other. It may help you to imagine that you can see the force flying from you to the other. The imagination properly used helps very much in these matters, for it creates a mental path over which the force may travel.

You must not act awkwardly when sending out the Thought-Waves, but converse in an ordinary manner, sending your Thought-Waves between your speeches, when the other person is talking to you, or at any pause in the conversation. It is always well to send first a powerful Thought-Wave before the conversation is opened, preferably while you are approaching the person. And it is likewise well to terminate the interview with a "parting shot" of considerable strength. You will find that these Thought-Waves are of far greater power than spoken words, and then again, you can in this way send out impressions that you could not utter in spoken words for obvious reasons.

And now do you see how you have been affected by persons who have influenced you at times in your past life? Now that you know the secret you will be in a measure immune from further impressions from others. And when you read our concluding chapter, entitled "Self-Protection," you will be able to surround yourself with a protective armor through which the Thought-Waves cannot penetrate, but which will turn aside the shafts directed toward you.

7

Hypnotic Influence

As we have mentioned in the previous lesson, there is a general resemblance between the manifestation of Mental Influence, known as "Fascination," and that known as Hypnotic Influence. In the manifestation known as Fascination, the influence is exerted solely by Thought-Waves passing from mind to mind without a physical medium or channel other than the ether. In Hypnotic Influence, on the contrary, the influence is heightened by means of passes, stroking or eye-influence.

In Hypnotic Influence the mind of the person affected, whom we shall call the "subject," is rendered passive by a flow of mental energy calculated to render it more or less drowsy or sleepy, and therefore less calculated to set up powers of resistance to the Thought-Waves of the person using the influence.

But the power employed is the same in all cases, no matter whether they fall under the classification of Fascination or whether that of Hypnotic Influence. The two classes of manifestation, as a matter of fact, really blend into each other, and it is difficult to draw a dividing line in some cases.

Hypnotic Influence is a form of that which was formerly termed Mesmerism, which name was given to it in honor of its discoverer, Frederick Anton Mesmer, who practiced this form of Mental Influence during the latter half of the Eighteenth Century. As a fact, however, the force and its use was known to the ancients centuries before Mesmer's time, the latter person having merely rediscovered it. Mesmer taught that the power was based upon the presence of a strange universal fluid which pervaded everything, and which had a peculiar effect upon the nerves and brains of people. He and his followers believed that it was necessary to put the subjects into a sound sleep before they could be influenced. But both of these ideas have given way to the new theories on the subject now held by investigators and students of the subject.

It is now known that the "magnetic fluid" believed in by Mesmer and his followers is nothing else than the currents of Thought-Waves emanating from the mind of the operator. And it is also known that the "deep sleep" condition is not necessary to render the will of the subject subservient to that of the operator. It is also now known that the nerves of the arms and fingers afford a highly sensitive conductor for the mental currents, which may be propelled over them to the mind of the subject, or to his nerves and muscles. This fact is explained by the well-known scientific fact that the material of which the nerves are composed is almost identical with that of the brain—in fact the nervous system may be spoken of as a continuation of the brain itself. It is now also known that the eye has a peculiar property of transmitting the mental currents along the rays of light entering it and from thence to the eyes of the other person. The above fact explains the phenomena of hypnotic influence, as it is now known to science. The question of "Suggestion" also has a bearing on the subject, as we shall see presently.

Modern operators do not produce the "deep sleep" condition usually except in cases when it is desired to produce some form of psychic phenomena apart from the subject of Mental Influence—that is, in which they are merely inducing the deep hypnotic condition in order to get the subject into a psychic condition in which the phenomena mentioned may be manifested or exhibited. We shall not enter into this phase of the subject in this book, for it is outside of the immediate subject. The modern hypnotic investigator merely induces a passive state in the mind, nerves or muscles of the subject sufficient to reduce the powers of resistance, and then he gives his orders or "verbal suggestions" accompanied by a projection of his Thought-Waves into the mind of the subject.

In order to illustrate the subject, we will give you a few experiments, which may be easily performed by anyone manifesting the power of concentration and thought-projection. There is of course a great difference in the degrees of impressionability of different persons to hypnotic influence—that is to say, difference of degrees resistance. Some persons will interpose a strong resistance, while others will set up a very feeble resistance, which is easily beaten down by the will of the operator. In the following experiments you had better begin by getting some person who is perfectly willing for the experiment, and who will not interpose a resistance but who is willing to become passive. Some person friendly, to you and interested in the experiments, we mean.

Begin by having the person stand before you. Then make sweeping passes in front of the person from head to foot. Then make a few passes in front of the face of the subject, then along his arms. Then take hold of his hands and hold them a little while, looking him straight in the eyes. Make all passes downward. Avoid levity or laughter and maintain a serious, earnest expression and frame of mind.

Then standing in front of the subject tell him to take his will off of his legs and stand perfectly passive and relaxed. Then looking him straight in the eyes, say to him: "Now, I am going to draw you forward toward me by my mental power—you will feel yourself falling forward toward me—don't resist but let yourself come toward me—I will catch you, don't be afraid—now come—come—come—now you're coming, that's right," etc. You will find that he will begin to sway toward you and in a moment or two will fall forward in your arms. It is unnecessary to say that you should concentrate your mind steadily upon the idea of his falling forward, using your will firmly to that effect. It will help matters if you hold your hands on each side of his head, but just in front of him, not touching him, however, and then draw away your hands, toward yourself, saying at the same time: "Come now—come—you're coming," etc. Standing behind the subject and drawing him backward may reverse this experiment. Be sure and catch him in your arms when he falls to protect him from a fall to the floor.

In the same manner you may fasten his hands together, telling him that he cannot draw them apart. Or you may start him revolving his hands, and then giving him orders that he cannot stop them. Or you may draw him all around the room after you, following your finger that you have pointed at his nose. Or you may make him experience a feeling of heat and pain by touching your finger to his hand and telling him that it is hot. All of the familiar simple experiments may be performed successfully upon a large percentage of persons, in this way, by following the above general directions. We shall not go into detail of the higher experiments of Hypnotism, as that forms a special subject by itself. We give the above experiments merely for the purpose of showing you that the phenomena of Hypnotic Influence does not require any "magnetic fluid" theory, and is all explainable upon the hypothesis of Mental Influence by means of Thought-Waves and Mental Induction.

In the above experiments, be sure you "take off" the influence afterward, by making upward passes, and willing that the influence pass off. Do not neglect this.

In your experiments, if you care to undertake them, you will soon discover the power of your eye upon the other persons. You will be able to almost feel the force passing from your gaze to theirs. And this is true in the case of the passes and stroking of the hands. You will feel the vibratory waves flowing from your hands into their nervous system. It is wonderful what power is aroused in a person after conducting a few experiments along these lines. Those who care to follow the subject further are referred to a forthcoming book of this series, to be issued shortly, and which will be called "The New Hypnotism," in which full instructions will be given in the higher phenomena, in complete detail.

And now a word of warning. Beware of people who are always putting their hands on you, or patting or stroking you, or wishing to hold your hands a long time. Many persons do this from force of habit, and innocently, but others do so with the intention of producing a mild form of hypnotic influence upon you. If you meet such persons, and find them attempting anything of this sort, you can counteract their influence by sending them a strong thought current (as stated in our last chapter), sending them the thought: "You can't affect me—I am too strong for you—you can't play your tricks on me." It is a good plan to practice this counteracting force when you are shaking hands with a "magnetic" person who seems to affect people. You will soon be able to distinguish these people by a certain force about them and a peculiar expression in their eyes, at the same time using your protective will upon them.

Caution young girls against allowing young men to be too free in using their hands in caressing them, and a word of advice to young men in your family would not be out of place in this respect. There are many cases of sex-attraction, leading to very deplorable results, arising from a conscious or unconscious use of this simple form of Hypnotic Influence. The danger lies in the fact that it renders one passive to other influences, and more readily led into temptation and to yield to the desires or will of the other person. A word to the wise should be sufficient. The use of this power for immoral purposes is a terrible crime and brings down upon the user deplorable results, which all occultists know and teach. Everyone should learn to resist such influences when exerted upon them. Forewarned is Forearmed.

8

Influencing at a Distance

In the two preceding chapters we invited your consideration of the manifestation of Mental Influence when the user of projector of the force was in actual contact with, or in presence of, the person or persons he was aiming to influence. In this chapter, and the one immediately following it, we shall pass on to a consideration of the manifestation of the influence when the persons affected are removed in space from the person using the influence.

The general public is familiar in a general way with the phenomena of hypnotism, and to a lesser degree with the phenomena of Fascination in its more common forms of Personal Magnetism, etc. But as regards the use of the influence at a distance people are more or less skeptical owing to a lack of knowledge of the subject. And still every day is bringing to the mind of the public new facts and instances of such an influence, and the teaching of various cults along these lines is now awakening a new interest in the subject, and a desire to learn something regarding the laws and principles underlying the same.

As strange as it may appear at first glance, the principles underlying Mental Influence at a distance are precisely the same as those underlying the use of influence when the persons are in the presence of each other. A little thought must show the truth of this. In the case of present influence the mental-currents flow across an intervening space between the two minds—there is a space outside of the two minds to be traversed by the currents. And a moment's thought will show you that the difference between present influence and distant influence is merely a matter of degree—a question of a little more or less space to be traversed by the currents. Do you see this plainly?

Well, then, this being so, it follows that the methods used must be identical. Of course, in the case of personal influence the added effect of the voice, manner, suggestive methods, the eye, etc., are present, which render the result more easily obtained, and causes the "rapport" condition to be more easily established. But with this exception the methods are identical, and even the advantages accruing from the exception mentioned may be duplicated by practice and development in the case of distant influence.

There are a number of methods given by the authorities in this matter of distant influencing, but they are all based upon the same principles named in the previous chapters of this book, i.e. Vibrations, Thought-Waves, Mental Induction, Concentration and Mental Imaging—in these words you have the key to the subject—the rest is all a matter of practice and development, and variation.

One of the most elementary, and yet one of the most effective methods known to occultists is that of creating a Mental Image of the person "treated" (for that is the common term among modern writers on the subject) in the sense of imagining him to be seated in a chair in front of the person treating him at a distance. The treater proceeds to give both verbal commands, and at the same time directs Thought-Waves toward the imaginary person seated before him. This process establishes a psychic condition between the treater and the actual person, although the latter may be removed from the treater by many miles of space. This was the method of the ancient magicians and wonder-workers, and has always been a favorite among persons pursuing these experiments, of desirous, of mentally influencing others at a distance.

A variation of the above, very common in former days, was to mould a clay or wax figure, calling it by the name of the person treated, and identifying it in the mind and imagination with the other person. A variation is also noticed in the cases where a photograph, lock of hair, article of clothing, etc., is used in this way as a psychic connecting link between the two persons. The practitioners of Black Magic, Witchcraft and other nefarious perversions of Mental Influence seemed to prefer these methods, although, on the contrary, they are used with the very best results today by many in giving beneficial treatments to absent patients, friends and others whose welfare is desired. The only effect the Mental Image of the person, or the picture, etc., has is the fact that by these means a psychic connection link is set up along which the Thought-Waves travel more readily.

In the above forms of treatment the treater treats the Mental Image, picture, etc., precisely as he would if the person were actually present. He forgets for the time being that the person may be hundreds of miles away, and concentrates his influence on the image, or picture, etc., because the latter is really the starting point of the psychic chain, which leads direct to the person. The treater sends his Thought-Waves toward the object, and in some cases actually talks (mentally) to the person by means of the medium mentioned. He may give commands, arguments, remonstrance, persuasion, etc., just as if the person were actually present. In short, he acts as if the person were sitting before him, wide-awake, and receptive to his influence.

Another way, employed by some, is to begin darting Thought-Waves toward the other person, forming in the imagination a gradual lengthening "psychic-wire" composed of thought-vibrations. Those practicing this form state that when the psychic-wire is projected sufficiently far (and it travels with incredible speed) and cones in contact with the mind of the other person, the treater feels at once that contact has been established, by a peculiar faint "shock" similar to that of a very mild galvanic current. Then the treater proceeds to send his thought-currents along the psychic-wire in the same manner as if the person were actually in his presence, as described under the head of "Fascination," in a preceding chapter. In fact, such treatments, and the others mentioned in this chapter, are really and practically "long-distance Fascination."

Another form of distant treatment consists in forming "astral-tube," mentioned in other books of this series. The astral-tube is set up in a similar manner to the "psychic-wire," and projected toward the person desired to influence. It is formed in the imagination as a "vortex-ring," similar to the little ring of smoke puffed out by the cigar smoker, only larger—about six inches to one foot wide—or, better still, like the ring of smoke ejected from the stack of a locomotive sometimes when it is puffing rapidly. This vortex-ring is then seen, in the imagination, by the use of the will, to lengthen out in the shape of a tube which rapidly extends and travels toward the person treated, in a manner identical with that of the psychic-wire. This tube is known to occultists as the "astral-tube," and is employed in various forms of occult and psychic phenomena, such as clairvoyance and other forms of "Psychomancy," as described by us in our volume of this series, so entitled.

Those following this method of distant influencing report that they recognize the completion of the tube by a sensation of stoppage and a feeling of "rapport" having been established between themselves and the other person.

In some cases they report that they are able to faintly "see" the figure of the other person in miniature at the other end of the tube, but this is undoubtedly due to the possession of "psychomantic" powers, suddenly awakened in to effect. The tube once established the treatment is proceeded with as if they were in the actual presence of the person treated. In many respects the "psychic-wire" and the "astral-tube" methods are similar, and a statement concerning one is generally true of the other.

There are two other methods frequently used in distant influencing which we shall now briefly describe.

The first of these two methods consists in sitting or standing in a quiet place, or rather in some place in which you can concentrate (the advanced occultist can find peace in the midst of the noise) and then directing your Thought-Waves toward the other person, forming in the imagination a mental picture of the force flying from you toward the other, like tiny sparks of electricity, or of a subtle fluid. This mental picture tends to give a concentrative force to the current which renders them powerful, and sends them direct to the desired spot.

The second of these two methods is that used by the most advanced occultists who have advanced beyond the use of the methods described just now. These people simply stand or sit quietly and concentrate their minds until they attain the state of Mental Calm known to many as "the Silence." Then they create a strong mental picture of the person treated, surrounded by the conditions desired created, or doing the things desired to be done. This is one of the highest forms of Mental Influence and really approaches a higher phase of influence than that of the mental plane as generally known. A picture of a person held in the mind in this way—the person being seen in perfect, robust health, and happy and successful—tends to materialize the same conditions in the person in real life. This form of treatment, however, is possible only to those of great concentration, and who have mastered the act of Mental Imaging, and who also possess Creative Willpower to a marked degree. Some degree of success in it, however, is open to nearly every student who practices along these lines. Before practicing any of these experiments, read what we have said in the chapter on "Magic Black and White," and guard against employing the power for evil purposes, for the fate of the Black Magician is a sad one.

9

Influencing En Masse

In our last chapter we considered the manifestation of Mental Influence at a distance in so far as was concerned the influencing of one or more persons by another. There is another phase of the subject that must not be overlooked, and that is the influencing of large numbers of people by some active, strong projector of Mental Influence. This form of the manifestation of the power is known as "Mental Influencing En Masse"—"En Masse," of course, means "in a body"—or "in a crowd," and Mental Influencing En Masse means the use of the influence in the phase of exerting a strong attracting or directing power to the mind or "the crowd," or rather, "the public," or a large number of people.

This form of the use of the power is that consciously or unconsciously exerted by the great leaders of men in the fields of statesmanship, politics, business, finance or military life. You will at once recall a number of the so-called "great men" of history from ancient times down to our own times who seemed to exert a wonderfully, almost miraculous, effect upon the minds of the people, causing men to see things through the eyes of the strong man, and making of all instruments to carry out the ideals, will or desires of these great masters of Mental Influence. And on a smaller scale are the majority of the successful people who depend upon public support. In fact, this influence in some degree is used by nearly all who succeed in any form of business or profession, in which success calls for the attraction of other people toward the occupation of the person in question. This may seem like a strange thought to many, but occultists know it as the truth, notwithstanding.

The most common form of Influencing En Masse is the lesser degree manifestation, along unconscious lines, manifested by a majority of people by reason of their desire for the success of certain things. By desire we do not mean the mere "wanting" or "wishing" state of mind, but rather that eager longing, craving, demanding mental state that evinces a hungry reaching out for the desired thing. You will notice that the men and women who "get things" are generally those who are possessed of a strong, burning desire for the things in question, which prompts them to be more or less aggressive in the search for satisfaction of the desire possessing them. These people are constantly sending out strong waves of thought-vibrations, which has a drawing, attracting influence upon all with whom they come in contact, and tending to draw such persons toward the center of attraction, which is, of course, the mind of the person sending out such thoughts. And in the same way a person possessed of a strong Fear of a thing will send out similar attracting waves, which have a tendency to attract or draw to him the people calculated to bring about the materialization of the thing feared. This may sound paradoxical, but the secret lies in the fact that in both the case of Desire and Fear the mind forms the Mental Image, which tends to become materialized. Fear, after all, is a form of "expectation," which, alas! too often tends to materialize it. "The thing that I have feared, hath come upon me," says Job, and in that saying he has stated the experience of the race. The way to fight things you may fear is to create a burning desire for the opposite thing.

Other persons who have either studied the principles of Mental Influence, or else have stumbled upon certain facts concerning the same, improve upon this elementary form of Influencing En Masse just mentioned. They send out the Thought-Waves consciously and deliberately, erecting the mental image, and holding strongly to it, so that in time their sweeps of mental currents reach further and further away and bring a greater number of people under the influence and into the field of attraction. They "treat" the public "en masse" by holding the strong mental picture of that which they desire, and then sending out strong thought-currents of desire in all directions, willing that those coming within their radius shall be attracted toward the ideas expressed in the Mental Image projected in all directions.

The constant dwelling upon some special object or subject, by men who have developed concentration, strong wills and fixity of purpose has the effect of sending out from the mind of that person great circles, constantly widening, of Thought-Waves, which sweep ever outward like waves in a pond caused by dropping in a stone. These waves reach and affect a great number of people, and will render them at least "interested" in the object or subject thought of, and the indifference has been overcome. Other appeals to the minds of these people will be far more likely to reach them than otherwise, for "interest" is the first step toward attention, and attention is another step toward action.

Of course, there are very many people sending out circles of Thought-Waves, and these currents come in contact with each other and tend to neutralize each. But now and then a particularly strong man will send out waves that will persist even after meeting other currents, and will reach the minds of the public in spite of the opposition. These thought-currents have the personality of the sender, and reflect the character of his will, be it strong or weak. The Mental Influence sent out by a strong business man in a town will soon make itself felt in a subtle manner, and the store becomes a center of attractive influence, although the public does not understand just why. In the same way some lawyers spring into public favor, although not possessing greater ability than their legal brethren. And popular preachers make their influence felt in a community in similar ways, although often they are not conscious of just what force they are using, their only knowledge being that they have a feeling of inward strength and an attractive influence over people, and at the same time a burning ardent desire to draw people their way, and a strong will to back it up with. And these are just the mental qualities that create and manifest the strongest kind of Mental Influence. And, besides, these people almost invariably "know just what they want"—there is no mere vague "wishing" about them—they make a clear mental picture of the things that they wish to bring about, and then they bend every effort toward materializing the picture. Everything they do towards accomplishing their ends gives an additional impetus to their constantly widening and constantly strengthening circle of power and influence.

Some masters of this art of influencing the public create a mental picture of themselves sending out great volumes of Thought-Waves for a time, and then afterward mentally imparting a rotary motion to the waves, until at last they form a mental whirlpool rushing round and round and always sucking in toward the center. An effort of this kind acts on the mental plane just as a physical whirlpool acts on the physical plane, that is it draws into its power all that comes in contact with its force. This is one of the most powerful forms of Influencing En Masse, and is used with great effect by many of the "strong men" of this age, who have acquainted themselves fully with the secrets of the ancient occultists. Ancient Occultism and Modern Finance seem far apart, but they are really working together to further the interests of some of these powerful minds of the day—and the public is paying the bill.

You will readily see from what has been said that an individual who has cultivated the faculty of concentration and has acquired the art of creating sharp, clear, strong mental images, and who when engaged in an undertaking will so charge his mind with the idea of success, will be bound to become an attracting center. And if such an individual will keep his mental picture ever in his mind, even though it may be in the background of his mind, when he is attending to the details and planning of his affairs—if he will give his mental picture a prominent place in his mental gallery, taking a frequent glance at it, and using his will upon it to create new scenes of actual success, he will create for himself a center of radiating thought that will surely be felt by those coming within its field of influence.

Such a man frequently "sees" people coming to him and his enterprises and falling in line with his plans. He mentally "sees" money flowing in to him, and all of his plans working out right. In short, he mentally imagines each step of his plans a little ahead of the time for their execution and he concentrates forcibly and earnestly upon them. It is astonishing to witness how events, people, circumstances and things seem to move in place in actual life as if urged by some mighty power to serve to materialize the conditions so imaged in the mind of the man. But, understood, there has got to be active mental effort behind the imaging. Daydreamers do not materialize thought, they merely dissipate energy. The man who converts thought in activity and material being, throws energy into the task and puts forth his willpower through the picture on the slide. With the rays of the will there will be no picture projected, no matter how beautifully the imagination has pictured it. Thought pictured in mental images and then vitalized by the force of the desire and will tend to objectify themselves into material beings. That is the whole thing in a nutshell.

10

The Need of the Knowledge

Although the true scientific principles underlying the subject of Mental Influence have been but recently recognized and taught to the general public, still the knowledge is far from being new. The occultists of the old civilizations undoubtedly understood the underlying principles and used them in practice, thus gaining an ascendancy over the masses. And more than this, the masses themselves had a more or less comprehensive knowledge of the working principles of the subject, for we find among all peoples, in all times, records of the use of this power. Under one name or another—under one form or another—Mental Influence has been operated and used from the earliest times. And today, even in the most remote portions of the globe, and among the most savage and barbarous races we find instances of the employment of this force.

The forms of the manifestation of Mental Influence are many and varied. In some cases it manifests under the form of a fascinating, attracting power exerted by some people, which causes such persons to draw or attract other persons to them. Persons are allured or "charmed" by others possessing this power, and their affections are taken captive by this mysterious force. Some persons are spoken of as "fascinating," "possessing powers of charming," "having winning ways," having "great personal magnetism," etc.

Others exert another form of the power in the driving of and compelling others to do their bidding, and people speak of them as having "a compelling will," being able "to work their will" on those around them, possessing "dominating powers," etc. We are also brought face to face with the wonderful effects of "Mental Science" under one form or another, under this name or that term, with the many forms of "treatments" followed by the different schools and cults. Then we read in the pages of history about the mysterious powers recorded under the name of Witchcraft, Hexes, Voodoo, and Black Magic, including the Hawaiian "Kahuna" work. And turning back the pages of history to Ancient time, Greece, Persia and Egypt, not to speak of India, ancient and modern, we find innumerable instances of the employment of, and knowledge of, Mental Influence in some of its forms.

And although many will seek to deny the fact, scientific investigators and students realize that there is but one real underlying principle under and back of all of the various forms of manifestation. The good results, and the evil results, all arise from the employment of the same force, strange as it may appear at first thought. The secret lies in the fact that this Mental Influence is a great natural force, just as is electricity or any other natural forces, it may be, and is, used for both good and evil purposes. The electricity which runs our machines, lights our houses and performs countless other beneficent tasks in the service of man is also used to electrocute criminals, and the unfortunate person who touches a "live wire" may be struck with instant death. The sun, which warms our earth and renders life possible, also kills countless persons exposed to its rays on the desert, or even in our large cities. Fire, that great friend of man, which has been one of the most potent factors in the evolution of the race from barbarism to civilization, is also a mighty enemy, destroying both property and lives. Water, that most necessary element, which renders life possible, and which is necessary to grow our grain and to perform countless other good services for us, also acts as an enemy at times, drowning people and sweeping away their homes. Gravitation, which holds all things in place, from suns and stars down to the tiniest atom of matter, also causes people to fall to their death from high places, or brings down on their heads objects from above them. In short, every natural force or power is capable of producing either beneficent or baleful effects to man, according to the circumstances of the case. We recognize these things, and accept them as a law of nature. And yet some would deny the identity of the power of Mental Influence as manifested in its good and bad uses.

There will be people who ascribe to God all the good qualities of Mental Influence, and ascribe to the Devil all of its evil uses. These people have primitive minds. Their counterparts are seen in those who would credit God with the helpful rain or sun, and who ascribe to the Devil the same things when there occurs a flood or a drought. Such reasoning is worthy only of the savage mind. The forces are natural forces, and work according to their own laws, imminent in their constituent qualities and nature, and are in that sense "above good and evil." When they work for man's interest and comfort man calls them "good"—when they work harm and discomfort to him man calls them "bad"— but the force remains unchanged, being neither "good" nor "bad." And thus it is with the power of Mental Influence—it is above "good" and "bad" in it—it is a great natural force, capable of being used for either weal or woe to mankind. But, remember this, there is a difference. While the force in itself is neither good nor bad the individual who employs it may be, and is, "good" or "bad," according to its use. Just as a man commits a good or bad act when he uses his gun to slay a wild beast attacking another man, or else turns it upon his brother or neighbor, as the case may be—so is a man good or bad according to his use of Mental Influence. The merit or demerit lies in the intention and purpose of the user, not in the force or power employed by him. Therein lies the difference.

On all sides of us we may see the manifestation of the possession of Mental Influence. We see men who are able to sway those around them in some mysterious and wonderful way, either by their powers of persuasion or by their dominant willpower. Some spring into prominence and power suddenly, in a way unaccountable to those who are ignorant of the secret of Mental Influence. As we have said in a previous chapter, certain people seem to have "something about them" that makes them attractive or successful in their relations with other people. The "personal magnetism" of leaders manifests itself strongly, some having this power to such an extent that the masses follow them like a great flock of sheep after the "bellwether" with the tinkling bell around his neck.

We have all come in contact with the "agent" or salesman who managed in some way to sell us things that we did not want and had no use for, and after he had gone we wondered and wondered how it all happened. If we had but understood the laws of Mental Influence this could not have happened.

We have all felt ourselves, at some time or another in our lives, in the presence of individuals who almost compelled us to do what we knew in our hearts we should not do. Knowledge of the laws of Mental Influence would have enabled us to overcome the temptation.

And not only in the case of personal interviews have we been affected. There is a far more subtle and dangerous use of the power, i.e., in the shape of "distant influence," or "absent treatment," as it had been called. And the increase in the interest and knowledge of Occult matters during the past twenty years has resulted in a widely diffused knowledge of this great force, and its consequent employment, worthily and unworthily, by many people who are thereby enabled to gain an influence over their neighbors and fellow men, who are not familiar with the laws of the force. It would surprise many people if they knew that some of the multi-millionaires of the country, and some of its greatest politicians and leaders, were secret students of Occultism, and who were using their forces upon the masses of the people.

Not only this, but there are Schools of Occultism which teach their pupils the theory, practice and art of Mental Influence, under one name or another—under this guise or that—the result being that there are a greater number of people equipped for the use of this force and instructed in the practice of employing it turned out every year than is generally imagined. There are Schools for Salesmanship giving disguised instruction in the art of Mental Influence. Nearly every large concern employing selling agents has private instructors for their men, who teach them the principles of Mental Influence disguised under the name of "Psychology of Business," or some such name.

And besides these, there are a number of people who have studied at the feet of some of the great metaphysical, semi-religious cults of the day, who have received instruction in Mental Influence disguised under the name of some creed or religious teachings, who have departed from the moral principles inculcated by their teachers, and who are using their knowledge in the shape of "treatments" of other persons for the purpose of influencing them to accede to their wishes or to act so as to bring financial gain to the person giving the treatment. The air is full of this Black Magic today, and it is surely time that the general masses were instructed on this subject. And this is the purpose of this little book, published and sold at a popular price in order to bring it within the reach of the purses of the "plain people," who have been exploited and influenced by those who have acquired a knowledge of the principles of Mental Influence, and who are using it unworthily upon their fellow men.

There is self-protection possible to all, and this little book purposes to teach you how to use it.

11

Magic Black and White

The use of the word "Magic" in connection with Mental Influence is quite ancient. Occultists make a clear distinction between the use of Mental Influence in a manner conducive to the welfare of others, and its use in a selfish, base manner calculated to work harm on others. Both forms are common and are frequently mentioned in all occult writings.

White Magic has many forms, both in its ancient manifestations and in these latter days of revived occult knowledge. The use of Mental Influence in this way generally takes the form of kindly "treatments" of persons by others having their welfare at heart. In this particular class fall the various treatments of the several cults and schools of what is known as Mental Science, or similar names. These people make a practice of giving treatments, both "present" and "absent," for the purpose of healing physical ailments and bringing about a normal Physical condition of health and strength. Similar treatments are given by some to bring about a condition of Success to others, by imparting to the minds of such persons the vibrations of courage, confidence, energy, etc., which surely make for success along the lines of material occupation, etc. In the same way one may "treat" adverse conditions surrounding others, bringing the force of the mind and will to bear on these conditions with the idea of changing the prevailing vibrations and bringing harmony from in-harmony, and success from failure.

The majority of persons, not informed along these lines, are surrounded by a mental atmosphere arising from the prevailing mental states, thoughts, feelings, etc., and also arising from the thought-currents which they have attracted to them by the Law of Mental Attraction. These Mental Atmospheres, when once firmly settled around a person, render it most difficult for him to "break away" from their vibrations. He struggles and fights, but the prevailing vibrations are beating down upon him all the time and must produce a strong effect upon even persons of strong will, unless indeed they have fully acquainted themselves with the laws of Mental Influence and have acquired the power of Concentration. The habit of a lifetime, perhaps, has to be overcome, and besides the constant suggestive vibrations from the mental atmosphere are constantly bringing a pressure to bear upon the person, so that indeed he has a mighty task before him to throw off the old conditions, unaided and alone. And, so, while individual effort is preferable, there comes a time in the lives of many people when "a helping hand," or rather a "helping mind," is of great service and aid.

The person coming to the mental aid of a person needing his or her services is performing a most worthy and proper act. We hear a great deal about "interfering with other people's minds" in such kind and worthy "treatments," but in many cases there is but little real interference done. The work of the helper is really in the nature of neutralizing and dissipating the unfavorable. Mental Influence surrounds the other person, and thereby giving the other person a chance to work out his own mental salvation. It is true that everyone must do his or her own work, but help of the kind above indicated is surely most worthy and proper.

In these White Magic treatments the person giving the treatments forms the Mental Picture of the desired condition in his mind, and then sends his thought-currents to the other person endeavoring to reproduce the Mental Picture in the mind or thought-atmosphere of the other person. The best way of doing this, of course, is to assert mentally that the desired condition actually exists. One may be of great help and aid to others in this way, and there is no good reason why it should not be done.

And now for the reverse side of the shield. We wish it were possible to avoid even a mention of this hateful form and manifestation of Mental Influence, but we feel that ignorance is no protection, and that it is useless and foolish to pursue the policy of the ostrich which sticks its head in the sand when pursued, that not seeing the hunter the latter may not see him. We believe that it is better to look things in the face, particularly where it is a case of "forewarned being forearmed."

It is a fact known to all students of occultism that Black Magic has been frequently employed in all times to further the selfish, base aims of some people. And it is also known to advanced thinkers today that even in this enlightened age there are many who do not scruple to stoop to the use of this hateful practice in order serve their own ends, notwithstanding the punishment that occultists know awaits such persons.

The annals of history are full of records of various forms of witchcraft, conjuration and similar forms of Black Magic. All the much talked of forms of "putting spells" upon people are really forms of Black Magic, heightened by the fear and superstition of those affected.

One has but to read the history of witchcraft to see that there was undoubtedly some force at work behind all of the appalling superstition and ignorance shown by the people of those times. What they attributed to the influence of people "in league with the devil" really arose from the use of Black Magic, or an unworthy use of Mental Influence, the two things being one. An examination of the methods used by these "witches," as shown by their confessions, gives us a key to the mystery. These "witches" would fix their minds upon other people, or their animals, and by holding a concentrated mental picture there, would send forth Thought-Waves affecting the welfare of the persons being "adversely treated," which would influence and disturb them, and often bring on sicknesses. Of course, the effect of these "treatments" were greatly heightened by the extreme ignorant fear and superstition held by the masses of people at the time, for Fear is ever a weakening factor in Mental Influence, and the superstitions and credulity of the people caused their minds to vibrate in such a manner as to render them extremely passive to the adverse influences being directed against them.

It is well known that the Voodoos of Africa, and similar cults among other savage races, practice Black Magic among their people with great effect. Among the natives of Hawaii there are certain men known as "Kahunas," who pray people sick, or well, whichever way they are paid for. These instances could be multiplied had we the space and inclination to proceed further with the matter.

And in our own civilized lands there are many people who have learned the principles of Mental Influence, and who are using the same for unworthy purposes, seeking to injure others and defeat their undertakings, or else trying to bring them around to their own (the "treater's") point of view and inclinations. The modern revival of occult knowledge has operated along two lines. On the one hand we see and hear of the mighty power for good Mental Influence is exerting among the people today, raising up the sick, strengthening the weak, putting courage into the despondent and making successes of failures. But on the other hand the hateful selfishness and greed of unprincipled persons in taking advantage of this mighty force of nature and prostituting it to their own hateful ends, without heeding the dictates of conscience or the teaching of religion or morality. These people are sowing a baleful wind that will result in their reaping a frightful whirlwind on the mental plane. They are bringing down upon themselves pain and misery in the future.

At this point we wish to utter a solemn warning to those who have been, or are tempted, to employ this mighty force for unworthy purposes. The laws of the mental plane are such that "as one sows so shall he reap." The mighty Law of Attraction acts with the accuracy of a machine and those who seek to entangle others in a net of Mental Influence sooner or later are caught by their own snare. The Black Magician involves him to pieces. He is sucked down into the whirlpool of his own making, and is dragged down to the lowest depths. These are not idle remarks, but a statement of certain laws of nature, operation on the mental plane, which all should know and heed.

And to those who may feel appalled at this mention of the existence and possibilities of Black Magic we would say that there is one thing to be remembered, and that is that GOOD always overcomes EVIL on the mental plane. A Good thought always has the power to neutralize the Evil one, and a person whose mind is filled with Love and Faith may combat a multitude whose minds are filled with Hate and Evil. The tendency of all nature is upward and toward Good. And he who would pull it back toward Evil sets himself against the law of Spiritual Evolution, and sooner or later falls a victim to his folly.

And then, remember this, Thought-Waves find entrance only to those minds that are accustomed to think similar thoughts. He who thinks Hate may be affected by Hate thoughts, while he whose mind is filled with Faith and Love is surrounded by a resistant armor which repels the invading waves, and causes them to be deflected, or else driven back to their senders. Bad thoughts, like chickens, come home to roost. Thoughts are like Boomerangs, in their tendency to return to their sender. To the poison of Black Magic Nature gives the antidote of Right-Thinking.

12

Self-Protection

The reader of the preceding chapters will see the power of Mental Influence in its various phases of manifestation, and will recognize the possibility of the force being used to influence himself. The question that will naturally arise in the mind of every student and investigator of this important subject, and which comes to all at sometime, is: "How may I protect myself from the use of this power against myself—how may I render myself immune from these influences which may be directed against me?"

It is true that we, and other writers on the subject, have shown you that one is far less liable to influence if he will maintain a mental atmosphere of high vibration—that is keeping oneself surrounded by a thought atmosphere filled with vibrations of the highest kind of thoughts and free from thoughts and desire of a base, selfish character, which tend to attract similar thoughts. In this way one creates a state of mental hygienic cleanliness which renders him immune from the "contagious thoughts of the selfish plane of desire," etc. This should be remembered and taken advantage of by everyone, for just as physical cleanliness gives no congenial lodgment for the germs of disease, so mental cleanliness refuses to admit the mental microbes.

But there is a method far more efficacious than even the above-mentioned plan.

And this method is really that employed by the adepts in Occultism, and the method and practice taught the initiates of the occult brotherhoods and lodges all over the world. Let us consider it here.

In the first place, without entering into a statement of the details of the high occult teachings, we wish to inform you that the Basic Principle of all such teaching and instruction is the fact that within each of us, in the very center of the being of each individual—in the very heart of hearts of the Immortal Ego— is what occultists know as the Flame of the Spirit. This is what you recognize in consciousness as the "I AM" consciousness—that consciousness of being which is far above the consciousness of personality, or the things of personality. It is that consciousness which informs each individual, unmistakably, that he IS actually an Individual Being. This consciousness comes to the individual by reason of his contact with the great One Life of the Universe—it is the point of contact between the PART and the ALL.

And in this part of a man's consciousness, coupled with the sense of BEING an "I," there resides a spark from the Divine Flame of Life and Power, which is what has been called the WILL of man. Now, do not mistake us and confuse this with the so-called Will of personality, which is merely a Desire, or else a certain firmness, which often is little more than Stubbornness. This inner Will is Real Power, and when once recognized may be drawn upon as a source of unending and unfailing Strength. The occult adepts have developed the consciousness of this Power Within, and use it freely. This is the result of years of practice, and correct living and thinking. But, still, each and every person may draw upon this source of strength within them to aid them in life and to repel the thought-vibrations of the lower plane.

This consciousness may be developed by a realization of its existence, and by a practice of bringing the idea in everyday consciousness, by thought, meditation and practice. The very fact of having called your attention to its existence has awakened within the mind of You who are reading these lines a new strength and sense of power. Think a moment and see whether you do not feel a dawning sense of Strength within you that you have not realized so fully before this moment! A continued recognition in your everyday consciousness of this Something Within will develop your ability to manifest it. Particularly in an hour of need will it spring to your assistance, giving you a sense of a part of yourself crying out to you in words of encouragement: "I Am Here! Be Not Afraid!"

It is very difficult to give you this method in written or printed works, but if you will enter fully into a recognition of this Inward Power you will find yourself developing a new power of resisting outside influences that will astonish you.

When you come in contact with people who are seeking to influence you in any of the ways mentioned in the preceding chapters of this book, or in other ways, you will find yourself able to defy their mental attacks by simply remembering the strength imminent in your "I," aided by the statement (made silently to yourself): "I am an Immortal Spirit, using the Will within my Ego." With this Mental Attitude you may make the slightest mental effort in the direction of throwing out from your mind vibrations, which will scatter the adverse influences in all directions, and which, if persisted in, will cause the other person to become confused and anxious to let you alone.

With this consciousness held in mind, your mental command to another, "Let me alone—I cast off your influence by the power of my Spirit," will act so strongly that you will be able to actually see the effect at once. If the other person is stubborn and determined to influence you by words of suggestion, coaxing, threatening, or similar methods, look him or her straight in the eyes, saying mentally "I defy you—my inner power casts off your influence." Try this the next time that anyone attempts to influence you either verbally or by Thought-Waves and see how strong and positive you will feel, and how the efforts of the other person will fail. This sounds simple, but the little secret is worth thousands of dollars to every individual who will put it into practice.

Above all, put out of your mind all Fear of other persons. The feeling of fear prevents you from manifesting the power within you to its full extent. Cast out fear as unworthy and hurtful.

Not only in the case of personal influence in the actual presence of the other person may be defeated in this way, but the same method will act equally as well in the matter of repelling the mental influence of others directed against you in the form of "absent treatments," etc. If you feel yourself inclining toward doing something which in your heart you feel that is not to your best interests, judged from a true standpoint, you may know that, consciously or unconsciously, someone is seeking to influence you in this way.

Then smile to yourself and make the statements mentioned above, or some similar one, and holding the power of the Spirit within your "I" firmly in your mind, send out a mental command just as you would in the case of the actual presence of the person himself or herself. You may also deny the influencing power out of existence by asserting mentally: "I DENY your power to influence me—you have no such power over me—I am resting on my knowledge of Spirit and its Will within me—I deny your power out of existence." This form of denial may be used either in the case of absent influence or personal influence. The rule is the same in all cases.

In repelling these absent influences you will at once experience a feeling of relief and strength, and will be able to smile at the defeated efforts of the other person. If you feel sufficiently broad and full of love for mankind you may then "treat" the other person for his error, sending him thoughts of Love and Knowledge with the idea of dispelling his ignorance and selfishness, and bringing him to a realization of the higher truths of life.

You will doubtless have many interesting experiences arising from thus repelling these attacks. In some cases you will find that the next time you meet the person in question he will appear confused and puzzled and ill at ease. In other cases the person will begin to manifest a new respect and regard for you, and disposed to aid you instead of trying to influence you to his way and desire. In other cases the person will still have the desire, and will endeavor to "argue" you into doing that which he has tried to influence you into doing by Mental Influence, but his efforts will "fall flat," and without effect, particularly if you give him "another dose" of the assertion of the Power of the Spirit within you.

In the same way you should call upon your Higher Self for aid and strength when you feel yourself being affected by any of the great Mental Waves of feeling or emotion sweeping over the public mind, and which have a tendency to "stampede" people into adopting certain ideas, or of following certain leaders. In such case the assertion of the "I" within you will dissipate the influence around you, and you will find yourself standing in a center of Peace surrounded on all sides by the ocean of mental tumult and agitation which is sweeping over or circling around the place. In the same way you will be able to neutralize the unpleasant mental atmospheres of places, localities, houses, etc., and render yourself positive to and immune from the same. In short, we have given you here a recipe that may be used in any and every instance of the employment of Mental Influence. It may sound simple to you, but a little use of it will make you deem it the most important bit of practical knowledge you may possess.

LOOK ALOFT!

The old sailor's advice—The warning cry—Peace and content—Mental balance recovered—The glory of the Universe—All governed by Law—The Law manifests everywhere—A reverent feeling of calm, peaceful faith—Look aloft.

I recently heard a little tale about a boy who went to sea, in the old days of the sailing vessel. One day he was ordered to go aloft, and was urged on until he reached the highest possible point on the mast. When he found that he could go no farther, he glanced down. The sight terrified him and almost caused him to lose his grip and fall headlong on the deck, far below. He felt dizzy and sick, and it seemed almost impossible for him to maintain his hold on the mast. Far below was the deck, looking so small as compared to the wide expanse of water on all sides of it. The motion made him feel as if he was suspended between heaven and earth, with nothing substantial to support him. He felt his brain reeling and his senses leaving him, and all seemed lost, when far away from the deck below, he heard an old sailor cry, "Look aloft, lad! Look aloft!" Turning his eyes from the scene below the boy gazed upward. He saw the blue sky, the fleecy clouds passing peacefully along, looking just the same as they did when he had looked at them while lying on his back on the green grass of the meadows in his country home. A strange feeling of peace and content came over him, and the feeling of dread, terror and despair passed away. His strength and presence of mind came back to him, and soon he was able to slide down the mast until he grasped a friendly rope, thence to the lower rigging, and on until the deck was again reached.

He never forgot the old sailor's advice given in the hour of need, and when he would feel dazed and fearful of danger, he would invariably look aloft until he recovered his mental balance.

We may well take a leaf from the old sailor's note-book, and impress his wisdom upon our minds. There's nothing so good in hours of trial, doubt, sorrow and pain, as to "look aloft." When we feel that we cannot see clearly with our spiritual vision—that our spiritual sight is blurred and dim—that we lose faith and confidence, hope and courage—that we feel the deadly sensation of despair and hopelessness creeping over us and benumbing our senses, stilling our heart—then is the time for us to listen to the warning shout: "Look aloft, lad; look aloft!"

When all seems lost—when darkness is closing around us—when we seem to have lost our foothold and have no way of regaining it—when all appears hopeless, gloomy and dreadful—when faith seems to have deserted us, and the chill of unbelief is on us—then is the time for us to shout to ourselves, "Look aloft—look aloft!"

When we try to solve the riddle of the universe—the problem of existence—by the aid of the intellect, unsupported by faith. When we ask our intellects, "Whence come I? Whither go I? What is the object of my existence? What does Life mean?" When we travel round and round the weary path of intellectual reasoning, and find that it has no ending. When we shout aloud the question of Life, and hear no answer but the despairing echo of our own sad cry. When Life seems a mockery—when Life seems to be without reason—when Life seems a torment devised by a fiend—when we lose the feeling of nearness to the Infinite Power that has supported us in the past—when we lose the touch of the Unseen Hand. These are the times for us to look upward to the source of Wisdom and Light. These are the times for us to heed the cry of the Soul: "Look aloft; look aloft; look aloft!"

Some clear night, when the moon is not shining, go out into the darkness, and gaze upward at the stars. You will see countless bright spots, each of which is a sun equaling or exceeding in size the sun which gives light and life to our little earth—each sun having its circling worlds, many of the worlds having moons revolving around them, in turn. Look all over the heavens, as far as the eye can reach, and endeavor to grasp the idea of the countless suns and worlds. Then try to imagine that in space, far beyond the reach of human vision, even aided by the telescope, are millions upon millions of other worlds and suns—on all sides of us, on and on and on throughout the Universe, reaching into Infinity. And then remember that all these worlds hold their places and revolve according to Law. And then remember that the microscope shows that Law manifests itself in the smallest thing that can be seen by its use. All around you, you will see nothing but the manifestations of Law. And then, remembering that the Infinite, which has us all in charge, takes note of the fall of the sparrow, what has become of your fears and doubts and worries? Gone is your despair and unbelief, and in their place is found a reverent feeling of calm, peaceful Faith.

Aye, there is much good sense in the old sailor's maxim. "When you get rattled, LOOK ALOFT!"

THE SECRET OF SUCCESS

Contents

1

The Secret of Success

It is with some hesitation that we bring ourselves to write this little book, entitled "The Secret of Success." Not that we are not in sympathy with the subject—not that we do not believe that there is a "Secret of Success"—but because there has been so much written on the subject of "Success" that is the veriest twaddle—masses of platitudinous wordiness—that we hesitate to take the position of a teacher of Success. It is so easy to fill pages of paper with good advice—it is so much easier to say things than to do them—so much easier to formulate a code of precepts than to get out into the field of active endeavor and put into practice the same percepts. And, you may imagine why we hesitate to assume a role which would lay us open to the suspicion of being one of the "do as I tell you, and not as I do" teachers of the Art of Success.

But there is another side of the question. There is, besides the mere recital of a List of Good Qualities Leading to Success—a list with which every school-boy and reader of the magazines is acquainted—a Something Else; and that Something Else, is a suggestion that the Seeker for Success has a Something Within himself which if expressed into activity and action will prove of great value to him—a veritable Secret of Success, instead of a code of rules. And, so we propose to devote this little book to unfolding our idea of what this Something Within is, and what it will do for one who will unfold it and thus express it into action. So, therefore, do not expect to find this book a "Complete Compendium of Rules Conducive to Success, Approved of and Formulated by the Successful Men of the World who became acquainted with these Rules only after they had Attained Success, and consequently had Time and Inclination to Preach to Others." This is not a book of that sort. It is Quite Different. We hope you will like it—it will do you good in any event.

All people are striving and seeking Success. Their idea of Success may differ, but they have all agreed upon the desirability of Attainment. "Attainment"—that is the word, which embodies the essence of that which we call Success. It is the "Getting-There" idea—the idea of Attainment—of Reaching the Goal for which we set out. That is the story—Attainment.

Many men and women have endeavored to point out the way to Success, and while some have rendered valuable service to those who were following them on the Path of Attainment, yet none have been able to tell the whole story of Success. And this is not to be wondered about, for the reason that on the road to Success each and every individual must be, in a measure a law unto himself, or herself. No two temperaments are exactly alike—Nature delights in variety; no two sets of circumstances are precisely the same—infinite variety manifests here also. And so it would be folly to attempt to lay down rules of universal application, which would surely lead all to the great goal of Success. One has but to look around him on all sides and see the different needs of the different individuals composing the crowd, in order to recognize the futility of any attempt to lay down lines of universal instruction on this subject. Each and every man who has succeeded has done so in a different way—generally along some original lines of action—in fact, the faculty or characteristic known as Individuality, seems to have played an important part in the success of the majority of persons who have attained it. And Individuality renders those possessing it to a marked degree to be likely to depart from any set of rules or laid-out courses of action. And so, it may be stated as a general principle that each must work out his own Success along the lines of his own Individuality, rather than by following any set rule or line of conduct.

In view of what we have just said, it may seem strange that feeling as we do we have ventured to write a little book entitled "The Secret of Success," particularly as we have started the said book by declaring the impossibility of laying down any set rules on the subject. This may seem like a paradox, but a little examination will show you that it is not so. It is true that we believe that each and every person must work out his own Success, along the lines of his own Individuality, instead of along some cut-and-dried plan. And right here is where the "Secret of Success" comes in. "Along the lines of his own individuality," we have just said—then it must follow that one must possess Individuality before he may work along its "lines." And in the measure that he possesses Individuality, so will he possess the first prerequisite to Success. And that is what we mean by "The Secret of Success"—INDIVIDUALITY.

Every person possesses dormant and latent Individuality—but only a few allow it to express itself. The majority of us are like human sheep trotting along complacently after some self-assertive bellwether, whose tinkling bell serves to guide our footsteps. We have absorbed the notion somehow that these bellwethers possess the sum and substance of human knowledge and power, and ability to think and instead of unfolding our own dormant powers, and latent possibilities, we allow them to remain in obscurity, and we trot along, jogitty-joggity-jog after our pet bellwether. People are very much like sheep in this way; they are obedient and imitative animals, and rather than assume the responsibility of directing their own footsteps, they wait until someone takes the lead, and then away they stampede after him. Is it any wonder that the leaders claim the choicest pickings for themselves, and allow the flock to get only the scrubby grass? Not a bit of it—they have earned the choice bits by reason of lack of Individuality and Initiative on the part of those following them—in fact, they were chosen as leaders because of this self-assertive, and self-directive quality. If they had stood back in a modest, mild manner, they would have been pushed aside by the flock that would disclaim them as leaders, in favor of others who knew how to push to the front.

Now, in this little book we shall not endeavor to awaken a spirit of "bell-wetherism" in you, nor to urge you to strive to lead the flock—there is nothing in the mere leading of people other than vainglory and petty self-satisfaction. The desirable thing is to possess sufficient Individuality and Initiative to be your own bellwether—to be a law unto yourself, so far as other men are concerned. The great men—the strong men—care nothing for the flock, which so obediently trots along after them. They derive no satisfaction from this thing, which pleases only inferior minds, and gratifies only petty natures and ambitions. The big men—the great spirits of all ages—have derived more satisfaction from that inward conviction of strength and ability which they felt unfolding into activity within themselves, than in the plaudits of the mob, or in the servility of those imitative creatures who sought to follow in their footsteps.

And, this thing called Individuality is a real thing. Inherent in each of us, and which may be developed and brought into activity in each one of us if we go about it right. Individuality is the expression of our Self—that Self which is what we mean when we say "I". Each of us is an Individual—an "I"—differing from every other "I" in the universe, so far as personal expression is concerned. And in the measure that we express and unfold the powers of that "I", so are we great, strong and successful. We all "have it in us"—it depends upon us to get it out into Expression. And, this Individual Expression lies at the heart of the "Secret of Success". And that is why we use the term—and that is what we shall tell you about in this little book. It will pay for you to learn this "Secret".

2

The Individual

In our last lesson we stated that we considered the "Secret of Success" to consist principally of the Free Expression of the Individual—the "I." But before you will be able to apply this idea successfully, you must first awaken to a realization of what the Individual—the "I" within you—really is. This statement may appear ridiculous at first to many of you, but it will pay you to acquaint yourself fully with the idea behind it, for upon the true realization of "I" comes Power.

If you will stop and take stock of yourself, you will find that you are a more complex being than you had at first considered yourself to be. In the first place there is the "I," which is the Real Self or the Individual, and there is the "Me," which is something attached to and belonging to the "I"—the Personality. For proof of this, let the "I" take stock of the "Me," and it will find that the latter consists of three phases or principles, (i.e. 1. The Physical Body; 2. The Vital Energy; 3. The Mind). Many people are in the habit of regarding their bodies as the "I" part of them, but a little consideration will show them that the body is but a material covering, or a machine through which and by means of which the "I" is able to manifest itself. A little thought will show that one may be vividly conscious of the "I Am" part of himself while totally oblivious of the presence of the physical body. This being so, it follows that the "I" is independent of the body, and that the latter falls into the "Me" classification. The physical body may exist after the "I" has left it—the dead body is not the "I." The physical body is composed of countless particles which are changing places every moment of our lives—our body of today is entirely different from our body of a year ago.

Then comes the second principle of the "Me"—the Vital Energy, or what many call Life. This is seen to be independent of the body, which it energizes, but it, too, is transitory and changeable, and readily may be seen to be but a something used to animate and energize the body—an instrument of the "I," and therefore a principle of the "Me." What, then, is left to the "I" to examine and determine its nature? The answer that comes naturally to the lips is, "The Mind," by which I know the truth of what you have just said. But, stop a moment, you have said, speaking of the mind, "by which I know"—have you not, in saying this, acknowledged the mind to be a something through which the "I" acts? Think a moment—is the mind YOU? You are aware that your mental states change—your emotions vary—your feelings differ from time to time—your very ideas and thoughts are inconsistent and are subject to outside influences, or else are molded and governed by that which you call "I," or your Real Self. Then there must be something behind Mental States, Ideas, Feelings, Thoughts, etc., which is superior to them and which "knows" them just as one knows a thing apart from itself but which it uses. You say "I" feel; "I" think; "I" believe; "I" know; "I" will; etc., etc. Now which is the Real Self? The Mental States just mentioned or the "I" which is the subject or Real Cause of the mental phenomena? It is not the Mind that knows, but the "I" which uses the Mind in order to know. This may seem a little abstruse to you if you have never been made a study of the subject, but think it over a little and the idea will clearly define itself in your mind.

We are not telling you these things merely to give you an idea of metaphysics, philosophy, or psychology—there are many books that go into these matters at length and in detail—so it is not for that reason. The real reason is that with a realization of the "I" or Real Self, comes a sense of Power that will manifest through you and make you strong. The awakening to a realization of the "I," in its clearness and vividness, will cause you to feel a sense of Being and Power that you have never before known. Before you can express Individuality, you must realize that you are an Individual. And you must be aware of this "I" within you before you can realize that you are an Individual.

The "Me" side of you is what is called Personality, to the outer appearance of yourself. Your Personality is made up of countless characteristics, traits, habits, thoughts, expressions and motions—it is a bunch of peculiarities and personal traits that you have been thinking was the real "I" all this time. But it is not. Do you know what the idea of Personality arose from? Let us tell you. Turn to the pages of any good dictionary, and you will see that the word originated from the Latin word "Persona," meaning "a mask used by actors in ancient times," and which the word in turn was derived from two other words, "sonare," meaning to "sound," and "per," meaning "through," the two words combined meaning "to sound through"—the idea being that the voice of the actor sounded through the mask of the assumed personality or character. Webster gives the following as one of the meanings of "Person," even to this day: "A character or part, as in a play; an assumed character." So then, Personality means the part you are playing in the Great Play of Life, on the Stage of the Universe. The real Individual concealed behind the mask of Personality is YOU—the Real Self—the "I"—that part of you which you are conscious when you say "I AM," which is your assertion of existence and latent power. "Individual" means something that cannot be divided or subtracted from—something that cannot be injured or hurt by outside forces—something REAL. And you are an Individual—a Real Self—an "I"—Something endowed with Life, Mind, and Power, to use, as you will.

A poet named Orr wrote:

Lord of a thousand worlds am I,
And I reign since time began;
And night and day, in cyclic sway,
Shall pass while their deeds I scan.
Yet time shall cease ere I find release,
For I AM the soul of Man.

3

Spiritedness

To many of you, the title of this lesson—Spiritedness—may seem to have some connection with "spirits," "disembodied entities," or else the "soul" or some higher part of it, to which the name Spirit is often applied. But, in this case, we use the word in a different sense, and yet in a sense approved by many advanced teachers and investigators of the occult and spiritual. One of the meanings of the word "spirit" as given by Webster is as follows: "Energy, vivacity, ardor, enthusiasm, courage," etc., while the same authority defines the word "spirited" as: "Animated; full of life and vigor, lively," etc. These definitions will give you a hint of the sense in which we are now using the term, but there is still more to it.

To us the word Spirit expresses the idea of the real essential nature of the Universal Power, and which is also manifested in man as the center of his being—his essential strength and power, from whence proceeds all that renders him an Individual. Spiritedness does not mean the quality of being ethereal, "goody-goody," spiritual, otherworldly, or anything of that sort. It means the state of being "animated," meaning, "possessed of life and vigor"—so that the state is really that of being filled with Power and Life. And that Power and Life comes from the very center of one's being—the "I AM" region or plane of mind and consciousness.

Spiritedness is manifested in different degrees among different men—and even among the animals. It is an elementary, fundamental, primitive quality and expression of Life, and does not depend upon culture, refinement or education. Its development seems to depend upon such instinctive or intuitional recognition of the Something Within—the Power of the Individual which is derived from that Universal Power of which we are all expressions. And even some of the animals seem to possess it.

A recent writer on the "Taming of Animals" expresses instinctive realization of Spiritedness among some of the higher animals as follows: "Put two male baboons in the same cage, and they will open their mouths, show all their teeth, and 'blow' at each other. But one of them, even though he may possess the uglier dentition, will blow with a difference, with an inward shakiness that marks him as the underdog at once. No test of battle is needed at all. It is the same with the big cats. Put two, or four, or a dozen lions together, and they also, probably without a single contest, will soon discover which one of them possesses the mettle of the master. Thereafter he takes the choice of the meat; if he chooses, the rest shall not even begin to eat until he has finished; he goes first to the fresh pan of water. In short he is 'king of the cage.' Now, then, when a tamer goes into a den with a big cat that has taken a notion to act 'funny,' his attitude is almost exactly that of the 'king beast' above mentioned would be toward a subject rash and ill-advised enough to challenge his kingship."

You will notice in the above quotation, that the writer states clearly that it is not always the baboon with the fiercest tusks that is the master, neither does the "king lion" necessarily assert his dominion by winning a physical fight—it is something far more subtle than the physical—it is the manifestation of some soul quality of the animal. And so it is with men, it is not always the biggest and strongest physically who rule—the ruler becomes so by reason of the mysterious soul quality which we call Spiritedness, and which men often call "nerve," or "mettle," or "sand." When two individuals come into contact with each other there is mental struggle—there may not be even a word uttered—and yet soul grapples with soul as the two pairs of eyes gaze into each other, and a subtle something in each engages and grapples with a subtle something in the other. It may be all over in a moment, but the conflict is settled for the time, and each of the mental combatants knows that he is victor or defeated, as the case may be. There may be no feeling of antagonism between the parties engaging, but nevertheless there seems to be an inward recognition on both sides that there is something between them that always leads. And this leadership does not depend upon physical strength, intellectual attainment, or culture in the ordinary sense, but upon the manifestation and recognition of that subtle quality that we have called Spirit.

People unconsciously assert their recognition of quality in themselves and others, by their use of the term. We often hear of people "lacking spirit"; being "spiritless"; and of others having had "their spirit broken"; etc. The term is used in the sense of "mettle." A "mettled" horse or man is "high-spirited," according to the dictionaries; and the same authorities define "mettlesome" as "full of spirit," so you see the term is used as we have employed it—but the explanation of the source of the "spiritedness" is not given. Breeders of thoroughbred racing horses will tell you that a horse having "spirit" will run a gamer race and will often outdistance and out-wind a horse having higher physical characteristics, but less "spirit" or "class." Horsemen insist that the possession of "spirit" in a horse is recognized by the other horses, who are affected by it and become discouraged and allow themselves to be beaten, although often they may be better racing machines, physically. This spirit is a fundamental vital strength possessed by all living things in degrees—and it may be developed and strengthened in one's self. In our next lesson we shall recite a few instances of its manifestation among men.

Oliver Wendell Holmes, in one of his books, gives the following vivid description of the conflict of spiritedness between two men: "The Koh-i-noor's face turned so white with rage that his blue-black mustache and beard looked fearful against it. He grinned with wrath, and caught at a tumbler, as if he would have thrown its contents at the speaker. The young Marylander fixed his clear, steady eye upon him, and laid his hand on his arm, carelessly almost, but the Jewel felt that he could not move it. It was no use. The youth was his master, and in a deadly Indian hug in which men wrestle with their eyes, over in five seconds, but which breaks one of their two backs, and is good for three score years and ten, one trial enough—settles the whole matter—just as when two feathered songsters of the barnyard, game and dunghill, come together. After a jump or two at each other, and a few sharp kicks, there is an end to it; and it is 'After you, monsieur,' with the beaten party in all the social relations for all the rest of his days."

Fothergill says: "Emily Bronte sketched out her ideal of a being possessed of immense willpower in a thorough ruffian—Heathcliff. A massive, muscular brute! Well, it was a girl's conception of a strong man; but I think I have seen some quiet, inoffensive-looking men in spectacles, who could very soon have shown the ruffian where the superiority lay."

A celebrated historical example of Spiritedness, under apparently overwhelming odds, is that of the interview between Hugo, Bishop of Lincoln and Richard Coeur de Lion, in the church of Roche d'Andeli. In his desire to prosecute the war in Normandy, Richard demanded additional supplies and money from his barons and bishops, but Hugo refused to furnish men or money. He claimed that although the See of Lincoln was legally bound to supply men and money for military service within the four seas of Britain, the war in Normandy did not come under that head, and he defied the king. King Richard, called the Lion-Hearted, was a dangerous man to defy, and so when he summoned Bishop Hugo to Normandy, and the latter went forth to beard the lion in his den, few doubted the outcome, and the bishop's downfall was taken as a matter of course. When the bishop landed in Normandy two friendly barons who informed him that the king was in a terrible rage against him, and who advised him to send some humble, conciliatory message to him before entering the royal presence. But the bishop refused to do this, and proceeded boldly to meet his monarch. Richard was sitting at Mass when the bishop entered. Hugo walked up to him, and disregarding his frown, said, "Kiss me, my lord King!" Richard turned wrathfully away, withholding his salute. But Hugo, gazing into his eyes, and shaking the royal shoulder vigorously, repeated his demand. "Thou hast not deserved it," roared the king in anger and chagrin. "I have," retorted Hugo, shaking the royal shoulder the harder. The king gradually dropped his eyes from those of the bishop, and gave the kingly salute and kiss, and the bishop passed on calmly to take part in the service. Hugo afterward defied the king in his council chamber, and persisted in his refusal, and even ventured to rebuke his royal master for infidelity to the queen. The council was astounded, for knowing Richard's courage and fiery temper they expected to see Hugo crush in a moment—but instead he emerged the victor in the struggle of Spiritedness. The historian says: "The Lion was tamed for the moment. The King acknowledged nothing, but restrained his passion, remarking afterward, 'If all bishops were like my lord of Lincoln, not a prince among us could lift his head among them.'"

And this was not the first time that this doughty Bishop of Lincoln had vanquished a king. In his earlier days, shortly after King Henry Plantagenet had created him bishop, he became involved in a fierce dispute with that monarch. Henry was at Woodstock Park surrounded by his courtiers when Hugo approached. The king feigned not to see the bishop, taking no notice whatsoever of him. After a few moments of strained silence, the bishop, pushing aside a powerful earl who was seated by the king's side, took his place beside the king. The king pretended to be mending his leather glove. The bishop cheerfully and lightly said: "Your Majesty reminds me of your cousin at Falaise." Falaise was the place at which Henry's ancestor Duke Robert met Arlotta, the daughter of a tanner of leather, who bore him his illegitimate son who was afterward known as William the Conqueror. The Bishop's impudent allusion to the king's ancestry was too much for the latter, and he was badly worsted in the encounter and later acceded to the wishes of the bishop.

But as Fothergill truly says: "It is a great mistake to suppose that this Will is disposed to air itself on all occasions; far from it. It often has a tendency to conceal itself, and is not rarely found under and exterior of much pleasantness. There are men, and women, too, who present an appearance of such politeness that they seem to have no will of their own; they apparently exist merely to do what is agreeable to others; but just wait till the time comes, and then the latent willpower is revealed, and we find under this velvet glove the iron hand—and no mistake about it. It is the secret of the diplomatist. Talleyrand possessed it to a remarkable degree, and was a cool, bold, successful diplomat; Cavour also possessed this power and used it wisely. The blusterer and bragger are devoid of it." It is a subtle, tenuous Power, resting latent beneath the surface and out of evidence—but when needed it flashes forth like the dynamic electric spark, driving all before it. It is an elemental force, of irresistible power.

4

Latent Powers

The majority of you know by actual experience in everyday life that we have within our physical organism that which we call "second-wind." We have essayed some physical task, and after a bit found ourselves "winded," that is short of breath, and we are tempted to stop and rest our panting bodies. But, we have also found by experience that if we will stick to the task at hand the feeling of physical distress will usually pass away, and we will gain what is called our "second-wind." Now just what this "second-wind" is, is a matter that has long perplexed physiologists, and even today they have not been able to hand us down a very good guess at the underlying cause of the phenomenon. It seems to be a fresh start acquired by reason of the opening up of reserve stores of vital energy—latent physical power stored away for such emergencies. All persons who have engaged in athletic sports know very well the details of this peculiar physiological phenomenon—its actuality is too firmly established to admit any doubt.

And, as is often the case, examination shows a curious parallel between the working of Nature on the mental plane and on the physical. Just as there is a physical "second-wind," so is there a mental reserve force or latent energy upon which we can draw and thus get a fresh start. The phenomena attendant upon physical "second-wind," as noted above, is almost exactly duplicated by certain mental phenomena. We may be jaded while performing some tedious bit of mental work, and we begin to feel that we are "all in," when lo! some new in—and away we are off with a full mental "second-wind" doing our work with a freshness, vigor and enthusiasm far surpassing the original effort. We have tapped into a fresh source or supply of mental energy.

The majority of us have little or no conception of the reserve mental energies and forces contained within our being. We jog along at our customary gait, thinking that we are doing our best and getting all out of life that there is in it—think we are expressing ourselves to our utmost capacity. But we are living only in the first-wind mental state, and behind our working mentality are stores of wonderful mental energy and power—faculties lying dormant—power lying latent—awaiting the magic command of the Will in order to awaken into activity and outward expression. We are far greater beings than we have realized—we are giants of power, if we did but know it. Many of us are like young elephants that allow themselves to be mastered by weak men, and put through their paces, little dreaming of the mighty strength and power concealed within their organisms. Those of you who have read our little manual entitled "The Inner Consciousness" will recall what we said therein regarding the regions above and below the plane of the ordinary outer consciousness. And on those hidden planes of the mind, are untold possibilities—the raw materials for mighty mental tasks and achievement—the storage batteries of wonderful accomplishment. The trouble with us is that we do not realize the existence of these faculties. We think that we are merely what we manifest in our ordinary dogtrot gait. Another problem is that we have not had the incentive to take action—we have lacked the interest to do great things—we haven't wanted to hard enough. This "want-to-hard-enough" is the great inciting power in life. Desire is the fire which rouses up the steam of Will. Without Incentive—and that means Desire—we accomplish nothing. Given the great, earnest, burning ardent Desire as an animating force—the great incentive to take action, and we are able to get up this mental "second-wind"—yes, third, fourth, and fifth winds—tapping one plane of inward power after another, until we work mental miracles.

We wonder at the achievements of the great men in all walks of life, and we are apt to excuse ourselves by the sad remark that these people seem to "have it in them," while we have not. Nonsense, we all have it in us to do things a hundred times greater than we are doing. The trouble is not in greater than we are doing. The trouble is not in the lack of power and mental material, but in the Desire and Interest, and Incentive to arouse into activity those wonderful storehouses of dynamic power within our mentality—we fail to call into our disposal, and which is like all other natural powers and forces eager and anxious to be manifested and expressed. Yes, that's what we said "anxious and eager," for all natural forces, penned up and in a static condition seem to be bursting with desire to manifest and express into outer dynamic activity. This seems to be a law of life and nature. Nature and all in it seems to be eager for active expression. Have you not been surprised at yourselves at times, when under some slightly higher pressure and incentive Something Within you seemed to break its bounds and fairly carry you off of your feet in its rush into active work? Have you not accomplished tasks under the stress of a sudden urgent need, that you would have deemed impossible in cold-blood. Have you not carried all before you when you "warmed-up" to the task, whereas your ordinary self would have stood around doing nothing under ordinary circumstances.

Earnestness and Enthusiasm are two great factors in bringing into operation these latent forces, and dormant powers of the mentality. But one need not stand by and wait until you work yourself into a fit of fervor before the energies spring into action. You can by a careful training of the Will—or rather, by a careful training of yourself to use your Will—manage to get hold of the mental throttle, so that you may pull it down and turn on a full head of steam whenever necessary. And when you have once mastered this, you will find that you are not any more tired when running under full pressure, than when you are crawling along—this being one of the Secrets of Success.

To many a person, the term "The Will," means merely a firm, steadfastness of mind, akin to Determination and Fixity of Purpose. To others it means something like Desire. To others, it means "the power of choice," etc. But to occultists, the Will is something far more than these things—it means a Vital Power—an Acting Force of the Mind—capable of dominating and ruling the other mental faculties as well as projecting itself beyond the mental organs of the individual and affecting others coming within its field of influence. And it is in this sense that we use the word "Will" in this lesson.

We have no desire to take the reader into the dim realms of metaphysics, or even into the lighter but still arduous paths of scientific psychology, but we must acquaint him with the fact of the existence of this thing that we call Willpower, and its relation to the "I." Of all the mental faculties or powers, that of the Will is the closest to the "I" or Ego of the person. It is the Sword of Power clasped in the hand of the Ego. One may divorce himself in thought from the other mental faculties and states, but when he thinks of the "I" he is bound to think of it as possessing that power which we call Will. The Will is a primal, original power of the "I" which is always with it until the end. It is the force with which he rules (or should rule) his mental and physical kingdom—the power of which his Individuality manifests itself upon the outside world.

Desire is the great motive power inciting the Will to action in life. As we have shown you the action of Will without the motive power of Desire is unthinkable, and therefore it follows that the culture and right direction of Desire carries with it the channel of expression and manifestation of the Will. You cultivate certain Desires, in order that the Will may flow out along these channels. By cultivating the Desire along certain lines, you are making channels along which the Will may flow in its rush toward expression and manifestation. So be sure to map out your Desire channels clearly by making the proper Mental Images of what you want—be sure and make the Desire channels deep and clear-cut by the force of repeated attention and autosuggestion.

History is filled with examples of men who have developed the use of the Will. We say "developed the use" rather than "developed Will," for man does not develop his Will—his Will is always there ready for use—a man develops his ability to use the Will—perfects himself in its use. We have frequently used the following illustration, and have not been able to improve upon it: Man is like a trolley car, with the upraised trolley-pole of his mind reaching out to the live wire of Will. Along that wire is flowing the current of Willpower, which it "taps" and draws down into his mind, and by which he is able to move, and act and manifest power. But the power is always in the Wire, and his "developing" consists in the ability to raise the pole to the Wire, and thus "tap into" its energy. If you will carry this idea in your mind, you will be able to apply this truth more easily in your everyday life.

A great promoter of the steel-pen, and electroplating industries, possesses this quality to a marked degree. It has been said of him that: "He had, to begin with, a strong, powerful, almost irresistible Will; and whoever and whatever he opposed, he surely conquered in the end." Buxton said: "The longer I live, the more certain I am that the great difference between men, between the feeble and the powerful, the great and the insignificant, is Energy—Invincible Determination—a purpose once fixed, and the Victory or Death. That quality will do anything that can be done in this world—and no talents, no circumstances, no opportunities, will make a two-legged creature a man without it. In this last quotation and the one preceding it, the idea of Persistence and Determination is identified closely with that of Will. And they are closely identified, the idea being that the Will should be held close, fast, and steadily against the task to be accomplished, just as the steel chisel is held firmly up against the object on the lathe, until its work is accomplished. It is not the mere Determination or Persistency that does the work—these would be of no avail unless the Will were there to do the cutting and shaping. But then again, there is a double-aspect of Will here—the Will in one phase does the work, while in another it forces the mind to hold it up against the task. So, in a sense the Will is the power back of Determination and persistency, as well as the force doing the work—the cutting-edge of the chisel, as well as the firm hand that holds it to its work.

Simpson has said: "A passionate Desire, and an unwearied Will can perform impossibilities, or what would seem to be such, to the cold and feeble." Disraeli said: "I have brought myself by long meditation to the conviction that a human being with a settled purpose must accomplish it, and that nothing can resist a Will which will stake even existence upon its fulfillment." Foster says: "It is wonderful how even the casualties of life seem to bow to a spirit that will not bow to them, and yield to subserve a design which they may, in their first apparent tendency, threaten to frustrate. When a firm, decisive spirit is recognized, it is curious to see how the space clears around a man and leaves him room and freedom." Mitchell has said: "Resolve is what makes a man manifest; not puny resolve; not crude determination; not errant purpose—but that strong and indefatigable Will which treads down difficulties and danger, as a boy treads down the heaving frost lands of winter, which kindles his eye and brain with a proud pulse-beat toward the unattainable. Will makes men giants."

So, raise that mental trolley-pole, and touch the live wire of Will.

5

Soul-Force

You often have heard the word "Enthusiasm" used—have used it often yourself. But have you ever thought of what the word really means—from what source it originated—what is its essential spirit? Few have. The word "Enthusiasm" is derived from the Greek term meaning "to be inspired; to be possessed by the gods, etc.," the term having been originally used to designate the mental state of an inspired person who seems to be under the influence of a higher power. The term originally meant, "Inspired by a superhuman or divine power; ecstasy; etc." It is now used, according to Webster, in the sense of: "Enkindled and kindling fervor of soul; ardent and imaginative zeal or interest; lively manifestation of joy or zeal; etc." The word has acquired a secondary, and unfavorable meaning in the sense of "visionary zeal; imaginative fervor; etc."; but its real and primary meaning is that ardent, lively zeal and interest in an inner force of one's nature. Real enthusiasm means a powerful mental state exerted in favor of, or against, some idea.

A person filled with Enthusiasm seems indeed to be inspired by some power or being higher than himself—he taps on to a source of power of which he is not ordinarily conscious. And the result is that he becomes as a great magnet radiating attractive force in all directions and influencing those within his field of influence. For Enthusiasm is contagious and when really experienced by the individual renders him a source of inductive power, and a center of mental influence. But the power with which he is filled does not come from an outside source—it comes from certain inner regions of his mind or soul—from his Inner Consciousness. Those who have read our little manual entitled "Inner Consciousness" will readily understand from what part of the mentality such power is derived. Enthusiasm is really "soul power," and when genuine is so recognized and felt by those coming within its field of influence.

Without a certain amount of Enthusiasm no one ever has attained Success, and never will do so. There is no power in personal intercourse that can be compared to Enthusiasm of the right sort. It comprises Earnestness, Concentration, and Power, and there are a very few people that cannot be influenced in some degree by its manifestation by another. Few people realize the actual value of Enthusiasm. Many have succeeded by reason of its possession, and many have failed by reason of its lack. Enthusiasm is the steam that drives our mental machinery, and which indirectly thus accomplishes the great things in life. You cannot accomplish tasks properly yourself unless you manifest a degree of interest in them, and what is Enthusiasm but Interest plus Inspiration— Inspired Interest, that's what Enthusiasm is. By the power of Enthusiasm the great things of life are brought to expression and accomplishment.

Enthusiasm is not a thing, which some possess and others lack. All persons have it potentially, but only a few are able to express it. The majority is afraid to let themselves "feel" a thing, and then to let the "feeling" express itself in powerful action like the steam in an engine. The majority of persons do not know how to get up the steam of Enthusiasm. They fail to keep the fires of Interest and Desire kindled under their mental boiler, and the consequence is they fail to get up the steam of Enthusiasm. Enthusiasm may be developed, by cultivating interest and love of your task. Interest, confidence, and desire arouse Enthusiasm, and it remains for you to either concentrate it so that its effect will be directed straight toward the object, person or thing that you wish to move, or else allow it to dissipate itself in the air without result. Like steam, Enthusiasm may be dissipated or used—by concentrated direction it produces results; and by foolish waste and dissipation it fails to do so. The more interest you take in a thing, the greater does your confidence and desire grow—and from these arise the steam of Enthusiasm. So remember always that Interest is the mother of Enthusiasm.

The enthusiastic man naturally tends toward the optimistic frame of mind, and by doing so he diffuses an atmosphere of confident, cheerful expectation around him which tends to inspire confidence in others, and which aids him in his endeavors. He surrounds himself with a mental aura of Success—he vibrates Success—and those into whose presence he comes, unconsciously take on his vibrations. Enthusiasm is very contagious, and one filled with the right quality, kind and degree of it unconsciously communicates his interest, earnestness and expectations to others. Enthusiasm plays an important part in that which is called Personal Magnetism. It is a live, warm, vital mental quality, and it quickens the pulse of the one using it, and those who are affected by it. It is different from the cold-blooded indifference that one meets with so often in business, and which causes many a sale to be lost, and many a good thing to be "turned down."

The man who lacks Enthusiasm is robbed of more than half his force of Personal Influence. No matter how good his arguments may be—no matter how meritorious his proposition may be—unless he posesses the warm vital quality of Enthusiasm, his efforts are largely wasted, and his result impaired. Think over the salesmen who have approached you and remember how some of them produced the chilling effect of a damp cellar upon you, while others caused you to sit up and take notice in spite of yourself by reason of their earnest interest and enthusiasm. Analyze the impression produced upon you by the different people with whom you have come in contact, and then see how great an influence Enthusiasm exerts. And then remember the effect it produces upon yourself, when you feel it. Enthusiasm is Mental Steam—remember that.

A few days ago there was erected a tablet, in one of the great colleges of the land, as a memorial to a former student in its halls. This young man saved the lives of seventeen people during a great storm on the lake. He swam out after them, one by one, and brought them all in alive. He fainted away from exhaustion, and when he recovered consciousness, his first words were, "Boys, did I do my Best?"

The words of this young man express the great question that should urge every true seeker after Success to so live and act that he may be able to answer it in the affirmative. It is not so much a question of "did I do so much," or "did I do as much as someone else?" as it is matter of "DID I DO MY BEST?"

The man who does his best is never a failure. He is always a success, and if the best should be but a poor pretty thing, still the world will place the laurel wreath of victory upon his brow when he accomplishes it. The one who does his best is never a "quitter," or a "shirker"—he stays right on his job until he has bestowed upon it the very best that there is in him to give at that particular time. Such a man can never be a failure.

The man who does his best is never heard asking the pessimistic question, "What's the Use?" He doesn't care a whole lot about that part of it—his mind is fixed upon the idea that he is "on his job," and is not going to be satisfied with anything less than his Best. And when one really is able to answer the great question with an honest, "Yes, I did my Best," then verily, he will be able to answer the "What's the Use" question properly—it is "of use" to have brought out the Best work in oneself, if for no other reason than because it is a Man Making process—a developer of the Self.

This infernal "What's the Use" question seems to have been invented by some pessimistic imp of darkness to use in discouraging people making desperate struggles or leading forlorn hopes. It has brought down many a man into the Mire of Despondency and Failure. Chase it out of you mind whenever it appears, and replace it with the question, "Am I doing my Best," knowing that an affirmative answer settles the other question also. Anything is "Of Use" if it is in the right spirit, in a worthy cause, and because one's own manhood demands it. Yes, even if one goes down to death in the doing of it still it is a Success. Listen to this story, told in a recent magazine article: It is a story of a sailor on the wreck of a German kerosene steamer, which dashed against the rocks of the Newfoundland coast in the early part of 1901. She had taken fire, and had been run ashore on a submerged reef about an eighth of a mile from the coast. The coastline itself was a wall, some four hundred feet high. When morning dawned, the fishermen on shore saw that her boats were all gone, and all the crew and officers had apparently been lost—all except three men. Two of these three men were standing on the bridge—the third was aloft, lashed to the rigging. Later, the watchers saw a tremendous wave strike the vessel, sweeping away the bridge and the two men who had been standing on it. Several hours later they saw the man in the rigging unlash himself and beat his arms against his body vigorously, evidently to restore the circulation, which had been almost stopped by the lashing and the extreme cold. The man then took off his coat, waved it to the fishermen on top of the cliff and then plunged into the sea. The first thought was that he had given up the fight and committed suicide—but he was not that kind of a man. He struck out for shore, and reaching it made three separate attempts to secure a foothold on the rocks at the bottom of the cliff. But, he failed—three times was he swept away by the surf, and finally, seeing the futility of his efforts, he swam away again, toward the ship. As the narrator well says: "At that crisis in the struggle ninety-nine men out of a hundred would have given and allowed themselves to drown; but this man was not a quitter."

After a fierce battle with the waves the man gained the ship, and after a desperate struggle managed to board her. He climbed again into the rigging and waved his hand to the fishermen high up on the cliff, who were unable to help him. He lashed himself fast, and until dark could be seen signaling the fishermen above, to show them that he was still alive and game. When the following morning broke the fishermen saw that his head had fallen to his breast—he was motionless—frozen during the night. He was dead—his brave soul had gone forth to meet its Maker, and who can doubt that when that man confronted his Maker his eyes were looking firmly and bravely toward the Presence, and not bowed down in shame or fear. Such a man was indeed worthy to face his Maker, unabashed and unashamed. As the writer, George Kennan, has said in words that make one thrill: "That man died as a man in adverse circumstances ought to die, fighting to the last. You may call it foolish, and say that he might better have ended his sufferings by allowing himself to drown when he found that he could not make a landing at the base of the cliff; but deep down in your hearts you pay secret homage to his courage, his endurance, and his indomitable will. He was defeated at last, but so long as he had consciousness neither fire nor cold not tempest could break down his manhood."

The Caucasians have a favorite proverb that says: "Heroism is endurance for one moment more." And that one moment more tells the difference between the "quitter" and the man who has "done his Best." No one is dead until his heart has ceased beating—and no one has failed so long as there is one more bit of fight in him. And that "one moment more" often is the moment in which the tide turns—the moment when the enemy relaxes his hold and drops back beaten.

6

The Power of Desire

What is Desire? Let us see! Webster tells us that it is: "The natural longing to possess any seeming good; eager wish to obtain or enjoy," or in its abnormal or degenerate sense: "excessive or morbid longing; lust; appetite." "Desire" is a much-abused term—the public mind has largely identified it with its abnormal or degenerate phase, just mentioned, ignoring its original and true sense. Many use the word in the sense of an unworthy longing or craving, instead of in the true sense of "aspiration," "worthy craving and longing," etc. To call Desire "aspiration" renders it none the less Desire. To apply to it the term "laudable aim and ambition" does not take away from its character of Desire. There is no sense in endeavoring to escape the fact that Desire is the natural and universal impulse toward action, be the action or good or bad. Without Desire the Will does not spring into action, and nothing is accomplished. Even the highest attainments and aims of the race are possible only when the steam of Will is aroused by the flame and heat of Desire.

Some of the occult teachings are filled with instructions to "kill out desire," and the student is warned to beware of it even in its most insidious and subtle forms, even to the extent of "avoiding even the desire to be desireless—even desire not to desire. Now this is all nonsense, for if one "wishes," or "wants," or "is inclined," or "thinks best to," or "is pleased to" Kill Out Desire—in any of these cases he is but manifesting a Desire "not to desire," in spite of his use of other names. What is this "wishing to; wanting to; feeling like; inclination; being pleased to;" and all the rest, but just plain, clear, unadulterated Desire masquerading under some of these names. To proceed to "kill out desire" without "desiring" to do so is like trying to lift oneself by pulling on his own bootstraps. Folly. What is really meant is that the occultist should proceed to kill out the lower desires that he finds within his nature, and also to kill out the "attachment" for things. Regarding this last we would say that all true occultist know that even the best "things" are not good enough to rule and master one—nothing is good enough for the soul to allow itself to be unduly attached to it so that the thing rules the soul instead of the soul mastering the thing. That is what the teachings mean—avoidance of "attachment." And in this the occult teachers are clearly right. Desire is a frightful master—like fire it sweeps away the supports of the soul, leaving nothing but smoldering ashes. But, also like Fire, Desire is a splendid servant and by its harnessed power we are able to generate the steam of the Will and Activity, and to accomplish much in the world. Without proper Desire the world would be without activity. So do not make the mistake of using Desire any more than you would refuse to use fire—but in both cases keep the mastery in your own hands, and avoid allowing the control to pass from you to Desire.

Desire is the motivating force that runs the world; as little as we care to admit it in many cases. Look around you and see the effects of Desire in every human act, good or bad. As a writer has said: "Every deed that we do, good or bad, is prompted by Desire. We are charitable because we Desire to relieve our inner distress at the sight of suffering; or from the Desire of sympathy; or from the Desire to be respected in this world, or to secure a comfortable place in the next. One man is kind because he Desires to be kind—because it gives him satisfaction to be kind; while another man is cruel from precisely the same kind of motive. One man does his duty because he Desires to do it—he obtains a higher satisfaction from duty well done than he would from the neglecting of it in accordance with some weaker desires. The religious man is religious because his religious desires are stronger than his irreligious ones—because he finds a higher satisfaction in religion than in the pursuits of the worldly-minded. The moral man is moral because his moral desires are stronger than his immoral ones—he obtains a greater satisfaction in being moral than in being the contrary. Everything we do is prompted by Desire in some shape or form—high or low. Man cannot be Desireless and act in any way. Desire is the motivating power behind all actions—it is a natural law of life. Everything from the atom to the monad; from the monad to the insect; from the insect to man; from man to Nature, acts and does things by reason of the power and force of Desire, the Animating Motive."

All the above at the first glance would seem to make of man a mere machine, subject to the power of any stray desire that might happen to come into his mind. But this is far from being so. Man acts not upon EVERY desire, but upon the STRONGEST Desire, or the Average of his Strongest Desires. This Average of Desires is that which constitutes his Nature or Character. And here is where the Mastery of the "I" comes in! Man need not be a slave or creature of his Desires if he will assert his Mastery. He may control, regulate, govern and guide his Desires in any directions that he pleases. Nay, more, he may even CREATE DESIRES by an action of his Will, as we shall see presently. By a knowledge of psychological laws he may neutralize unfavorable Desires, and grow and develop—yes, practically Create New Desires in their place—all by the power of his Will, aided by the light of his Reason and Judgment. Man is the Master of his Mind.

"Yes," but some close reasoning critic may object; "yes, that is true enough, but even in that case is not Desire the ruling motive—must not one Desire to create these new Desires before he can do so—is not Desire always precedent to action?" Very close reasoning this, good friends, but all advanced occultists know that there is a point in which the Principle of Desire shades and merges into companion Principle, Will, and that a close reasoner and mental analyst may imagine a mental state in which one may be almost said to manifest a WILL to Will, rather than to merely Desire to Will. This state must be experienced before it can be understood—words cannot express it.

We have stated that it was in the power of man to Create Desire—not only to be its master when created, but also to actually Create it by bringing it into being. And the statement is absolutely true, and is verified and proven by the most recent experiments and discoveries of modern psychology. Instead of man being a creature of Desire—and this indeed he is in many cases—he may become Master of Desire and even a Creator of it. By knowledge and Will he may reverse the ordinary order of things and, displacing the intruder from the throne, he may seat himself there in his rightful place, and then bid the late occupant to do his will and obey his bidding. But the best way for the new occupant of the throne to bring about a reorganized court is to dismiss the old objectionable creatures of his mind and create new ones in their places. And here is how it may be done: In the first place, one must think carefully over the tasks that he wishes to accomplish, then, using his judgment carefully, judicially and impartially—impersonally so far as is possible—he must take mental stock of himself and see in what points he is deficient, so far as the successful accomplishment of the task is concerned. Then let him analyze the task before him, in detail, separating the matter into as many clear defined divisions as possible, so that he may be able to see the Thing as It Is, in detail as well as in its entirety. Then let him take a similar inventory of the things, which seem necessary of the accomplishment of the task—not the details that will arise only as the work progresses, day by day—but the general things, which must be done in order that the task is brought to a successful conclusion. Then having taken stock of the task, the nature of the undertaking, and one's own qualifications and shortcomings—then Begin to Create Desire, according to the following plan: The first step in the Creation of Desire is that of the forming of a clear, vital Mental Image of the qualities, things and details of the undertaking, as well as of the Completed Whole. By a Mental Image we mean a clear-cut, distinct mental picture in the Imagination of the things just named. Now, do not turn away with an impatient motion at the mention of the word Imagination. That is another word that you have only a mistaken idea of. Imagination means far more than the mere idle, fanciful use of that part of the mind that is believed by people to be "all there is to it." It isn't all, by a long way—in fact, the fanciful part may be said to be merely a shadow of the real Imaginative effort. Imagination is a real thing—it is a faculty of the mind by which it creates a matrix, mold, or pattern of things, which the trained Will and Desire afterward, materializes into objective reality. There has been nothing created by the hands and mind of man which did not have its first origin in the Imagination of someone. Imagination is the first step in Creation—whether of worlds or trifles. The mental pattern must always precede the material form. And so it is in the Creation of Desire. Before you can Create a Desire you must have a clear Mental Image of what you need to Desire.

You will find that this task of creating a Mental Image is a little harder than you had expected at the start. You will find it hard to form even a faint mental picture of that which you need. But be not discouraged, and persevere, for in this, as everything else, Practice makes perfect. Each time you try to form the Mental Image it will appear a little clearer and more distinct, and the details will come into a little more prominence. Do not tire yourself at first, but lay aside the task until later in the day, or tomorrow. But practice and persevere and your need becomes just as clear as a memory picture of something you have already seen. We shall have more to say on this subject of Mental Imagery and Imagination in subsequent lessons.

Then, after having acquired the clear Mental Image of the things you wish to Desire, and thus attain, cultivate the focusing of the Attention upon these things. The word attention is derived from the Latin word "Attendere," meaning "to stretch forth," the original idea being that in Attention the mind was "stretched forth," or "extended" toward the object of attention, and this is the correct idea for that is the way the mind operates in the matter. Keep the ideas before your attention as much as possible, so that the mind may take a firm grasp upon them, and make them a part of itself—by doing this you firmly impress the ideas upon the wax tablet of the mind.

Thus having fixed the idea clearly in your mind, by means of the Imagination and Attention, until as we have said, it becomes a fixture there, begin to cultivate an ardent DESIRE, LONGING, CRAVING DEMAND for the materialization of the things. Demand that you grow the qualities necessary for the task—demand that your mental pictures materialize—Demand that the details be manifested as well as the Whole, making allowance for the "something better" which will surely arise to take the place of the original details, as you proceed—the Inner Consciousness will attend to these things for you.

Then Desire firmly, confident, and earnestly. Be not half-hearted in your demands and desires—claim and demand the WHOLE THING, and feel confident that it will work out into material objectivity and reality. Think of it, dream of it, and always LONG for it—you must learn to want it the worst way—learn to "want it hard enough." You can attain and obtain many things by "wanting them hard enough"—the trouble with most of us is that we do not want things hard enough—we mistake vague cravings and wished for earnest, longing, demanding Desire and Want. Get to Desire and Demand the Thing just as you demand and Desire your daily meals. That is "wanting it the worst way." This is merely a hint—surely you can supply the rest, if you are in earnest, and "want to hard enough."

7

The Law of Attraction

There is in Nature a great Law—the Law of Attraction—by the operations of which all things—from atoms to men—are attracted toward each other in the degree of the common affinity of common use. The reverse of this law—which is merely another manifestation of its power—is what is called Repulsion, which is but the other pole of Attraction, and by the operations of which things tend to repel each other in the degree that they are unlike, opposing, and of no use to each other. The Law of Attraction is Universal, on all the planes of life, from the physical to the spiritual. Its operations are uniform and constant, and we may take the phenomena of one plane and thereby study the phenomena of another plane, for the same rule applies in each case—the same Law is in operation in the same way.

Beginning with the tiny corpuscles, electrons, or ions, of which the atoms are formed, we find manifested the Law of Attraction—certain electrons attract each other, and repel others still, thereby causing to spring into existing groups, combinations and colonies of electrons which being in agreement and harmony manifest and constitute what are called atoms, which until recently were supposed to be the primal form of matter. Passing on the atoms themselves, we find many degrees of affinity and attraction existing between them which cause them to combine and form into molecules of which all masses of matter consists. For instance, every drop of water is composed of countless molecules of water. And each molecule is composed of two atoms of Hydrogen and one atom of Oxygen—the combination always being the same in every molecule of water. Now, why do these atoms combine in just this way—the same invariable grouping and proportion? Not by chance, surely, for there is no such thing in Nature—there is a natural law back of every phenomenon. And in this case it is the Law of Attraction manifesting in the case of these atoms. And it is so in all chemical combinations—it is called Chemical Affinity. Sometimes an attached atom will come in contact with, or in proximity to, another atom, and then bang goes the explosion of the molecule as the atom flies away from its partners and into the arms of the other atom for which it has a greater affinity. There are marriages and divorces in the world of atoms, you will notice. And in the cases of the molecules, it is found that certain molecules are attracted to others of the same kind, under what is called Cohesion, and thus masses of matter are composed. A piece of gold, silver, tin, glass, or other form of matter is composed of countless molecules held together tightly by Cohesion—and this Cohesion is merely another form of the Law of Attraction—the same that draws all things together. And, underlying the Law of Attraction is to be found our old Principle of Desire and Will. You may shrug your shoulders at this mention of desire and Will in connection with electrons, atoms, molecules— all forms of matter, but just wait a bit and see what the leading scientific authorities have to say on the subject.

Prof. Haeckel, one of the world's greatest scientists—a materialist who would sneer at the teachings of Mental Science—even this man, naturally prejudiced against mentalist theories, finds himself compelled to say: "The idea of chemical affinity consists in the fact that the various chemical elements perceive the qualitative differences in other elements—experience pleasure of revulsion at contact with them, and execute specific movements on this ground." He also positively and distinctly states that in the atoms there must be something corresponding to Desire for contact and association with other atoms, and Will to enable the atom to respond to the Desire Law is constant throughout Nature, from atom to man—physical, mental and spiritual.

But what has all this to do with the Secret of Success you may ask? Simply, that the Law of Attraction is an important part in the Secret of Success, inasmuch as it tends to bring to us the things, persons and circumstances in accordance with our earnest Desire, Demand, and Will, just as it brings together the atoms and other particles of matter. Make yourself an atom of Living Desire and you will attract to yourself the person, things and circumstances fitting in with the accomplishment of your Desire. You will also get into rapport with those who are working along the same lines of thought, and will be attracted them and they to you, and you will be brought into relations with persons, things and environments likely to work out the problem of your Desires—you will get "next to" the right persons and things—all by the operation of this great natural Law of Attraction. No Necromancy or Magic about it at all—nothing supernatural or mysterious—just the operations of a great Natural Law.

You can do little by yourself in Life, be you ever so strong and able. Life is a complex thing, and individuals are interdependent upon each other for the doings of things. One Individual, segregated from all the other Individuals, could accomplish little or nothing along the lines of outer activity. He must form combinations, arrangements, harmonies and agreements with others, and in accordance with environments and things, that is, he must create and use the proper environments and things, and draw to himself others with whom he must form combinations, in order to do things. And these persons, things and environments come to him—and he to them—by reason of this great Law of Attraction. And the way he sets into operation this great Law of Attraction is by the operation of his Desire, and along the lines of Mental Imagery. Do you see the connection now? So be careful to form, cultivate and manifest the right Desires—hold to them firmly, strongly and constantly, and you will set into operation this great Law, which forms an important part of the Secret of Success.

Desire-Force is the motive power leading the activities of Life. It is the basic vital power, which animates the minds of living things and urges them forth to action. Without strong Desire no one accomplishes anything worthy of the name—and the greater the desire the greater will be the amount of energy generated and manifested, everything else being equal. That is to say, that given a dozen men of equal intellect, physical health and mental activity—equal in everything else except Desire, in short, the ones in whom the greatest Desire resides and is manifested will outstrip the others in attainment—and of these winners the one in who Desire burns like an unquenchable flame will be the one who will Master the others by the force of his primitive elementary power.

Not only does Desire give to the man that inward motive which leads to the enfoldment of the power within himself, but it does more than this; it causes to radiate from him the finer and more subtle mental and vital forces of his nature, which, flowing forth in all directions like the magnetic waves from the magnet, or the electric waves from the dynamo, influencing all who come within the field of force. Desire-Force is a real, active, effective force of Nature, and serves to attract, draw and bring to a center that which is in line with the nature of the Desire. The much talked of Law of Attraction, of which so much is heard in Mental Science and the New Thought, depends largely upon the force and power of Desire. Desire-Force is at the center of the Law of Attraction. There is a tendency in Nature to attract and draw to the center of a Desire the things, which are needed to fulfill that Desire. One's "own will come to him" by reason of his natural force, which lies behind and underneath the entire phenomena of Mental Influence. This being so, does it not become at once apparent why one who wishes to accomplish anything should be sure to create a strong Desire for it, and at the same time be sure to acquire the art of

Visualization so as to form a clear Mental Picture of the thing Desired—a clear mold in which the materialized reality may manifest?

Have you ever come in contact with any of the great men of modern business life? If you have seen these people in action, you will have become conscious of a subtle, mysterious something about them—a something that you could actually feel—a something that seemed to draw you to fit in to their schemes, planes, and desires almost by an irresistible force. These people are all people of the strongest kind of Desire—their Desire-Force manifests strongly and affects those with whom they come in contact. Not only this, but their Desire-Force flows from them in great waves, which occultists inform us soon manifests a circular, or whirlpool-like motion, swinging around and around the center of the Desire—these men become actual cyclones of Desire into which nearly everything that comes within its sweep is affected and swept into the vortex. Have we not evidences of this in the cases of all the great leaders of men—can we not see the operation of that mighty law of attraction which brings to them their own? We are apt to call this Willpower, and so it is in a way, back and under the Will in such cases is to be found the ardent, burning Desire that is the motive force of the attractive power.

This Desire-Force is a primitive, elemental thing. It is found in the animal kingdom, and among the lower races of men, perhaps more clearly than among the higher types of men, but only because in such instances it is seen stripped of the covering, sheaths, disguises and masks that surround the more civilized forms and planes of life. But remember this well, the same principle is manifested under and beneath the polished veneer of civilized life—the Desire-Force of the cultured leader of men is as elemental as that animating the fierce and shaggy caveman or the wild Berserker who, naked and half-mad, rushed upon overwhelming hordes of his enemy, brushing them aside like flies—that is, if you will but look beneath the polished surface. In the old wild days Desire manifested its force on the physical plane—now it manifests on the Mental Plane—that is the only difference, the Force is the same in both cases.

While we write, there has just been produced on stage a new play that illustrates this principle. The heroine, the daughter of an old New York family of high social standing and wealth, has a dream of her life in a former incarnation, in which she sees herself torn from the arms of her cave-dweller father by the mighty arms of a fierce savage chief, whose desire is manifested through the physical. She awakens from her dream, and to her horror soon discovers the face of her dream-captor on a man who comes into her father's life in New York. This man comes from the West, forceful, resourceful and desirous, beating down all before him in the game of finance. As of old, he places his foot not on the neck of his enemies—but on the mental-plane, this time, instead of the physical. The same old Desire for power is strong within him—the same old masterfulness manifests itself. This man says: "I have never quit; I have never been afraid." The same old Desire then flamed up in the savage now manifests in the Master of Wall Street, and between the force of its Attraction and the coupled and allied force of his Will, he repeats the performances of his previous incarnation—but on the plane of mental forces and achievement this time—mind, not muscle, being the instrument through which the Desire manifests.

We give the above example merely as an illustration of the fact that Desire is the motivating force that moves the Will into action, and which causes the varied activity of life, men and things. Desire-Force is a real power in life, and influences not only tracts, influences and compels other persons and things to swing in toward the center of the Desire sending forth the currents. In the Secret of Success, Desire plays a prominent part. Without a Desire for Success, there is no Success, none. The Law of Attraction is set into motion by Desire. The majority of the principles advanced in this book have been in the nature of Positive injunctions—that is, you have been urged to do certain things rather than to not do the opposite or contrary. But here we come to a place in which the advice must be given along the negative lines—we must urge you not to do a certain thing. We allude to that great poison of the mind and Will known as Fear. We do not allude to physical fear—important though physical courage may be, and as regrettable as physical cowardice may be considered, still it is not a part of the purpose of this book to preach against the latter and advise a cultivation of the former quality—you will find much of that elsewhere. Our purpose here is to combat that subtle, insidious enemy of true Self-Expression which appears in the shape and guise of mental fear, forebodings which may be considered as Negative Thought just as the other principles mentioned in this work may be considered as Positive Thought.

Fear thought is that condition of the mind in which everything is seen through blue glasses—in which everything seems to bring a sense of the futility of endeavor—the "I Can't" principle of mentality, as contrasted with the "I Can and I Will" mental attitude. It is the noxious weed in the mental garden, which tends to kill the valuable plants to be found therein. It is the fly in the ointment—the spider in the cup of the Wine of Life. So far as we know the first person to use the word "Fear-Thought"—which has now passed into common use—was Horace Fletcher, the well-known writer, who coined it to supplant the use of the word "Worry" in a certain sense. He had pointed out that Anger and Worry were the two great hindrances to a well-balanced, advanced and progressive mentality, but many misunderstood him and urged that to abolish Worry meant to cease taking any consideration of the morrow—a lack of common prudence and forethought. And so Fletcher coined the word "Fear-Thought" to express a phase of his idea of "Forethought without Worry," and he entitled his second book on the subject, "Happiness, as found in Forethought minus Fear-Thought," a very happy expression of a very happy idea. Fletcher also was the first to advance the idea that Fear was not a thing-in-itself, but merely an expression of Fear-Thought—a manifestation of the state of mind known as Fear-Thought. He and others who have written on the subject, have taught that Fear might be abolished by the practice of abolishing Fear-Thought from the mind—by driving it out of the mental chamber—and the best teachers have taught that the best way to drive out Fear (or any other undesirable mental state) was by cultivating the thought of the opposite quality of mind by compelling the mind to dwell upon the mental picture of the desirable quality, and by the appropriate auto-suggestions. The illustration has often been stated that the way to drive darkness from a room is not to shovel it out, but to throw open the shutters and let the sunlight stream in, and that is the best way to neutralize Fear-Thought.

The mental process has aptly been spoken of as "vibrations," a figure that has a full warrant in modern science. Then, by raising the vibration to the Positive pitch, the negative vibrations may be counteracted. By cultivating the qualities recommended in the other lessons of this book. Fear-Thought may be neutralized. The poison of Fear-Thought is insidious and subtle, but it slowly creeps through the veins until it paralyzes all useful efforts and action, until the heart and brain are affected and find it difficult to throw it off. Fear-Thought is at the bottom of the majority of failures and "going down" in life. As long as a man keeps his nerve and confidence in himself, he is able to rise to his feet after each stumble, and face the enemy resolutely—but let him feel the effects of Fear-Thought to such an extent that he cannot throw it off and he will fail to rise and will perish miserable. "There is nothing to fear except Fear," has well been said.

We have spoken elsewhere about the Law of Attraction, which operates in the direction of attracting to us, that which we Desire. But there is a reverse side to this—it is a poor rule that will not work both ways. Fear will set into motion the Law of Attraction just as well as Desire. Just as Desire draws to one the things he pictures in his mind as the Desired Thing, so will Fear draw to him the thing pictured in his mind as the Thing Feared. "The thing that I feared hath befallen me." And the reason is very simple, and the apparent contradiction vanishes when we examine the matter. What is the pattern upon which the Law of Attraction builds under the force of Desire? The Mental

Image, of course. And so it is in the case of Fear—the person carries about the Mental Image or haunting picture of the Feared Thing, and the Law of Attraction brings it to him just as it brings the Desired Thing. Did you ever stop to think that Fear was the negative pole of Desire? The same laws work in both cases.

So avoid Fear-Thought as you would the poisonous draught that you know would cause your blood to become black and thick, and your breathing labored and difficult. It is a vile thing, and you should not rest content until you have expelled it from your mental system. You can get rid of it by Desire and Will, coupled with the holding of the Mental Image of Fearlessness. Drive it up by cultivating its opposite. Change your polarity. Raise your mental vibrations. Someone has said, "There is no Devil but Fear"—then send that Devil back to the place where he properly belongs, for if you entertain him hospitably he will make your heaven a hell in order that he may feel at home. Use the mental Big Stick on him.

8

Personal Magnetism

We hear much about Personal Magnetism these days. It is a peculiar quality of the mental being of the individual that serves to bring other persons into a mood or state of mind sympathetic with that of the magnetic person. Some men have this quality developed to a wonderful extent, and are able to bring about a harmonious agreement on the part of other persons in a short time, while others are almost entirely deficient in this respect and their very presence tends to arouse antagonism in the minds of others. The majority of people accept the idea of Personal Magnetism without question, but few will agree upon any theory attempting to account for it. Those who have studied the matter carefully know that the whole thing depends upon the mental states of the individual, and upon his ability to cause others to "catch" his mental vibrations. This "catching" is caused by what is known as Mental Induction. Induction, you know, is "that property or quality, or process by which one body having electrical or magnetic polarity produces it in another without direct contact." And Mental Induction is a manifestation of similar phenomena on the mental plane. People's mental states are "catching" or "contagious," and if one infuses enough life and enthusiasm into his mental states they will affect the minds of persons with whom they come in contact. We have explained this matter in detail in the little book of this series entitled, "Mental Influence. "

It seems to us that the prime factor in successful Mental Induction, or manifestations of Personal Magnetism, is Enthusiasm. In another lesson in this book we have told you about Enthusiasm, and when you think of Personal Magnetism, it will be well for you to read what we have said about Enthusiasm also. Enthusiasm gives Earnestness to the person, and there is no mental state so effective as Earnestness. Earnestness makes itself felt strongly, and will often make a person give you attention in spite of himself. Walter D. Moody, a well-known writer on the subject of Salesmanship, says, truthfully, "It will be found that all men possessed of personal magnetism are very much in earnest. Their intense earnestness is magnetic." And nearly every student of the subject has noted this fact. But the earnestness must be more that a firm, confident, honest belief in the thing being presented to the attention of the other person. It must be a live, contagious earnestness, which can best be described as Enthusiasm—Enthusiastic Earnestness, that's the term.

This Enthusiastic Earnestness has much emotion in it—it appeals to the Emotional side of human nature, rather that to the Thinking-Reasoning side. And yet an argument based upon reason and conducted upon logical principles, may be presented with Enthusiastic Earnestness with much greater effect than if the appeal to the reason is conducted in a cold, unemotional way. The average person is so constituted mentally that he thaws out under a manifestation of live, enthusiastic "feeling," under the term of Personal Magnetism. The "feeling" side of mentality is as important as the "thinking" side—and it is far more common and universal, for the majority of people really think very little, while everyone "feels."

A writer in the "early seventies" of the last century said: "All of us emit a sphere, aura, or halo, impregnated with the very essence of ourselves; sensitive knows it; so do our dogs and other pets; so does a hungry lion or tiger; aye, even flies, snakes and the insects, as we know to our cost. Some of us are magnetic—others not. Some of us are warm, attractive, love inspiring and friendship making, while others are cold, intellectual, thoughtful, reasoning, but not magnetic. Let a learned man of the latter type address an audience and it will soon tire of his intellectual discourse, and will manifest symptoms of drowsiness. He talks at them, but not into them—he makes them think, not feel, which is most tiresome to the majority of persons, and few speakers succeed who attempt to merely make people think—they want to be made to feel. People will pay liberally to be made to feel or laugh, while they will begrudge a dime for instruction or talk that will make them think. Pitted against a learned man of the type mentioned above, let there be a half-educated, but very loving, ripe and mellow man, with but nine-tenths of the logic and erudition of the first man, yet such a man carries along his crowd with perfect ease, and everybody is wide-awake, treasuring up every good thing that falls from his lips. The reasons are palpable and plain. It is heart against head; soul against logic; and is bound to win every time."

If you will notice the man and woman who are considered the most "magnetic," you will find that almost invariably they are people who have what is called "soul" about them—that is, they manifest and induce "feeling," or emotion. They manifest traits of character and nature similar to that manifested by actors and actresses. They throw out a part of themselves, which seems to affect those coming in contact with them. Notice a non-magnetic actor, and you will see that although he may be letter perfect in his part, and may have acquired the proper mannerisms, gestures and other technical parts of his art, still he lacks a "certain something," and that something may be seen to be the ability to communicate "feeling." Now, those who are in on the secret know full well that many of the successful actors, who seem to burn with passion, feeling and emotion on the stage, really feel but little of these qualities while acting—they are like phonographs, giving off sounds that have been registered in them. But if you will investigate still further, you will see that in studying their parts and practicing the same privately, these people induced a stimulated emotion, such as the part called for, and held it firmly in their minds, accompanying it with the appropriate gestures, etc., until it became firmly "set" there—impressed upon the tablets of the mentality as the record of a phonograph is likewise impressed upon the wax. Then, when afterward they played the part, the outward semblance of the feelings, with the motions, gestures, emphasis, etc., reproduced itself and impressed the audience. It is said that if an actor allows himself to be actually carried away with his part so that he feels the same keenly, the result will not be advantageous, for he is overcome with the feeling and its effect is upon himself rather than upon his audience. The best result is said to be obtained when one has first experienced and felt the emotion, and then afterward reproduces it in the manner above stated, without allowing it to control him.

We mention the above facts for the use of those who do not naturally possess the faculty or quality of Personal magnetism to the required degree. Such people will find it to their advantage to endeavor to work up the desired feeling of Enthusiastic Earnestness, in private, fixing the mental impression by frequent private rehearsals and practice, until it becomes registered in their "habit mind," to be reproduced upon occasions when needed. Be a good actor—that is the advice in such cases; and remember this, that frequent practice and private rehearsal makes the good actor. It is a far better thing to be able to induce feeling and enthusiasm in this way, rather than be lacking of it, on the one hand; or to be an "emotional inebriate" on the other hand. One may be rationally Enthusiastically Earnest, without being filled full of "slushy gush" or maudlin emotionalism. We think that the careful student will see just what is meant here, and will not misunderstand us. And remember, that through this repeated "acting" the desired quality will often become real and "natural."

9

Attractive Personality

We have explained in our lesson on "Individuality" that what is known, as the "Personality" was not the real "I" of the Individual, but that instead it formed the "Me" part of oneself—the outward appearance of the Individual. As we have told you, the word Personality really means the "mask" aspect of the Individual, the outward appearance of the part in the great drama of life that he is playing. And just as the actor may change his mask and costume, so may the Individual change, alter and replace his Personality by other features found desirable.

But nevertheless, while the Personality is not the real "I," it plays an important part in the drama of life, particularly as the audience pays more attention to the Personality, as a rule, than it does to the real Individual behind the mask. And so it is proper that every Individual should cultivate and acquire a Personality that will prove attractive to his audience, and render him acceptable to them. No, we are not preaching deception—we regard Individuality as the Real Self, and believe that one should build himself up to his highest and best according to the laws of Individual Unfoldment—but, nevertheless, so long as one must wear a Personality about him as he goes through life, we believe that it is not only to his advantage, but is also his duty to make that Personality as pleasing and attractive as he is able to. You know that no matter how good, intelligent and high-minded a man may be, if he wears the mask of an unattractive and unpleasant Personality he is placed at a disadvantage, and drives away people whom he might benefit and who would be glad to love him if they could see behind his unattractive mask.

Nor are we speaking of one's personal physical appearance when we speak of unattractive and attractive masks. While one's physical appearance goes a good way in some cases, there is a charm of Personality that far transcends that fleeting appearance. There are many persons having beautiful faces and forms whose personality is far from charming, and who repel rather than attract. And there are others whose faces are homely and whose forms are far from shapely, who have, nevertheless, that "winning way about them" that attracts others to them. There are people whom we are always glad to see, and whose charm of manner makes us forget that they are not beautiful, in fact, even their homely faces seem to become transfigured when we are in their presence. That is what we meant by Personality, in the same way in which we are now using it. It bears a very close relationship to "Personal Magnetism," of which we spoke of in our preceding lesson.

One of the first things that should be cultivated by those wishing to develop the Charm of Personality is a mental atmosphere of Cheerfulness. There is nothing so invigorating as the presence of a cheerful person—nothing so dispiriting as one of those Human Wet Blankets that cast a chill over everyone and everything with whom they come in contact. Think of your acquaintances and you will find that you will naturally place them in two classes—the Cheerful ones and the Gloomy ones. Sunny Jim is always preferred to Gloomy Gus—the one you will welcome, and the other you will fly from. The Japanese understand this law of Personality, and one of the first things that they teach their children is to preserve a cheerful, sunny exterior, no matter if their hearts are breaking. With them it is considered one of the most flagrant offenses against good form to carry their sorrows, grief and pain into the presence of others. They reserve that side of their life for the privacy of their own chamber—to the outside world they present always a happy, sunny smile. And in this they are wise, for a number of reasons: (1) that they may induce a more buoyant and positive state of mind in themselves; (2) that they may attract cheerful persons and things to them by the Law of Attraction; and (3) that they may present an attractive Personality to others, and thereby be welcome and congenial associates and participants in the work of life. There is little welcome or help for the Gloomy Gus tribe in everyday business life—they are avoided as a pestilence—everyone has troubles enough of his own without those of other people added thereto.

Remember the old lines:

> Laugh and the world laughs with you;
> Weep and you weep alone.
> For this sad old earth is in need of mirth,
> And has troubles enough of its own.

So cultivate the Smile that Won't Come Off. It is a valuable asset of Personality. Not the silly, idiotic grin, but the Smile that means something—the

Real Thing. And such a smile comes from within, and is more that skin deep. If you want a Verbal Pattern upon which to model the mental state that will produce this outward appearance of Personality, here it is: "BRIGHT, CHEERFUL, AND HAPPY." FRAME IT AND HANG it in a prominent place in your Mental Art Gallery. Commit it to memory and Visualize it, so that you may be able to see it before you like an illuminated electric sign—"BRIGHT, CHEERFUL AND HAPPY"—then endeavor to materialize the idea into reality within your mind. Think it out—act it out—and it will become real to you. Then will you have Something Worthwhile in the shape of Personality? This may seem simple and childish to you—but if you will work it out into actuality, it will be worth thousands of dollars to you, no matter what walk of life you may be in.

Another valuable bit of Personality is that of Self Respect. If you have real Self Respect it will manifest itself in your outward demeanor and appearance. If you don't have it, you had better start in and cultivate the appearance of Self Respect, and then Remember that you are a MAN, or a WOMAN, as the case may be, and not a poor, crawling Worm on the Dust of a Human Door Mat. Face the world firmly and fearlessly, keeping your eyes well to the front. HOLD UP YOUR HEAD! There is nothing like a stiff backbone and a raised head for meeting the world. The man with bent head seems to apologize for living and being on the earth—and the world is apt to take such at their own valuation. An erect head enables one to walk past the dragons at the door of Success. A writer gives the following good advice on this subject: "Hold your ear lobes directly over your shoulders, so that a plumb line hung from the ears describes the line of your body. Be sure also not to carry the head either to the right or left, but vertical. Many men make the mistake, especially while waiting for a customer to finish some important piece of business, of leaning the head to the right or left. This indicates weakness. A study of men discloses the fact that the strong men never tilt the head. Their heads sit perfectly straight on strong necks. Their shoulders, held easily, yet firmly, in position, are inspiring in their strength—indicating poise. Every line of the body, in other words, denotes the thought of the bearer." The value of this advice lies not only in the fact that it gives to you the "appearance" of Self Respect (no trifling matter, by the way), but also that it tends to cultivate a corresponding mental state within you. For just as "Thought takes form in Action," so do Actions develop mental states— it is a rule that works both ways. So think Self Respect and act Self Respect. Let the "I AM" within you manifest itself. Don't crawl—don't cringe—don't grovel—but do be a Real Human Being. Another bit of Personality worth cultivating is the Art of Taking an Interest in Others. Many people go through the world so wrapped up in their own affairs that they convey the impression of being "apart" and aloof from others with whom they come in contact. This mental state manifests in a most unpleasant form of Personality. Such people are not only regarded as "cold" and lacking heart and soul, but they also give others the impression of selfishness and hardness, and the public is apt to let such a person alone—to leave him to his own selfish moods and mental states. Such a one never becomes popular—never becomes a good mixer among men. Taking an Interest in Others is an art that well repays the student of Success to cultivate it. Of course one must always keep the main chance before him and not allow his own interests to suffer by reason of his interest in others—that goes without saying, for unreasonable altruism is just as one-sided as undue selfishness. But there is a middle course. You will find something of interest in every person with whom you come in contact, and if you will but turn your attention to that interest it will manifest itself in such a way that the person will be conscious of it, will appreciate it, and will be glad to respond by taking an interest in you. This is not deceit, or time serving, or flattery—it is the Law of Compensation working on the mental plane—you get what you give. If you will stop and think a moment you will find that the people whose Personality seems the most attractive to you are the people who seem to Take an Interest in your own personality.

This Taking an Interest in Others manifests itself in many ways, one of which is in making you a Good Listener. Now, we do not mean that you should allow yourself to be made a dumping ground for all the talk of all the people with whom you come in contact—if you do this you will have time for nothing else. You must use ordinary judgment and tact in regulating the time you give to others, depending upon the person and the particular circumstances of the case. What we do mean is that while you're listening you should Listen Well. There is no subtler compliment that one person can pay to another than Listening Well to him or her. To Listen Well is to Listen with Interest. And that is something that cannot be very well taught in a book. Perhaps the best way to express the idea is to say, "Listen as you Would be Listened unto." The Golden Rule may be applied to many things and ideas, with benefit and good results. The man who listens well is well thought of by those to whom he listens. In this connection we are always reminded of the old story of Carlyle, who, as everyone knows, was reputed to be a crusty, crabby old chap, prone to sarcastic remarks and brusque treatment of those with whom he engaged in conversation. The tale goes that one day a man called upon Carlyle—and the man understood the Art of Listening Well. He so turned the conversations as to get Carlyle started on a subject dear to his heart—and then he kept quiet and Listened Well. Carlyle talked "a straight streak" for several hours, and grew quite enthusiastic over his topic. When at last the visitor arose to depart, he was forced to actually tear himself away from Carlyle, who, following him to the door, manifested unusual enthusiasm and good spirits, and bidding him good-bye, said warmly: "Come again, mon—come again and often—ye have a wonderfully bright mind, and I've enjoyed your conversation very much indeed—ye are a most delightful conversationalist."

Be careful not to bore people with your personal experiences—better forget your personal self in talking to others, except when it is right to the point to bring yourself in. People do not want to hear what a wonderful fellow you are—they want to tell you what wonderful people they are, which is very much more pleasant to them. Don't retail your woes, nor recite your many points of excellence. Don't tell what a wonderful baby you have—the other people have babies of their own to think about. You must endeavor to talk about things of interest to the other person, if he wants to do the talking himself. Forget yourself and Take and Interest in the Other Person.

Some of the best retail merchants impress upon their salespeople the advantage of cultivating the mental attitude and personality that you will give the customer the impression that you are "on his side of the counter"—that is, that you are taking a personal interest in his being well-served, suited, well-treated and satisfied. The salesman who is able to create that impression is well advanced on the road to success in his particular line. This is a difficult thing to describe, but a little observation and thought and practice along the lines laid down in the preceding lessons will do much for you in this direction. A recent writer truthfully says on this subject: "Suppose, for instance, you are in trade or a profession, and wish to increase your business. It will not do, when you sell goods or services, to make the matter a merely perfunctory transaction, taking the customer's money, giving him good value and letting him go away feeling that you have no interest in the matter beyond giving him a fair deal and profiting thereby. Unless he feels that you have a personal interest in him and his needs, and that you are honestly desirous to increase his welfare, you have made a failure and are losing ground. When you can make every customer feel that you are really trying to advance his interests as well as you own, your business will grow. It is not necessary to give premiums, or heavier weights, or better values than others give to accomplish this; it is done by putting life and interest into every transaction, however small." This writer has stated the idea clearly, forcibly and truthfully, and you will do well to heed his advice and to put it into actual practice.

Another important point in Personality is Self-Control, particularly in the matter of Keeping your Temper. Anger is a mark of weakness, not of strength. The man who loses his temper immediately places himself at a disadvantage. Remember the old saying: "Those whom the gods would destroy, they first make angry." Under the influence of anger a man does all sorts of foolish things that he afterwards regrets. He throws judgment, experience and caution to the winds, and acts like a crazy man. In fact, anger is a sort of madness—a phase of insanity—if you doubt this look carefully at the face of the first angry man you meet and see how irrational he looks and acts. It is a well-known fact that if one keeps cool while his opponent is angry, he has decidedly the best of the matter—for he is a sane man dealing with an irrational one. It is the better policy to allow the other fellow to "stew in his own fat" of anger, keeping cool yourself at the same time. It is a comparatively easy matter to cool down an angry man without becoming angry with you—and as it takes two to make a quarrel, the matter is soon over. You will find that a control of the outward expression will give you control of you inner mental state. You will find that if you are able to control your voice, keeping it calm, steady and low-pitched, you will not fly into a passion, and more than this, you will find by so doing that the voice of the other fellow will gradually come down from its loud, boister- ous tones, and in the end both of you will be pitching your voices in the same key—and you have set that key-note. This is worth remembering—this control of the voice—it is a secret well worth knowing and practicing.

While we are on the subject of voice, we would like to call your attention to a further control of voice, or rather a cultivation of voice. A man having a well-controlled, even, pleasant voice has an advantage over others having equal abilities in other directions, but lacking that one quality. The value of a vi- brant, resonant, soft and flexible voice is great. If you have such a voice, you are blessed. If you lack it, why start to work and cultivate it. Oh, yes, you can! Did you ever hear of Nathan Sheppard, the well-known public speaker? Then listen to these words of his, telling of his natural disadvantages of voice, and how he overcame them and became a great speaker. He says: "When I made up my mind to devote my mind and body to public speaking, I was told by my teach- ers and governors that I would certainly fail; that my articulation was a failure, and it was; that my organs of speech were inadequate, and they were; and that if I would screw up my little mouth it could be put into my mother's thimble, and it could. Stinging words these certainly were, and cruel ones. I shall never forget them; possibly, however, they stung me into a persistency that I would have never known but for these words. At all events, that is the philosophy of the 'self made' world of mankind. I may not have accomplished much; I do not claim to have accomplished much. It is something I have made a living out of,

my art for twenty years, and that I do claim to have done in spite of every obstacle and every discouragement, by turning my will upon my voice and vocal
organs, by cultivating my elocutionary instincts and my ear for the cadences
of rhetoric, by knowing what I and my voice and my feelings were about, by
making the most of myself." After these words, anything that we might add
regarding the possibility of acquiring a good voice by will, practice and desire
would be superfluous. Pick out the kind of voice that you think best adapted
to your work, and then cultivate it by practice, determination and desire. If
Mr. Sheppard could become a famous public speaker with such obstacles as
these, then for you to say "but I can't" is to stamp you as a weakling.

It has been suggested to us that we have a few words to say regarding the
carriage or physical bearing of the person, as an important part of Personality—
particularly in the phase of Walking. But we do not think that is necessary to
add to what we have said in this lesson regarding the subject, in connection
with what we have also said regarding the mental state of Self Respect. The
main thing is to cultivate the Mental State of Self Respect, and the rest will
follow as a natural consequence. Thought takes form in Action, and the man
who has Self Respect imbedded in his mind will surely so carry and demean
him that he will give evidence of his mental state in his every physical action,
gesture, carriage and motion. He must have it within, as well as without. One
must pay attention to the exterior aspect of course, particularly in the matter
of dress. One should cultivate Cleanliness and Neatness, of both body and
clothing. To be well dressed does not mean to me showily clad—in fact, the
person who is best dressed is inconspicuously dressed. Cultivate a quiet, refined
taste, expressed in quality rather than in showiness. And above all—be Clean.

In conclusion, let us impress upon you again and again that which we call
Personality is but the outer mask of the Individual Within. The mask may be
changed by an effort of the Will, aided by an intelligent discrimination. First
find out what kind of Personality you should have, and then set to work to
cultivate it—to grow it, in fact. Form the Mental Image of what you want to
be—then think of it—desire it ardently—will that you shall have it—then Act
It Out, over and over again; rehearsal after rehearsal, until you will actually
materialize your ideal into objective reality. Make a good mental pattern or
mold, and then pour in your mental material steadily, and slowly! From the
mold will come forth the Character and Personality that you desire and need.
Then polish up this newborn Personality until it becomes radiant with the
brightness of Culture.

You can be what you want to be—if you only want to hard enough. Desire
is the mother of the Actuality. Remember once more the old rule—EARNEST

DESIRE—CONFIDENT EXPECTATION—FIRM RESOLVE—these are the three things that lead to ACCOMPLISHMENT. And now that we have given you this little Secret of Success—USE IT. "It is Up to You" to "Make Good." We have "pressed the button—you must do the rest!"

Afterword

On reading the foregoing pages after they have been set up in type, we are impressed with the idea that in spite of our determination, as expressed in the first few pages, not to attempt to lay down a code or rules or a course of conduct which should be considered as an infallible Guide to Success—in spite of our vowed determination not to pose as a teacher or preacher—we have nevertheless managed to do considerable in the direction of "laying down the law" so far as is concerned naming of things to be done, or avoided.

However, we feel that the advice given is good, and that the various examples quoted are calculated to arouse within the mind of the reader the Spirit that leads to Success. And, with this thought, we send forth these pages to those who may attract them to themselves, or who may be attracted to them— under the Law of Attraction. But we feel that we shall not have completed our task unless we, once more, remind the reader that Success is not to be gained by a blind and slavish following of anyone's rules or advice, our own any more than any other persons. There is no Royal Road to Success—no Patent Process by which the unsuccessful are to be magically transformed into Captains of Industry or Magnates of Wall Street. There is nothing more amusing, or pitiful, according to how one views it, than the bulk of Success Talk given to the public by self-appointed teachers and preachers. There is no one who can in a few pages point out to seekers after Success an infallible method whereby each and everyone may attain the Success and Attainment that their hearts crave. It is a cold, hard truth that each and every man must work out his own salvation in the matter of Success. Rules and advice may greatly assist—and they undoubtedly do this—but the individual must accomplish the real work. He must carve out his own Destiny, and there is no power above or below that will do the work for him if he refuses to perform it himself.

The old saying that "God helps him who helps himself" is true in more senses than one. It is true in the sense that the Higher Aid seems to refuse to come to the assistance of one who is not willing to strike out for him and do his best. But it is true in another sense—this Aid does come to one who will throw heart and soul into the task set before him, and who will do each days work the best he know how, with hope in his soul, and a confident expectation of better things right ahead, around the turn of the road. The wise man is the one who takes courageously the step right ahead of him, planting his foot firmly and confidently upon it, although he is unable to see further ahead. To such a one step after step is illuminated as he proceeds, and he reaches his goal, whereas the shrinking ones, who have feared to take the obvious step because they could not see beyond it, are still waiting for something to turn up. This waiting business is a poor policy—as Garfield said: "Don't wait for something to turn up—go out and turn something up." Take the step before you boldly and hopefully, and the next step will then appear. The thing to do is that which lies right before you to be done—do it the best you know how, feeling assured that in its doing you will be making progress toward the better things for which your heart has been longing. New ideas come while you are in action—in the doing of things comes the inspiration for the doing of greater things. You can always get a better "running start" when in action, which will give you an advantage over the best "standing start" imaginable. Get into action and motion.

In this little work we have endeavored to call your attention to something of far greater importance than a mere code of rules and general advice. We have pointed out to you the glorious fact that within each of you there is a Something Within, which if once aroused would give you a greatly increased power and capacity. And so we have tried to tell you this story of the Something Within, from different viewpoints, so that you might catch the idea in several ways. We firmly believe that Success depends most materially upon a recognition and manifestation of this Something Within—we think that a study of the character and work of all successful men will show you that differ as they do in personal characteristics, they all manifest that consciousness of that Something Within them that gives them an assurance of Inward Power and Strength, from which proceeds Courage and Self-Confidence. You will find that the majority of successful men feel that there is a Something helping them—back of and behind their efforts. Some have called this Thing by the name of "Luck" or "Destiny," or some such term. But it is all a form of the same recognition of an Inward Power that they are "helped" in some way, although they are not quite sure of the nature of the helper—in fact, the majority of them do not stop to speculate upon its nature, they are too busy and are content with the knowledge that It is there. This Something Within is the Individual—the "I" in each of them—the source of the power which men manifest when they express it.

And this little book is written in the hopes that to many it may be the first step toward the recognition, unfoldment and manifestation of this Inward Power.

We earnestly urge upon you to cultivate this "I AM" consciousness—that you may realize the Power Within you. And then there will come naturally to you the correlated consciousness which expresses itself in the statement, "I CAN and I WILL," one of the grandest affirmations of Power that man can make. This "I Can and I Will" consciousness is that expression of the Something Within, which we trust that you will realize and manifest. We feel that behind all the advice that we can give you, this one thing is the PRIME FACTOR in the Secret of Success.

THE HUNGER OF
THE SOUL

The soul, as well as the body and mind, requires nourishment—The want, a promise of the fulfillment—The law of unfoldment—Nourishment provided when it is needed—Provided for in the Divine Plan—The feast of good things.

The Soul, as well as the body and the mind, requires nourishment. We have felt that hunger for spiritual knowledge which transcended our hunger for bread—exceeded our craving for mental sustenance. We have felt soul-hungry and knew not with what to appease it. The Soul has cried out for food. It has been fed upon the husks of the physical plane for so long that it is fairly starving for the proper nourishment. It seeks this way and that way for the Bread of Life and finds it not. It has asked this authority and that authority for information as to where this food may be had—where could be obtained the food that would nourish the Soul—but it has been given nothing but the stone of Dogma and Creeds. At last it sank exhausted and felt that perhaps there was no bread to be had. It has felt faint and weary and almost believed that all was a delusion and a will-o'-the-wisp of the mind—that there was no reality to it. It felt the chill of despair creeping over it and all seemed lost.

But we must not lose sight of the fact that just as the hunger of the body implies that somewhere in the world is to be found that which will satisfy it—that just as the hunger of the mind implies that somewhere is to be found mental nourishment—so the mere fact that this soul-hunger *exists* is a proof that somewhere there is to be found that which the Absolute has intended to satisfy it. The *want* is the prophecy of the fulfillment. Yes, and the want and its recognition afford the means of obtaining that which will satisfy the want. When, in the course of unfoldment either on the physical, mental or spiritual plane, it becomes necessary for the well-being of the unfolding Ego to draw to itself certain things which it requires in the process of evolution, the first step toward the obtaining of that necessary thing is the consciousness of a great and pressing want—the birth of a strong desire. And then the desire grows stronger and stronger, until the Ego becomes desperate and determines to obtain the necessary thing at any cost. The obtaining of that thing becomes the prime object in life. Students of evolution realize this fact perhaps more than the rest of us. The subconsciousness of the plant or animal becomes surcharged with this great desire, and all the conscious and subconscious power of the living thing is put forth to obtain that which is necessary for its development.

And on the mental plane the same thing is true. The hunger for knowledge, when it once possesses a man, will cause him to cut loose from old environments, surroundings and everything else which has held him, and he forces himself to the place where that knowledge may be obtained—and he obtains it. If he only wants it hard enough he gets it. When we think of Lincoln in his boyhood days, painfully and laboriously striving for knowledge, lying on his side before the log fire and reading his book by the light of its flames—and this after a hard day's work such as only the boy on the farm knows—when we think of this we may understand the effects of a strong desire possessing the mind of man or boy, woman or girl.

And this hunger for spiritual knowledge and growth, from whence comes it? When we understand the laws of spiritual unfoldment we begin to understand that the Ego is growing and developing—unfolding and casting off old worn-out sheaths. It is calling into operation new faculties—exploring new regions of the mind. In the super-conscious regions of the Soul are many faculties lying dormant, awaiting the evolutionary hour of manifestation along conscious lines. As the faculties approach the hour of birth into the new plane they manifest an uneasiness which is communicated to the subconscious and conscious planes of the mind, causing a restlessness and uneasiness which is quite disturbing to the individual in whom they are manifesting. There is a straining for expression—a reaching forward for development—a desire for growth which produces something akin to pain. All growth and development is accompanied by more or less pain. We speak of the beautiful growth of the plant—of the lily—and wish that we could grow as easily and as painlessly as it does. But we forget that *all* growth means a breaking down—a tearing away—as well as a building up and adding to. The lily's growth appears painless to us, but if we were endowed with keen enough vision—with clear enough sight—with a power enabling us to feel that which is going on within its organism, we would be made aware that there is a constant change going on—a tearing down of tissue, a using up of cells, a pressing upon and breaking through of confining sheaths—all meaning growth, development and unfoldment. We see only the birth of the new parts and lose sight of the pain and destruction preceding it. All through life is manifested the "growing pains" of development. All birth is attended with pain.

And so it is with the birth into consciousness of these unfolding spiritual faculties. We feel an uneasiness, dissatisfaction, yea, even pain, as we strive to call into conscious life these children of the Soul. We feel that desire for something needed by our inner self and we seek for it in all directions. We exhaust all of the pleasures of life, so-called, and find no satisfaction there. We then endeavor to find comfort and solace in intellectual pursuits, but without obtaining that which we seek. We pore over the writing of the philosophers and learned writers of the past and present, but find them as but husks to the hungering soul. We seek in creeds and dogmas that comforting something, the need of which we feel, but of the nature of which we are ignorant—but we find no satisfaction there. We, perhaps, go from creed to creed, from philosophy to philosophy, from one scientific theory to another scientific theory, but still we hunger. At last we get to a position in which we feel that life is not worth the living and that all is a ghastly mockery. And so we go on and on, seeking—ever seeking—but the quest is fruitless.

Man on the physical plane has a comparatively easy time of it. He lives as does the animal—he thinks as does the animal—he dies as does the animal. The problems of life fret him not. He does not even know of the existence of the problems of life. He is happy in his way, and it almost seems a pity that he must be disturbed from his state of animal content. But he *must* be disturbed, not by you or by me perhaps, but by the inevitable Law, which is working around and about him, and in him. Sooner or later in the course of his development he must be awakened. And he awakens upon the mental plane, and here his troubles begin. On the mental plane everything seems beautiful for a time. Man finds himself a new being and he goes on and on, feeling himself a very god and reveling in his intellectual powers. But after a time these things cease to satisfy him. The unfolding of the higher faculties begin to annoy him, particularly as he cannot explain them. His intellectual training has perhaps taught him to believe that there was nothing higher than the mind—that religious feelings were nothing but the result of the emotional nature and that he had outgrown all that. But still he feels that Something Within, never ceasing to annoy him—never ceasing to intrude upon his intellectual consciousness certain *feelings* entirely contrary to his theories. He has grown to doubt the existence of a Supreme Being, and having read Haeckel's "Riddle of the Universe" feels that the question has been satisfactorily settled for all time, and that the answer to all of life's problems may be found in the tenets of his creed—Materialism.

But, somehow, he is not at ease. He feels the pressure of the growing Something

Within and becomes quite restless. This goes on from time to time and he seeks the Truth in all directions, rushing from one thing to another in his desire to satisfy the cravings of the Soul, but all the time denying that there is anything to be found. After a time he becomes aware of a new state of consciousness developing within him, and in spite of his mental revolts against any good thing coming from within, he is forced to accept himself in his growing state, and to realize that he may possess a Knowing other than that of the intellect. It may take him a long time to accept this, but so long as he rebels against it and struggles, so long will he feel pain. And only when he catches a glimpse of the true state of affairs does he open himself up to the Divine Unfoldment going on in his Soul, and joyfully welcome the tearing away of confining mental sheaths, which destruction enables the newly born faculty to force its way into the conscious mentality. He learns to even aid in the unfoldment by holding the thoughts conducive to spiritual development, and thus assists in the bringing forth of the new leaf or flower of the Soul. It has always been so. Man has gone through stage after stage of unfoldment, suffering pain each time as the old sheaths are burst asunder and discarded. He is prone to hold on to the old sheaths and to cherish them long after they have served their purpose in his growth. And it is only when he has reached the stage that many men are now coming into a knowledge of that he understands the process of growth and is willing and glad to aid in the development instead of attempting to oppose it. He falls in with the workings of the Law instead of trying to defeat it.

Life is motion. We are moving onward and upward throughout the ages. Man has passed over miles of The Path, but he will have to travel many more before he sees the reason of the journey. But he has now reached the stage where he may see that it all means something—all is a part of a mighty plan—that this is a necessary stage of the journey, and that around the bend of the road are to be found shady trees, and a brook at which he may quench his thirst and wash away the dust of the last few miles.

This hunger of the Soul is a real thing. Do not imagine that it is an illusion—do not endeavor to deny it. If you feel it you may rest assured that your time is coming, and that there will be provided that which will satisfy it. Do not waste your energy in running hither and thither seeking for bread. The bread will be provided when it is most needed. There is no such thing in Life as spiritual starvation. But instead of seeking without for that which will nourish you, look within. At each stage of the journey the traveler will find enough to nourish him for the hour—enough to sustain him until he reaches the next stage. You cannot be denied this nourishment. It is part of the Divine Plan that it be provided for you. If you will look for it in the right place you will always find it, and will be saved much seeking and worrying. Do not be impatient because the feast is not set before you at this stage. Be satisfied with that which is given, for it suffices your needs at the present moment. By and by you will reach the stage when the feast of good things will have been earned, and you will be invited to feast and rest until you are ready for the next stage of the journey.

The great spiritual wave which is now sweeping over the world brings with it great wants, but it also carries with it the means of satisfying those wants. Do not despair.